The Soviet Scene

The Soviet Scene

A Geographical Perspective

James H. Bater

Professor of Geography and
Dean of the Faculty of Environmental Studies
University of Waterloo

Edward Arnold

A division of Hodder & Stoughton

LONDON   NEW YORK   MELBOURNE   AUCKLAND

© 1989 James H. Bater

First published in Great Britain 1989

British Library Cataloguing in Publication Data

Bater, James H.
   The Soviet scene : a geographical
   perspective.
   1. Soviet Union. Human geographical
   features
   I. Title
   304.1′0947

   ISBN 0-7131-6613-4
   ISBN 0-7131-6420-4 Pbk

Typeset in 11/12 pt Bembo by Colset Private Limited, Singapore
Printed and bound in Great Britain
for Edward Arnold, the educational academic and medical publishing division of
Hodder and Stoughton Limited, 41 Bedford Square, London WC1B 3DQ by
Bookcraft, Avon

TO
Linda, Lisa, Steven, Kevin and Ian

Contents

List of Tables

List of Figures

Preface

This small book is intended to serve as an introduction to the Soviet Union for the undergraduate student and general reader alike. It assumes no previous knowledge of the Soviet Union, or Russia before it. Two basic themes run throughout the contents. The first is that an historical perspective is essential if one is even to come close to understanding the present. The second theme is that in the Soviet Union there is frequently a gap between ideal and reality, the explanation for which requires some appreciation of the decision-making process. In an introductory survey such as this, it is possible to cover only a selection of possible topics. To a large extent what has guided the selection of topics is the author's own interests. If the book's subject matter serves to stimulate further enquiry its purpose will have been served.

This is not a regional geography of the Soviet Union in the traditional sense of providing a detailed discussion and description of the major groupings of landscape and peoples. It is a systematic survey, with the integrating themes noted above, which may serve as a point of departure for further study of any one of the more comprehensive geographies listed below. In a book such as this there is little that represents original research. Rather the content is very much a distillation and synthesis of other people's research and writing. While the text has been intentionally kept free of references and footnotes, each chapter includes a list of recommended readings which the interested reader may wish to consult. Books rather than journal articles have been cited since these may be more readily accessed in most libraries. However, the journal literature should not be overlooked by anyone wishing to pursue a particular topic in greater depth. The Social Sciences and the Humanities Indexes are a good place to start a bibliographic search.

There are a number of important sources available in translation which may be found in most university libraries. Pride of place for the study of the geography of the Soviet Union belongs to *Soviet Geography*, published ten times a year from 1960 until the spring of 1987 under the indefatigable editorship of the late Ted Shabad. Its publication continues fortunately. Many insights into contemporary Soviet affairs may be gleaned from *The Current Digest of the Soviet Press*. Published weekly since 1949 its pages are currently replete with unusually frank discussions of many topics owing to the impact of the policy of *glasnost'*, or openness, introduced by Mikhail Gorbachev, the present Soviet leader. There is a wide array of other translated materials, some of the potentially more useful of which for the novice student of the Soviet Union are listed below as well.

Much of the statistical information included in this book has been drawn from the series, *Narodnoye Khozyaystvo SSSR*, the annual statistical yearbook. As noted already, Soviet newspapers are an especially rich source of information at the present, a change for which all Soviet enthusiasts are grateful. Compared to the rather barren pages of earlier years, there is much that can now be culled which is of inestimable value in attempting to square Soviet ideals with present realities. Soviet atlases are also of generally high quality, and a couple of hours learning the cyrillic alphabet will open the door to a wealth of cartographic information. The transliteration of place names cited in this book follows the style used in *Soviet Geography*.

Whatever merit this book may have owes much to the efforts of other people. On the technical side I would like to acknowledge the assistance of Barry Levely and Gerry Boulet who drew the maps and charts. Susan Shantz has typed the text probably more times than she cares to think about, but always fitting this task into a busy schedule with good humour. The editorial assistance at Edward Arnold is much appreciated.

Waterloo   James H. Bater
June 1988

Some basic geography texts

Balzak, S.S., Vasyutin, V.F., Feigin, Ya., *Economic Geography of the USSR* (New York: Macmillan, 1949), a classic Soviet view.

Baransky, N.N., *Economic Geography of the USSR* (Moscow: Foreign Language Publishing House, 1956), another classic Soviet study.

Cole, J.P., *Geography of the Soviet Union*. (London: Butterworths, 1983).

Demko, G.J., Fuchs, R.J. (eds.), *Geographical Perspective in the Soviet Union* (Columbus, Ohio: Ohio State University Press, 1974) for a Soviet view of geography.

Dewdney, J.C., *A Geography of the Soviet Union* (Oxford: Pergamon, 1970), 2nd ed.

Gregory, J.S., *Russian Land, Soviet People* (London: Harrap, 1968).

Gregory, J.S. (ed), *Geography of the USSR: An Outline* (London: Collet's, 1975).

Hooson, D.J.M., *The Soviet Union* (London: University of London Press, 1966) still a useful geographical regional synthesis.

Howe, G.M., *The Soviet Union: A Geographical Survey* (Estover, Plymouth: Macdonald & Evans, 1983) 2nd ed.

Jorre, G., *The Soviet Union: The Land and its People* (London: Longman, 1967) 3rd ed.

Kalesnik, V., Pavlenko, V.F. (eds), *Soviet Union: A Geographical Survey* (Moscow: Progress Publishers, 1976).

Lavrischev, A., *Economic Geography of the USSR* (Moscow: Progress Publishers, 1969).

Lydolph, P.E., *Geography of the USSR* (New York: John Wiley, 1977), 3rd ed. still the most complete survey.

Lydolph, P.E., *Geography of the USSR: Topical Analysis* (Elkhart Lake, Wisconsin: Misty Valley Publishing, 1979), an indispensable source.

Lydolph, P.E., *1988 Supplement to Geography of the USSR: Topical Analysis* (Elkhart Lake, Wisconsin: Misty Valley Publishing, 1988).

Mathieson, R.S., *The Soviet Union: An Economic Geography* (London: Heinemann, 1975).

Mellor, R.E.H., *The Soviet Union and its Geographical Problems* (London: Macmillan, 1982), 2nd ed.

Pokshishevskiy, V., *Geography of the Soviet Union* (Moscow: Progress Publishers, 1974).

Symons, L., *et al., The Soviet Union. A Systematic Geography* (Totowa, New Jersey: Barnes and Noble, 1983).

Some basic references and guides to literature

Brown, A., *et al.* (eds.), *The Cambridge Encyclopedia of Russia and the Soviet Union* (Cambridge: Cambridge University Press, 1982).

Dewdney, J.C., *USSR in Maps* (New York: Holmes & Meier, 1982).

Horak, S.M., *The Soviet Union and Eastern Europe: A Bibliographic Guide to Recommended Books for Small and Medium-Sized Libraries and School Media Centers* (Littleton, Colorado: Libraries Unlimited, 1985).

Horecky, P.L. (ed), *Russia and the Soviet Union: A Bibliographic Guide to Western Language Publications* (Chicago: University of Chicago Press, 1965).

Pallot, J., 'Recent Approaches in the Geography of the Soviet Union,' *Progress in Human Geography*, Vol. 7, No. 4, 1983, 519–42.

Sanchez, J., *Bibliography for Soviet Geography: with Special Reference to Cultural, Historical and Economic Geography* (Chicago: Council of Planning Librarians, 1985).

Some basic translations of Soviet material

The Current Digest of the Soviet Press
Soviet Geography
Soviet Sociology
The Soviet Review
Soviet Studies in History
Soviet Studies in Literature
Soviet and East European Foreign Trade
Soviet Law and Government

1 Introduction

Only slowly does the newcomer learn to think in contradictions; to distinguish, underneath a chaotic surface, the shape of things to come; to realize that in Sovietland the present is a fiction, a quivering membrane stretched between the past and the future . . .

Koestler, 1953.[1]

Contradictory. Paradoxical. Words like these readily spring to mind upon first acquaintance with things Soviet. Even after acquiring a reasonable understanding of the Soviet Union it is sometimes the case that such words still seem to be appropriate adjectives. Consider the following points. The Russian revolution of 1917 heralded the rise of the first socialist state, one in which the interests of the collective would take precedence over self-interest. Yet from the outset privatism and privilege were nurtured by the state for an elite which, while usually unobtrusive, remains part of the present-day Soviet scene. Indeed, during the Gorbachev era various forms of private entrepreneurial activity have been facilitated, if not lauded. For many people the revolution portended a level of personal freedom beyond reach in autocratic, imperial Russia. Yet there remain firmly in place various controls over the movement and activities of the citizenry. The revolution resulted in the nationalization of resources and the substitution of central planning for the market place. Yet the so-called 'second economy' of private production, distribution and sale persists. The Soviet Union has demonstrated the technological capability to explore space and to produce some of the most sophisticated military hardware. Yet in the countryside millions of peasants work with decidedly primitive equipment in an increasingly vain attempt to wrest planned levels of grain production from a generally begrudging soil. Of course, contradiction is sometimes more apparent than real, and may be detected in differing degrees in all societies. Put simply, ideals and realities are frequently at odds. What makes the Soviet Union so fascinating is in large part related to the fact that it began as a unique experiment in the management and

---

[1] Arthur Koestler, *The Invisible Writing: An Autobiography* (Boston: The Beacon Press, 1953), 53.

development of society, an experiment in which the solutions to many practical tasks still had to be worked out according to socialist principles. Contradiction between ideal and reality was inevitable under such circumstances.

The Soviet Union is clearly an important geographical entity. It is the largest state in the world in area and third largest in population. A federal state constitutionally, it is home to scores of different nationalities among whom Russians are only one, albeit the single largest in number. Notwithstanding the homogenizing effects of six decades of Soviet policies, the Soviet Union remains a land of distinctive regional landscapes – both natural and man-made. The Soviet Union is not just Moscow, not just European Russia. It is the Caucasus, Middle Asia,* Siberia, places separated by vast distances, places where the landscapes have been moulded over the centuries by peoples as different as the Christian Georgians and the Buddhist Buryat Mongols. To be sure, upon first setting foot on Soviet soil the first language to be seen and heard is Russian, and the pungent aroma of a *papirosa*, the ubiquitious Russian working-man's cigarette, is usually the first thing to be smelled.

It is the purpose of this small book to introduce the student to some selected facets of Soviet geography. In so doing two principal themes have played an important part in the organization and content of what follows. The first is historical continuity and change. An appreciation of the past is absolutely imperative if we are even to come close to understanding the present. The second integrating theme is that of decision-making. Who makes decisions, how they are implemented, what is the relationship between policy and practice – all will be dealt with in as much detail as possible. Clearly, the topics selected and the facts and interpretations presented reflect an element of personal choice and bias. But if the book sheds some light on how the system works, on how the system has helped to shape the landscape, and at the same time serves to promote, or provoke, further enquiry, its purpose will have been satisfied.

The focus of our inquiry

In developing the thesis that a sense of history is prerequisite to understanding the contemporary geography of the Soviet Union, it is important that 1917 not be seen as a hard and fast watershed. The revolution obviously produced a major transformation of society. But if the results of more than six decades of Soviet development are to be properly assessed, then it is necessary to have some appreciation of Russia before the revolution. Thus, the next chapter will sketch, in fairly broad strokes, the principal features of the agrarian system, the urban-industrial economy and the currents of social and political change in the late imperial era.

Chapter 3 describes the political-administrative system which the Russian revolution of 1917 spawned. The structure of the Soviet planned economy and the nature of the decision-making process which have evolved over the years are also discussed. The Soviet approach to economic development traditionally generated high rates of

---

* Throughout this book the designation Middle Asia refers to the territory embraced by the following republics: Kazakh, Uzbek, Kirgiz, Tadzhik and Turkmen. See Fig. 10, p. 48

growth. Having become accustomed to quite respectable annual increases in gross domestic production, the chequered record since the early 1970s is especially troublesome to planners. To reverse the trend of flagging labour productivity and faltering output is one of the single most important tasks confronting the Soviet Union for the next decade. Part of the reality of the Soviet economic system is periodic, and unpredictable, shortage. It is in this context that the 'second economy' comes into play. Without it some goods and services would be denied consumers. The chapter concludes with a brief assessment of the importance of the 'second economy' in the contemporary Soviet scene.

The demographic, distributional and ethnic characteristics of the Soviet population are outlined in Chapter 4. Reliable information on population trends is important in all economies irrespective of political ideology, but it is especially important for those which are centrally planned. This is so for a number of reasons, not the least of which being the need for decision-makers to have some reasonable appreciation of future labour supply since this affects fundamental allocations of investment. The management of human resources, however, has been less straightforward than planners might wish. The chapter concludes with an overview of the urbanization process and settlement system.

The Soviet socialist city, home to two-thirds of the country's 1988 total population of 285 million, has long been regarded as an important element in the process of directed social change. It was to reflect egalitarian principles in design, it was to facilitate the dissolution of the various strata of society and the fusion of the country's many national minorities, and it was to create some of the necessary conditions for the emergence of a communist ethos. In Chapter 5 the nature of the Soviet socialist city is examined and the relationship between town planning theory and practice, between ideal and reality, is assessed.

From the standpoint of natural resource endowment the Soviet Union ranks amongst the world's richest countries. Chapter 6 provides a broad overview of the way in which socialist ideology has influenced the perception and management of natural resources over the years. In the seventh chapter the management of one of the most important natural resources – agricultural land – is examined. Long exploited and substantially undercapitalized, in recent years agriculture has garnered a progressively larger share of total investment capital. But this development has not yet produced the desired result. Predictable returns from soil which sometimes suffers from too much, but more often too little, moisture, have been elusive, and perhaps more to the point, during the last decade frequently have fallen short of planned targets.

Harnessing rivers to generate electricity has long figured prominently in Soviet energy schemes, but as the discussion of energy resources in Chapter 8 makes plain, historically hydroelectric power has received rather more publicity than its share of the energy balance would warrant. In recent years nuclear energy has been thrust into the limelight, principally because of the disastrous meltdown of the reactor at Chernobyl' in 1986. Publicity aside, for the remainder of this century oil and natural gas development on the Siberian frontier will be the central issue in the energy scene. The controversy surrounding the Soviet Union's ability to meet its own fast growing energy needs – let alone its sizeable export commitments to Eastern

Europe and the West – will be set against a discussion of the energy resource base and development policy and practice.

Regional industrial development strategy and the Soviet approach to reducing regional disparity are reviewed in Chapter 9. In theory a centrally planned economy affords some distinct advantages in terms of the ability to direct investment to particular regions. However, the need to make the most efficient use of limited financial resources frequently runs counter to notions of regional equality, a dilemma scarcely peculiar to the Soviet Union. In Chapter 10 the discussion focuses on what is labelled social justice and the quality of life. Such topics as levels of income, social benefits, quality of environment, public health care, recreation and leisure, and their regional and rural-urban variations, will be examined. In the final chapter a brief summary of some of the more pressing problems which will confront the Soviet leadership in the years down to the turn of the century will be presented.

While all of these topics are important, they obviously represent just a small selection of what might be discussed. Nonetheless, if the book is to convey something of a sense of place, it is necessary to have an appreciation of the physical setting which bears the impress of Soviet development, and Russian before it.

The physical environment

The two most striking features of the territory embraced by the Soviet border are size and northerliness. Covering 22.5 million square kilometres of the earth's surface, it is more than twice the area of its closest rival, Canada. The sheer size of the Soviet Union is often difficult to comprehend. It stretches more than 10,000 kilometres from west to east, embracing in the process eleven time zones, and is more than 4,800 kilometres from north to south. To travel by train from Leningrad in the northwest to Vladivostok in the far east, for example, takes a full week (Fig. 1). As Vladivostok is a major naval base it, until recently, was closed to foreigners. Thus a trans-continental rail journey for them typically ended, or began, at the small port of Nakhodka, a few score kilometres to the east along the coast of the Sea of Japan, from which there is a regular passenger steamship service to Yokohama. For many people such a trip is enormously appealing. But few would likely choose to make the eight-day journey more than once. The customary fare offered in the dining car usually pales long before journey's end, and this combined with the seemingly permanent line up to get in, is sufficient reason for tourists to adopt the Soviet habit of taking as much food on board at the outset as possible. Fortunately for the novice traveller, with some practice it is possible to purchase supplementary foodstuffs from peasant vendors on the station platforms at scheduled stops. Speed, not discrimination in purchase, is the primary objective in such transactions. Given the time required to travel across the Soviet Union by train, and the difficulties in booking a seat in the first place, the greatest volume of trans-continental passenger service is handled by Aeroflot, the quite satisfactory – and for foreigners decidedly inexpensive – domestic air service. Whether people or goods are moved by air, land or water transport, the huge distances involved impose costs which ultimately must be absorbed by the state. However, it would be shortsighted to think of the vast territorial extent of the Soviet Union purely in terms of cost. After all, within its lengthy borders are found virtually all resources required by a modern industrial economy. And on more than one occasion in the past sheer distance has been turned to military advantage. Napoleon and Hitler both learned how risky it was to extend supply lines into the heart of European Russia. How much more costly would it be to extend such lines into Siberia or Middle Asia? Even in an era of intercontinental ballistic missiles, defence in depth is still of significance in military strategy. In short, enormous territorial extent bestows a variety of benefits which need to be set against the obvious costs associated with overcoming distance.

As Fig. 1 reveals, the Soviet Union is a distinctly northern state. High latitude means that during the winter most ports are ice-bound. Some ports, for example, Riga on the Baltic Sea, Odessa on the Black Sea, and Vladivostok on the Sea of Japan can be kept open by ice breakers, but clearly at some expense. Too few ports are like Murmansk on the Kola peninsula, which benefitting from the tail end of the warm Gulf Stream is open year round. As Fig. 1 indicates, much of the Soviet Union's ecumene, or permanently settled and developed territory, has limited access to the sea, a situation in marked contrast to the United States, or for that matter, Canada.

What Fig. 1 does not show is the considerable uniformity of landform within the Soviet Union. To be sure, there is a variety of different natural landscapes including tundra, tayga, steppe, alpine, desert and oasis ecosystems, some bearing ample evidence of the impact of man, others hardly any at all. But owing to the basic geological structure, and the huge distances covered, for the trans-continental traveller the landscape visible from the train window is characterized by uniformity. A bed of hard crystalline rock of igneous and metamorphic origin underlies much of the country. In European Russia, that is, west of the Ural mountains, glacially-eroded outcrops occur most notably in the northwest near the border with Finland, and in pockets of the south Ukraine (Fig. 2). Over the rest of European Russia the bed of crystalline rock is buried under several score metres of sedimentary deposits, the physical forms of which bear mute testimony to the last continental ice sheet. To the south of the ice sheets' furthest extent, fine dustlike yellowish material, called loess, was carried by the winds off the moraines and deposited to considerable depth, further muffling ground relief. Consequently, most of the European Russian landscape is gently rolling. Where rivers have eroded sedimentary deposits and loess, the results on occasion can be spectacular. But after a day or so on an eastbound train out of Leningrad, for example, it is the uniformity of landscape which is the dominant impression.

Proceeding east the first physiographic exception to this vast expanse of plain is the Ural mountain range. Much eroded by the succession of ice sheets during the Pleistocene period, rarely do the Urals exceed 2,000 metres in elevation. In most places they are only 600–700 metres above sea level and in age and general appearance are similar to the Appalachians of the eastern United States. Numerous broad valleys in the middle of the range facilitate links with Siberia. Passengers on the trans-Siberian railroad follow a northerly route across the Urals, reaching a maximum elevation of 400 metres above sea level, before descending the eastern flank of the range to the city of Sverdlovsk. After watching kilometre after kilometre of gently rolling plain and plateau, dissected by ravine and valley, but all dressed in similar vegetation, little relief, figuratively or literally, is occasioned by the journey across

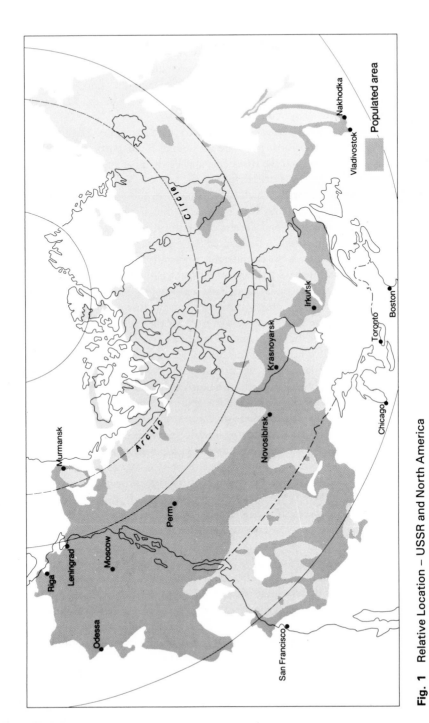

Fig. 1 Relative Location – USSR and North America

Source: Adapted from A. Brown *et al.* (eds.), *The Cambridge Encyclopedia of Russia and the Soviet Union* (Cambridge: Cambridge University Press, 1982), 339.

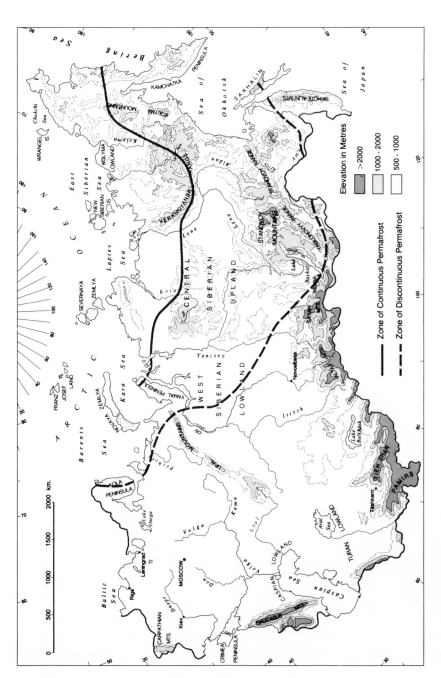

Fig. 2 Physical Geography

Source: Adapted from Paul E. Lydolph, *Geography of the USSR* (New York: Wiley, 1970, 2nd ed.), 12.

the Urals. For the next thousand kilometres there is more of the same. To the east of the Ural mountains the underlying bed of hard crystalline rock continues, giving physical form to the West Siberian Lowland and the Central Siberian Upland. To the south it finds expression in the plateaux and lowlands of Middle Asia (Fig. 2).

Leaving the Urals behind, the trans-Siberian traveller crosses the Tobol' river and passes on through the Ishim steppe before reaching the city of Omsk. The steppe is only periodically disturbed by stands of pine or birch, or by marshes supporting aspen and willow – a landscape, like that before it, always dominated by the sky. To the north lies the West Siberian Lowland. This vast expanse of sedimentary strata laid down during tertiary and quaternary times when the Arctic Ocean reached deep into the middle of the Eurasian land mass, is remarkably flat. Poorly drained by the Ob' and Irtysh rivers, the West Siberian Lowland presents a panorama of forest, bog, swamp and meadow. Only recently has its vast potential as a source of oil and natural gas been recognized and developed. From Omsk on the Irtysh river the trans-Siberian railroad crosses the Baraba Steppe, which because of its multitude of swamps and shallow lakes, occasionally fresh, more often brackish, is visually more of a waterscape than a landscape. Eventually Novosibirsk is reached, and once past this major city of 1.5 million people the southwestern extremity of the rugged Siberian Upland and then the tayga itself slowly come into view. Evidence of man's attempt to wrest a living from the soil diminishes accordingly.

The Central Siberian Upland covers most of the territory between the Yenisey and Lena rivers (Fig. 2). Plateaux of about 700 metres elevation, heavily dissected by several major drainage systems, are the principal element in the landscape. Only to the east of the Lena river, and along most of the southern borders of the Soviet Union, do mountains prevail. As first Krasnoyarsk, and then Irkutsk, are left behind, the terrain becomes rougher. But it is only east of Lake Baykal that one is aware of being in a mountainous region, an event perhaps all the more impressive by virtue of having waited so long. Once over the Yablonovyy range, which lies a few hundred kilometres east of Lake Baykal, all rivers drain to the Pacific. However, from Chita, the first major city on this eastern flank of the watershed, it is still 3093 kilometres to Vladivostok. Put another way, the train trip will last another two and a half days. Eventually the tayga is left behind and deciduous forest of the eastern region, or Primoriye, takes over. By now the enormous size of the Soviet Union will have registered on even the most unobservant of travellers. For those who began the trip in Leningrad, disembarking at Nakhodka is usually a welcome event.

More than two-thirds of Soviet territory is less than 3,000 metres in elevation, only the southern and eastern perimeter of the country being typically alpine (Fig. 2). The mountain ranges of the Caucasus, Middle Asia, and Eastern Siberia, however, do offer some truly spectacular scenery. Some peaks in the Pamir-Alay and Tyan Shan mountains of Middle Asia, for example, exceed 6,000 metres.

The combination of limited relief, huge territorial expanse and high latitude clearly influences the climatic regime of the Soviet Union. Dominant air streams are westerly. While air masses move across European Russia largely unimpeded, vast regions are simply too distant to benefit much from those systems originating over the Gulf Stream. Thus, annual total precipitation generally declines from west to east. Moreover, precipitation also declines to the north and south. In Middle Asia high mountain ranges serve as an effective barrier to moisture-bearing air masses originating over the southern seas and ocean. The potential moderating influence of the eastern ocean and seas is similarly diminished by mountain ranges (Fig. 2). Put simply, the climate of the Soviet Union is primarily continental – winters are long and not infrequently extremely cold, summers are warm and all too short.

Few countries have such a uniform climate. Even fewer have such burdensome winters. Rare is the place in the Soviet Union which is spared frost and snow during the winter months. Indeed, more than half of the country experiences average temperatures of 0° celsius, or lower, for at least six months. Arctic air masses penetrate deep into the southern reaches of the country, bringing periods of bitter cold even to the oasis settlements of Middle Asia. Over Siberia and the Far East a pronounced high-pressure system develops during the winter, which draws cold Arctic air down from the north into the maritime zone of the Soviet Far East, thereby further inhibiting any moderating influence of the Pacific Ocean and ice-free eastern seas. In the centre of this very intense high-pressure system clear skies and calm air prevail. This facilitates heat loss and record low temperatures result. Conditions in Verkhoyansk, a mining centre in the middle of this high-pressure area, are often cited to illustrate the severity of the winter. Average January temperatures are usually in the order of – 50° celsius. Winter temperatures gradually moderate as one moves from the northeast to the southwest. Indeed, on the Caucasian shores of the Caspian and Black Seas there are even a few regions where a humid subtropical climate prevails. The southern fringe of the Crimean Peninsula, closer to the heart-land of the Soviet Union, offers the advantages of a Mediterranean climatic regime. But these are among the very few spots having a mid-winter average temperature which is above freezing. Notwithstanding the ever-present threat of frost, their popularity as winter retreats is easy to appreciate.

Winter is the dry season in the Soviet Union, and it seldom brings more than 13 centimetres of precipitation. The principal exceptions to this pattern are found in Middle Asia, (where what little precipitation there is accumulates as snow on the mountains and foothills), and in the aforementioned enclaves of subtropical and Mediterranean climate around the Black and Caspian Seas. One measure of the severity of the climate is that permafrost conditions extend over half the country (Fig. 2), a phenomenon which reflects continentality and northerliness. Winter ranges from a month or two in the south Ukraine to ten or more months in the northerly reaches of the far east. For the substantial number of people living on the northern margin of the ecumene, or permanently settled zone, continentality means extreme cold, while the high latitude means there is limited daylight during the long winter months.

Summer comes quickly over most of the country, spring being a brief spell of dirty snow and much mud. Historically, spring was the time of *bezdorozhnaya* or road-lessness. Indeed, as many rural roads are still unpaved they remain largely impassable for a period in the spring and sometimes again during heavy autumn rainfalls. Sun or frost is still necessary to transform an impenetrable sea of mud into a more or less negotiable maze of ruts. During the summer it is generally warm and not infrequently very hot. Even in northeastern Siberia where January record low temperatures are recorded the short summer still offers a reasonable number of days in the upper 20° celsius range (and on occasion higher still). As the land mass warms a low pressure system replaces the winter's dominant high and helps to draw moist air masses off the Atlantic onto Soviet territory. But the vast west to east expanse of the country limits the moderating influence. Therefore, the western region receives the bulk of the rainfall. Summer is the wet season in most parts of the country. In European Russia and West Siberia there are usually 25 centimetres of precipitation, much of it produced by thunderstorms. The Chinese monsoon brings heavy rains to the southeastern corner of the Soviet far east, especially during August and September, and in this region precipitation is often as much as 60 centimetres over the summer. Few other areas are so wet, though it is the subtropical Colchis Lowland on the Georgian coast of the Black Sea which holds pride of place in terms of the total rainfall. Although summer is the wet season, for agriculture rainfall is rarely abundant. Less than one quarter of the country receives as much as 50 centimetres of precipitation annually. In the United States, for example, more than one half of the country falls in this category. What is more, in the Soviet Union precipitation during the summer is highly variable. In summary, precipitation decreases from west to east and to the north and to the south. While over much of the Soviet Union July average temperatures are in the mid 20° celsius range, few areas have anything like an ideal balance between adequate heat and moisture for growing crops.

The distribution of natural vegetation is portrayed by Fig. 3 and like the climatic zones is broadly latitudinal. The tayga or boreal forest, covering about 30 per cent of the country, constitutes an enormous reserve of softwood. Larch and spruce prevail amongst the conifers, the former on the poorly drained podzolic soils of Siberia and the far east, the latter in European Russia. Forestry operations, however, are largely confined to the more accessible western and southern regions. To the north climatic severity increases, until tree growth can no longer be sustained and tundra dominates the landscape. The tundra makes up about one-tenth of Soviet territory. Man's presence there is evident, but most notably in terms of settlements based on mineral exploitation. Compared to the northern parts of other polar states, the Soviet Union has staked a far more permanent claim. Noril'sk, a city of 250,000, is the largest settlement north of the Arctic circle anywhere, but is just one of a number of major northern Soviet cities. To the west and south the tayga gradually gives way to a zone of mixed forest, which in turn blends into the wooded steppe and steppe. Each of these natural ecosystems has been substantially modified by man. For example, more than half of the mixed forest of European Russia has been axed. Since their gray-brown podzolic soils offer some potential for agriculture there was considerable pressure to clear the mixed forest zone long before the Soviet era. The wooded steppe, with its river-bottom tree growth amidst open grassland, and the steppe proper, are largely coincident with chernozem, or black earth, soils, long valued for their natural fertility. It is here that man's impact on the land has been greatest. Virtually all of these soils have been put under the plough. The wooded steppe and steppe together are threefold the area of mixed forest, but they still comprise less than one-sixth of the Soviet territory. Notwithstanding the rich chernozem soils of the steppe and wooded steppe, the climate which helped to produce them is fickle. Thus, bountiful harvests cannot be taken for granted. To the south of the steppe the climate becomes drier still. The chestnut-brown soils of the semi-desert zone are

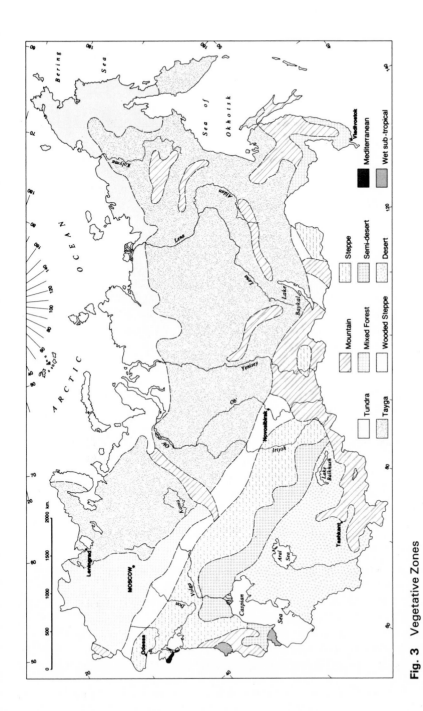

Fig. 3   Vegetative Zones

Source: David J.M. Hooson, *The Soviet Union* (London: University of London Press, 1966), 43.

productive when adequate moisture is available. But they are friable and easily wind-eroded if cultivated without proper regard to arid land soil-conservation practices. Historically this was the realm of the nomadic herdsman and until the Soviet era the plough was rarely seen. Huge areas have since been cultivated, but not without some untoward consequences, as we shall see in a later chapter. Four per cent of Soviet territory is semi-desert. While this is a relatively small fraction, in absolute terms it represents a huge expanse of semi-desert. Desert is nearly three times as extensive, and like the tundra, gives evidence of man's activity where the resource base has warranted development. Mountains and foothills occupy a further quarter of Soviet territory. For Middle Asia the mountains are the source of the life-sustaining water for the oasis settlements of the semi-desert and desert. The distinctive landscapes of the southern portion of the Crimean peninsula and the Caucasian littorals of the Black and Caspian Seas comprise the remaining zones of natural vegetation – Mediterranean in the former, humid sub-tropical in the latter.

Man has modified many of these landscapes over the centuries, but he has not done so with equal impact. Natural conditions have not always been very accommodating for settlement based on agriculture. In very general terms, the zone north of the narrow belt of wooded steppe and steppe suffers from a short growing season and surplus moisture. In the sunnier south there is often a water shortage. Certainly where minerals or other resources have warranted exploitation, settlement has followed irrespective of the natural environment. But as Fig. 1 makes plain most of the Soviet Union's population live within the triangle bounded by Leningrad, Odessa and Irkutsk. Before the revolution a far larger proportion of the population lived west of the Ural mountains than is the case now. Six decades of Soviet development have indeed reshaped the distribution of human activity. Still, as exploration, surveying, and mapping of the Soviet resource base proceeds, the long-standing imbalance between the distribution of resources, or supply, and the distribution of population, or demand, becomes more pronounced.

The Russian revolution obviously transformed the economic, political and social structures which existed during the imperial era. Put simply, it portended a new geography. But before we can appreciate change, or indeed, continuity, it is necessary to have some basic understanding of what existed before. It is the purpose of the next chapter to provide this essential point of reference.

Recommended reading

Berg, L.S., *Natural Regions of the USSR* (London: Macmillan, 1950).

Borisov, A.A., *Climates of the USSR* (Edinburgh: Oliver and Boyd, 1965).

Lydolph, P.E., *Climates of the Soviet Union* (Oxford: Elsevier Science Publishing, 1977). Vol. 7 in *World Survey of Climatology*.

Nalivkin, D.V., *Geology of the USSR* (Edinburgh: Oliver and Boyd, 1973).

Newby, E., *The Big Red Train Ride* (London: Penguin, 1984).

Parker, W.H., *The World's Landscapes: 3, The Soviet Union* (London: Longman, 1969).

2 Modernization of the Russian Empire: The Seeds of Contradiction

Industrial life probably means progress in Russia, but at present it is a very rough-and-tumble and creaking kind.

Williams, 1914.[1]

The process of modernization in Russia was intimately bound up with urban-industrialization, with the penetration of capitalism into a society which had evolved under conditions of an absolute autocracy. But modernization was not easily accommodated by institutional systems designed to perpetuate the authority of the Tsar, by a society whose elites were bent upon maintenance of the status quo, by patterns of behaviour which were often quintessentially rural and not urban. At the turn of the century Russia was already the largest country in the world in terms of area, and the largest European state in terms of population. In many ways it was also one of the more backward of European countries. Outstanding achievements in science, in the humanities, in the world of culture in the broadest sense, combined with the pomp and splendour of the imperial court to belie the harsh and impoverished conditions of daily life and labour for so many of the Empire's inhabitants. The trappings of modernization lay like a thin veneer over much that was Russian. On the eve of the First World War the vast majority of the Empire's more than 160 million subjects were peasants. Many could recall from personal experience the reality of serfdom, which was formally abolished in 1861. Prior to that date a large proportion of the population of the Russian Empire, which then numbered about 60 million, was the personal property of a small elite or of the state itself. Indeed, wealth was usually measured in terms of number of male peasants, or souls as they were called, which one owned. Thus, compared to countries like Britain, France or Germany modernization had come late to Russia. Its impact was no less profound for the delayed start, however. In this chapter we will examine the process of modernization in the

---

. [1] Harold V. Williams, *Russia of the Russians* (New York: Scribner, 1914), 388.

context of the agrarian and urban-industrial economies, and describe some of the social and political changes set in motion. Before doing so, however, it is appropriate that the territorial expansion of the Russian Empire from the early Middle Ages to the eve of the First World War, and the ethnic composition of the population which came to be embraced by its ever-expanding borders, be briefly surveyed.

Emergence of Empire

The expansion of the Russian Empire depicted in Fig. 4 suggests that frontier and colonization played an important role in Russian history. And indeed they did. From the first settlement of Slavic peoples in the territory around the upper Volga river and its tributary the Oka in the twelfth century, the process of territorial expansion continued through the nineteenth century.

The earliest Slavic settlements developed as quasi-independent princedoms in the mixed forest of the upper Volga region. Independence ended with the invasion of the Tatars, or Mongols, in the early 1200s. With the notable exception of Novgorod, all of these early princedoms were brought under Tatar control. The princes of Moscow eventually gained the favour of the Great Khan, and while serving him as a tax gatherer they at the same time were able to extend their hold over other princedoms. As the wealth and prestige of the Principality of Muscovy increased, so too did the so-called Tatar Yoke begin to chafe. From the thirteenth to the fifteenth centuries the princes of Muscovy steadily expanded their territory, the subjugation of Novgovod in the late 1300s adding substantially to their domain to the north and northeast – the traditional hinterland of Novgovod's prosperous merchantry (Fig. 4). During this period of territorial expansion confrontation with the Tatars steadily escalated. It was not until the mid-sixteenth century, however, that Russia, as the Principality of Muscovy eventually became known, finally put paid to the last vestiges of external control by defeating the Tatars in the battle of Kazan' (1552). This victory was celebrated by Alexander IV through his commissioning the construction of St Basil's Cathedral in Moscow's Red Square. The Tatars remained a considerable threat, however. For example, in the 1580s they were able to muster sufficient forces to sack Moscow yet again. Still, the defeat of the Tatar Khanate based at Kazan' was significant. The Tatars no longer wielded influence as before and a major obstacle to the exploration and colonization of Siberia was removed.

Those peoples who inhabited the region between the Volga river and the Urals offered minimal resistance to the small bands of cossacks, soldiers and hunters who comprised the first wave of explorers, and who sought not to colonize so much as to collect fur. Sable, prized in Europe, and thus high in price, was the principal attraction. The vast expanse of Siberia across the easily traversed Ural mountains beckoned. Moving by river through the tayga, Russians reached the Sea of Okhotsk by 1649 and established there another colonial outpost (Fig. 4). Scattered in the forest behind them were numerous *ostrogi*, or fortresses. These were customarily small since the indigenous peoples had proven relatively easy to subjugate, and thus a token garrison force was usually sufficient to administer the collection of fur tribute or *yassak*. The fur trade brought trappers and traders, but few settlers. The Russian realm was limited to the forest, since in the steppe to the south nomads still held

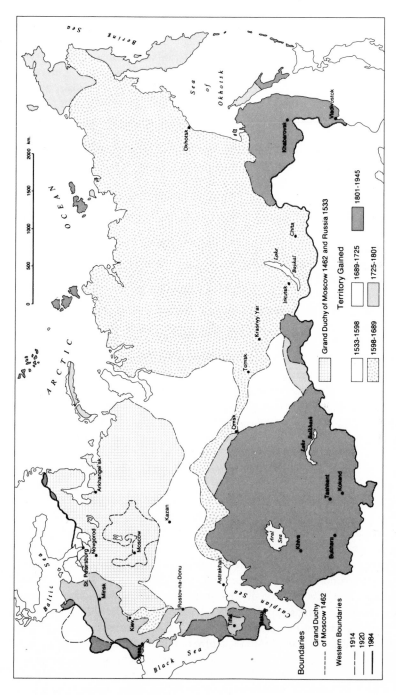

Fig. 4 Territorial Expansion of the Russian Empire and USSR

Source: Adapted from Paul E. Lydolph, *Geography of the USSR* (New York: Wiley, 1970, 2nd ed.), 6.

sway. Russian claim to this vast tract of Siberian tayga was formally acknowledged by the Treaty of Nerchinsk concluded with China in 1689. The Stanovoy mountains served as the boundary between the Russian and Chinese spheres of influence in the east. The wealth of the fur trade had drawn Russians to the Pacific. Potential profits from trade in seal skins would soon lure Russians onto North American soil as well. Expansion of the Russian Empire during the seventeenth century was by no means confined to the eastern regions, although as Fig. 4 clearly reveals, territorial gains in Siberia greatly exceeded all others.

The consolidation of Russian control over the steppe region of European Russia, and to a lesser extent in the Siberian steppe, was one of the major developments during the eighteenth century (Fig. 4). For centuries permanent settlement had been confined to the poorer soils of the forest zone of European Russia. Save for a few fortified cossack settlements the rich soils of the steppe could not be cultivated because of the constant threat of attack by the nomads. With the defeat of the Crimean Tatars in the late eighteenth century the historic grip by a war-like nomadic people over the Ukrainian steppe was finally broken. But this did not result in widespread colonization by Slavs. By the late eighteenth century serfdom had been legally entrenched in Russia for more than a century. Free colonization, the authorities feared, would simply undermine the existing social, economic and political order. Thus, foreigners, including Mennonites, Hutterites and other minorities from Europe were invited to settle these new lands. Settlement of the steppe by subjects of the Empire remained closely monitored. Meanwhile, on the western frontier of the Empire European powers steadily gave way to Russian expansion, most notably in terms of the creation of the Grand Duchy of Warsaw (the Russian spoils from the late eighteenth-century process of partitioning Poland with Prussia and Austro-Hungary) and control over the Baltic region.

Nineteenth-century territorial acquisitions brought large numbers of non-Slavic peoples into the Empire. Finland was acquired from Sweden in 1809 and also given the status of Grand Duchy. The Georgians and Armenians of the Caucasus were ostensibly rescued from the Turks and Persians during the first quarter of the century. In extending control over the Caucasus region the Russian Empire had to absorb a vast array of peoples differentiated by race, religion and language. However, the rugged, mountainous terrain afforded numerous opportunities for minorities to seclude themselves from external influence. Thus, many groups were able to perpetuate a cultural identity despite having been incorporated into an Empire noted for Great Russian chauvinism. The rugged physical environment also facilitated armed resistance to Russian suzerainty by some minorities, something which took years to eradicate. In the second half of the century Russian military penetration into Middle Asia began in earnest. This first of all opened the way for colonization in Siberia of the southern reaches of the steppe and the northern margins of the semi-desert, a zone previously controlled by nomadic peoples. Across the deserts of Middle Asia were the Moslem Khanates and Emirates centred on oasis and montane valley. One by one they fell under Russian control – the city of Tashkent in 1865, the city of Samarkand in 1868, the Emirate of Bukhara in 1868, the Khanate of Khiva in 1873. The mountain perimeter of Middle Asia, and British India beyond, forestalled further Russia advance.

In the far east the weakening authority of the Manchu Empire prompted Russian incursion into Chinese territory after mid-century. Russian settlements on the Pacific shores, to say nothing of those in Russian Alaska or in northern California, had long proven to be extremely difficult, and costly, to supply. Thus, the presumed agricultural potential of the Amur and Ussuri river valleys was especially attractive. But these lands were beyond the Stanovoy mountains, the boundary between Russia and China established in 1689. The region proved too enticing to forego, and therefore was simply annexed. Permanent settlement was required and colonization was promoted by the state in consequence. The formal abolition of serfdom in 1861 had created a vast pool of potential colonists, and the construction of the trans-Siberian railroad in the last years of the nineteenth century opened the door to the lands of Siberia and the far east. Large numbers of Ukrainian peasants, amongst others, came to farm in the Amur region. Access to the far east was greatly facilitated when Russia gained the right in 1894, through negotiations with a further weakened China, to build the last section of the trans-Siberian railway across Manchuria to the Russian port of Vladivostok. Indeed, for a short period the whole of Manchuria was in Russian hands.

The Russo-Japanese War of 1904–05 brought to a close Russian territorial expansion in the far east. Defeat by Japan resulted in Manchuria passing out of Russian hands. As well, the southern half of Sakhalin Island, acquired from Japan in 1875 in exchange for the Kuril Islands, was ceded to Japan. It was not until World War II that control over all of Sakhalin was regained.

The zenith of Russian territorial expansion had been reached by the early 1900s (Fig. 4). The partitioning of Poland and the acquisition of Finland pushed Russian borders to their furthest western extent. The Lesser Caucasus mountains separated Russia from the domain of Turks and Persians to the south. In Middle Asia mountains separated British colonial India from Russian colonial Middle Asia. The abandonment of the Californian outposts and the sale of Alaska to the United States in 1867 signalled the end of Russian territorial interests across the Pacific. The Arctic realm, of course, had been under the Russian flag for centuries. The pattern of territorial expansion depicted by Fig. 4 has on more than one occasion been reduced to single, simple historical explanations – the search for warm-water ports, the felt need to unite all Slavic peoples being but two examples. Historical reality, as usual, defies such simplistic interpretations.

Of the more than 160 million people living within the extensive borders of the Russian Empire on the eve of the First World War, a considerable number were neither Russian, nor indeed even Slavic, as the data drawn from the census of 1897 presented in Table 1 indicate. Aside from the East Slavs, that is, Russians, Ukrainians and Belorussians, who comprised about three-quarters of the total population, there were more than 170 other distinct nationalities. Some of these national minorities could claim only a few score thousand members. The indigenous peoples of Siberia and the north such as the Chukchi, Koryaks or Kamchadals are examples. Other groups were both sizeable in number and restive subjects of the Tsar. For example, more than 12 million people lived in the Grand Duchy of Warsaw. Attempts to Russify the Poles during the latter part of the nineteenth century prompted concerted resistance to Russian authority. The obligatory substitution of

Table 1: Nationalities by language group, 1897

Nationality	Number (000)	Per cent of total
Russia, total	124,200	100
Slavs		
Russian	55,600	44.8
Ukrainian	22,800	18.4
Belorussian	5,800	4.7
Moldavian	1,120	.9
Balts		
Estonian	1,000	.8
Latvian	1,430	1.2
Lithuanian	1,660	1.3
Transcaucasian		
Armenian	1,170	.9
Azeri	1,470	1.2
Georgian	1,310	1.1
Muslim		
Kazakh ⎫ Kirgiz ⎭	4,280	3.4
Tadzhik	850	.7
Turkmen	630	.5
Uzbek	2,790	2.2
Tatar	2,230	1.8
Jews	3,770	3.0

Source: Basile Kerblay, *Modern Soviet Society* (New York: Pantheon Books, 1983), Table 10, 40. Translated by Rupert Swyer.

Russian for Polish in Polish schools was especially offensive, but was just one example of Russification. Resistance increased, and so too did the stream of Polish nationals exiled to Siberia. In Finland, Russian rule was much more tolerant of local interests. Greater sensitivity in dealing with Finland did not preclude the emergence of a Finnish nationalist movement, however. Estonians, Latvians and Lithuanians did not have the separate juridical status of Poles and Finns, but by virtue of language and religion they were equally separate and distinguishable culture groups. Across the vast expanse of the Empire there were many other such minorities.

While most minorities suffered in one way or another from Slavic, or more commonly Russian, chauvinism, it is doubtful if any were more oppressed than the Jews. Living for the most part in a region straddling the western reaches of the Ukraine and European Russia and spilling over into part of the Baltic provinces, the geographical and social mobility of the Empire's Jewish population was limited by statute. Denied the right to live where they wanted, denied the freedom to pursue certain professions, denied in any sense the rights of self-determination, Jews were certainly amongst the most persecuted of minority groups. Notwithstanding the many legal shackles imposed upon them and the widespread anti-Semitism, Jews still became a major force in industry and commerce, and figured prominently in a number of professions.

Not all minorities caught up in the historical expansion of the Russian Empire had much contact with Russians or with the Empire's colonial administration. In the Caucasus, for example, most Georgians, Armenians and Azeris carried on very much as they had always done. Indeed, Russian culture was not always regarded as being of a higher order, and the intellectual elites of some national minorities perceived Russians as inferior. In Middle Asia the ten million or so Muslims vastly outnumbered the emigrant Slav colonists who had arrived during the last decades of the imperial era. In the few cities, Russian colonial administrators created a built environment based on the European model, segregated from the hotch-potch of adobe structures which made up the traditional Middle Asian urban settlement, much as the British did in India. In the countryside, strict segregation of colonists from the indigenous population was also the rule.

The Emancipation of the Serfs in 1861, the construction of the trans-Siberian railroad, and the Stolypin Agrarian Reform, about which we will say more later, all served to spur migration from the overpopulated lands of European Russia to Siberia. Migration to Siberia, of course, was not a new phenomenon. In earlier times hundreds of thousands of peasants fled to escape the injustices of serfdom. Scores of thousands more sought religious freedom, seeing in Siberia a possible refuge from the intolerance of establishment Eastern Orthodox religious principles and practice. And always Siberia had been the place of exile. Tens of thousands of people of all classes and nationalities had been forced to trek across the Empire to a place of internment somewhere in the distant reaches of the Siberian realm. Some exiles never did return, choosing instead to stay in Siberia upon completion of their sentence. For them, and many others, life in a region known then (and now) for an independence of spirit and action was preferable to the surveillance and oppression associated with the autocracy and European Russia. By 1914 more than ten million people lived in the enormous area stretching from the Ural mountains to the Pacific. The indigenous populations, always small in number, were now completely submerged by recent migrants, most of whom were Russians and Ukrainians. Notwithstanding the enormous scale of the late nineteenth–early twentieth century exodus to the east, many regions in European Russia remained acutely overpopulated. Save for the oasis-based settlements in Middle Asia, population density east of the Urals was seldom very great. Most of the Empire's inhabitants lived west of the Urals and earned a livelihood from the land. Unfortunately, the soil there provided but a bare subsistence existence for the majority, little changed from decades, if not centuries, before.

The agrarian scene

Serfdom was legally entrenched in Russia in a code of laws adopted in 1649. It lasted until 1861. From that year on peasants could no longer be bought, sold or mortgaged. They could not be forced to labour free of charge on the landlord's estate or serve as domestic servants. They no longer had to pay for the privilege of departing the village, temporarily, to seek work elsewhere in the countryside or in the city. Put simply, trade in human capital ended with the Emancipation Act of 1861. But the peasantry paid a heavy price for their newly acquired freedoms. Serf owners had to be recompensed by the state for their loss, and for future income foregone. The peasantry was thus saddled with an additional annual tax, or redemption payment as it was called, to continue for 49 years to compensate the state for having made a financial settlement with the serf-owning gentry. Furthermore, the Emancipation Act required that peasant lands be formally separated from those of the former landlord. Since tradition, rather than legal documentation, often differentiated the areal extent of the peasants' agricultural operations from the landlord's there was certainly scope for manipulation in the land allocation process. And, indeed, it appears that this occurred on a fairly wide scale. So far as available data are accurate, they indicate that the average peasant land holding was about 4 per cent less after the Emancipation than before it. In those regions where soil productivity was high, and therefore where estate owners had a vested interest in acquiring land customarily cultivated by the peasants for their own needs, peasant landholdings were as much as 20 per cent less. Thus, not only was there the new burden of redemption payments after the Emancipation, but peasant households had less land on average from which to generate the income to pay them. For a great many peasants the burden was such as to further promote rural–urban migration in search of wage employment. The Emancipation produced a major transformation of the legal underpinnings of the rural social structure, but this did little to change the appearance of the countryside.

Although by the time of the Great War some peasants had acquired their own farms, and the large estates of the land-owning gentry were still an important feature in the rural landscape, most rural inhabitants were villagers and members of a rural commune, or *mir*. Thus, the village remained the customary settlement form in rural Russia and the commune the primary form of social organization outside the family. A sense of group solidarity no doubt had been nurtured by the peculiar demands of serfdom. However, even before becoming enserfed there appears to have been a sizeable element of collective decision-making within the village. The Emancipation did not alter this time-honoured pattern of behaviour.

Within the village commune, or *mir*, an elected group of elders took decisions on behalf of all members. For example, they allocated land to spring crops, winter crops and fallow in accordance with the principles of the three-field system. Collective actions like these were taken in hundreds of thousands of villages across Russia, though it should be noted that such expressions of collectivism were more common in the central European Russian core than in the peripheral regions of the Empire. The allocation of the individual strips of land within the cultivated 'fields' was also governed by collective decision-making. The number of strips allocated to each household was usually determined by the number of mouths to feed. Strips were distributed in as equitable a fashion as possible. Each household was to share the good, bad or indifferent soils and would travel roughly similar distances to work them. The actual distribution of one household's allocation of strips is portrayed in Fig. 5A. In some parts of Russia strips of land were periodically re-allocated in order to reflect changes in household membership. In the Baltic region, in the south Ukraine and in the steppe region of Siberia, however, strips were customarily hereditary allotments, that is, they were not periodically re-distributed. Cultivating scattered parcels of land was clearly inefficient. The Emancipation, however, did not improve agricultural efficiency in the peasant domain. Indeed, the government had a vested interest in preserving the status quo.

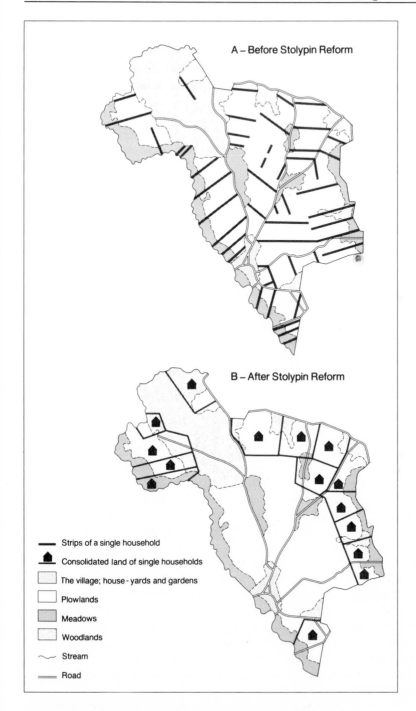

A – Before Stolypin Reform

B – After Stolypin Reform

Strips of a single household

Consolidated land of single households

The village; house-yards and gardens

Plowlands

Meadows

Woodlands

Stream

Road

Fig. 5 Rural Transformation at the Time of the Stolypin Reform

Source: Adapted from G.R. Robinson, *Rural Russia Under the Old Regime* (New York: Macmillan, 1967, sixth printing), 217.

The communal *mir* had administrative functions in addition to determining land allocations. As a rule it administered the selection of recruits for the army and was responsible for the collection of taxes. Indeed, not only did the *mir* collect taxes, it was also liable for the taxes of all households in the village. Thus, should one household default the village as a whole was responsible for making up the tax obligation. Consequently, the village community had a vested interest in superintending the migratory habits of individual village members. Prior to the Emancipation, peasants could leave the village only with the necessary authorization of the *mir* and consent of the landlord. After the Emancipation permits issued by the *mir* were still required. To be sure, from time to time some peasants left the village without the approval of the *mir*. However, because of tax obligations, and tradition, there was considerable peer-group pressure to preserve the village community structure.

Rural–urban migration increased in volume in the decades following the Emancipation. Most peasants sought work in the city on a seasonal basis, or as their permits dictated. However, growing numbers of peasants, mostly males, managed to stay in the city for periods of years, and slowly acquired some characteristics of a working-class culture. But ties with the village, both legal and familial, remained strong. The numerous religious holidays facilitated journeys back to the village at regular intervals where distances, or cost of travel, were not too great. Even amongst the growing number of peasants who had become part of the permanent urban workforce, many retained more than a passing interest in village affairs. After all, the village was potential refuge in times of hardship, where tradition ensured that those in need would be looked after. The sense of collective was deeply embedded in the peasant mentality, perpetuating rural customs on the one hand, and because of the nature of the rural–urban migration process, helping to shape the urban milieu itself on the other.

Traditional peasant agriculture was largely subsistence. Therefore, it could contribute relatively little to grain exports, which were so important in financing industrial development. Peasant agriculture had helped to meet domestic and foreign demand for grain, by expanding the area under cultivation, in particular by bringing the new lands of Siberia and Middle Asia into production. However, the technology employed, and the organization of agriculture itself, dictated that yields remained low. Of course, not all Russian agriculture was in the hands of peasant households. From the estates of the land-owning gentry substantial amounts of grain moved to both domestic and foreign markets. Following the Emancipation, some estate owners adopted technological innovations and substituted capital for the labour that was no longer free. With sufficient acreage economies of scale were also possible. In the Baltic region and the south Ukraine capitalist agriculture took firm root on many estates, the very best comparing favourably in terms of management, technology and production with advanced agricultural operations in Europe and America. But the dead weight of the peasant agricultural economy ensured that average yields for the Empire as a whole remained comparatively low.

By the turn of the nineteenth century growing population pressure made even more difficult the task of wresting a living from the soil. The occasional natural calamity meant that life itself was sometimes at risk. On occasion, the *mir* was able to extend village lands by purchase or lease, often from former landlords. In most cases, however, it was confronted with the task of sharing out a fixed amount of land amongst more mouths. The average size of peasant land allotments steadily declined, incomes shrivelled, poverty intensified. A growing number of peasants showed physical manifestations of an impoverished existence. For example, one-fifth of the military conscripts called up between 1899 and 1901 was rejected as physically unfit. The impoverishment of the peasantry was in no sense a universal phenomenon, however. Indeed, a class of wealthy peasants emerged. Some peasants prospered by virtue of greater ability as farmers, others were able to augment their income from non-agricultural sources, others simply at the expense of the growing number of households with subsistence-size allotments or less. Thus, the peasantry itself was increasingly stratified according to wealth, creating in the process further grounds for grievance.

Peasant dissatisfaction reached the breaking point by the turn of the century. An economic depression prevailed throughout most of the 1880s, and from 1898 the Russian economy was caught up in yet another. From 1900 to 1904 hundreds of peasant disturbances, revolts, and uprisings took place in Russia. Some were minor, but a good number were serious. In 1905 peasant disturbances combined with widespread strike activity in the cities. The catalyst in sparking what is customarily labelled the '1905 revolution' was the Russo-Japanese War. Initiated with much popular support in 1904, the incompetent management of the war effort culminated in an ignominious settlement which was forced on Russia in 1905. This brought the grievances of workers and peasants alike to a head. Tsar Nicholas II was obliged to introduce some major reforms in order to stem the tide of unrest. In 1906 a constitutional government, or *Duma*, was created, legitimizing for the first time the existence of political parties in Russia. Workers in the factories were given the right to strike. In the countryside the pressure for change was every bit as acute as in the city. Inadequate allotments, restrictions on access to woodlot and pasture imposed by landowners on what before the Emancipation had been part of the peasant agricultural realm, and the continuing authority of the *mir*, all served to perpetuate subsistence agriculture, and thus inhibit development of market oriented agricultural production. Propagandists and agitators advocating change found more and more receptive ears amongst the villagers. Conscripts' first-hand accounts of the debacle on the far eastern front simply fired further the discontent. That preservation of the status quo in the countryside was weakening, not bolstering, the basis for the auto-cracy was now conventional wisdom amongst many of the Tsar's key advisors. Thus, beginning in 1906 Tsar Nicholas II signed into law a series of measures which are commonly referred to as the Stolypin Agrarian Reform.

In recognition of the impoverished state of the mass of the peasantry the Tsar already had issued a decree in late 1905 cancelling all further redemption payments to the state. The main thrust of the agrarian reform, however, was still to come. The Emancipation of 1861, as we have emphasized, perpetuated traditional – and highly inefficient – agricultural practices by reaffirming the authority of the communal *mir*. In decrees passed in 1906, however, the right of the individual peasant to leave the village at will, to consolidate the household's allotment of strips, and to receive title to this land, was confirmed in law. What the state intended to create by the Stolypin

Agrarian Reform was a new class of independent, land-owning peasant farmers. The vested interest of this class would entail support of the Tsar and government to whom it would owe its independence, if not its prosperity. The reform's attraction was greatest for the roughly nine-million-odd peasant households belonging to communes in which the strips of land were not hereditary holdings, but were periodically re-distributed, or repartitioned, according to local custom. As this group comprised about three-quarters of all peasant households the potential impact of the reform was clearly enormous.

Available data suggest that between 1906 and 1915 some 2.5 million households gained title to land previously held by the commune. That represents more than one-quarter of all households involved in repartitional communes. Such conversions of title, however, did not necessarily result in the consolidation of strips into a single holding. Indeed, while some conversion of titles brought both consolidation of strips and the creation of new independent farms as indicated by Fig. 5B, this was an exception, although an important exception to be sure. While the communal *mir* no longer had the legal authority to direct the actions of peasant members, the fact is there was not a wholesale conversion of landholdings of the type depicted in Fig. 5A to that described by Fig. 5B. Such consolidation, of course, afforded those participating households the opportunity to decide for themselves which crops to sow, how much land should be left fallow, and so on. Consolidation occurred most often in the peripheral regions of the Empire where the communal system was not as well established. Consolidation also offered the possibility of greater efficiency. No longer was there weed-infested waste land separating strips under the plough. No longer was it necessary to travel to a score or more individual strips. No longer was there a disincentive to improve soil quality through fertilization because the improved strips might be assigned to another household at the next repartition. Even in the absence of financial capital and knowledge of such agrarian innovations as improved seeds, consolidation helped to raise productivity. There were limits to what could be achieved, however.

The difficulty of deciding how to consolidate strips of differing soil qualities and locations no doubt persuaded some peasants to persist with the old ways even when they could see advantage to consolidation. For others, indeed, perhaps the majority, their daily lives were so deeply embedded in traditional ways that they simply did not want change. There was after all a measure of security in belonging to the commune. Thus, over much of Russia, especially European Russia, agriculture carried on after the Stolypin Reform much as it had before. Each dawn witnessed millions of peasants trudging off to tend individual strips of land, a scene transcending the revolution of 1917, continuing in fact down to the collectivization drive initiated by Stalin in the late 1920s. Still, to dismiss the Stolypin Agrarian Reform as having had little, or no impact, would be incorrect. Peasants had much more personal freedom after the reform than before it. Free now to stay in the village or to leave, huge numbers decided to migrate to the frontiers of settlement, to colonize. Even larger numbers abandoned the village for the factory and the city. After the Stolypin Reform there occurred a period of economic growth unparalleled in Russian history. Perceived opportunities for a better life outside the village unleashed an unprecedented wave of rural–urban migration. In the following pages we will discuss some features of the urban-industrialization process which helped to stimulate migration and outline some of its consequences.

Industrialization

At the turn of the century, three-quarters of the Empire's labour force were employed in agriculture. Manufacturing engaged perhaps a tenth of the total. However, its share was growing quickly and in any event greatly understated the importance of industrialization. While the development of industry was late in comparison with the major European powers and the United States, this was not because of an inadequate industrial resource base.

All of the basic materials necessary for industrialization in the nineteenth century were available within Russia. For example, iron ore, coking coal, even oil deposits were being tapped – with profit – at the turn of the century. Indeed, in the case of oil, production from the Baku region in the Caucasus was the largest in the world. While the enormous resource potential of Siberia was still largely unrecognized, within European Russia there were sufficient mineral and energy resources to sustain industrialization. Russia also had a huge handicraft production, albeit largely peasant in origin and therefore closely tied to the village. There was therefore a sizeable population familiar with some facets of the manufacturing process. Still, industrial development in Russia was not just comparatively late, it was also distinctive because of the degree of state involvement, the scale of enterprise, the location, and the role of foreign capital.

State involvement in industry was of long-standing importance despite some notable efforts by Tsar Peter I (1682–1725) to foster private enterprise, both Russian and foreign. But in a state in which the few people capable of assuming the responsibility for industrial development more often than not spurned industry (and sometimes commerce as well), for a position in the state bureaucracy, both entrepreneurial talent and financial resources were at a premium. Thus, from the outset industrial development necessitated the purchase of foreign technology and administrative personnel. State orders, guaranteed profits, protective tariffs, conscription of state-owned serfs to labour in factory or mine, and encouragement of education, science and technology, all were intended to nurture industrialization. However, as each new military encounter with European powers served to illustrate, Russian industry and armaments remained weak links in the defence of the state. The ability of the state to defend its borders was further compromised by the policy of Tsar Nicholas I (1825–1855) not to modernize the internal transport system. At mid-nineteenth century, for example, the Empire had but a single railroad, that joining the capital St Petersburg with Moscow. A vast network of public highways and post-roads served the needs of internal transport at least during those seasons when movement was possible. When spring brought *rasputitsa*, or the time of mud, land transport came to a halt. Autumn rains produced the same state of *bezdorozhnaya* or roadlessness in Russia, a condition that lasted from several days to several weeks depending on prevailing climate and soil characteristics. River and canal transport was even more limited by the seasons than was the largely unpaved dirt-track road system. The consequences were more than just economic. The Crimean War of

1854–56 was resolved unsatisfactorily for Russia at least in part because road and river transport was inadequate to the task of supplying the forces on the Crimean peninsula. In war technological innovation was now just as important as the ability to muster men. Backwardness, not modernity, characterized much of the Empire's industrial structure, its military equipment and the internal transport system. But following the Crimean War, industrial development was promoted as never before, especially in terms of the construction of rail and rolling stock in Russia. The Emancipation of the Serfs played an obvious part in the state's plans for modernization.

By the middle of the nineteenth century there were about 10,000 manufacturing establishments with just over one-half million workers. In most important sectors of industry, however, private enterprise played a decidedly minor role. As before, the state was not only a major purchaser of industrial goods, it was a major producer as well. The changes set in motion by the post-Crimean War development policies culminated in a period of frenetic industrialization around the turn of the century. Although the figures are only approximations, the number of factories and employees increased threefold between 1850 and 1890. Nearly 1.5 million people were now working in over 30,000 factories. By 1913 about 2.6 million workers were employed in the Empire's manufacturing establishments, that is, nearly twice the figure of 1890. However, the number of factories had increased by only 50 per cent in the same period. The concentration of workers in large establishments, already a distinctive feature of Russian industrialization in 1890, was therefore accentuated. In 1910, for instance, more than half of the industrial workforce in Russia was employed in factories with more than 500 workers. In the United States, where economy of scale was the byword, barely one-third of the factory workforce was employed in such large enterprises. Amongst European countries the share was smaller still. Of course, modernization is not necessarily to be equated with the number of workers in a factory. Compared to both Europe and America the quality, and cost, of Russian labour was lower. Low wages, of course, reflected low productivity. But labour could be, and was, substituted in some production processes for more expensive machinery, and this was one reason for such large individual factory workforces. It has also been suggested that because managerial and technical personnel were scarce in late imperial Russia, concentration of production in a single enterprise made more efficient use of the limited available talent. Whatever the reasons involved, the fact is that there were many very large factories. Thousands of workers in a single factory was not uncommon. Indeed, in 1913 a number of factories employed more than 10,000 workers each.

State policies concerning industrialization in the nineteenth century were somewhat ambivalent. Positive endorsement appeared, for example, in the form of tariff protection (Russia had the highest average import duties of any major European industrial country in 1914), in the form of government purchase of domestic production at prices high enough to ensure large profits, and in the form of state involvement in industrial production, especially in the armaments sector. Yet there was no wish to have industrialization proceed without some measure of control. The experience in some European cities where a large 'lumpen-proletariat' had proven socially and politically disruptive was sufficient to worry those who sought to preserve the autocracy. Thus, after the Emancipation of 1861 the state attempted to

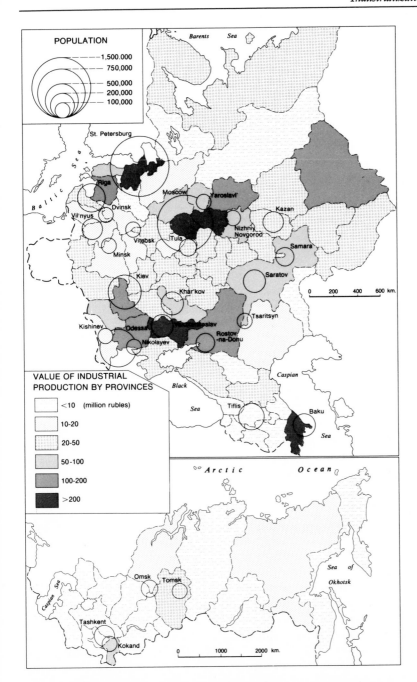

Fig. 6 Population Centres and Industrial Production – Russia 1910

Source: Based on W.H. Parker, *An Historical Geography of Russia* (London: University of London Press, 1968), 316; Peter I. Lyashchenko, *History of the National Economy of Russia to the 1917 Revolution* (New York: Macmillan, 1949), 595.

keep in place the means for controlling the movement of peasants. Endorsement of the communal *mir* and its authority to issue permits to peasants wishing to depart the village temporarily went hand in hand with the maintenance of a bureaucracy in the cities to monitor the 'coming and going' of such peasants. Factory workers in Russian cities were consequently slow to develop a sense of solidarity based upon long association with industrial production and permanent ties with the city. To be sure, when unions were legalized after 1905 the situation began to change, and quickly. But even so, many peasant factory workers retained close ties with the village.

The state had long encouraged factories to locate in the countryside. To some extent a rural orientation of industry was reinforced by handicraft activities, since these were mostly found in the villages, especially those of central European Russia where only marginal prospects for earning a livelihood from the land had long ago fostered the development of alternative, non-agrarian occupations. Thus, a potential labour supply could be tapped. But perhaps more important a reason for promoting rural industry was that many government officials reckoned it would be potentially less disruptive than urban industry. As it turned out, this hope was not always realized since strikes and labour unrest were by no means confined to the city. In encouraging industry to locate in the countryside state policy was in fact reasonably successful. By 1902, for example, only 41 per cent of the 1.9 million factory hands lived in cities. In 1914, there were few urban-industrial regions in Russia, St Petersburg, Moscow, and Riga being the most notable exceptions. Together these three areas accounted for about 18 per cent of the Empire's factory workforce.

As Fig. 6 indicates, there was considerable regional variation in the distribution of industrial activity in Russia in the early 1900s. The area around Moscow was the most heavily industrialized, yet even here the vast majority of people still worked the land. The Baltic ports of St Petersburg and Riga were major industrial centres, more spatially concentrated than the Moscow region, and more modern. The central industrial district, focused on the city of Moscow, was still dominated by textile manufacture, while in St Petersburg and Riga metallurgy and engineering accounted for most industrial jobs. Metallurgy, and food products industries, notably sugar beet processing, characterized the industrial structure of the Ukraine. In the Baku region the petroleum industry was particularly important, while in the Urals mineral resource exploitation was the source of most industrial employment.

As Table 2 reveals, by the early 1900s the Empire's industrial structure remained dominated by the traditional sectors – textiles and foodstuffs. Still, there were clear signs of modernization. The metallurgical industries, particularly steel and engineering, had developed quickly and now commanded a reasonably sizeable share of total industrial employment. The expansion of the metalworking and machinery sector was very much associated with the programme of railroad construction initiated after the abortive Crimean War. At mid-nineteenth century Russia could boast of barely 1,600 kilometres of railroad. By 1910 there were more than 66,000. The expansion of the rail network drew whole regions into the world of national, and indeed international, markets. The demand for rails and rolling stock helped to shift the traditional emphasis on production of consumers goods, such as textiles and clothing, to producers goods, that is, items which are not in themselves end-products, but

Table 2: Share of industrial employment and production, Russia 1897 and 1908

Industrial group	Workers per cent 1897	1908	Gross value of production per cent 1897	1908
Textiles	30.6	36.5	33.3	29.8
Food products	12.2	17.1	22.8	33.9
Mining and metallurgy	25.9 ⎱	24.5	13.9 ⎱	16.4
Metalworking and machinery	10.2 ⎰		10.9 ⎰	
Timber processing	4.1	4.1	3.6	3.7
Livestock products	3.1	2.8	4.7	3.5
Ceramics & building materials	6.8	–	2.9	–
Chemical	1.7	2.9	2.1	3.8
Paper	2.2	3.9	1.6	2.8
Other	3.2	8.2	4.2	6.1
TOTAL	100.0	100.0	100.0	100.0

Source: Olga Crisp, 'Labour and industrialization in Russia,' in Mathias, Peter and Postan, M.M.: (eds.) *The Cambridge Economic History of Europe; The Industrial Economies, Capital, Labour and Enterprise; The United States, Japan and Russia* (Cambridge: Cambridge University Press, 1978) Vol. VII, Part 2, 354.

which are used to manufacture other commodities. Consumer goods from rural handicraft, or *kustar'*, industries continued to find a market. Of course, when factory technology was applied to the manufacture of the same commodities *kustar'* production was rarely able to compete in terms of price and suffered accordingly.

The modernization of the industrial structure suggested by the growth of the metalworking, machinery and chemicals industries in Table 2 was made possible by a massive influx of foreign capital, especially from the late 1890s on. Foreign investment flowed in largest volume into those industries where growth potential and profits were greatest. Mining, electrical engineering, rubber, chemicals, petroleum production – all are examples of industries dominated by foreign capital. In many instances government support through tariff protection or lucrative contracts further boosted profits for foreign investors. In the early 1900s capital investment on the part of Russian entrepreneurs was still concentrated in the traditional areas of industrial enterprise – textiles, clothing, woodworking, tobacco and food products.

Only a small share of the Empire's total workforce actually toiled amidst the din and dust of the factory. But in absolute terms the numbers involved were still huge, and given the transient nature of at least a part of the factory labour force, many more people than the 2.6 million operatives counted in manufacturing establishments in 1913 would have had first-hand acquaintance with factory production. Of course, industrialization was much more than just factories and workers. For the recently arrived peasant whose life had been governed by the seasons, the daily regularity of habit dictated by the factory whistle and clock was often an entirely new, and not necessarily welcome, experience. The factory changed the conditions of employment for those who had some work experience in the city in trade, commerce or domestic service from the close personal relationships, good or bad, to impersonal, bureaucratic ones, thereby creating a void between owner or manager and employee. Industrialization required new financial structures; it required more transport facilities, if not new modes; it destroyed some handicraft activities and spawned others. Put simply, industrialization transformed in both subtle and obvious ways the whole of the national economy; it was both an example and an agent of modernization and there were few parts of the Empire which did not experience some of the changes set in motion. But it was in the Russian city that the impact of industrialization was most evident.

Urbanization

Russia's urban population was always small in relative terms. At mid-nineteenth century about 3.4 million people were classified as urban, barely 5 per cent of the total population. By 1914 there were more than 28 million people living in urban places, but this was still less than one-fifth of the total population. In England, France, Germany and the United States, for instance, urbanites now comprised 50 per cent or more of the total population. What is more, in Europe and America urban growth was more nearly synonymous with urbanization. Those who departed the countryside for the city usually did not return. Such migrants helped to change the city, and in turn their behaviour and attitudes were modified by the environment in which they now lived. In short, they became urbanized. In Russia, on the other hand, the development of cities and life within them was very much under the thumb of officialdom from at least the middle of the seventeenth century until well into the nineteenth. Peasant rural–urban migration was customarily monitored through permits and passes, and thus a peasant's sojourn in the city was intended to be short-term. The seasonal nature of residence in the city was by no means restricted to the peasantry, as we shall see shortly.

Urbanization, like industrialization, was both an example and an agent of modernization. The trappings of modern urban-industrialism, however, had little to do with the reality of the urban experience for perhaps the majority of the Russian city's inhabitants. On the eve of the First World War, for example, peasants comprised almost three-quarters of the total population in the Empire's two largest cities, St Petersburg and Moscow. This was nearly twice the share fifty years earlier, and resulted from the surge of peasant migration following the Stolypin Agrarian Reforms. The official *sosloviya*, or legal estates, were certainly not an accurate reflection of the urban class structure. But for the three-quarters of the inhabitants of St Petersburg and Moscow who belonged to the peasant *sosloviye*, or estate, it is not unreasonable to suggest that they were little urbanized and even less urbane. St Petersburg and Moscow were dual economies in the sense that international industrial enterprises, joint-stock banks, companies with world-wide business dealings and so on lay like a thin veneer over the peasant economy which more often than not involved the itinerant pedlar and bazaar. In the city there existed different social worlds as well as business ones, with prince and peasant representing opposite ends of the social class continuum. But in terms of sheer numbers the world of the peasant was absolutely dominant. Moving down the urban hierarchy from capital city to provincial centre to county town the social class structure of the population changed. Peasants comprised a smaller share of the population, the *meshchane*, or petty trading estate, increased in proportion. But the links with the countryside were still palpable.

The proportion of the Russian population living in towns was never very great. The role of the Russian city as a centre of cultural change was therefore different from its European and American counterpart. But who acquainted with the broad canvas of Russian history would assign to the city an importance commensurate with its share of the Empire's population? After all, the city was the scene of revolution. Indeed, it was in the city where the fundamental contradictions between the old and new, between the traditional values of Russian society and the forces of modernization, were to be seen in boldest relief. In the next few pages we will explore, albeit briefly, a few of these contradictions and some of their consequences.

After a long period of comparative neglect the eighteenth century witnessed a renewed interest in the city on the part of the autocracy. Peter I (1682–1725) and Catherine II (1762–1796) in particular, busied themselves with the creation of an ordered, and orderly, urban environment. The founding of St Petersburg in 1703, and its development after 1712 as the planned capital of Russia, served as a model for new town development elsewhere in the Empire. While what was accomplished there was rarely achieved in other settings, it nonetheless reflected the prevailing values of the autocracy.

Throughout the eighteenth and early nineteenth centuries the principal emphasis in urban development was on external form. However, the fascination with the geometry and symmetry of the town plan tended to mask the fact that it was more than simply a technical working document. Within the city land-use segregation was a first priority. This went far beyond simply banishing polluting industry to peripheral locations, or dispatching industry to the countryside. The plan usually included provisions for the enforcement of social class segregation. While attempts to separate the various constituents met with only limited success owing to the costs involved and the less than perfect enforcement, the important point is that the town plan was used to reinforce the existing social order.

Despite the hundreds of plans created to guide the development of new towns and the re-construction of existing ones, by the middle of the nineteenth century the Russian city rarely gave much evidence of close adherence of ideal with reality. The fabric of the typical Russian town was still largely wooden. Even in the imperial capital, St Petersburg, wooden buildings prevailed, notwithstanding requirements to build with stone, bricks and mortar. Countless imperial edicts stressing the need for architectural consistency and harmony in the design of public and private buildings alike did little to alter the appearance of ancient cities like Kiev, Novgorod or Moscow where the main impression remained one of a rich confusion of design and construction materials. The smaller, more remote the town, the less did such regulations have any real meaning. Moreover, as the frontiers of the Empire came to embrace growing numbers of non-Slavic peoples, regional differences in urban form and fabric were accentuated. Cities of the Baltic region such as Reval' (Tallinn), Riga and Vil'na (Vilnyus) had their own distinctive architecture. So, too, did more recently acquired Caucasian cities like Tiflis (Tbilisi), Yerevan and Baku. Still to be brought into the Empire were the ancient urban settlements of Middle Asia, but at mid-century the frontier was fast approaching them (Figs. 4 and 6). While few cities were actually developed with close adherence to town-planning principles, they, like St Petersburg itself, often symbolized the aims and aspirations of the autocracy.

The essence of planned development of cities was controlled, predictable growth. As urban-industrialization took hold in the latter part of the nineteenth century, the bureaucratic machinery for supervising rural–urban migration was severely tested. During the period from mid-nineteenth century to the Great War the increasing tempo of urban growth demanded that more attention be given by the authorities to the material conditions under which people lived, and that less attention be given the plan and external appearance of the Russian city. But despite a conscious shift in emphasis, it came too late. Cities lacked autonomy, lacked finances and consequently lacked sufficient municipal services to meet demands. From sewage systems to water supply networks to public transport to primary education, the urban infrastructure was inadequate, antediluvian, or both. When the Stolypin Agrarian Reforms unleashed an unprecedented flood of rural migrants any remaining possibility of an orderly development of the Russian city simply disappeared. Instead there ensued a crisis of numbers. The urban population of Russia may not have been very large in relative terms on the eve of the First World War, but the rate of increase, and the sheer mass of humanity it represented, simply outstripped the urban system's capacity to absorb it.

In the Russian city males were numerically dominant, unlike European and American cities where females customarily outnumbered males. The principal reason for this demographic pattern was the Russian practice of permitting peasants to depart the village only for limited periods. Even after the Stolypin Agrarian Reform when families could migrate to the city at will, the acute housing shortage helped to perpetuate sex-selective rural–urban migration. To be sure, the demographic profile of the Russian city was slowly changing as more single females, and indeed wives and families, left the countryside for the town. But on the eve of the First World War there were many married men with reasonably secure city jobs paying higher than average wages who still maintained a family in the countryside. Even when tradition no longer governed behaviour, the crisis in housing forestalled the creation of a normal family life in the city for a great many working men.

Throughout Russia the signs of an impending housing crisis were evident already in the 1860s. The rapid conversion of previously uninhabited cellars, the year-round occupancy of suburban summer *dachi*, or cottages, the constant carving up of the existing housing stock into smaller and smaller rental units until in all too many instances people were forced to live, literally, in just a corner of a room, all of this and more testified to the deterioration of the housing scene. Rents escalated, and in their wake appeared more and more jerry-built tenements. In the early 1900s there were three times as many people per apartment in St Petersburg and Moscow as in Vienna, Paris, Berlin or London.

In addition to the hardships produced by the acute housing shortage, there was disease, the spread and persistence of which were causally linked to deficient municipal services, especially water supply and sewage networks. Throughout urban

Russia the onset of spring was regarded as a mixed blessing, for the easing of the icy grip of winter was sure to bring infectious disease. Maintaining satisfactory standards of public health was perhaps the most important task confronting municipal government. Cities large and small alike, however, generally failed to fulfil this particular mandate. Ports like Odessa, Baku, Astrakhan, and even the capital, St Petersburg, were notorious bastions of infectious disease. But serious epidemics rarely spared cities further inland. For example, in the short period from 1883 to 1917 the citizens of Moscow were ravaged by no less than 32 outbreaks of smallpox, cholera and typhus. In the smaller provincial towns, municipal services such as centralized water supply and sewage systems were usually quite limited. This situation had a pronounced impact on rates of mortality. As the data for the city of Kazan', located at the confluence of the Volga and Kama rivers, reveal (Fig. 7), population growth during the nineteenth century was very erratic.

In few other countries were cities so hazardous to live in. The brunt of epidemic disease was of course borne by the masses who were descending upon the Russian city in ever greater number in the early 1900s. Infectious disease regularly accounted for a third or more of all deaths in cities. While births exceeded deaths on a more regular basis in the late nineteenth century, even in the early 1900s it was not unusual for cities to register more annual deaths than births.

Migration was the principal source of urban growth throughout most of the imperial era. In light of the abysmal state of public health those who came to the city had little reason to stay very long. Indeed, for those members of urban society who had some choice in the matter, residence in the city was often very much a seasonal affair. For the social elites, especially the nobility, winter was the time to sojourn in the city since it was during that period that the social season was in full swing. With the arrival of spring many of those who could, departed for the *dacha* or estate. Peasants too had limited attachment to the city, though as we have noted, for rather different reasons than elites. But whether because of social custom, expiry of permit, inadequate or too costly housing, or the legitimate fear of being caught up in the regular outbreak of epidemic disease, transience was an ingrained feature of urban life in Russia. Indeed, even those who ostensibly had some claim to permanent urban residence were very much on the move. Frequent changes of address (made easier owing to the very high proportion of rental accommodation in the housing stock), were common for those people listed in the city directory. High levels of transience meant many things, and among them were less commitment to the city, less concern with its management and its resultant environmental quality.

Change usually associated with rapid urban-industrialization was in Russia inhibited by technological backwardness and by ingrained social custom. Technological backwardness was manifested in many ways in the Russian city. For example, the limited development of public transport meant that the voluntary residential segregation of particular groups, especially the elites and emerging middle classes, in socially homogeneous suburbs was severely restricted. In contrast to many European and North American cities where the process of residential segregation had long since left an indelible stamp on urban form, in some of the larger Russian cities a kind of three-dimensional residential segregation occurred. In the multi-storeyed built environment of central St Petersburg, for example, the lower classes were often

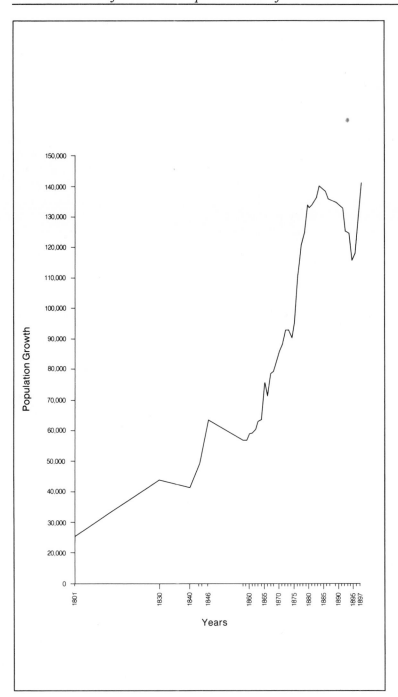

Fig. 7   Population Change – Kazan'

Source: M.V. Kazanskiy, *Putevoditel' po Kazani* (Kazan': Tipo-Litografiya Imperatorskogo Universiteta, 1899), 126–7.

forced to live in the cellars and garrets. On the floors in between lived a heterogeneous mix of social groups. Toward the periphery of the city, land-use intensity fell off, and the proportion of the lower classes amongst the population increased correspondingly. Ability to pay was as often reflected in the size of the apartment and the manner in which it was furnished as it was through an exclusive claim to territory. In effect the lavish decoration of living space might help to insulate social elites from the poor who might be housed above and below in the same building. But once on the street social elites were dependent upon the time-honoured personal symbols of rank and status, that is upon uniform or dress, to proclaim their place amidst the seeming confusion of classes and activities. However, on the eve of the First World War such symbols no longer guaranteed a deferential response from the burgeoning masses. Indeed, at a time when the status-quo in Russian society was increasingly being called into question, such personalized symbols of rank and class might well have heightened resentment. Deficient municipal services and hypercongestion had already made the Russian city uncommonly hazardous in terms of public health. For the social elites and the leading government bureaucrats, residence in the city was becoming increasingly hazardous in other ways as well.

Reform, revolution and civil war

Alexander II, the Tsar who had 'liberated' the serfs by passing the Emancipation Act of 1861, was assassinated in 1881. Thereafter, despite a vastly expanded network of police, spies and agent-provocateurs, the government was unable to stem the anarchist and revolutionary movements. Of course, many legitimate grievances served to generate support for groups advocating social, economic and political reform, whether by peaceful or violent means. As was noted earlier, at the turn of the century Russia was in the grip of a severe depression. Famines, and then riots, spread across the countryside. In the cities the cost of living was rapidly outstripping the rise in wages. Unions were illegal, strikes were illegal. There was no real mechanism for legitimately voicing the concerns and aspirations of the majority of the population. In the city there was elected municipal government. However, under the highly restrictive franchise imposed by the state usually less than one per cent of a city's population was entitled to vote. Few bothered. Thus the potential for social reform on the part of municipal government was severely limited. From time to time strikes occurred, invariably to be put down by brute force. Resentment festered. After the turn of the century each year witnessed more instances of resistance to authority. A growing list of prominent people fell victim to assassination. Years of economic depression and growing social unrest culminated in 1905 in widespread strikes and mass demonstrations to publicize perceived injustices and inequities, as we have already seen. The debacle of the Russo-Japanese War had brought matters to a head. The social, economic and political upheaval which occurred in 1905 was in every sense a revolution. It was not the first revolution in Russia, nor was it to be the last.

The Stolypin Agrarian Reforms were one manifestation of Tsar Nicholas II's attempt to mollify public opinion and accommodate change. An equally significant gesture was the creation in 1906 of a *Duma*, or Consultative Assembly, to which members would be elected. The existence of a State *Duma* meant that political parties were now legal in the Empire. Still, the authority of the Tsar was not entirely emasculated. On issues deemed vital to national interests the Tsar had veto power over legislation passed by the *Duma*. Indeed, the very existence of a *Duma* was dependent upon imperial goodwill. For example, after elections to the first *Duma* revealed a strong liberal sentiment amongst its members, it was disbanded by the Tsar and the election procedures were changed. Manipulation of the franchise resulted in a political complexion more or less satisfactory to the Tsar and his advisors. All parties including Lenin's Bolsheviks, now had a legal, and public, forum in which issues could be raised and debated.

Through a combination of reforms, conciliatory gesture and, where necessary, brute force, the upheaval of 1905 was finally subdued. In the process, grass-roots organizations of workers called 'soviets' were abolished. These had appeared spontaneously during 1905. Aside from coordinating strikes, the soviets on occasion helped to maintain public order where local government and police had fallen into disarray. During 1905 the formation of soviets became a more formal democratic process. All factories and trades, for instance, were encouraged to elect delegates to local soviets on the basis of one delegate for every 100 workers. The network of soviets was centred on the capital, St Petersburg. The spread of an overtly socialist, grass-roots organization had been rapid. Clearly it could not be tolerated under an autocracy. But it proved simpler to suppress the formal trappings of this organization than it did the idea.

In the years following the revolution of 1905 the process of urban-industrialization quickened perceptibly. But the fundamental contradictions inherent in an autocracy persisted. And so, too, did the privation experienced both by large numbers of urban workers and by millions of peasants dependent for a living upon marginal land. As the demand for labour increased, vast numbers departed the countryside for the town, only to be confronted by an inflationary spiral in which wages lagged behind the already high costs of food, fuel and housing. Social unrest was always a potential threat to the stability of the Empire.

The outbreak of the First World War in 1914 fired the nationalism of political leaders and general populace alike. Amidst the initial outburst of enthusiasm to defend the interests of Slavs everywhere, the name of the capital itself was changed from St Petersburg to Petrograd in deference to anti-German sentiment. However, as the war effort dragged on, as casualties mounted, eventually reaching the millions, as management of the armed forces, domestic economy and government became increasingly inept, dissatisfaction rose. From 1914 to 1917 the annual number of strikes increased from fewer than 100 to 1300, and this was just in those factories subject to government inspection. As the domestic economy deteriorated, food shortages grew worse, and food riots in the cities became commonplace. The cost of living soared. Hours of work in factories increased as overtime was demanded of the labour force, a growing proportion of which was made up of women and children. The mobilization of 14 million men left factory and farm short of labour in general, and it seriously depleted the ranks of skilled workers in particular. In the growing chaos political activism by socialist and revolutionary groups increased. Meanwhile from the State *Duma* came appeals to maintain, indeed augment, the war effort.

These increasingly fell upon deaf ears. Government was ineffectual. The personal involvement of Tsar Nicholas II in military strategy was a failure. Surrounded by sycophants, poorly advised, uncertain in action and dependent upon the advice of his wife Alexandra, who in turn was manipulated by the infamous Gregory Rasputin, Nicholas II and all he stood for was discredited. He abdicated in March 1917.

Failure to find a successor to Nicholas II created an unprecedented crisis. Just a few days before abdicating Nicholas dissolved the fourth, and last, State *Duma*. The Empire now had neither Tsar nor government. As an interim measure a Provisional Government was formed. But the Provisional Government was handicapped by the very circumstances giving rise to it – world war, a national economy in near ruin and political conflict. Though committed to the task of bringing into existence a democratically elected Constituent Assembly, the exigencies of the times and the absence of any tradition of consensual politics made a daunting task all the more difficult. Election of the new Constituent Assembly was eventually set for the autumn of 1917. However, a revolutionary solution to the domestic chaos in Russia had already been set in motion.

The economic chaos during the war and the abdication of the Tsar were sufficient conditions for the re-emergence of the system of soviets. Indeed, during the eight months of Provisional Government real political power rapidly built up in the network of soviets, once again centred in the capital. Lenin returned to Russia in the spring of 1917 after a long period of exile in Europe. While abroad he shaped the policies and programmes of the Bolsheviks, a faction of the Russian Social Democratic Workers Party he had led since its formation in 1903. Having recognized the political significance of the fast expanding soviets, Lenin added the slogan 'All power to the soviets,' to the Bolshevik calls for an end to the war and a redistribution of agricultural land. Most probably the call to end the war and to redistribute land would have been more comprehensible to the masses than 'All power to the soviets'. But as the soviet system spread from factory to armed forces to the countryside, its significance began to be appreciated by a growing number of people, including those in the Provisional Government. Indeed, before long important policy decisions taken by the Provisional Government had to be approved by the soviet in Petrograd.

The Bolsheviks twice attempted to overthrow the Provisional Government in 1917. The first effort in July was a failure and resulted in Lenin fleeing Petrograd to take refuge in nearby Finnish territory. In early autumn he secretly returned to Petrograd. With a growing Bolshevik presence in the key soviets in the factories and garrisons of the capital, Lenin was able to plan another attempt to overthrow a weakened and increasingly demoralized Provisional Government, a government with no real popular support, a government in name only. This occurred on 25 October 1917, on the eve of the Second All Russian Congress of Workers and Soldiers Deputies. The Bolshevik forces met with scarcely any resistance. With the Provisional Government now gone, the Congress, comprising delegates from the soviets which had spread across much of the country, was confronted with a successful *coup d'état*. A motion was adopted to the effect that the Executive Committee of the Congress should administer the country until the election of the Constituent Assembly. This had been set for 25 November by the now defunct Provisional

Government. The 'revolution' of 25 October, 1917 did not immediately give power to the Bolsheviks. Indeed, within the soviets across the country Bolsheviks were customarily a minority. But in the Congress's Executive there were a number of Bolsheviks, including Lenin himself. Thus, political power was determined not so much by the number of delegates, but by control over the vital centres of decision-making. It was in this context that the Executive of the Congress was so singularly important.

The election of a Constituent Assembly took place as planned. But it demonstrated that throughout Russia support for the Bolsheviks was limited. Still, as the real political power came increasingly into the hands of the soviets, and especially the executive, this was not a major problem. By early 1918 Lenin mustered support for a decree to dissolve the newly elected Assembly. Political authority now resided in the network of soviets, over which the Bolsheviks exercised control. By the summer of that year a new constitution was adopted in which the soviet became the key element in the new political reality. Peace had been declared on 25 October 1917, but it was only in March 1918 that the war with Germany was formally concluded by the Treaty of Brest-Litovsk. Peasants needed little encouragement to displace estate owners and distribute the land following the decree of 26 October, 1917 to nationalize land. Thus, in a matter of a few short months the Bolsheviks had realized three key objectives – giving political power to the soviets, redistributing land, and ending Russia's involvement in the Great War.

The revolution of 1917 confirmed the demise of autocracy and ensured the same fate for capitalism. It also triggered nationalist aspirations amongst a number of the minorities who had been incorporated into the Russian Empire during the centuries-long process of territorial expansion, because the Bolsheviks, led by Lenin, decreed the right of all nationalities to self-determination on 25 October. Finland, Latvia, Lithuania and Estonia won their independence after the war, while republics were declared, but not sustained in the Ukraine and the Caucasus. Other territories on the western flank of the old Empire, most notably Poland, were lost in the process of creating the new states of Eastern Europe following the Treaty of Versailles. Within the new Soviet state, however, the economy was in chaos. Even political control was questionable as civil war erupted in the summer of 1918.

The Bolsheviks had finessed their way to power, rather than winning outright majority support. Coalitions with other socialist parties had helped, but these were fragile arrangements and soon crumbled. Meanwhile resistance to socialists in general, and Bolsheviks in particular, mounted. The anti-Bolshevik forces were varied in their political complexion. The Mensheviks (created at the time of the factionalization of the Russian Social Democratic Workers' Party in 1903, which produced the Bolshevik, or literally if not accurately, the majority element of the same party), and the Socialist Revolutionaries criticized, but were not counter-revolutionary in action. Parties of the centre and right, especially those supportive of the monarchist and now dispossessed landed gentry, were in forcible opposition. These anti-Bolshevik, or White, coalitions and groups under such leaders as Wrangel, Denekin and Kolchak reduced the Bolshevik-controlled territories to a core area of European Russia focused on Moscow. But they lacked popular support, especially amongst the peasantry who had been only too willing to 'redistribute' estate lands. As the Red

Army was reorganized, largely through the efforts of Trotsky, the anti-Bolshevik forces were slowly pushed back. The direct intervention of some Allied countries during the summer of 1918 further complicated matters. Ostensibly Allied intervention was intended to prevent the German forces acquiring munitions supplies located in Russia. But some moral support was also provided the Whites. Certainly the reconstitution of an eastern front was a widely shared objective amongst the Allied countries, but their intervention also played into the hands of the Bolsheviks, who quickly capitalized on the opportunity to embark on a propaganda war against Allies and Whites alike. The civil war probably would have been concluded earlier were it not for the Allied intervention. In any event, it was not until the autumn of 1920 that the last of the anti-Bolshevik forces was defeated.

In the years of civil war following the revolution the fabric of society and economy alike was pulled apart. Many Bolshevik policies, however, simply exacerbated the disintegration of the domestic economy. In the attempt to remove capitalist structures and replace them with socialist forms, a number of irrational elements were introduced into the economy. The years from 1918 to 1921 are referred to as the period of War Communism. The revolution of 1917 was thus just one element, albeit a vitally important one, in the process of change. It was not until the mid 1920s that conditions in the new Soviet state assumed a measure of normalcy. The old order was no more; but what socialism actually meant had still to be determined.

Recommended reading

Anderson, B., *Internal Migration During Modernization in Late Nineteenth Century Russia* (Princeton: Princeton University Press, 1980).

Bater, James H., *St. Petersburg: Industrialization and Change* (London: Edward Arnold, 1976).

Bater, James H., French R.A., (eds), *Studies in Russian Historical Geography* (London: Academic Press, 1983), 2 vols.

Becker, S., *Nobility and Privilege in Late Imperial Russia* (Dekalb: Northern Illinois University Press, 1985).

Blackwell, W.L., *The Industrialization of Russia. An Historical Perspective* (New York: Thomas Y. Crowell, 1970).

Blum, J., *Lord and Peasant in Russia From the Ninth to the Nineteenth Century* (New York: Atheneum, 1961).

Bradley, Joseph, *Muzhik and Muscovite Urbanization in Late Imperial Russia* (Berkeley: University of California Press, 1984).

Brooks, J., *When Russia Learned to Read* (Princeton: Princeton University Press, 1985).

Chamberlain, W.H., *The Russian Revolution 1917–1918* (Princeton: Princeton University Press, 1987, first published 1935), 2 vols.

Crisp, O., *Studies in the Russian Economy Before 1914* (London: Macmillan, 1976).

Fedor, T., *Patterns of Urban Growth in the Russian Empire During the Nineteenth Century* (Chicago: University of Chicago Department of Geography Research Paper, No. 163, 1975).

Glickman, R.L., *Russian Factory Women. Workplace and Society 1880–1914* (Berkeley: University of California Press, 1984).

Guroff, G., Carstenson, F.V. (eds), *Entrepreneurship in Imperial Russia and the Soviet Union* (Princeton: Princeton University Press, 1983).

Hamm, M.F. (ed), *The City in Late Imperial Russia* (Bloomington: Indiana University Press, 1986).

Harcave, S., *First Blood: The Russian Revolution of 1905* (New York: Macmillan, 1964).

Kaiser, D.H., *The Workers' Revolution in Russia, 1917. The View From Below.* (Cambridge: Cambridge University Press, 1987).

Kanatchikov, S.I., *A Radical Worker in Tsarist Russia: The Autobiography of Semen Ivanovich Kanatchikov* (Reginald E. Zelnik ed. and trans.) (Berkeley: University of California Press, 1986).

Keep, J., *The Russian Revolution: A Study in Mass Mobilization* (New York: Norton, 1976).

Lyashchenko, P.I., *History of the National Economy of Russia to the 1917 Revolution* (New York: Macmillan, 1949).

Pares, B., *A History of Russia* (New York: Alfred A. Knopf, 1964).

Parker, W.H., *An Historical Geography of Russia* (London: University of London Press, 1968).

Rabinowitch, A., *The Bolsheviks Come to Power: The Revolution of 1917 in Petrograd* (New York: Norton, 1976).

Riasanovsky, N., *A History of Russia* (Oxford: Oxford University Press, 1984), 4th ed.

Ransel, D. (ed.), *The Family in Imperial Russia* (Urbana: University of Illinois Press, 1978).

Rieber, A., *Merchants and Entrepreneurs in Imperial Russia*, (Chapel Hill: University of North Carolina Press, 1982).

Smith, S.A., *Red Petrograd: Revolution in the Factories, 1917–1918* (Cambridge: Cambridge University Press, 1983).

Sumner, B.H., *Survey of Russian History* (London: Methuen, 1961).

3 The Nature of the Soviet System

For the first time in history, the working man has become master of the country, the creator of his own destiny.

Gorbachev, 1985.[1]

The revolution of 1917 heralded the rise of an entirely new order, one in which many values and relationships had to be worked out according to socialist principles. The prospects were exciting, but they were also uncertain since there was no existing socialist system to use as a model and only vague guidelines in the theory available on socialism. In the process of transforming imperial Russia into a socialist state the Communist Party and the soviets were destined to play important roles. Fundamental changes soon occurred. All resources, including land, were nationalized shortly after the Bolsheviks seized power. The state also assumed control over many sectors of the economy, including banking and foreign trade. Some elements of privatism were immediately abolished and most others were to follow. In the place of privatism the ethos of collectivism was to be cultivated instead. To usher in the new order required that plans be formulated, decisions taken, results monitored. All of this demanded new bureaucracies and countless officials to staff them. The existence of a bloated bureaucracy was nothing new in the history of imperial Russia. What would be new would be the degree to which bureaucrats intruded themselves into the affairs of ordinary citizens. The population was now out from under the thumb of patrimonial, autocratic Russia, but there was a long road between the reality of day to day life in 1917 and the utopian existence portended by the revolution.

We will begin this chapter with a description of the political and governmental structure of the Soviet Union. The framework for, and process of, economic decision-making will then be outlined. In this discussion attention will be accorded

[1] Mikhail Gorbachev, 'Communique on the Plenary Session of the Central Committee of the Communist Party of the Soviet Union,' *Pravda* and *Izvestiya*, 24 April, 1985, 1, in *The Current Digest of the Soviet Press*, Vol. 37, No. 17, 1985, 3.

both the formal and informal sectors of the Soviet economy; included as well will be a brief assessment of the performance and problems of the contemporary Soviet economy.

Governance and the Party

The adoption of a constitution for the Russian Soviet Federative Socialist Republic in July 1918 enshrined the Soviet in the new political reality. This served as a model for the constitution ratified for the Union of Soviet Socialist Republics in January, 1924. The Communist Party (as the Bolshevik faction of the Russian Social Democratic Workers' Party came to be known after March 1918) played a central role in these developments. Before considering the structure for government, it is necessary first of all to have some sense of how the Communist Party functions.

At no time has the membership of the Communist Party been very large, at least in terms of the relative proportion of the total population. In November 1917 there were perhaps as many as 150,000 Bolsheviks. At the time the Empire's total population was in the order of 160 million. The Bolsheviks were clearly a very small political group. Their success in overthrowing the Provisional Government is even more remarkable when it is recognized that the Party membership was probably no more than 20,000 in early 1917, though clearly it grew rapidly during the summer and autumn of that year. During the Soviet era the Communist Party has played a central role in the economic, social and, of course, political life of the country. But even now the nearly 19 million Communist Party members, including those in a probationary status, comprise a shade less than 7 per cent of the total Soviet population. Indeed, there are presently probably more full-time Party officials than there were Party members at the time of the revolution in November 1917! The bureaucratization of the Party began shortly after the death of Lenin in 1924 and continued apace until the Gorbachev era when the possibility of paring back the Party bureaucracy was raised for the first time.

The clandestine nature of Bolshevik activities in the early years of its existence gave credence to the need for strict discipline and a sense of hierarchy. But it was not until the Stalin era that the typically free-wheeling, vigorous debate over ideological and policy matters within the Party was forcibly curtailed. Under Stalin policies were increasingly determined at the top, while the mandate of those below was to implement, not to question. Greater discipline was achieved not just by squelching dissident opinion, but by purging those who held dissenting views. Mass arrests, particularly during the 1934–38 period, political trials, exile and execution on an unprecedented scale ensured a measure of compliance amongst Party members in particular and within Soviet society in general. Some attributes of totalitarianism were certainly present at this time including the monopolization of power based on the ever more inflexible ideology underpinning the Communist Party, the bureaucratization of society, the obliteration of dissenting views, mass mobilization of society to attain common goals, usually, but not exclusively related to production targets, and so on. The Communist Party that emerged out of this process of change was one in which the predispositions, indeed, the whims, of one person, Josef Stalin, often shaped policy and practice. Yet even during the Stalin era the notion that the

USSR represented a totalitarian model of society is overly simplistic. Interest groups still continued to press for advantage within the Party and the system, though to be sure the process was less public, and frequently only really comprehended by the cognoscenti. Totalitarianism may have been the goal of some, but Soviet society under Stalin was in reality much more complex than the totalitarian model suggests. The passage of time tends to mute what life must have been like for many people during this era, but Arthur Koestler's *Darkness at Noon* (1940) goes some way toward conveying the sense of unease which seems to have characterized this perverse period of Soviet history. Stalin's manipulation of Party affairs continued until his death in 1953.

Soviet society since Stalin has become increasingly complex with a host of internal pressure groups representing everything from the Party to nationalities to social classes, all complicated further by the replacement of one generation with another. The Communist Party has increased in membership and shifted from the dominance of a single individual to what is usually described as a collective leadership. The basic structure of the Party is outlined in Fig. 8. The hierarchical framework corresponds to the political-administrative organization of the state. At the top of the Party hierarchy is the Politburo, the key decision-making body. Its membership is small, sometimes no more than a baker's dozen in number, but it nonetheless comprises several different interest groups. The Communist Party Central Committee has emerged since Stalin's time as an influential forum for debating policy alternatives. With 300-odd full members a much broader range of viewpoints was likely to be found on any specific issue than was the case in the Politburo, if only because the median age of Politburo members was for so long so much higher than in the Central Committee and therefore the shared experience of the past tended to play a more important role in shaping perceptions. However, the arrival of Mikhail Gorbachev has brought change. He is the first youthful leader in decades. In consolidating his position he has appointed a number of younger men to the Politburo and retired a number of the most elderly. As noted earlier, the Party bureaucracy itself is enormous. Within it an elite has emerged with a voice in Party affairs.

Despite the demise of the 'cult of the personality', the rise of a collective leadership, and the appearance of various interest groups and forums for discussion, an essentially top-down decision-making process still characterizes Party affairs. The Politburo convenes at least once a week, while the Central Committee which, in theory, elects it, meets twice a year. The Party Congress in turn elects the Central Committee, but the roughly 5,000 delegates to the Congress as a rule assemble only once every five years. The special Congress held in June 1988 to affirm the Gorbachev plan for restructuring the economy and its management was a rare break from past practice. Thus, the Politburo remains the key element in the decision-making process even if diversity of opinion and consultation with other groups, including the middle echelon of the Party membership, is now tolerated. The role of the Party is indeed as pervasive as Fig. 9 implies and it ought to be borne in mind that in the Soviet Union there has only ever been one political party.

To become a Party member requires more than simply filling out a form and paying monthly dues. Although the total membership is now around 19 million, it was and remains by definition something of an elite. To join requires approval, and

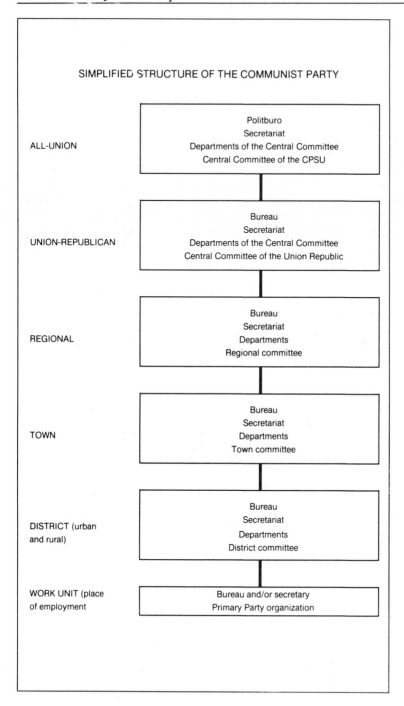

Fig. 8   Simplified Structure of the Communist Party

Source: A. Brown *et al.* (eds.), *The Cambridge Encyclopedia of Russia and the Soviet Union* (Cambridge: Cambridge University Press, 1982), 296.

this is usually the culmination of a long process of moving from youth group to the *Komsomol'*, (the All-Union Leninist Communist Union of Youth), to 'probation-ary' Party status. However, success in some fields of endeavour is often recognized through an invitation to join. Once a member of the Party, public and private behaviour is expected to conform to established norms, and each year witnesses the expulsion of some people for various transgressions. Ostensibly Party membership is monitored to ensure that all strata of Soviet society are adequately represented. As in most societies, however, participation in elitist organizations is usually sought by those wishing to get ahead, and over the years joining the Communist Party has been widely perceived as facilitating this objective.

Clearly, the Communist Party controls the government (Fig. 9). In less obvious ways it intrudes itself into every other facet of the Soviet scene as well. To this end the Party maintains a register of politically dependable people, and a list of positions in which political reliability is deemed essential. The *nomenklatura*, as this list is known, is just one way through which control is exercised. Within the Party itself are organizations which parallel, for example, those of the government, economy, culture, education, military and police. Thus, Party members will be found in key positions in factories, state farms, ballet companies, and so on. The responsibility of Party members so employed is to monitor, to cajole, to manipulate as necessary in order to fulfil directives initiated above. However, as Soviet society becomes more sophisticated, as consumer expectations rise, the task of making the system work effectively becomes more difficult. In this context, one of the most pressing dilemmas for the leadership is the extent to which autonomy in decision-making should be decentralized.

While the Party and its extensive bureaucracy are mandated to facilitate the realization of national objectives, there was growing, irrefutable evidence that it was becoming an obstacle to change itself. Under Gorbachev rather radical remedies have been proposed. Instead of a life-time sinecure, Party officials are to have limited terms of office and are to be democratically elected to them rather than just appointed. This is to apply to the office of general secretary of the Communist Party, Gorbachev's own position, down to the 300-odd members of the Central Committee. After nearly three-quarters of a century of sinecured positions, save for the Stalin era purges, the unease such a proposed change caused amongst the Party's officialdom might be easily imagined. However, amongst the public at large the proposal found much favour since the privileges of Party officials were the object of considerable envy, if not criticism. Gorbachev's pursuit of greater democracy, under the banner of *glasnost'*, or openness, unleashed enormous public debate on many aspects of the reality of the Soviet scene which previously were taboo subjects. The privileges and sinecured positions of Party functionaries were certainly amongst them. The idea of contested elections was another. From Party, to academia, to government, to the shop floor, the election of officials from a slate of candidates is now possible. The Soviet populace at large is still warming to the task at hand since such democratic processes were to a large extent a lost art. The process of democratization began first with Gorbachev's efforts to resuscitate the national economy. Here the by-words were *perestroyka*, or restructuring, and *uskoreniye*, or acceleration. But before we turn our attention to this issue, the political-administrative framework for governance

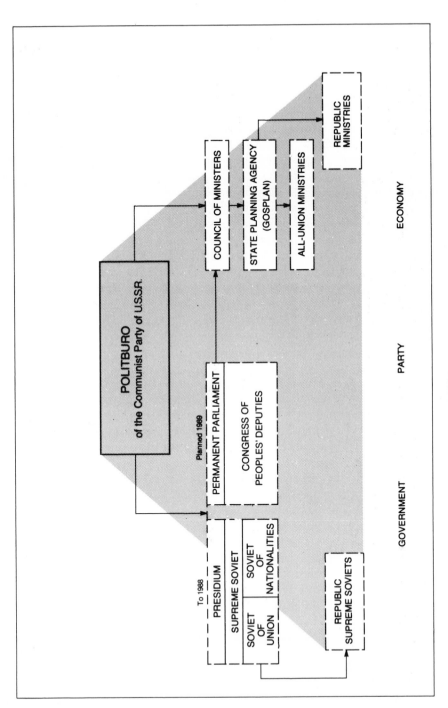

Fig. 9 Simplified Structure of Decision-Making in the USSR

Source: James H. Bater, *The Soviet City. Ideal and Reality*, (London: Edward Arnold, 1980), 38.

and for managing the economy requires brief elaboration.

As a federal system the USSR currently embraces 15 Soviet Socialist Republics, which in turn contain 20 Autonomous Soviet Socialist Republics, eight Autonomous Oblasts and ten Autonomous Okrugs (see Fig. 10). The highest-order unit is the Soviet Socialist Republic. According to the Soviet constitution the nationalities so represented have all the rights of a sovereign state, including the right to secede. For that reason all such republics are peripheral to the Russian Soviet Federative Socialist Republic, as a careful inspection of Fig. 10 reveals. A number of nationalities residing within the Russian Federative Soviet Socialist Republic have Autonomous Soviet Socialist Republic status although they outnumber several of the minorities having full republic status. Theoretically, the titular nationality of a republic comprises the majority of the population, but this is not the case for the Kazakh and Kirgiz peoples. Given the reality of the Soviet system, the *de jure* constitutional right to secede, to establish separate foreign relations and so on, is academic. Nonetheless, because of the nature of the Soviet constitution, and some apparently persuasive argument at the time the United Nations was created, the USSR was granted three seats, and thus three votes. The USSR and two republics, the Ukraine and Belorussia are still full voting members of the United Nations.

Since the late 1930s government authority has resided in the Supreme Soviet (Fig. 9). This bicameral legislature comprises the Soviet of the Union, to which members are elected on the basis of one delegate for every 300,000 people, and the Soviet of Nationalities, to which members are elected according to the status of political-administrative unit. Those nationalities represented in Fig. 10 have the right to send delegates in the following numbers: 32 for each Soviet Socialist Republic; 11 for each Autonomous Soviet Socialist Republic; five for each Autonomous Oblast; and one for each Autonomous Okrug. There are many other nationalities in the Soviet Union, but owing to their lower political-administrative status they are not directly represented in the Soviet of Nationalities. Until the Gorbachev-era reforms the delegates sent to the Supreme Soviet were invariably Communist Party nominees, and elections, while displaying near perfect turnouts, were from the standpoint of the Western observer politically uncontested. How far the system will go in accommodating contested elections and non-Party delegates remains to be seen.

Administrative functions of government are largely carried out by the Council of Ministers, a body elected from the Supreme Soviet and responsible to it, or the Presidium. The latter, which is also elected from the Supreme Soviet, is like an inner cabinet and can exercise legislative authority between sessions. In theory, the Supreme Soviet, which meets only occasionally, could revoke measures adopted by the Council of Ministers. In practice it does not, although on occasion it will recommend revisions. Thus, the day-to-day business of government at the national level falls very much on the shoulders of executive committees of one kind or another. The Council of Ministers has about 100 members and meets four times a year. It includes not just those responsible for various ministries, but since the late 1970s the chairmen of the State Committees as well. Until 1978 the numerous State Committees were under the jurisdiction of the Council of Ministers. Committee chairpersons are now members of the Council and hence their profile and potential influence is much greater. State Committees deal with a great many concerns; for

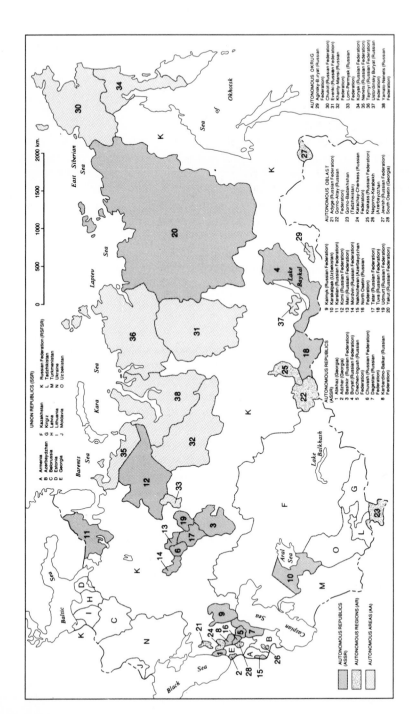

Fig. 10 Political-Administrative Regions – USSR

Source: A. Brown *et al.* (eds.), *The Cambridge Encyclopedia of Russia and the Soviet Union* (Cambridge: Cambridge University Press, 1982), 306–7.

example, there is Gosplan, the key state planning agency; the KGB or internal police; science and technology; environmental protection; and the protection of mother and child. The basic administrative structure of the Supreme Soviet, Council of Ministers and so on is replicated in each Soviet Socialist Republic.

While this basic political-administrative structure has a long history it is not immutable as the discussion and debate during the extraordinary Party Congress held in late June 1988 indicated. In addition to legitimizing *glasnost', perestroyka* and *uskoreniye* recommendations to modify the political system were adopted and later endorsed, or perhaps more aptly, cautiously articulated by the Politburo. What is intended is a more explicit leadership role for the Party and its bureaucracy, and less interference in the management of the economic system in particular and in affairs of day to day life in general. A modification of the existing Supreme Soviet, Council of Ministers and Presidium structure is regarded as a central element in the Gorbachev-era reform. Instead of the present arrangement whereby the Supreme Soviet meets twice a year and day-to-day management proceeds as described above, a new bicameral assembly is to come into being as early as spring 1989. Comprising 2250 members elected by secret ballot from slates of candidates, the proposed Congress of Peoples' Deputies would convene but once a year. Of its total membership, 750 representatives could be elected from various civic organizations such as professional groups or trade unions and therefore need not be Party members. By definition the remaining representatives would be, and therefore Party members would still comprise the majority. Each elected representative is to be limited to two five-year terms.

The principal distinction between what currently exists and what is proposed is that some 400-odd members of this bicameral assembly would be elected to a new permanent parliament which would debate and enact both domestic and foreign-policy legislation. The Council of Ministers and Presidium of the current system would thus disappear in their present guise, and direct Party involvement in the management of domestic affairs would wane. All of this is to be facilitated by a legal reform which would provide the necessary independence of state from Party. The strategic planning role of the Politburo would continue, however. In keeping with these changes at the national level, the apparatus of government at the Republic and lower levels would similarly change. A recurring theme during the Gorbachev era has been the restoration of proper authority to city and regional Soviets. But this is not a new issue as the discussion of past efforts to mobilize the statutory authority of the city Soviets in Chapter 5 will make plain.

While the June 1988 extraordinary Party Congress permitted an unprecedented degree of free public debate and criticism of present and past Party officialdom, it should not be construed as a quest for a fundamental restructuring of the existing socialist system. Many of the recommendations ultimately adopted, and later interpreted by the Politburo remain rather fuzzy as to actual intent and procedure – perhaps intentionally so. Certainly the call for a legal reform has yet to be spelled out in much detail. As will be noted in subsequent chapters, it is often far easier to change the legal apparatus, including that of government, than it is human values and habits. Decades of insulating the various elites from public scrutiny, and indeed public accountability, will not be readily aborted. The call to separate more clearly

Party and state which was so often heard during the June 1988 Congress may remain just that – a call.

Managing the economy

Economic planning has been administered through a hierarchy of ministries, committees, and departments for most of the Soviet era (Fig. 11). Basic policy decisions are taken by the Politburo, whose actions are accountable not to the government, that is, the Supreme Soviet, but to the Party Congress. In the realm of economic planning *per se*, the role of Gosplan is key. It is chaired by a deputy premier thereby ensuring a high profile. Once basic development priorities have been set by the Politburo, Gosplan translates them into plan-instructions for the ministries. As is apparent from Fig. 11, economic planning is a multi-faceted process in the Soviet Union. Theoretically, information required for economic planning passes up through the administrative hierarchy, while directives go down. The reality of the process is scarcely so simple. The following describes the nature of the planning process up until the 1980s when the Gorbachev reforms were initiated.

Ministries exist at three levels – All-Union, Union-Republic, and Republic – are numerous in number, and are in a constant state of flux. At present about 60 are concerned with economic matters. Plan-instructions usually cover a five-year period and theoretically determine for each year what is to be produced, how and by what means, where, when and to whom it is to be delivered, and at what price it is to be sold. Prices, both 'wholesale' and 'retail', in the absence of a market are established by the State Committee on Prices. The price structure is characterized by rigidity, is generally based upon estimated costs of production rather than resource scarcity, and is therefore of limited use in re-directing resource allocation. In practice central planning authorities do not make most of the detailed decisions regarding management of the economy. If they did the system simply would not work as well as it does. What has emerged, therefore, is something of a balance of real decision-making authority between ministries and central planners. Central authorities specify goals, set plans, and it is up to the ministerial decision-makers to do what is necessary to make the system work. The reality of the economic decision-making process is closer to what Alec Nove has called 'centralized pluralism'. In this context, ministries almost inevitably become interest groups. But some ministries, and ministers, are economically and politically more important than others. Nevertheless, within any particular ministry all decision-makers have a vested interest in at least appearing successful. Hence, in order to meet output targets ministerial decision-makers have tended to bring under their control as many inputs as possible. Where they are not able to control all the essential components for increasing production themselves, systems of mutually beneficial personal contacts have been developed to take up the slack. Where semi-legal bartering or exchange between production units fails to garner the necessary supplies, production targets are not fulfilled, bottlenecks occur, and positions of authority become increasingly tenuous. Even those in charge of important ministries have been dismissed for perceived failures. Thus, throughout the whole system all participants in the decision-making process have a real stake in making things work. While there is no question that the economy functions, and in

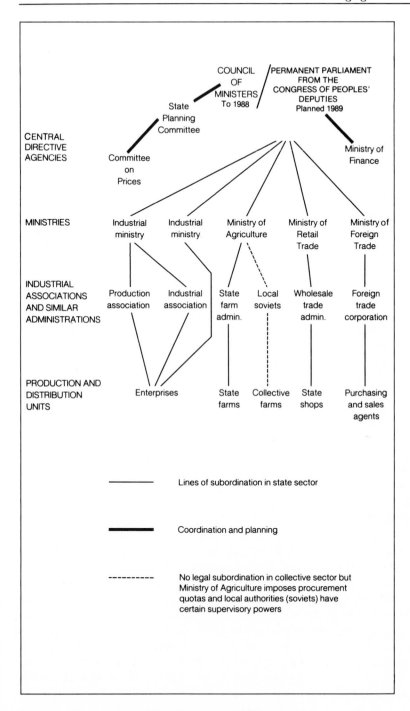

Fig. 11   The Framework for Managing the Economy

Source: Adapted from A. Brown *et al.* (eds.), *The Cambridge Encyclopedia of Russia and the Soviet Union* (Cambridge: Cambridge University Press, 1982), 356.

some sectors exceedingly well, there is also no question that the nature of the decision-making system produces a number of conflict situations.

In all economic systems there are tensions between regional and sectoral interests. During the Soviet period this tension has been exacerbated somewhat owing to the absence of any spokesperson for regional interests equivalent to that of the minister of a branch of the economy. This does not mean to say that the regional dimensions of economic development have been ignored. In fact, from the outset regional planning concepts played an important part in Soviet strategies for economic development. Probably the most widely publicized regional planning scheme in the immediate post-revolutionary period was the State Plan for the Electrification of Russia (GOELRO). This plan owed much to Lenin's enthusiasm for the generation of electric power as the essential lynch-pin in the programme of industrial development. The GOELRO scheme incorporated regional electric power grids as the basis for regional planning. But as was so often to occur during the early Soviet period, there was rather more theory than there was practice. The national economy, of course, had been devastated by World War I and the years of Civil War which followed. It was only in 1921 that internal political conditions stabilized to the point that rebuilding the national economy became a practical necessity. It was at this time that Lenin introduced his New Economic Policy. This pragmatic accommodation with reality encouraged small-scale private enterprise in both town and countryside, a measure critical to the ultimate success of the Soviet Union in regaining the levels of domestic production which existed in 1914. Such levels of output were generally not attained until the mid-1920s. Meanwhile, direct state intervention in the economic system in terms of regional planning remained at a comparatively low level.

Lenin's death in 1924 precipitated an internal power struggle in the Soviet Union out of which Stalin eventually emerged the central figure. He introduced the Five Year Plan in 1928, and along with it the initial apparatus of the ministerial system. There were some important regional development schemes initiated at this time, but these we will discuss in a later chapter. The point to be made here is simply that with the end of the New Economic Policy in 1928, and with it most vestiges of private enterprise, a sectoral rather than regional decision-making structure was embedded in the system. The arrival of the national economic planner provided an opportunity for regional planning, but it went largely unheeded.

The centralization of decision-making in economic matters paralleled the centralization of control over the Party, a feature which characterizes much of the Stalin era. It was not without a measure of success either. In terms of economic growth some impressive gains were registered during the 1930s. Annual rates of growth of industrial production, for example, frequently exceeded 10 per cent. During the world-wide depression of the 1930s the Soviet economic experiment attracted much favourable attention, and many otherwise unemployed European and North American technical and professional personnel took jobs in the Soviet Union. The 1940s witnessed the colossal destruction wrought by World War II and the ensuing vast programme of reconstruction during the Fourth Five Year Plan, 1946–50. By the early 1950s real economic growth resumed. But as was the case before the War, it was based on a narrow spectrum of activities, notably those related to basic industries such as iron and steel. Indeed, in many instances the Soviet

Union lagged behind developments in the West. The energy sector, for example, remained heavily dependent upon coal well into the 1950s, whereas in Europe and America oil and natural gas were increasingly important sources of energy. Agriculture and the consumer goods sector were intentionally given short shrift in the allocation of scarce investment capital, just as they had been before the war. In short, the Soviet economy registered rapid annual growth, but it was locked into a pattern established in the early 1930s. Modernization of some sectors was much needed, and so too was a better integration of development plans framed in an explicitly sectoral mode. What brought the need for more effective regional economic planning to the fore in the early 1950s was the widespread recognition that the existing decision-making structure was no longer working satisfactorily. The many criticisms of the ministerial system included the following: it resulted in bottlenecks and shortage of goods; it contributed to unacceptably high levels of cross-hauling of material supplies; it tended to emphasize quantitative, rather than qualitative aspects of production; and it fostered what was called ministerial autarchy.

Ministerial autarchy, or self-sufficiency, however was a logical response to two features of the Soviet decision-making environment; the constantly changing (usually higher) production targets set by central planners, and the uncertainty associated with dependence upon other ministries for critical material supplies. Thus, the more control a ministry had over inputs for the production process, including labour, the greater the potential for a successful, adaptive response to changing production targets set by central planners. While striving for self-sufficiency was perfectly rational at the ministerial and sub-ministerial level, this pattern of behaviour was frequently objectively irrational, and very costly, when viewed from the perspective of the state. It not only led to ministries producing goods properly the mandate of other ministries (which reduced the potential economies of scale in production for the latter), it also contributed to cross-hauling. The Soviet press is thick with accounts of the same good being transported in opposite directions often between two quite distant places, each origin and destination of movement determined by separate ministries. A broader perspective on demand and source of supply would highlight the complementary nature of each ministry's requirement. The compelling logic of each ministry meeting the need of the other by means of a local exchange is obvious. But logic and reality in decision-making are not always the same. The burden that unnecessary cross-hauling placed on the Soviet railroad system was enormous. Another obvious diseconomy associated with the ministerial drive for self-sufficiency was 'hoarding' labour. This resulted in the under-employment of an important resource in many factories. The long-standing pre-occupation with meeting those targets set in physical output terms in the easiest possible manner inevitably led to poor quality. The widespread habit of managers consciously underestimating what their particular factory was capable of producing when submitting information about plant output potential to higher planning authorities, and the latter's anticipation of this behaviour by way of even higher targets for production being imposed, frequently resulted in critical shortages when the targets set really did exceed what was physically possible to produce. All of these problems, and more besides, dictated that the decision-making process be re-examined.

The death of Stalin in 1953 provided an opportunity for serious discussion of fundamental reform of the Soviet economy. The problems were apparent, the solutions less so. Following the assumption of control by Nikita Khrushchev several potentially significant changes in the management and structure of the economy were instigated in 1957. Despite being well into the Sixth Five Year Plan, it was aborted. A Seven Year Plan, designed to carry development strategies through until 1965, was adopted instead. With the strong endorsement of Khrushchev the Seven Year Plan witnessed the dismantling of all but a handful of key All-Union ministries and the creation of over 100 regional economic councils, or *sovnarkhozy*, to take their place. Each *sovnarkhoz* was responsible for planning, managing and budgeting for virtually all economic activities in the region. Certainly there had long been a clear need for better integration of sectoral planning in a regional context. With so much authority vested in ministerial offices located in Moscow, or to a lesser extent in Republic capitals, there was often legitimate reason for contending that local requirements, or potentials, were being overlooked. The fact that the political importance of ministers heading up powerful All-Union Ministries would be emasculated in this restructuring of the decision-making system was perhaps not an insignificant benefit to someone like Khrushchev. He had survived the political in-fighting which followed Stalin's death, as opposed to having been immediately and enthusiastically acclaimed as leader.

The radical transformation of the decision-making structure initiated by Khrushchev was not without some potential pitfalls, however. The decision-making responsibility for achieving targets was widely decentralized geographically, and therefore the relationship between plan and reality was even more difficult to monitor. The basic industrial structure of the Soviet Union was also altered in several important ways at this time. Such changes usually prove problematic. We need only note at this point a couple of examples. In the energy sector the long-standing emphasis on coal production was changed. Instead the development of oil, and especially natural gas, which until this date had largely gone unused as an energy source, was promoted. Consumers goods, and related items like housing, municipal services, and so on were given a substantial fillip. Finally, putting authority into the hands of decision-makers at the regional level risked feeding nationalist aspirations, because the regions used as *sovnarkhozy* were political-administrative in origin, and therefore reflected the distribution of the various national minorities. Some minority groups needed little encouragement to put their interests ahead of those of the state as a whole. The Baltic Republics, which had been independent in the inter-World War period, and the peoples of the Caucasus, for example, were well known for their separatist tendencies. The *sovnarkhoz* experiment offered considerable scope for putting local interests ahead of the state's, notwithstanding the fact that the Party apparatus existed at all levels of the political-administrative cum regional system and ought to have been able to squelch such nationalist tendencies as came to the fore. In fact some of the regional Party bureaucracies did succumb to nationalist tendencies. For a variety of reasons the *sovnarkhoz* experiment soon came upon rocky ground.

Within a few years the clumsiness of decision-making vested in more than 100 regional economic councils took its toll. The number of *sovnarkhozy* was steadily reduced and finally consolidated into 47 larger regions. Centralized state committees were created in an effort to establish control from 'above', and discussion of other reform options proceeded apace. One such option involved redirecting emphasis from the quantitative fulfilment of planned targets, which was the essence of the Material Balance Planning method used by Soviet authorities since the 1930s, to meeting contracts with 'customers', thereby focusing more attention on the quality of goods produced. The measure of success would be the volume of sales and associated surplus of revenue over costs, or what might in the Soviet context be seen as profit. To encourage participation in this new approach to economic management the economist E.G. Liberman, with whom it is most frequently associated, proposed that a share of the profit be used in a discretionary system of bonuses for workers and managers alike. Toward the end of the Seven Year Plan some limited experimentation with the Liberman method was approved.

All of this rather radical, at least by Soviet standards, discussion and experimentation took place during a period of general liberalization of the Soviet system introduced by Khrushchev. Not only were economists free to debate the merits of various schemes for improving the performance of the economy, artists, writers and others were permitted freedom of expression not seen for decades. For instance, Solzhenitsyn's *One Day in the Life of Ivan Denisovich* was published in the premier literary journal *Novy Mir* in 1962 and signalled the state's tolerance of public assessment of the Stalin era. Khrushchev had earlier set in motion a widespread programme of de-Stalinization, which included rewriting history and the geography of place names. Across the Soviet Union public recognition of Stalin was purged, the renaming of countless streets, squares, cities being but one manifestation of the process. For many thousands of Soviet citizens the easing of restrictions on internal migration provided a new lease on life. Thus, the Khrushchev period is notable for considerable experimentation, a general relaxation of control over individual behaviour and a frank assessment of the Stalin era. But many of the schemes with which he was closely associated were not successful. In consequence, he was ousted in 1964. The assumption of power by L. Brezhnev and A. Kosygin brought management of the economy nearly full circle.

In 1965 a major economic reform was announced, though given the tenor of the debate which characterized the last years of the Khrushchev period it could scarcely be regarded as radical. The now discredited experiment with regional economic councils (*sovnarkhozy*) was shelved. The ministerial system was put back in place along with an expanded system of State Committees – but with some potentially important differences. The number of plan indicators central authorities used to monitor performance of individual enterprises was to be reduced drastically. More autonomy was given decision-makers at the grass-roots level to manage their affairs so as to best satisfy national priorities as set by central planners. Of course, the five year plans continued to serve medium-term development strategies, while fifteen or twenty-year planning scenarios were intended to keep the national economy abreast of technological changes and social needs. The annual plan, frequently altered, almost always unpredictable, remained the principal management tool. The 1965 reform, which the Eighth Five Year Plan beginning in 1966 officially introduced, included some concepts advocated by the economist Liberman. These included an emphasis on sales, profitability and discretionary incentive funds, all of which were intended to foster innovation and higher quality goods produced more efficiently.

Given the importance attached to enterprise profitability in the 1965 reform, a major price revision was required if there was to be anything like a rational accounting of profit. This occurred in 1967. As noted earlier, both retail and wholesale prices are established by the State Committee on Prices. While scarcity does play some part in price determination, most prices are set with state policy and social needs in mind. In other words, price is not regarded as an autonomous factor in resource allocation. For example, despite huge increases in the cost of providing public transport, the fares charged have remained unchanged for more than a quarter century. In such an environment a realistic assessment of cost, and profit, is bound to be elusive. The 1965 reform also introduced a charge on investment capital advanced by state banking institutions to some sectors of the economy. This charge, perhaps most readily likened to our notion of interest, was intended to bring about a more efficient use of financial capital. It was often the case that huge sums were allocated 'free of charge' to capital projects such as hydroelectric power stations. Many were not completed until years after they were scheduled to begin operation. Meanwhile, state investment capital drew no return. In a similar vein the assignment of industrial materials supply planning to the State Supply Committee was supposed to offset the autarchic tendencies of the ministerial system. By giving this committee a higher profile, material flows were supposed to be more predictable, and from the national perspective, less wasteful.

Some features of the 1965 economic reform implied a loosening of control from above. Perhaps not too surprising is the fact that such initiatives did not always meet with widespread enthusiasm since they were often direct challenges to well ensconced vested interests in the Soviet system. For nearly 40 years the locus of decision-making had been based in the upper echelons of the hierarchical structure in party, government and economic planning (excepting in this latter case, of course, the Khrushchev-initiated *sovnarkhozy* experiment). After some initial success with the 'new' ministerial structure several of the traditional problems reappeared. The number of performance indicators steadily grew, and thus eroded such local autonomy as had existed. Ministries resisted materials supply planning by the State Supply Committee, preferring instead to achieve a measure of self-sufficiency with all of the attendant inefficiencies already described. The revision of industrial wholesale prices in 1967 did not bring all the changes desired either. Given the rigidity of the price structure, innovation continued to be frustrated. It was frequently more 'profitable' for a plant to manufacture an old product than introduce new lines, where the margin between cost and sale price was less. Indeed, the distribution of enterprise profits soon became less a discretionary bonus to workers for higher productivity than an expected regular supplement to the monthly wage packets. Put simply, the introduction of profitability did not radically improve the propensity to innovate, nor did the creation of bonus funds bring about a fundamental change in the attitude toward work as evidenced by the various measures of labour productivity. The 1965 economic reform brought some improvements, but it did not mark a divergent trend away from centralized decision-making in economic planning. By the early 1970s it was recognized that something else had to be done.

In a complex economy many important development opportunities lie at the interface of traditional industrial sectors, which in the Soviet Union are customarily set up as separate ministries. The Soviet decision-making structure announced in 1965 did little to facilitate inter-ministerial initiatives. Indeed, as the economy expanded the sheer number of individual enterprises, be they factories, warehouses, or scientific research institutes, grew correspondingly, and so too did the task of centrally coordinating them all. Not infrequently by-products of one manufacturing process which could be used as input in another simply ended up as waste owing to the lack of integration of enterprises belonging to different ministries. The loss to the national economy was sizeable, and thus in 1973 a new organizational unit was created – the *obedineniye*, or association. Intended to replace the individual enterprise (*predpriyatiye*) as the basic administrative unit in the industrial and resource development sectors, the association conceivably could include design, production and distributional functions previously under the jurisdiction of several ministries. There were two types, production associations and industrial associations, but their common purpose was to promote greater efficiency through economies of scale and, because of their legal status, to minimize bureaucratic interference in production. But even here the apparent benefits were not sufficient to alter behaviour of institutions and individuals alike. Since 1973 ministries have been adept at protecting their turf, and attempts to transfer real decision-making to the *obedineniye* have been successfully resisted. Most of the problems giving rise to the *obedineniye* still exist.

The 1965 economic reform and the creation of the *obedineniye* in 1973 were both intended to provide greater scope for grass roots initiative, while at the same time facilitating central planning. Fostering grass-roots initiative is one thing, weakening the central planning function is quite another. The dilemma for the state is that to the extent real control from the centre is given up, central planning becomes more problematic. In any event, the inertia, or resistance to change, within the Soviet system is considerable, and has in fact served to frustrate most decentralization efforts in the past. The ministerial apparatus, the Party bureaucracy, and probably even a large segment of the population itself, is disinclined to readily accommodate such change. To do so perhaps raises the possibility of losing power, working harder for less certain gain, or both. Notwithstanding the difficulties involved in attempting to plan such a complex and, indeed, increasingly sophisticated economy, there is as yet no suggestion that the basic centralized decision-making structure be dismantled. Indeed, economic policy changes since 1965 have consistently affirmed the role of central planning and are intended to facilitate it, not to undermine it. In 1978 Brezhnev endorsed the need for central planning by arguing for more not less authority for Gosplan. A year later a formal decree confirmed the sanctity of central planning. Since the 1979 decree other measures have been introduced to further improve the central planning function.

Another revision of basic industrial wholesale prices was undertaken in 1982. Some retail prices were also increased substantially at this time. The retail cost of gasoline, for example, was about doubled. But for the growing number of people who own a car this was less traumatic than might initially appear, since it is estimated that close to half of all gasoline consumed by the private sector comes from other than 'official' channels. In other words, it is acquired illegally through purchase, barter or outright theft. The increase in gasoline prices at the pump is but one instance of the attempt by the state to facilitate central planning of resource development and allocation through a more realistic price structure intended to encourage conservation and more efficient consumption.

Balanced regional development has figured prominently in Soviet economic development theory. Obviously, the continual affirmation of the ministerial system and central planning does not solve the problem of integrating sectoral plans with regional needs. In response to this issue the role of the major economic regions in the Soviet Union was redefined in 1982. There has always been a network of economic regions. Except for the brief experiment with the *sovnarkhozy*, however, the system of economic regions which has existed in one form or another throughout the Soviet period has been a tool for statistical reporting and planning as opposed to economic management and decision-making. The 1982 decree did not change that essential feature, though in order to strengthen the regional perspective in central planning a Gosplan official and support staff have now been seconded to each of the regions outlined in Fig. 12. This regional system, with the exception of a few minor boundary changes, has been in place since 1961. The Gosplan representatives supposedly make recommendations to ensure better integration of sectoral plans and coordinate regional development planning within each region. How well this will work out in practice remains to be seen.

With the death of A. Kosygin in 1980, and then of L. Brezhnev in 1982, new opportunities for change arose. The selection of Y. Andropov as Soviet leader portended a campaign against corruption and slack labour discipline. And, indeed, the former head of internal security, the KGB, was responsible for both decree and action in this area. The forcible assault on drunkenness, 'parasitism' (or voluntary unemployment), graft and the widespread casualness concerning hours of work did produce some positive results. Labour productivity increased dramatically during the early months of the Andropov era (from November 1982 to February 1984), but failing health precluded a sustained effort on Andropov's part. Upon his death K. Chernenko assumed control. Aged and infirm, Chernenko continued most of the Andropov initiatives, but he possessed few of the attributes of the true reformer. His passing away in March 1985 brought Mikhail Gorbachev to the fore. As noted earlier, he has quickly consolidated his position and introduced the prospect of wide-reaching change throughout the Soviet system. As chairman of the Politburo and the Secretariat of the Party Central Committee he is well placed to shape events. The call for improved management of the economy through *perestroyka, glasnost'* and *uskoreniye* is being espoused with vigour. And not without reason as our review of current economic performance shortly will make clear.

In speech after speech Gorbachev has made the relationship between improvement of the material conditions of the Soviet population and economic performance his central theme. The following excerpts from a May 1985 report on the upcoming 27th Communist Party Congress are typical:

> The development of Soviet society will be determined, to a decisive extent, by qualitative changes in the economy, by its switch onto the tracks of intensive growth and by an all-out increase in efficiency. . . .
>
> It is known that, along with the successes that have been achieved in the

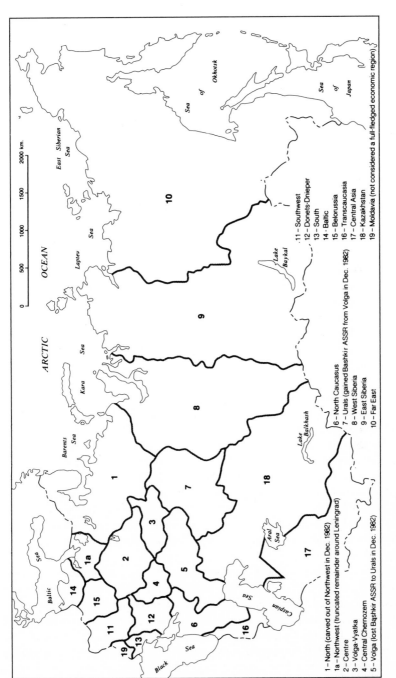

Fig. 12 Major Economic Regions

Source: Theodore Shabad, 'News Notes', *Soviet Geography: Review and Translation*, Vol. 24, No. 3, March 1983, 250–1.

1 – North (carved out of Northwest in Dec. 1982)
1a – Northwest (truncated remainder around Leningrad)
2 – Centre
3 – Volga-Vyatka
4 – Central Chernozem
5 – Volga (lost Bashkir ASSR to Urals in Dec. 1982)
6 – North Caucasus
7 – Urals (gained Bashkir ASSR from Volga in Dec. 1982)
8 – West Siberia
9 – East Siberia
10 – Far East
11 – Southwest
12 – Donets-Dnieper
13 – South
14 – Baltic
15 – Belorussia
16 – Transcaucasia
17 – Central Asia
18 – Kazakhstan
19 – Moldavia (not considered a full-fledged economic region)

economic development of the country, in the past few years unfavourable tendencies have intensified, and a good many difficulties have arisen.

. . . Life is making even higher demands on planning, which is the core of management. It should become an active lever for the intensification of production and the implementation of progressive economic decisions, and it should ensure the balanced and dynamic growth of the economy. At the same time, the plans of association and enterprise must drop a great many indices and make broader use of economic normatives, which open up scope for initiative and enterprise.

. . . We must sharply restrict the number of instructions, regulations and rules, which sometimes give wilful interpretations of Party and government decisions and fetter the autonomy of enterprises.[1]

At the Party Congress in early 1986 Gorbachev continued to espouse these same points. Additionally, he called for further centralization of decision-making, especially in the context of creating several super-ministries to better coordinate strategic planning across key sectors of the national economy. At the same time, greater reliance is to be placed upon loosening controls from above, as implied in the foregoing quotations. There is clearly some potential for confused signals. Gorbachev has proposed, and the Party and government have endorsed, a series of new initiatives. Control from the centre will be relaxed. Enterprises will be given the freedom, indeed will be encouraged, to arrange contracts and establish prices for some goods. Thus, the role of the State Committee on Prices will be trimmed. It will concentrate on determining prices in priority sectors. Where there is already adequate supply of goods – or services – enterprises will be permitted to set prices within upper and lower ranges. It is expected that greater resource-use efficiency will result from this development, which is scheduled to take effect in the new Five Year Plan in 1991. Enterprises are to be judged by their profitability. If they record a loss they will be permitted to go bankrupt. This is a major change inasmuch as the state has put huge amounts of financial capital into the account of non-profitable enterprises each year in the past. By the end of the 1980s all factories are to have switched to self-financing, in anticipation of major price reform in 1991. Meanwhile, more foreign capital will be enticed into the country on a joint venture basis, with majority control of course being vested in the Soviet counterpart. These latter initiatives have seen everything from advanced technology to fast-food operations gain a foothold in the Soviet Union.

One of the most successful, and controversial Gorbachev initiatives has been the fostering of cooperatives. By 1988 150,000 people worked in the 14,000 cooperatives which have been created. While most are in the consumers goods and services sector, a few are engaged in manufacturing intermediate goods for Soviet industry itself. Their success is measured by the huge incomes many members have been able to earn, in some cases ten to twelve times the average monthly wage of a white-collar

---

[1] Mikhail Gorbachev, 'Communique on the Plenary Session of the Central Committee of the Communist Party of the Soviet Union,' *Pravda* and *Izvestiya*, 24 April, 1985, in *The Current Digest of the Soviet Press*, Vol. 37, No. 17, 1985, 3, 6.

worker. The Soviet income tax system was not geared up for such a phenomenon. In the first year the levy was in the range of 2 to 3 per cent. By the third year it increased to 10 per cent. But with personal incomes of several thousand rubles per month a new class of wealthy Soviet citizen was in the making. The Party and Council of Ministers responded by introducing a much greater tax, up to 90 per cent at the highest rate, that is, on monthly incomes in excess of 1,500 rubles. Oddly enough given the usually passive role of the Supreme Soviet in passing such legislation, the maximum rate was deemed too high when it was referred to this body. Incentive, it was contended, would be dampened with such a high tax rate! Whatever the success of cooperatives they still represent a tiny step toward satisfying the basic goal of making more efficient the Soviet economy at large. It is estimated that cooperatives might account for one-eighth of national income generation by the turn of the century. Individual entrepreneurs might contribute an additional twentieth by this date.

All told, the changes portended – if realized to the full – are significant. But it always needs to be borne in mind that the Gorbachev initiatives, while pointing in some new directions, nonetheless follow on the heels of several other major economic reforms. All have failed to live up to expectations. Some, such as the *sovnarkhozy* experiment of the Khrushchev era, disappeared altogether. The Soviet system has proven enormously resilient when it comes to absorbing, diluting and fundamentally emasculating past efforts to reform it. Inertia and vested interests should never be underestimated as barriers to change.

Thus far the Gorbachev era has witnessed both intense debate about how to improve economic efficiency and some new and major policy reforms. Shedding surplus labour raises the spectre of unemployment, at least until retraining can occur. Millions of people may well be affected. Indeed, some estimates indicate that as many as 16 million people will have been assigned new positions by the turn of the century. For many therefore the prospect of a lower salary, less prestigious occupation and residence in a less desirable locale looms large. In the Turkmen republic in Middle Asia, for example, some 5,000 administrative positions are scheduled to be abolished by the end of the first stage in the process in 1990. As nearly one-fifth of the total socially productive labour force is engaged in administration and management there is ample scope for some reallocation of labour. *Perestroyka* in the Turkmen republic, as elsewhere, portends some rather fundamental changes inasmuch as not all managers and administrators will willingly embrace work in production. In Moscow itself, about 60,000 people are to be re-assigned. The state planning agency, Gosplan, will lose about two-fifths of its staff positions by 1990. Retraining is not always a practicable option for those near retirement and therefore the prospects of maintaining income and status for this group are not always good. Given the Soviet history of proclaiming effective full employment and jobs for all, the loss of previously sinecured, if unproductive positions, is certainly causing hardship. But while there is no official unemployment, on a regional scale there are already severe problems of underemployment, especially in rural Middle Asia. How to tap this potential has been accorded very frank attention in the Soviet press.

In the formulation of the most recent Five Year Plan (1986–1990) therefore there are some new initiatives as well as slogans. However, only so much can be squeezed out of any system through appeal to public conscience, and only so much can be done to trim the bureaucracy. And more draconian measures such as those initiated by Andropov and continued by Gorbachev against 'idlers' and 'parasites' rarely have long-term effect. Indeed, the initial gains in labour productivity which the Andropov campaign generated have proven temporary. On balance the growth of the Soviet economy is slowing down. And this is the major challenge for Soviet planners.

The rate of growth of Soviet national income during the 1930s probably exceeded 5 per cent per annum, rates of industrial growth 10 per cent. Following World War II, and the subsequent period of reconstruction, these annual rates were once again achieved. But since the 1950s there has been a perceptible decline. This is the result of several factors. The basic economic structure was consciously diversified, the consumers goods sector garnered a larger share of investment funds, and from the 1960s agriculture has come to claim a much larger share of investment capital. All of these developments, and others as well, have served to dampen the return on investment, the rate of growth of industrial production and national income. The 1965 economic reform was a response to this decline in the rate of annual economic growth. But it, and measures since, to promote efficiency and higher rates of growth have not altered these basic trends. As Fig. 13 indicates, since 1966 the average annual rate of growth of national income by five-year planning periods has slipped from close to 8 per cent to less than four. These are the official figures. There are suggestions from some leading Soviet authorities that the situation was actually much worse, that by the early 1980s the annual growth of the economy had slipped to zero.

The problem is not simply attributable to the attitude of workers, but includes such things as the style of management and long-standing patterns of investment. For example, for years the preferred route to higher production levels was through investment in new plant. Reconstruction, modernization and maintenance of existing plants was a distinctly lower priority amongst managers. Past failure to technically re-equip and update existing enterprises has caught up with planners and managers alike for the return on all assets is in decline. The task now is to find ways of substantially augmenting investment in reconstruction of existing plants without seriously impairing development plans which do require new facilities, especially those of a high-technology kind. Simply put, past practice has been one of extracting from existing facilities as much as possible without putting anything back. Of course, for the typical manager, shutting down a production line in order to modernize meant that overall production that year would probably drop, with the obvious negative impact on profitability and bonus income for all concerned. Given the continual emphasis on achieving targets set by central planners such strategies were clearly impractical. Hence, short-term, rather than even medium-term, strategic management decision-making was encouraged. Much of Gorbachev's early speech-making has been directing attention to the folly of such behaviour.

The current dilemma faced by Soviet planners is thus far from straightforward. Since the reform of 1965, increased reliance on foreign technology has been a common strategy in economic development. But here too the plans have come upon hard times. Imported technology, especially from western countries, usually requires payment in hard currency. Barter is possible, but not always feasible. Since 1965

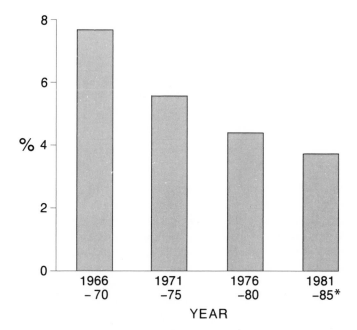

Growth of National Income **

Average Annual % Change

Based on actual figures for 1981 - 84 and plan for 1985 *

Net material product produced **

Fig. 13   Growth of National Income

Source: Adapted from 'Inside Comecon. A Survey', *The Economist*, April 20, 1985, 3.

much of the hard-currency earnings have been derived from the sale abroad of energy resources, notably oil and natural gas. It is no longer so easy to plan on increased oil exports; indeed, there is some question as to their being sustained at current levels owing to depleted reserves and growing domestic consumption, a topic we will return to in a later chapter. Moreover, once committed to sales abroad international economic forces have to be accommodated, and the decline in the price of oil on international markets in the past few years has had an adverse effect on Soviet hard-currency earnings. As if this were not problem enough, hard-currency reserves, which had been so assiduously accumulated through the sale of such commodities as oil, gas, gold and, whenever possible, manufactured goods, have been eroded because of the failure of Soviet agriculture to perform according to plan in recent years. Since 1971–72 the Soviet Union has been consistently a net importer of grain, in some years of a very considerable quantity. The inability of Soviet agriculture to meet planned output targets has thus been an unanticipated drain on hard-currency reserves. One opportunity cost accruing from buying western grain is less western technology. It is small wonder that all Soviet leaders have bemoaned the performance of the agricultural sector over the past decade, regularly pointing up shortfalls despite the huge increase in the relative share of available investment capital being directed toward the countryside since 1965. With Gorbachev's long-standing involvement in the agricultural sector (he is trained in both law and agronomy) it will be interesting to watch developments over the next few years.

Still, lest it should be thought that the system is in a state of collapse it should be reiterated that the system works and has brought substantial material improvement to the lives of all Soviet citizens, especially over the past four decades. But not all of these gains are the result of central planning. The existence of the so-called 'second economy' plays an important role in making life a little better for all.

The second economy

In the discussion of the Soviet economy thus far we have focused attention on the formal sector, that is, the state sector which is centrally planned. There is another dimension to the Soviet economic scene which is not planned, but which is nonetheless important and deserving of at least brief consideration. This is the informal sector, or second economy, which, while far from the absolute importance of the planned economy in terms of rubles of output, trade turnover or whatever other measure might be employed, is nonetheless significant because it helps to bridge the gaps. In any economic system there will be occasional scarcity of some goods or services. The Soviet Union is no exception to this generalization. Indeed, as is implicit in some of the foregoing discussion, the very nature of central planning in a complex economy is likely to produce scarcity – either artificial or real. To a not inconsiderable extent the second economy helps to offset shortages in both the producers and consumers goods sectors. The activities embraced by the second economy run the gamut from those which are legal and sanctioned by the state, to those which are legal but merely tolerated as an interim necessity, to those which are simply illegal and therefore subject to criminal prosecution when uncovered. In this brief discussion of the second economy we will concentrate on the first two types of activity.

The central planning of the Soviet economy is obviously a formidable task. The system functions, but it is in the very nature of the decision-making structure that periodic shortages occur and for the successful management of the economy these must be overcome. Scarcity of both producers and consumers goods is thus a fact of life. Unlike those economic systems in which prices charged for goods and services reflect to some degree supply and demand, the official Soviet price system to date has not been governed by the market but by bureaucrats. As we have noted, the price system is rigid, only infrequently revised, and for ideological reasons does not always reflect scarcity. Soviet managers and Soviet consumers, however, are not without considerable talent in working within and around the existing system. We might consider first the case of producers goods shortages.

The penchant of Soviet enterprise managers to finesse as much as possible by way of inputs to the productive process out of central authorities has already been discussed, along with the consequences in terms of waste and inefficiency. Waste and inefficiency occur when inputs are used in excess of the necessary minima. An example is that of labour input, and this is one of the reasons for the typically lower level of labour productivity registered by the Soviets in most international comparisons. But as a managerial strategy, padding the labour supply makes good sense since demands for higher levels of output by central planners might be more easily accommodated if there is a 'reserve' labour pool available. *Perestroyka* is intended to change this ingrained practice. To acquire, in similar fashion, more raw materials, semi-processed goods and so on than is really required in the production of a particular commodity also provides a certain flexibility in this regard. Thus, despite repeated attempts to establish norms which really do reflect the minimum input requirements for industrial production, the typical Soviet manufacturing process registers a higher level of resource consumption than western industrial states. For example, compared to West Germany, the Soviet Union uses about 2 1/2 times the amount of steel per $1,000 of gross domestic product. The acquisition of excess supplies can have a purpose other than simply facilitating an adaptive response to increased output targets imposed by central planners. It can play a part in the extensive bartering that goes on between enterprises. Bottlenecks in materials supply are endemic to the Soviet system of central planning. These are at least partially overcome by means of 'unplanned' resource re-allocations. Successful managers are those who are able to accumulate surpluses of something they do not require in order to exchange them for something they do. The intermediary in this process is the so-called *tolkach*, or pusher. This is the plant employee whose formal job designation is usually something other than what is done, namely expediting. It is his or her skill in finding other enterprises with which to enter into semi-official exchanges of mutually required commodities which helps to make the system function. Central authorities are clearly not oblivious to this type of activity. While it has historically operated outside the officially sanctioned inter-enterprise flow of material, the customary inability of the system to deliver what is required when needed has resulted in such activities being tolerated. Indeed, with each move toward enabling enterprises to enter into formal contracts to accommodate such transfers the state moves another step closer to institutionalizing formally what goes on anyway. As a rule these unplanned transactions are strictly barter, with no financial payment made. The redistributive process is seldom so straightforward as to involve only two participants in the barter. The longer the chain the more important the skill of the *tolkach*. Clearly a resource in short supply relative to others available for barter will command a premium regardless of the official price.

It is in the consumer goods sector, including food supply, where there is the greatest variety of second-economy enterprise and initiative. There is also the greatest potential for personal reward with least risk. To be sure, enterprise plays an important part in the successful management of a factory with the concomitant benefit of bonuses for meeting planned output targets. But bonuses have official limits and are relatively straightforward to monitor. We might illustrate how difficult it is to control personal income in some of the legally sanctioned markets which comprise the second economy outside the producers goods sector. The collective farmers market is one case in point.

Ever since the 1930s peasants in the collective farm sector, and some other categories of rural inhabitants as well, have been able to sell surplus products from their personal plot and privately owned livestock. The evolution of this form of free enterprise we will examine in some detail in a later chapter, but suffice it to say at this juncture that the flow of such foodstuffs to the urban market to be sold at prices which reflect supply and demand conditions and not the state price for the same commodity, has been an important supplement to the diet of the typical city family. To be sure, there is some monitoring of the prices charged, and theoretically even in times of acute shortage peasants are not supposed to charge in excess of three times the official state price, but this is frequently ignored. Thus, there is considerable scope for peasant entrepreneurs to exploit shortage. Many do, and the standard of living of some peasant families with access to urban markets is of a very high order indeed.

Within the state retail sector shortages are sometimes used to advantage by the sales personnel. It is a simple matter to advise friends or relatives of an incoming shipment of goods customarily difficult to obtain. Holding back a commodity for sale at the official price for someone who will then either use it, or, more likely, resell it at whatever the market will bear and share the proceeds, is commonplace. In such cases, the second economy functions to allocate goods in short supply to those who are willing to pay a premium price. The opportunities for such manipulation by state employees is limited only by imagination – and the police. The greater the risk the higher the price, of course. But much of what commonly goes on is borderline in terms of legality.

Rental housing, especially but not exclusively holiday accommodation, is another example of where private enterprise operates. Rental accommodation helps to fill an important niche in the Soviet system, but the line between legitimate rent and gouging is far from clear. Here again the price charged for a scarce resource is determined very largely by what the market will bear. The absence of clear guidelines on rent to be charged and inadequate means of enforcement enable the marketplace to exist. The sale of flowers by individuals in railroad and subway stations or in pedestrian underpasses is another common activity which is perfectly legal. Yet who determines whether the price charged and income received exceed guidelines? Similarly, each city has at least one second-hand, or flea, market at which supplementary income generation is possible. In short, whether renting – or buying – an apartment or house, purchasing food at the collective farmers market, hiring a repairman 'nalevo' or on the side, or buying flowers on the street, there are innumerable instances of individual enterprise bridging the gaps which almost inevitably are associated with the central plan. Ignoring entirely all activities which are clearly illegal, the second economy performs an important service for the state. In recent years especially this has been recognized, and to some degree endorsed. For example, there has been positive support of the personal sector in agriculture during the past few years, and this is not restricted to just collective farmers' auxilliary operations, as we shall see in a later chapter. Additionally, the state has given its blessing to the development of consumers services by private 'entrepreneurs' and cooperatives. How far the state is willing to proceed in this direction is not clear since there has been considerable discussion in the press of the legitimacy of large earned, but not state-source, personal incomes. The proposed maximum tax rate of 90 per cent on personal income from cooperatives noted earlier is a case in point.

The Soviet economic system is far from perfect. There are deficiencies. The question at the moment is whether or not they can be corrected by policy shifts within the context of central planning or whether some major revision of the structure of the decision-making system itself is in order. At this point in time there is nothing to suggest that the latter will occur. Most people, it seems, have a vested interest in the status quo, not least of whom being the huge number of Party members. Historically, the system has shown remarkable tenacity and inertia. Improvement is what is being called for, not fundamental reform of the basic structure. After all, the Soviets have been inculcating the merits of the system, economic, social and political, for more than seven decades. The majority of the population may at times complain, but most have in fact experienced material progress in the quality of day to day life. Whether they wish to work much harder in return for future benefits is another matter. But in light of the manpower problems currently faced by Soviet planners, not to speak of the underlying demographic trends, there is every reason for encouraging them to do so.

The Soviet system has gone through several phases, and no doubt will go through several more. Much that we think of as being Soviet owes something to the past, even though the ideas and aspirations of the early Marxist thinkers have not always found expression in the Soviet version of socialism. To some current Marxist, but non-Soviet, writers it is merely some form of state capitalism which inhabits the territory embraced by Soviet borders. For others it is a model for economic development, though the number of states which look to the Soviet Union for instruction in this regard is dwindling.

The most exciting period in the emergence of the Soviet system was that which bridged the revolution of 1917, extending back to the turn of the century and forward to the Stalin era. Ideas and concepts were abundant, and were debated with vigour. Nothing was yet cast in stone. The Stalin era, however, witnessed a period of centralization of decision-making and an assault on free expression. Since Stalin the Soviet system has undergone various changes, but none have succeeded in really decentralizing the decision-making process, even if so intended. It should always be borne in mind, of course, that in Soviet as well as other societies, the gap between ideal and reality is often sizeable. In the Soviet case it is not infrequently because one or another group within society refuses to accommodate prescribed change. The record of Soviet planners in managing the nation's human resource is a case in point.

Recommended reading

Aganbegyan, Abel, *The Challenge: Economics of Perestroika* (London: Hutchinson, 1988).

Bergson, A., Levine, H.S. (eds), *The Soviet Economy: Toward the year 2000* (London: George Allen and Unwin, 1983).

Bornstein, M. (ed), *The Soviet Economy, Continuity and Change* (Boulder: Westview Press, 1981).

Buck, T., Cole, J., *Modern Soviet Economic Performance* (Oxford: Blackwell, 1987).

Buston, T.G., *Gorbachev. A Biography* (New York: Stein and Day, 1985).

Churchward, L.G., *Soviet Socialism. Social and Political Essays* (London: Routledge and Kegan Paul, 1987).

Cracraft, J. (ed), *The Soviet Union Today. An Interpretative Guide* (Chicago: The University of Chicago Press, 1983).

Davies, R.W., *The Industrialization of Soviet Russia* (Cambridge, Mass.: Harvard University Press, 1979), 2 vols.

Dyker, D.A. (ed), *The Soviet Union Under Gorbachev: Prospects for Reform* (London: Croom Helm, 1987).

Federal Institute for East European and International Studies (ed), *The Soviet Union 1984–85. Events, Problems, Perspectives* (Boulder: Westview Press, 1986).

Harasymiw, B., *Political Elite Recruitment in the Soviet Union* (New York: St. Martin's Press, 1984).

Hewett, E.A., *Reforming the Soviet Economy. Equality Versus Efficiency* (Washington: Brookings Institution, 1987).

Hill, R.J., *Soviet Political Elites* (Oxford: Martin Robertson, 1977).

Hill, R.J., *The Soviet Union: Politics, Economics and Society. From Lenin to Gorbachev.* (London: Frances Pinter, 1985).

Hosking, G., *The First Socialist Society: A History of the Soviet Union from Within* (Cambridge, Mass.: Harvard University Press, 1985).

Joint Economic Committee, U.S. Congress, *Gorbachev's Economic Plans* (Washington: U.S. Government Printing Office, 1987), 2 vols.

Lane, D., *Soviet Economy and Society* (New York: New York University Press, 1985).

Lewin, M., *The Making of the Soviet System: Essays on the Social History of Interwar Russia* (New York: Pantheon, 1985).

Millar, J.R., *The ABCs of Soviet Socialism* (Urbana: University of Illinois Press, 1981).

Miller, R.F., Miller, J.H., Rigby, T.H. (eds), *Gorbachev at the Helm: A New Era in Soviet Politics?* (London: Croom Helm, 1987).

Nove, A., *The Soviet Economic System* (London: George Allen and Unwin, 1986), 3rd ed.

Pallot, J., Shaw, D.J.B., *Planning in the Soviet Union* (London: Croom Helm, 1981).

Rigby, T.M., Brown, A., Reddaway, P. (eds), *Authority, Power and Policy in the USSR* (London: Macmillan, 1981).

Schapiro, L., *The Communist Party of the Soviet Union* (London: Methuen, 1970).

Skilling, G., Griffiths, F., *Interest Groups in Soviet Politics* (Princeton: Princeton University Press, 1971).

White, S., *Political Culture and Soviet Politics* (London: Macmillan, 1979).

4 Soviet Peoples in a Planned Economy

The Communist Party and Soviet government attach great significance to the successful resolution of the demographic problem. . . .

Kiseleva, 1987.[1]

The population of the Soviet Union is the third largest in the world, exceeded only by China and India. With around 285 million inhabitants in 1988, the Soviet Union outnumbered the United States by nearly 45 million people. The Soviet system which evolved to manage this population has several distinguishing features, among which are the notion that the political leadership knows what is best for the people, that central planning can chart the most appropriate course of action to enhance national well-being, and that planning directives are implemented all the way down the line. A seemingly inevitable attribute of a Soviet-type political and economic system is a large and pervasive bureaucracy although the Gorbachev reforms are certainly intent upon reducing its size. In the area of planning industrial production, there is no logical reason to assume other than that the process is within the competence and control of state bureaucrats. But in the area of manpower planning, or managing basic demographic trends, the degree of control which can be exercised by planners is rather different. Intruding state policies into the daily lives of the Soviet populace is clearly a more complex task than planning iron and steel production. The state is not entirely helpless in this former endeavour, however. For instance, in instilling in the population a sense of collective responsibility, in laying the foundation for a communist ethos, the Soviet educational system can certainly claim a measure of success. But the record of government policy in shaping basic demographic trends is less clear cut, for on more than one occasion the Soviet peoples have proven rather resistant to state policies which directly impinge upon their private lives.

---

[1] G.P. Kiseleva, 'Propaganda Demograficheskikh Znaniy – Vazhnyy Element Demograficheskoy Politiki,' in Rybakovskiy, L.L., *et al* (eds), *Demograficheskoye Razvitiye v SSSR* (Moscow: Mysl', 1985), 17.

We shall begin this chapter with a description of Soviet population growth and demographic history. The expansion of the Russian Empire over the centuries brought within Russian, and now Soviet, borders a vast multi-national population. Demographic trends reflect the existence of different cultural values, and differences in the level of urbanization amongst the various nationalities. Both are topics to which we will devote some attention. Given the recent trends in national economic growth described in the preceding chapter, the prospect of reduced manpower availability is a major concern and reinforces further all efforts to secure greater labour productivity. As we shall see, the state has not abandoned programmes to encourage higher rates of natural reproduction. Who responds, however, is quite another matter.

The Soviet peoples are not only differentiated according to language, national culture and degree of urbanization, they are also differentiated according to occupation, education and income, in short, according to class or strata of society. In this chapter we will merely sketch in broad strokes the essential features of the social structure, returning to some of the consequences of the social reality in subsequent chapters.

Even a cursory re-examination of Fig. 1 (page 6) will be sufficient to underscore the fact that the Soviet population is far from evenly distributed across the country. But as was noted in Chapter 1, prior to the revolution a far greater proportion of the Empire's population lived west of the Ural mountains than is presently the case. This eastward shift in population is a direct consequence of Soviet development policies. During the early Soviet era internal migration was consciously channelled from village to city and from European Russia to the eastern and northern regions. Planners nowadays face many obstacles in attempting to direct manpower from regions of surplus to regions experiencing acute labour shortage. The basic patterns of migration described in this chapter will provide the essential background for the ensuing discussion of regional development strategies.

While the balance between rural and urban populations has been amenable to some manipulation by planning authorities, there are schemes for a more rational spatial distribution of the total population than currently exists. We will conclude this chapter with a brief review of some of the policies for re-shaping settlement patterns.

Demographic trends

The study of Soviet demographic trends has laboured under two inter-related handicaps. The first is that there is a general paucity of demographic data. During the Soviet period censuses have not been regularly conducted, have not always been published, and of late, have appeared in increasingly aggregate and summary form. The second handicap is that demographic enquiry itself has had a chequered history. Because early demographic research sometimes revealed trends which put the Soviet Union in a bad light or belied official ideological positions, the discipline was 'abolished' in the mid-1930s. Sociology and criminology suffered a similar fate. Clearly, if there was to be only limited, officially approved research, the need for demographic data diminishes accordingly. This situation prevailed until the 1960s when the study of demography, along with sociology and criminology, was resumed. What prompted the change was the realization, finally, that far more accurate information about the behaviour and values of the Soviet population was required for informed policy formulation on the part of Party and government. Miscalculations of projected population growth, flagging labour productivity, the impact of urbanization on social values, these were just a few of the factors which helped to make research into the reasons for, and dimensions of, demographic change once again a legitimate exercise. While censuses have deteriorated since 1959 in terms of the variety and volume of data made public, the results of large-scale social surveys have compensated to some degree. Still, as the following discussion will illustrate, our knowledge of current demographic trends is compromised by decisions to curtail enumerations of the population and restrict some kinds of research.

During the pre-Soviet period the single national census took place in 1897. The next censuses were not taken until 1920 and 1926; at the latter date there were just over 147 million people living within the new, and truncated, borders of the USSR. Between 1897 and 1926 the combined impact of World War I, revolution, boundary changes, civil war and wholesale emigration, make accurate population counts impossible. Nonetheless, the population loss for this period is generally reckoned to be in the order of 25 to 30 million. Even allowing for sizeable error, the scale of the loss is colossal by any standard of measure. Thus, the population base of the new Soviet socialist state was substantially smaller than its Tsarist counterpart. Moreover, it was not until the mid-1920s that pre-war fertility and mortality trends were re-established, and it was not until the Second World War that the boundaries of the USSR once again approximated those of the Russian Empire. Most war-time territorial changes occurred on the western flank of the country. Estonia, Latvia and Lithuania, which had gained independence during the turmoil of revolution and civil war, were 'repatriated' by the Red Army in 1940. In addition, from Finland in the north to Rumania in the south the border was pushed back and territory added (see Fig. 4; page 15) While the Second World War produced horrific population losses and long-term demographic consequences, the inter-war years were also witness to domestic policies and programmes which had a perceptible impact on the Soviet population.

A number of laws introduced in the wake of the revolution promoted the rights of women. Women gained the vote, divorce was simplified, abortion was legalized, and the legal distinction between legitimate and illegitimate births was erased. The demographic consequences of these policy changes, which in general constituted a challenge to the stability of the nuclear family, were greatest in the cities. It should be noted, however, that in 1926 only a shade more than 26 million people, or barely 18 per cent of the total population, were classified as urban, that is, living in a city or urban-type settlement.[1] Life for the vast majority of people who

---

[1] In general cities are currently defined as those places with more than 10-12,000 inhabitants (depending on the Republic). Urban-type settlements are defined as those places with a minimum of between 2,000 and 3,000 population in which between 60 and 85 per cent of the labour force are engaged in non-agricultural occupations, the particular threshold again varying by Republic.

still lived in the countryside carried on very much as before, at least until the onset of the Stalin-era Five Year Plans and collectivization.

Although rural–urban migration quickened during the early years of Lenin's New Economic Policy (1921–1928), not all migrants were able to secure jobs. And life for many of those who were employed was difficult. But as the domestic economy steadily improved, more and more people were attracted to the cities. Urban growth was given a real fillip with the introduction of the First Five Year Plan in 1928. This programme of forced industrialization was dependent upon rapid urban growth, which in turn was of necessity based upon migration. Coincident with industrialization was the campaign to collectivize the peasantry, about which more will be said in a later chapter. We need only note here that peasant resistance to collectivization was fierce, agricultural production collapsed as a result, famine took hold in parts of the Ukraine and Lower Volga regions (the traditional breadbasket of the country), and food rationing was introduced in the cities. Nonetheless, within five years the programme of collectivization was complete, but not before huge numbers of peasants had been killed as resisters, countless others had died of starvation, and the pattern of natural increase of the general population had been severely disrupted. To be without a job in the cities in the early 1930s usually meant denial of a food ration. In the ordinary family, to make ends meet husband and wife were both obliged to work. Raising children was a luxury many could not afford. Thus, owing to the widespread recourse to abortion, urban birth rates were often lower than the death rate. The growth of cities was therefore primarily attributable to in-migration, just as it had been in the nineteenth century. The impact of these troubled years on the structure of the population was soon evident.

A Soviet census conducted in 1937 apparently recorded a total population of about 164 million. Earlier forecasts presumed the population would be roughly 170 million at this date. The shortfall is attributed to several factors, among them being the precipitous decline in the crude rate of net natural increase,[1] especially in the cities, and the absolute loss of life brought about by the Soviet collectivization programme and the Stalin-initiated purges of Party members and others who held, or were presumed to hold, dissident opinions. Small wonder the 1937 census was never published and that the results of the next census, taken in 1939, were only published as residual columns in the 1959 census. While the state did little in terms of publishing census data, it responded to the population 'loss' by introducing a series of explicitly pronatalist policies.

Beginning in 1936 abortion on demand was abolished. It was thereafter only available through official channels by meeting stringent medical criteria. Abortion was otherwise deemed to be a criminal offence. Divorce was also made more difficult to obtain. At the same time the legal obligations of a father toward illegitimate offspring were relaxed. In short, the state introduced a series of measures intended to strengthen the nuclear family. Given the population loss which occurred during the 1930s, this would have been reason enough for the change. The catastrophic impact of the Second World War reinforced the need for such measures.

---

[1] This is the difference between unadjusted, crude rates of birth and death, usually expressed per 1,000 population.

The consequences of the Great Patriotic War, as World War II is called in the Soviet Union, are sufficiently well known as to require little comment. We need only be reminded of the fact that after allowing for border changes the population loss alone was between 25 and 30 million. Few Soviet families escaped the war untouched by disaster. More than 1,700 cities and 70,000 villages were damaged. In extreme cases, of which there were all too many, city and village alike were literally levelled. In all, about one-sixth of the total housing stock was damaged or destroyed. By the end of the decade a massive programme of post-war reconstruction had not fully repaired the physical destruction. The human costs are evident to this day in the age–sex pyramid of the population.

As Fig. 14 indicates, there is a dissymetrical balance between males and females in the older age groups. This feature rather coldly insinuates something of the war-time population loss, primarily but not exclusively the Second World War. A close inspection of Fig. 14 will reveal that there are also truncations of both males and females in particular age groups. The most obvious one is that which roughly defines the age group born during the Second World War, but distinguishable as well are similar contractions for those born during the troubled 1930s and during the years of World War I and ensuing civil war. Beginning in the 1960s there was a further contraction in the population base. Clearly, as the artifically reduced war-years age

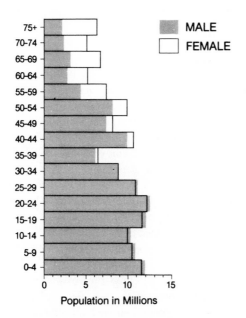

Age – Sex Profile 1979

Fig. 14 Population by Age and Sex 1979

Source: Adapted from Murray Feshbach, 'The Soviet Union: Population Trends and Dilemmas', *Population Bulletin*, Vol. 37, No. 3, August 1982, 33.

cohort entered the 1960s the number of births would have fallen independent of any change in female fertility patterns. But there was a significant increase in the absolute and relative importance of the urban sector during the post-war period (Fig. 15). In 1961 the urban sector finally overtook the rural, something which happened in a number of European states a half century or so earlier. In 1988 two-thirds of the country's 285 million inhabitants lived in cities or urban-type settlements. Historically, urbanization results in a lower per capita birth rate and, of course, as the urban share of the population increases relative to the rural, the potential impact of urban values on countryside customs is similarly enhanced.

In general there has been a downturn in both birth and death rates since the beginning of the century (Fig. 15). While we have the advantage of hindsight in discerning demographic trends, it seems that the sharp decline in the birth rate which began in the late 1950s caught Soviet planners unaware. Official projections of the Soviet population made in the latter half of the 1950s put the 1970 estimated total at 250 million. In the early 1960s this projection was revised to 248 million. But even that estimate proved far too optimistic as the 1970 census recorded only 241.7 million people. The difference may seem merely academic, but it ought to be borne in mind that in a planned economy long-term investment decisions frequently involve labour–capital ratios. Errors in projecting manpower supply obviously assume considerable significance in such circumstances.

Since the 1960s sociologists, demographers, economists and planners, amongst others, have sought to clarify reasons for the dramatic decline in the crude rate of net natural increase from 17.8 per 1,000 population in 1960 to 8.9 per 1,000 in 1969. The fact that abortion was again made available upon demand in the mid-1950s after nearly two decades of tightly circumscribed legal access was of some importance in accounting for the decline, thought this should not be overemphasized since recourse to illegal abortion as a means of contraception during the years of proscription was common. But on balance high rates of abortion, a greater propensity to divorce, planned deferral of marriage amongst the rapidly expanding urban population, and a growing preference to trade off maternal/paternal 'benefits' for a higher material standard of living combined during the 1960s with the arrival of the war-reduced age cohort to alter fundamentally previous patterns of fertility. The Soviet birth rate fell from 24.9 per 1,000 in 1960 to 17.0 in 1969, its lowest point thus far (Fig. 15). Urbanization certainly contributed to this decline, but it is notable that the downturn was even more precipitous in the rural sector than in the urban. The birth rate amongst the urban population dropped from 21.9 per 1,000 in 1960 to 15.3 in 1968, its lowest point. Amongst the rural population the birth rate declined from 27.8 per 1,000 in 1960 to 18.7 in 1969, its lowest point.

Fig. 15 indicates that since the late 1960s the Soviet birth rate has slowly edged upward, thus broadening the base of the age–sex profile (Fig. 14). During the 1970s the post-war baby-boom cohort entered the reproductive age. Thus, there were simply more prospective parents than in the early 1960s. But female fertility seemed to increase as well, at least to judge by the number of first births by females aged 15 to 19. State policy perhaps played some part in this development. For example, in the late 1960s the draft age was lowered and the length of military service reduced. This served to return men to civilian status at age 20 rather than 22

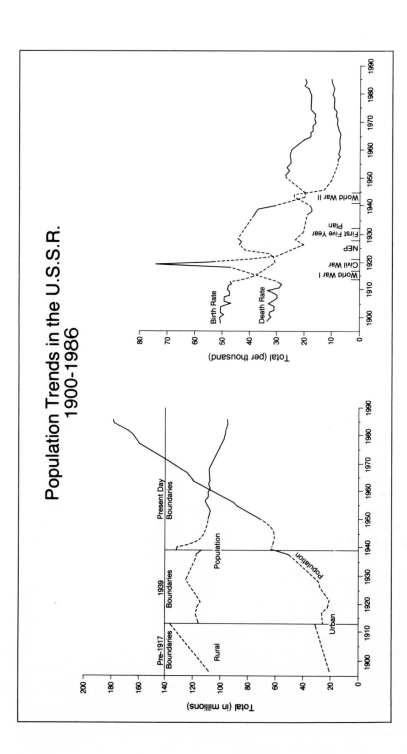

Fig. 15 Population Trends

Source: James H. Bater, *The Soviet City. Ideal and Reality* (London: Edward Arnold, 1980), 70; *Narodnoye Khozyaystvo v 1985 g* (Moscow: Finansy i Statistika, 1986), 31.

Table 3: Birth, death, crude rate of net natural increase* per 1,000 population 1970, 1981–86. Average family size 1979

REPUBLIC	1970 Birth	Death	CNNI*	1981 Birth	Death	CNNI*	1982 Birth	Death	CNNI*
Slavic									
RSFSR	14.6	8.7	5.9	16.0	10.9	5.1	16.6	10.7	5.9
Ukraine	15.2	8.9	6.3	14.6	11.3	3.3	14.8	11.3	3.5
Belorussia	16.2	7.6	8.6	16.3	9.6	6.7	16.3	9.6	6.7
Baltic									
Estonia	15.8	11.1	4.7	15.4	12.3	3.1	15.4	11.9	3.5
Latvia	14.5	11.2	3.3	14.0	12.6	1.4	14.6	12.2	2.4
Lithuania	17.6	8.9	8.7	15.1	10.3	4.8	15.2	10.0	5.2
Caucasus									
Armenia	22.1	5.1	17.0	23.4	5.3	18.1	23.2	5.5	17.7
Azerbaydzhan	29.2	6.7	22.5	26.3	6.9	19.4	25.3	6.7	18.6
Georgia	19.2	7.3	11.9	18.2	8.6	9.6	17.9	8.4	9.5
Middle Asia									
Kirgiz	30.5	7.4	23.1	30.8	8.0	22.8	31.2	7.8	23.4
Tadzhik	34.8	6.4	28.4	38.3	7.8	30.5	38.2	7.7	30.5
Uzbek	33.6	5.5	28.1	34.9	7.2	27.7	35.0	7.4	27.6
Turkmen	35.2	6.6	28.6	34.3	8.5	25.8	34.7	8.0	26.7
Kazakh	23.4	6.0	17.4	24.3	8.0	16.3	24.3	7.8	16.5
Moldavia	19.4	7.4	12.0	20.5	10.3	10.2	20.6	10.2	10.4
USSR	17.4	8.2	9.2	18.5	10.2	8.3	18.9	10.1	8.8

Source: Narodnoye Khozyaystvo SSSR 1922–1982 (Moscow: Finansy i Statistika, 1982), 29;
Narodnoye Khozyaystvo SSSR v 1982g (Moscow: Finansy i Statistika, 1983), 33;
Narodnoye Khozyaystvo SSSR v 1983g (Moscow: Finansy i Statistika, 1984), 33;

as had been the case, and more of them started families earlier than they would have done otherwise. The state has also come a long way in providing support services and direct economic benefits to those who have children. Family allowance payments were introduced during the Stalin era, but subsequently reduced in amount. In 1974, and again in 1981, payments have been increased quite substantially. Maternity leaves have been improved, and of considerable potential significance for urban families, eligibility for housing was linked to family formation and number of children in 1981. Current demographic trends are fascinating. To judge from the data for 1982 alone, for example, it would appear that the 1981 state policies did produce results (Table 3). The absolute increase in the number of births in 1982 delighted Soviet authorities, because for the first time since the 1960s the total number of children born in any one year exceeded five million. Moreover the percentage of women with three or more children is slowly edging upward again. The pattern continues. But the questions remain, what caused the birth rate to change, is the pattern consistent amongst all nationalities, can it be sustained and what are the implications for manpower supply? In providing some answers we need to, first of all, examine the general trend in the death rate, and secondly, assess changing educational levels and attitudes towards having children amongst Soviet women in general and amongst the various nationality groups in particular.

1983 Birth	Death	CNNI*	1984 Birth	Death	CNNI*	1986 Birth	Death	CNNI*	1979 Average family size
17.6	11.1	6.5	16.9	11.6	5.3	17.2	10.4	6.8	3.3
16.0	11.5	4.5	15.6	12.0	3.6	15.5	11.1	4.4	3.3
17.5	10.0	7.5	17.0	10.5	6.5	17.1	9.7	7.4	3.3
16.0	12.0	4.0	15.9	12.5	3.4	15.6	11.6	4.0	3.1
15.9	12.5	3.4	15.7	12.9	2.8	15.9	11.9	4.0	3.1
16.3	10.3	6.0	16.2	10.9	5.3	16.5	9.9	6.6	3.3
23.6	5.8	17.8	24.2	5.8	18.4	24.0	5.7	18.3	4.7
26.2	6.7	19.5	26.6	6.8	19.8	27.6	6.7	20.9	5.1
18.0	8.4	9.6	18.5	8.8	9.7	18.7	8.8	9.9	4.0
31.5	7.9	23.6	32.1	8.3	23.8	32.6	7.1	25.5	4.6
38.7	7.6	31.1	39.8	7.4	32.4	42.0	6.8	35.2	5.7
35.3	7.5	27.8	36.2	7.4	28.8	37.8	7.0	30.8	5.5
35.6	8.5	27.1	35.2	8.2	27.0	36.9	8.4	28.5	5.5
24.4	8.0	16.4	25.4	8.2	17.2	25.5	7.4	18.1	4.1
22.5	10.9	11.6	21.9	11.1	10.8	22.7	9.7	13.0	3.4
20.1	10.3	9.8	19.6	10.8	8.8	20.0	9.8	10.2	3.5

Narodnoye Khozyaystvo SSSR v 1984g (Moscow: Finansy i Statistika, 1985), 35;
Narodnoye Khozyaystvo SSSR za 70 Let (Moscow: Finansy i Statistika, 1987), 406–407;
David Lane, *Soviet Economy and Society* (Oxford: Blackwell, 1985), 118.

For most of the Soviet era the death rate has declined, though there are some notable exceptions highlighted in Fig. 15; for example, the devastations wrought by external factors such as world war, and internal policies such as collectivization. The death rate reached its nadir of 6.9 per 1,000 in 1964. As the consequences of earlier catastrophies have worked their way through the population structure, with the resultant gradual resumption of a normal age–sex composition, the death rate has steadily edged upward reaching 10.8 in 1984 before dropping slightly. In 1986 it was 9.8 per 1,000. While the initial rise in the death rate was regarded as a perfectly normal trend, the reasons for some deaths came to be of real concern during the 1970s. For example, life expectancy for Soviet males fell from the late 1960s until the early 1980s, a trend which stands in stark contrast to all other industrialized states. In the mid to late 1960s life expectancy of the Soviet male was about 66 years. By 1980 it had dropped to 62 years. By 1986 it had again risen to about 64. Simultaneously, infant mortality increased during the 1970s before dropping slightly in the 1980s. Statistical data for infant mortality and life expectancy were not published from the early 1970s to the mid-1980s. In the absence of sufficient data to permit a detailed analysis of actual trends, conventional wisdom at the time had it that the decline in life expectancy for males was related to health problems, especially those of a respiratory and alcohol-related kind. Infant mortality is a much more contentious matter – and may reflect real deficiencies in health-care delivery. Other reasons are equally plausible, however. Improved accuracy of reporting infant mortality in Middle Asia and changing definitions of what constitutes infant mortality are amongst the most often cited. We will return to the questions of life expectancy and infant mortality in Chapter 10. For our purpose here, we need only take note of the fact that as the death rate edges upward even more births per capita are required to compensate if the crude rate of net natural increase of the population is to be bolstered. Attitudes toward marriage, and especially child raising amongst urban women, therefore become of great importance. The trend in illegitimate births casts an interesting light on contemporary attitudes.

Over the last decade the proportion of illegitimate children born each year has increased from 7 to 10 per cent. Illegitimacy is scarcely a new phenomenon in Soviet and Russian history. For instance, after the revolution many of the policies introduced by the Soviet government undermined the legal and moral foundations of the family. With the disruption to normal family life resulting from civil war, famine, and so forth, the stage was set for a surge in illegitimate births. There arose a huge number of children who were parentless, and in number, and frequently in behaviour, beyond the capability of the few state orphanages to accommodate. It was, of course, a human tragedy and a visible testament to the breakdown of society at the time. The consequences of the Second World War were broadly similar. With the huge loss of life, especially amongst fighting men, illegitimacy was common. Indeed, up to the mid-1960s illegitimate children annually accounted for about a sixth of all births. The share then dropped precipitously. While the proportion of illegitimate births at present is therefore not especially notable in the context of Soviet history, the age distribution of the mothers is. Previously the most common age group of mothers having children out of wedlock was 17 to 18; the predominant age group now is 30 to 40. The past still casts a shadow over the balance of the sexes, for Soviet women outnumber men by some 18 million. Amongst those in the reproductive age group there is a better balance (Fig. 14). However, divorces are now running close to 400 per 1,000 marriages (and even higher in some of the major cities in the Slavic culture realm) up from 228 per 1,000 in 1960. As most divorced males are not remarrying, it appears that many older, presumably non-Muslim, women are choosing to have a child without being encumbered with a husband. This trend may owe something to the measures introduced in 1981. As we have noted, families with children have been accorded a number of benefits, including priority in respect of acquiring housing. Allowances for single mothers have also been raised substantially. Whatever the reasons for the increase in the number of children born out of wedlock, this phenomenon is not in itself of sufficient absolute importance in terms of the number of births to offset other national trends.

As Soviet women have acquired more education, have joined the urban labour force, in short, as women have become urbanized, they have chosen to have smaller families. Surveys of attitudes amongst non-Muslim urban women consistently indicate that the preferred family size is two children. But in many non-Muslim regions of the Soviet Union the single-child family is the norm. Conscious choice is obviously exercised in the determination of family size since abortions exceed births by a ratio of three to one in the cities, with no indication of a downward trend. Abortion rates are amongst the highest in the world. For every 1,000 women between 15 and 49 there were 150 abortions annually in the late 1960s. In the RSFSR in 1985 it was still in excess of 123 per 1,000. In England the comparable rate was 11.4, in the United States 27.5 in 1978–79. Thus, between the government's ideal family with three to four children and reality there is an obvious gap. The reasons for this are varied and have to do with such factors as availability of adequate day care and housing, and the respective responsibilities of males and females in household and child-raising chores. We will return to some of these issues in a later chapter. What needs to be borne in mind, however, is that in the Soviet Union attitudes toward family, children and the role of women vary markedly amongst national minorities.

The data presented in Table 3 provide a general overview of the demographic profile of each republic. These data do not accurately reflect differences between national minorities since, as we noted in an earlier chapter, the share of the titular group of the total republic population varies. Slavs have traditionally comprised the majority of migrants into non-Slavic republics. The demographic characteristics of this migrant population reflect its predominantly urban origin and destination. The net result is that its presence outside the home republic has usually dampened the birth rate in the non-Slavic host republic. Thus, amongst rural Middle Asians such as the Uzbeks and Tadzhiks the average family size is much larger than the average for the republic as a whole. Conversely, the 10 million or so Muslim people who live in the Russian republic no doubt bolster somewhat the per capita birth rate there. The impact of Slav migration into the Baltic republics can only be speculated upon, but as Estonians and Latvians are just barely replacing themselves the presence of Slavs in fact may even be enhancing the crude rate of net natural increase. At any rate, the principal message conveyed by the rather incomplete data in Table 3 is that it is the Soviet Middle Asian Muslim peoples who are increasing their numbers at the greatest rate. Differential patterns of fertility are the basic reason for the changing shares of the total Soviet population by major nationality groups.

In Table 4 the changing proportions of the total Soviet population according to major nationalities show some interesting trends. Over the period covered by the last three censuses the proportion of Slavs has steadily declined, while the Muslim population has increased, a trend which of course can be imputed from the demographic data presented in Table 3. The question yet to be answered is whether Muslims will follow the general demographic trends evidenced in all other modernizing states. Most are still rural, the cities of Middle Asia typically being dominated by Russians in particular and Slavs in general. Prying the indigenous peoples from countryside location and tradition has not proven easy. Yet the evidence from non-Slavic republics in which urbanization of the indigenous population has proceeded apace, for example Armenia, is that since 1959 the birth rate has fallen, the death rate has been stable, and thus the crude rate of net natural increase has declined. The changing ethnic balance of the population has caused some Soviet authorities to question, usually in a rather indirect fashion, whether or not pro-natalist policies should be universal, nationality or region specific. Universality, however, has prevailed as the guiding principle to date. The final column in Table 4 extrapolates population growth by major nationality groups to the end of the century. Russians would then be a numerical minority, though control over critical centres of decision-

Table 4: Population by major nationality 1959–2000

Nationality	1959 Number	1959 Per cent of total	1970 Number	1970 Per cent of total	1979 Number	1979 Per cent of total	2000* Number	2000* Per cent of total
USSR, total	208,827	100.0	241,720	100.0	262,436	100.0	300,000	100.0
Slavs	159,280	76.3	178,820	74.0	189,207	72.0	195,000	65.0
Russian	114,114	54.6	129,015	53.4	137,397	52.4	140,000	46.7
Ukrainian	37,253	17.8	40,753	16.9	42,347	16.1		
Belorussian	7,913	3.8	9,052	3.7	9,463	3.6		
Moldavian	2,214	1.1	2,698	1.1	2,968	1.1		
Balts	4,715	2.3	5,102	2.1	5,310	2.0	6,000	0.2
Estonian	989	0.5	1,007	0.4	1,020	0.4		
Latvian	1,400	0.7	1,430	0.6	1,439	0.5		
Lithuanian	2,326	1.1	2,665	1.1	2,851	1.1		
Transcaucasian, excluding Azeri	5,479	2.6	6,804	2.8	7,722	2.9		
Armenian	2,787	1.3	3,559	1.5	4,151	1.6		
Azeri	2,940	1.4	4,380	1.8	5,477	2.1		
Georgian	2,692	1.3	3,245	1.3	3,571	1.4		
Muslims, including Azeri	24,738	11.8	35,158	14.5	43,772	16.7	64,000	21.3
Kazakh	3,622	1.7	5,299	2.2	6,556	2.5		
Kirgiz	969	0.5	1,452	0.6	1,906	0.7		
Tadzhik	1,397	0.7	2,136	0.9	2,898	1.1		
Turkmen	1,002	0.5	1,525	0.6	2,028	0.8		
Uzbek	6,015	2.9	9,195	3.8	12,456	4.7		
Other Muslims	8,973	4.2	11,171	4.6	12,451	4.7		
of which Tatar	4,968	2.4	5,931	2.5	6,317	2.4		
Jews	2,268	1.1	2,151	0.9	1,811	0.7		

Source: Murray Feshbach, 'The Soviet Union: Population Trends and Dilemmas', *Population Bulletin*, Vol. 37, No. 3, (August 1982), Table 6, 22.

Table 5: Major nationalities and share speaking Russian as second language: 1970–1979

Nationality	1970	1979
Russian	100.0	100.0
Ukrainian	36.3	49.8
Belorussian	49.0	57.0
Moldavian	36.1	47.4
Estonian	29.0	24.2
Latvian	45.2	56.7
Lithuanian	35.9	52.1
Armenian	30.1	38.6
Azeri	16.6	29.5
Georgian	21.3	26.7
Kazakh	41.8	52.3
Kirgiz	19.1	29.7
Tadzhik	15.4	29.6
Turkmen	15.4	25.4
Uzbek	14.5	49.3
Tatar	62.5	68.9
Jews (Ashkenazi)	16.3	13.7

Source: Basile Kerblay, *Modern Soviet Society* (New York: Pantheon Books, 1983), Table 10, 40.

making will not likely diminish in similar fashion. Whether Muslims would remain geographically anchored to the Middle Asian countryside is a quite different matter.

Knowledge of Russian is an important factor in facilitating migration from village to city throughout the non-Slavic realm. As the data in Table 5 reveal, it is the Middle Asian and Caucasian peoples who have shown the least propensity to learn Russian. While in most cases there has been considerable progress in the last inter-censal period, one of the key problems confronting Soviet authorities is recruiting enough competent Russian-language teachers to fill the places available in Middle Asia in particular and in the non-Slavic rural countryside in general. In the Soviet press criticism is often directed at the qualifications of the available instructors.

Notwithstanding the trend toward inter-nationality marriage, producing the so-called fusion (*sblizheniye*) of peoples, which was one of the original goals of Soviet society, relations between national minorities are not always ideal. Over the years there have been unofficial reports of inter-nationality conflict in Middle Asian cities, usually triggered, it would appear, by some local problem such as a food shortage. In late 1986 there were widely publicized riots in Alma-Ata, the capital of Kazakhstan. These were the result of nationalist tensions related to the replacement of an indigenous Kazakh as Party leader in the republic by a Russian. The scale of the upheaval was unprecedented in the region in recent years. It reflects real problems at present, and portends certain difficulties for the future. There is no doubt that stereotypes do exist and these affect ethnic relations. For instance, in Middle Asia indigenous people are sometimes described pejoratively in Russian as '*zver'ye*', or animals. The question raised by some western analysts is, what will be the reaction to a large-scale influx of Muslim peoples into the dominantly Slavic Middle Asian cities? Indeed, what would a large-scale migration of Muslims to the labour deficient cities of the RSFSR portend? A substantial modification of the existing urban ethnic balance could well test some of the fundamental principles upon which contemporary Soviet society is based. As was the case in the late nineteenth century, Slavic and other migrants to the Middle Asian countryside customarily live apart from the indigenous peoples. Separate lives clearly facilitate perpetuation of cultural identity and afford an ideal environment in which to nurture nationalist aspirations.

The upheaval in Kazakhstan in 1986 was followed by an even more serious inter-nationality conflict in the Caucasus in 1988. On this occasion the focus of the dispute was the Nagorno-Karabakh Autonomous Oblast in the Republic of Azerbaydzhan. This area has a large Armenian population (about three-quarters of the total) amongst whom the sense of being dominated by the Azeri people whose cultural traditions are Muslim, not Christian is widespread. Public demonstrations in Yerevan, the capital of Armenia, were replicated throughout the republic. In the disputed region strikes and violence between Armenians and Azeris precipitated attacks on Armenians, or those presumed to be, in other cities of Azerbaydzhan but notably in the industrial centre of Sumgait near Baku. Soviet authorities refused to accede to the demand of the Armenians that the Nagorno-Karabakh Autonomous Oblast be removed from the Republic of Azerbaydzhan and turned over to Armenia. To some degree the Gorbachev emphasis on *glasnost'* has fueled such tensions by permitting public discussion in the media and massive public demonstrations.

While none of the outbreaks of inter-nationality conflict represents a new development since such tensions have a long history, and certainly predate the Soviet period, they nonetheless are a real source of concern to authorities whose public proclamations over the years have stressed harmonious relations. And indeed, for the vast majority of Soviet citizens inter-nationality relations are harmonious. But such events as have taken place in Middle Asia and the Caucasus in the late 1980s do have ominous overtones. The Soviet military, for example, is composed of multi-ethnic units. The growing proportion of Middle Asian and Caucasian youth drafted into the military is posing problems simply in terms of basic communication because so many from the countryside have an imperfect knowledge of Russian. As the preceding discussion of demographic trends revealed, the trend toward fewer Slavs and Baltic peoples and more Middle Asians and Caucasians will continue. The traditional pattern of dominance is thus being challenged by sheer weight of numbers. Such a trend when set against a background of more and more instances of inter-ethnic violent conflict can do little but worry Soviet officials.

Given all of the uncertainties associated with government efforts to enhance fertility and the conceivable dampening of the birth rate in the future owing to the urbanization of Middle Asians, the demand for labour is not likely to be satisfied through natural increase of the population. Indeed, a close examination of the data presented in Table 3 reveals that the 1981 pro-natalist policies had an inconsistent effect amongst non-Muslims. A comparison of the pattern of births and the crude rate of net natural increase in 1983 and 1984 indicates that the Slavic and Baltic peoples did not initially maintain the enhanced proclivity to reproduce themselves. By 1986 the trend was again of some consolation to manpower planners. However, the contrast with the Muslim and Transcaucasian peoples is self-evident (Table 3).

Between 1970 and 1985 the working-age population across the country increased at an average annual rate of 1.5 per cent. This was half the rate which prevailed during the years from 1955 to 1970. As a proportion of the total population the labour force is steadily shrinking as those on pension correspondingly increase. For instance between 1939 and 1987 the share over 60 years of age increased from 6.7 to 13.5 per cent of the total population. And it should be noted that women retire at 55. By the turn of the century those over 60 will comprise an even larger share. The cost of supporting an expanding population on pension is considerable. The current drive to enhance labour productivity assumes even greater significance when set against this demographic reality, the more so perhaps when it is recognized that three traditional sources of labour are no longer available.

With so many still living in the countryside until so recently, Soviet planners had been able to draw upon a huge pool of labour for the cities. However, by the early 1970s it was no longer possible to foster rural–urban migration indiscriminately. Yet with about one-third of the total population still in the countryside, at first glance it would appear that there remains a reserve to draw upon. However, the bulk of the rural labour force is female, and aged. Indeed, in marginal but still important agricultural regions there is now a severe labour shortage. Put simply, years of under-capitalization in many agricultural regions have come home to roost. The poor conditions in the village prompt the youth in such regions to depart for the city whenever possible, often encouraged by parents. In Middle Asia, of course, the opposite situation exists, but such surplus labour is not easily relocated.

Two other sources of labour were tapped until the 1970s. After the rural peasantry, the reserve of 'socially unproductive' females comprised the second most important labour pool. In the main this group was made up of housewives who did not work for the state, but occupied themselves instead with domestic chores. In the countryside they looked after the personal plot and livestock as well as the home. Most women now hold 'socially productive' jobs. Indeed, because of the predominance of females in the total Soviet population (53.1 per cent in 1985) women in fact occupy just over half of all jobs. Given the fact that at any one time some women are looking after infants, are engaged in some form of study or training, or because of cultural tradition are in effect tied to the household, there is no longer much flexibility left.

The third source of labour was the growing number of able-bodied pensioners. Normal age of retirement is 55 for women, 60 for men. In labour-deficient regions like Siberia there has been some success in persuading pensioners to rejoin the workforce. At present pensioners comprise about one-twentieth of the total Soviet labour force of about 131 million. The problem of labour shortage is quite acute in the major urban centres where in-migration is tightly controlled. In such cities the share of the population on pension is increasing more rapidly than for the country as a whole. But clearly, even allowing for a sizeable share of the growing number of pensioners staying on in the workforce this is not a solution to the general problem of labour shortage.

At any one time there are some two million jobs in industry which are unfilled. This helps to promote high rates of labour turnover, which see on average a fifth of

Table 6: Population characteristics by Republic, 1940, 1987

Republic	Total population 1940	Total population 1987	Per cent urban 1987	Per cent labour force* of total 1984
Slavic				
RSFSR	110,098	145,311	74	50.5
Ukraine	41,340	51,201	67	48.5
Belorussia	9,046	10,078	64	50.4
Baltic				
Estonia	1,054	1,556	72	50.5
Latvia	1,886	2,647	71	52.3
Lithuania	2,925	3,641	67	50.1
Caucasus				
Armenia	1,320	3,412	68	42.6
Azerbaydzhan	3,274	6,811	54	35.6
Georgia	3,612	5,266	55	47.2
Middle Asia				
Kirgiz	1,528	4,143	40	36.4
Tadzhik	1,525	4,807	33	29.9
Uzbek	6,551	19,026	42	33.2
Turkmen	1,302	3,361	48	36.3
Kazakh	6,148	16,244	58	42.8
Moldavia	2,468	4,185	47	47.3
USSR	194,077	281,689	66	47.2

Source: Narodnoye Khozyaystvo SSSR v 1983 g (Moscow: Finansy i Statistika, 1984), 8–9. *Narodnoye Khozyaystvo SSSR v 1984 g* (Moscow: Finansy i Statistika, 1985), 300, 411. *Narodnoye Khozyaystvo SSSR za 70 Let* (Moscow: Finansy i Statistika, 1987), 374, 378.
* includes *kolkhozniki*

all factory workers who hold jobs changing them in the course of a single year. As might be expected, the rate of job turnover is even higher in the frontier regions or in those industries popularly perceived to offer less desirable employment conditions.

Table 6 summarizes population growth by republic since 1940 and provides two other important types of information as well. Firstly, it points up the very considerable differences in urban population. These differences clearly have a direct bearing on many of the demographic trends we have already described. Secondly, the relationship between size of the labour force and total republic population underscores something of the problem confronting manpower planners. Where the population has been growing most rapidly is, generally speaking, not where labour is in greatest demand. And, of course, labour requirements usually amount to more than simply available hands; rather skills, and in an increasingly technological society, more of them, are what are needed. Thus, imbalances in labour supply, especially of skilled labour, pose one of several population problems for Soviet authorities. The growing materialism of the population and its resultant social stratification may well come to pose yet others.

The social class system

The Soviet peoples are differentiated according to nationality, culture, tradition, and level of urbanization, all of which impinge on demographic patterns. Differentiating the Soviet population as well is an official class structure. As in any society, however, individual preferences when shared tend to mediate relationships between particular groups of people, be they based on ethnicity, income, occupation or official ideology. The reality of the social class structure in the Soviet Union is thus complex, and we will do no more here than draw attention to some of its dimensions.

Compared to the Tsarist era, replete as it was with various bureaucratic methods for pigeon-holing the constituents of society, with numerous barriers to social mobility, and with a well ensconced system for defining the niceties of inter-personal and inter-class relationships, the revolution of 1917 really did open the door to a new social order. In the early years at least egalitarian precepts influenced the laws and decrees issued by the new Soviet government. With the nationalization of all resources, and with the abolition of all forms of privatism, the ultimate objective, a new society, was in the making.

In the Marxist analysis of capitalist society class positions are determined by the relationship to the means of production. Thus, the owners of the means of production are the ruling class who exploit the proletariat, who in turn are obliged to sell their labour under disadvantageous circumstances. Under capitalism the state sanctions the perpetuation of a system in which one class exploits another, and in which power and status of the industrial bourgeoisie mediate all the social relationships. The abolition of capitalism would, by definition, remove political and social inequality. As we have seen in the preceding chapter, however, the chaos created by world war and civil war forestalled a number of initiatives, and Lenin was obliged to introduce the New Economic Policy in 1921 to resuscitate the national economy. Thus, elements of private property, and private enterprise of a small-scale kind, continued until Stalin's Five Year Plan and nationalization programme of 1928. Notwithstanding Stalin's initiatives, some elements of private enterprise persist to the present day, most notably in the personal sector in Soviet agriculture. With Gorbachev's *perestroyka* individual entrepreneurs and cooperatives have also been given a fillip. There are also elements of private enterprise in what we have labelled the second economy, but if these involve control of the means of production and/or hiring labour, such activities are usually illegal. What should be borne in mind, however, is that despite the intent of the revolution some aspects of privatism persist. The door to a new social order had indeed been pushed open, but what lay inside was far from tidy.

In 1936 the USSR was officially designated a socialist society. But as the data presented in Table 7 indicate, there still existed a contingent of individual peasant farmers and *kustari*, or handicraftsmen. Still, the transformation of Soviet society was underway as the abolition of the bourgeoisie, traders and *kulaki* (or wealthy peasant class), category between 1926 and 1939 suggests. Social relationships henceforth were to be governed by the precepts of the Communist Party, not by ownership of property.

The new order comprised two social classes and one social stratum. The first

Table 7: Soviet social class structure percentage change 1928–1987

	1928	1939	1959	1979	1985	1987
WORKING CLASS	17.6	50.2	68.3	85.1	87.6	88.0
of which:						
Manual	12.4	33.7	50.2	60.0	61.6	61.8
Intelligentsia	5.2	16.5	18.1	25.1	26.0	26.2
COLLECTIVE FARMERS	2.9	47.2	31.4	14.9	12.4	12.0
INDIVIDUAL PEASANT	74.9	2.6	.3	–	–	–
FARMERS AND *KUSTARI*						
BOURGEOISIE, TRADERS	4.6	–	–	–	–	–
AND *KULAKI*						
TOTAL	100.0	100.0	100.0	100.0	100.0	100.0

Source: *Strana Sovetov za 50 Let* (Moscow: Finansy i Statistika, 1967), 3. *Narodnoye Khozyaystvo SSSR v 1984g* (Moscow: Finansy i Statistika, 1985), 7, *Narodnoye Khozyaystvo SSSR za 70 Let* (Moscow: Finansy i Statistika, 1987) 11.

official class is the working class, the second, collective farmers. As the former is no longer exploited by the owners of the means of production, it is by definition not a proletariat.[1] Collective farmers were deemed a separate class because they are involved in a form of production in which they at least nominally own the output. This situation will be described more fully in a later chapter. The third official group in Soviet society is the *intelligentsia*, which is distinguished from the working class by virtue of its being involved in intellectual as opposed to manual labour. Within each of the three official components of the new order is a plethora of occupations. For instance, within the *intelligentsia* the occupations run the gamut from clerks to authors to Party elite. As the data in Table 7 make plain, there has been a distinct change in the social class structure, which reflects, amongst other things, the urban-industrialization process. The official Soviet position is that the steps taken toward the complete abolition of private ownership of the means of production have removed any basis for class antagonisms.

The concept of social mobility, that is, moving up some type of social hierarchy in respect of material possessions, prestige and privilege, has traditionally been downplayed in the Soviet Union. But in fact there are preferred occupations which do bring different social status, income and privilege, and these in turn can foster class tensions. This facet of Soviet society has now been tacitly recognized since there is available a reasonably substantial body of research into such questions as occupational preference and mobility. The most desirable occupations are those which afford the opportunity to think creatively in a largely unstructured environment. The essential prerequisite for such positions is higher education, as is customary elsewhere. And over the past four decades the number of people who have achieved some form of higher education has grown exceedingly fast. Between 1939 and 1959 the pool grew

---

[1] It should be noted that within the manual working class category are state farm employees who in 1986 numbered approximately 12 million, or about one-eighth of the total.

from 1.2 to 3.8 million. In the next inter-censal period it more than doubled again, reaching 8.3 million in 1970. By 1987 there were 20.8 million Soviet citizens with some type of higher education. The true measure of this transformation is that at the time of the revolution about 70 per cent of the total population were illiterate. The Soviet Union now compares very favourably, on a per capita basis, with other industrialized countries in terms of the number of students pursuing post-secondary education. For example, in 1983–84 there were 5.3 million students registered in Soviet higher educational establishments, a ratio of 194 students per 10,000 population. The comparable ratio in the USA was 268 in 1980–81, 105 in Great Britain in 1979–80, 108 in West Germany in 1981–82 and 144 in Japan in 1982–83. But who are these Soviet students and do they reflect the full spectrum of official Soviet society?

It will come as no great surprise to learn that in the Soviet Union there tends to be a strong positive correlation between the educational attainment of children and the level of education of the parents. At various times in the past there have been major state initiatives to broaden the social class background of students in higher education. For example, under Khrushchev special priority was attached to work experience in the factory or on the farm in the entrance requirements to institutes of higher education, a reform specifically intended to favour children of classes other than the *intelligentsia*. At the time most members of the Soviet political hierarchy came from working-class backgrounds. As with so many other of Khrushchev's schemes, this one was also to prove short-lived. A diminution of standards in higher education was one of the perceived, unfavourable by-products of opening the door to workers. A more recent reform, in 1984, is intended to streamline high school education so as to better train those wishing a vocational education as well as those bent upon some form of higher education. Entrance to a university is now once again highly competitive and the academic requirements are very stringent. Still, over the years children from any socio-economic background who were bright and motivated could succeed. But if there is strong endorsement of education in the home, if the language around the kitchen table is Russian, and if the kitchen is in the apartment of an *intelligentsia* family in a major urban centre, the probability of success is naturally much higher than for the progeny of a non-Russian speaking, rural family. Most higher education requires comprehension of Russian no matter if the university or polytechnic is located in Riga or Dushanbe. Indeed, there is an internal pecking order within the Soviet system of higher education such that, as in other countries, a graduate of an institution such as Moscow State University will be more highly regarded than one from a provincial institution. Egalitarianism in education, especially higher education, remains a basic objective, but the fact is that opportunity for advancement through education is greatest for the *intelligentsia*. Thus, an intellectual elite does exist, and it is geographically concentrated in the major urban centres, most notably in the republic capitals. In those regions where urbanization has progressed least, educational opportunity for the indigenous population is more elusive. As higher education is the key to occupational and social mobility, there is a strong inter-generational and spatial bias to the present Soviet educational system.

As we have noted, education opens the door to occupational mobility. And this in the nature of things has produced a social class fabric rather more intricate in detail than is suggested by the official categories already described. Relationships between groups, social status and its public recognition, income and privilege, all were well articulated in imperial Russia. The revolution sought to change that by substituting egalitarian measures for those of an elitist kind. The initiatives were plentiful, but they did not bring forth the kind of utopian society intended. Pragmatic accommodation with the reality of particular historical circumstances has been a consistent feature of Soviet policies. We need look no further than Soviet policies regarding wages, salaries and the accumulation of wealth, all of which have some bearing on position in society.

After having squeezed wage differentials to a minimum ratio between lowest and highest of about 1.75 in 1919, during the 1920s they were widened to reflect skill requirements throughout all sectors of the economy. Piecework became commonplace in the factory during the 1930s, thereby linking higher production with higher remuneration. Salary and wage differentials were intended to foster an upgrading of skills, which in turn would result in a better educated working class. Wage differentials still exist, although since Stalin's time there has been a general trend toward levelling. For example, in the 1970s the difference between maximum and minimum rates in some industrial sectors was reduced to around 1:2. Two decades earlier the ratio in these same sectors was closer to 1:4. As well, the number of different wage scales has been rationalized with a view to evening out wage rates across the country. There still are differences, and the income earned at the top is not unimportant, but the base level has been improved substantially. And as we shall describe in a later chapter, a system of regional wage coefficients has long been in place to attract labour to remote and climatically harsh regions of the north and east. Thus, substantial income differences continue. However, in general, they are less important in connoting social status than in the United States or Great Britain for instance.

Under Stalin egalitarianism was abandoned as part of the drive to industrialize. The success of this drive was dependent upon the willing participation of that rather small portion of the labour force educationally and technically competent to run industry. Thus, salaries of managers were consciously increased so as to nurture incentive. Moreover, laws pertaining to inheritance were changed to permit the transfer of accumulated wealth in the form of, for example, furnishings, a *dacha* and money from one generation to another. This was intended to further co-opt the participation of the *intelligentsia* in the drive to industrialize. The basis for a middle class, materialistic in spirit and upwardly mobile in ambition, was being put in place. In the military, ranks were restored in the mid-1930s after having been abolished in a post-revolutionary flurry of egalitarian decrees. Thus, in a variety of different ways society was becoming more stratified by virtue of state policies affecting wages, salaries, accumulation of wealth, and recognizable status in the form of military and civilian rank. Indeed, the bourgeois and materialistic values of the *meshchanstvo* of the imperial era were being legally endorsed at the same time that the USSR was being proclaimed a socialist state. True egalitarianism would have to await the arrival of communism, the ultimate stage in the Marxist scheme for the evolution of society.

As we already noted, some jobs are more desired than others, and those people successful in acquiring them benefit accordingly. With the most highly valued occupations comes social status. For those jobs which the state deems especially important to society, there is a well developed system of perquisites. For example, access to better state housing, priority in acquiring a room in a holiday sanitorium, priority in food supply, a car, or indeed, a car, chauffeur and domestic help, all make life easier and more enjoyable. In an economic system in which periodic shortage is an endemic feature of daily life amongst the masses, such perks are not to be under-estimated and are often as important as the salary paid. Privilege has given rise to an elite, which some observers of the Soviet scene have estimated to range in size from several hundred thousand to several million, depending on the definition employed. While the existence of elites is clearly at the pleasure of the state, there is obviously pressure to ensure continuity from one generation to the next. By no means is this more easily achieved by what might be labelled the Party elite than other segments of Soviet society. Indeed, some western observers reckon the Party member's ability to perpetuate status is rather more problematic than for a member of the *intelligentsia* who is not directly beholden to the Party for position and privilege. In fact, the system supports elites from a wide cross-section of society, from academia, the military, the arts, industry and so forth. Small wonder that the spectre of being made redundant as a result of *perestroyka* is being resisted wherever possible by those who have something to lose.

Privilege is graded, and thus reflects officialdom's perception of the value of the contribution to the well-being and development of society as a whole. Some forms of privilege are manifested publicly, and perhaps in consequence serve to stimulate incentive to achieve. But in Soviet society, like that of Imperial Russia before it, status is conveyed in part by personal appearance. During the 1920s, for instance, ordinary jobs which required uniforms were generally preferred over those which did not. Uniforms are still common in contemporary Soviet society, and describe position clearly enough. During Stalin's time the dress and manners of the emerging middle class tended to connote station in life to all who cared to take notice. Subtle manifestations of status still exist amongst the growing middle class, and periodically campaigns are mounted to draw public attention to such matters. In recent years, for example, the press has criticized as unseemly ostentation the wearing of gold jewellery and the acquisition of gold teeth, with perhaps predictably little effect on public behaviour. Modish dress is not necessarily at odds with state objectives, of course. However, in the 1980s the recently arrived *kolkhoznik*, or peasant, is still as readily recognizable in the large city as he was in the past. And he is still at the bottom of the social order.

The creation of social groups outside the official tripartite model of Soviet society is regarded as an unhealthy tendency, though there is little evidence as yet to suggest that such social groups as may exist consciously dictate the behaviour of members. By the same token, the idealized harmonious interaction amongst, and between, manual workers, collective farmers and the *intelligentsia*, the social categories recognized by officialdom, does not appear to exist on a very large scale either, as we will illustrate in the next chapter. Clearly, in all societies there are different social networks. While the goal of Soviet society is to break down barriers between groups, and to promote social interaction amongst them, the process of socialization is still conditioned more by peer group interests than by, for example, who happens to occupy the apartment next door. Social justice for all remains an elusive goal, as we will illustrate in Chapter 10.

As we have noted before, the difference between ideal and reality in the Soviet Union is sometimes substantial. As Soviet society becomes more complex, perhaps more materialistic and acquisitive, it is not beyond the realm of possibility that some of the unofficial social groups will become fundamentally antagonistic. The system of privilege which supports a comfortable lifestyle for some members of society at the expense of others certainly has the potential to foster resentment.

The official categorization of Soviet society may be quite simplistic, but the changes in the relative shares of the various categories over the years nonetheless suggest a society very much on the move in terms of social mobility (Table 7). Education, and especially higher education, has opened the door to opportunity for literally millions of Soviet citizens. Party membership, and thus a greater chance of securing a *nomenklatura* position (those jobs throughout the Soviet system which are allocated by the Party), no doubt has helped to open the door a little wider. Soviet society has been very much on the move in other ways as well.

Internal migration

During the Soviet period there has been a fundamental change in the respective shares of rural and urban populations, as Fig. 15 indicates. With barely 18 per cent of the total population urban in 1926, the Stalin-initiated industrialization drive was largely responsible for the 150 per cent increase in the urban sector before World War II. By 1939 the urban sector represented 32 per cent of the total population. Rural–urban migration accounted for most of this growth, and was manipulated by the state to achieve specific objectives. The principal mechanism for manipulating internal migration – the internal passport system – was introduced in 1932.

The Soviet version of the internal passport was scarcely a novel concept. As we have noted in an earlier chapter, a similiar device was employed by the Tsarist government for essentially the same purpose, namely to control the movement of peasants from village to city. For those aged 16 or older leaving the countryside for the city without a passport during the Stalin era was not impossible, but it certainly was difficult. For the millions of adult *kolkhozniki*, that is, collective farm peasants who comprised the bulk of the rural population, it remained so for decades. It was not until the mid-1970s that they were legally entitled to an internal passport upon reaching age 16, something which clearly differentiated this group from the rest of Soviet society. But those *kolkhozniki* youth who had not reached 16 years could, and did, migrate to the city without difficulty, and often with the encouragement of their less mobile parents. It is only since 1981 that all Soviet citizens aged 16 and over have been required to have an internal passport. This document facilitates movement, both in terms of permanent relocation and holidaying. In the former case, it is a necessary document in seeking employment, and in the latter, is usually requested when purchasing airline and rail tickets. Aside from establishing identity the passport also provides authorities with information on place of residence, nationality, and all past places of residence. Because this covers any period of incarceration it reveals criminal records. Clearly, monitoring, if not actually controlling, internal population movement is more easily managed by virtue of the passport system. Without it the vast shift between rural and urban population shown in Fig. 15 doubtless would have been even greater. While the urban population presently accounts for about two-thirds of the total, it should be remembered that it was only in 1961 that it reached 50 per cent. But residence in a city is not assured simply because one possesses a passport. The second bureaucratic device for controlling urban growth is the *propiska*, or residence permit.

Each urban inhabitant must have a *propiska*, which is entered in the passport and which gives legal recognition of the right to live in a specific city. The *propiska* denotes whether residence is permanent or temporary. Temporary residence permits of between one and three years are in fact quite common, owing to the severe labour shortage in some cities, notably the larger ones. People who hold such temporary *propisky* are reckoned to comprise about 15 per cent of the labour force in the large Soviet city. Often referred to as *limitchiki* because of their temporary urban status, they represent a kind of legal lumpenproletariat. In theory, one cannot live in a city without a *propiska*, but in fact most major cities attract sizeable numbers of 'illegal' unregistered residents. Registered migrants are normally permitted a three month temporary *propiska* during which time they must secure a job if they arrived without one in hand. When credentials and employer's recommendation are in order, migrants may then obtain a permanent *propiska*, which allows them to be assigned accommodation. Given the general shortage of housing, prolonged waiting times are not unusual. For many this means that home continues to be a bed in a hotel, hostel, workers' barracks, a friend's apartment or even rented space in someone else's home. In summary, it requires little imagination to see how internal migration and urban growth might be 'administratively' manipulated through discretionary allocation of an internal passport and *propiska*. However, a lot more imagination and enterprise have been employed in overcoming such institutional barriers to internal migration.

In simple terms the major population movements during the Soviet period have been from west to east and from north to south. Since the turn of the century the absolute population increase east of the Volga river has been about twice that west of it. To be sure, part of this increase reflects those demographic features which differentiate the Middle Asian and Caucasian peoples who predominate east and south of the Volga from the Slavs and Baltic peoples of European Russia. But a substantial component of this population increase is the result of internal migration, both voluntary and involuntary. Development of the huge resource potential of the eastern regions was a major objective of the Stalin-era industrialization drive, as we shall explain in a subsequent chapter. There has continued to be a commitment to develop the eastern regions in the post-Stalin period. However, reliance on incentives has assumed more importance in attracting labour to the eastern and northern frontiers than simply assigning people to work there for indefinite periods as was commonplace with Stalin. The problem confronting Soviet manpower planners now is that despite sizeable wage differentials the eastern regions are generally characterized by very high labour turnover rates. In many industrial operations it exceeds 50 per cent per annum. Thus, not only does labour cost more than, say, in European Russia, there is the added burden of continually training new workers whose productivity is naturally much lower than seasoned employees.

While the absolute population change in the Siberian and Far East economic regions between 1939 and 1979 was nearly nine million (17.1 to 26.0 million), this represented both in-migration and out-migration, as well as natural increase. With the easing of the Stalin-era restrictions on internal migration in the late 1950s, substantial numbers of people decided to leave Siberia. Between the 1959 and 1970 censuses net out-migration from the West and East Siberian economic regions alone was close to 900,000. Thus, while the total population still grew as a result of natural increase, the scale of the outflow clearly posed some serious manpower problems. In the late 1960s regional wage incentives in the eastern zones were augmented. Combined with public appeals for Soviet youth to participate in the construction of massive projects such as the Baykal – Amur railroad (BAM), thousands of new workers have been drawn into the eastern regions from other parts of the country. Thus, net out-migration which characterized the 1960s appears to have been stemmed for the time being. While many of those who migrate to the eastern frontiers do not stay long, nonetheless, one of the major achievements of the Soviet era is the quite fundamental re-working of the distribution of population.

The shift in the centre of gravity of population from north to south while perhaps more subtle than that from west to east has been especially frustrating in terms of balancing supply and demand for labour. The Soviet equivalent of the sun-belt – Moldavia, the south Ukraine including the Crimea, the north Caucasus and Caucasian republics, and Middle Asia – not only is a region characterized by high rates of natural increase, over the years it has been the destination of a substantial number of migrants from the north. The majority of the migrants are Slavic and urban. For example, from the RSFSR alone more than one million people left for a sunnier southern clime between 1970 and 1979. Slavic migrants traditionally have found employment in urban industry, and often dominated the managerial ranks. But in recent years there are signs of a change in direction of migration. As Table 8 indicates, between 1979 and 1984 the RSFSR recorded a net in-migration of nearly three quarters of a million people. The data in Table 8 suggest that this is because of an out-migration from the southern republics. There are several possible reasons for this quite significant change in basic migration pattern. As Middle Asians themselves become more urbanized they are bringing pressure to bear on migrant worker and manager alike in terms of competition for jobs. And when indigenous people reach positions of power and authority there are often claims that they show favouritism toward their own kind, a scarcely surprising development but one which is resented by migrants. Ethnic tensions are conceivably another reason for the change in migration flow. The recent racial riots in Kazakhstan, noted earlier, were widely reported in the Soviet press and certainly will serve to dampen Slavic enthusiasm to move to Middle Asia. They are symptomatic of some fundamental problems and no doubt will spur even more Slavic migrants to return home. Still, it should not be forgotten that given the harsh winter which exists over much of the northern region the attraction of life in a southerly locale remains compelling.

Thus, the paths of migration in recent years raise some new problems. If the pattern depicted in Table 8 continues then the Slavic presence in the Middle Asian and Caucasian realm will diminish, something scarcely desired by the Party or the

Table 8: Natural increase and balance of migration in union republics between 17 January, 1979 and 1 January, 1984

Republics	Increase in population	of which	
		Natural increase	Balance of migration
Slavic			
RSFSR	4,566,000	3,819,000	+ 747,000
Ukraine	912,000	917,000	− 5,000
Belorussia	318,000	323,000	− 5,000
Baltic			
Lithuania	141,000	89,000	+ 52,000
Latvia	66,000	25,000	+ 41,000
Estonia	52,000	24,000	+ 28,000
Caucasus			
Georgia	152,000	240,000	− 88,000
Azerbaydzhan	478,000	582,000	− 104,000
Armenia	236,000	274,000	− 28,000
Middle Asia			
Uzbek	2,107,000	2,218,000	− 111,000
Kirgiz	357,000	413,000	− 56,000
Tadzhik	564,000	607,000	− 43,000
Turkmen	359,000	385,000	− 26,000
Kazakh	964,000	1,224,000	− 260,000
Moldavia	133,000	207,000	− 74,000

Source: Ann Sheehy, 'Population Trends in the Union Republics, 1979–1984,' *Radio Liberty Research Bulletin*, Vol. 29, No. 22, (3331), 29 May, 1985, 7.

government. The in-migration registered by the RSFSR would appear to be a positive development since this is the key labour deficit republic. But if it transpires that the principal destinations are the major cities of European Russia, the east and north will continue to be labour deficient. A return to the days of limited choice over job and its location, reminiscent of the early Stalin era in general and war-measures era in particular, is most unlikely. As restrictions on internal migration have eased since the late 1950s people have come to expect to exercise personal choice as a matter of course. The not uncommon pattern of migration from labour-scarce northern and eastern regions to labour-surplus southern locales is one instance of this attitude. The persistence young people in European Russia show in leaving the labour-short villages for the town is another.

To some degree migration has been managed in accordance with state policies. But there still are some unrealized objectives: for example, stabilizing rural populations in marginal, but still important, agricultural regions in European Russia; moving indigenous Middle Asians from the labour-surplus countryside to the city; promoting urban growth in particular regions and specific city size categories. These objectives, and more besides, comprise part of a strategy for the planned development of the whole settlement system. In the remaining pages of this chapter we will sketch in some of the main problems confronting Soviet planners in re-working the geography of settlement.

The settlement system

In a Soviet-type economy it is theoretically possible to manipulate population movement so as to conform with state objectives. The foregoing discussion has served to remind us, however, that when state objectives do not match individual preferences they are often confounded. This is perhaps nowhere more evident than in terms of where the average Soviet citizen chooses to live.

For more than four decades the notion of an optimal city size was widely accepted as an essential element in Soviet urban policy, though what was to be the optimal population was far from consistent. Early concepts articulated in the 1920s reckoned that a population of 50-60,000 was ideal since this was large enough to make the provision of the necessary goods and services economic, yet small enough to permit a sense of community and a communal, socialist ethos to be fostered and maintained. However, the Stalin-initiated industrialization drive brought about a seemingly unending circular and cumulative process of urban growth. Unable to hold city growth in check, ideas about what constituted the optimum size began to change. By the mid-1950s the most frequently cited figures ranged between 150,000 and 200,000, a rather pragmatic accommodation with the reality of urbanization, but also reflective of changing notions about the nature of urban economies. By the 1960s the optimum size had been bumped into the 200,000 to 300,000 range. Put simply, despite the steady inflation of what constituted the optimal size, the actual pace of urban growth far outstripped it. By the beginning of the 1960s the validity of the concept was being questioned by numerous Soviet writers. Events since have put paid to its utility in planning theory and practice.

From Table 9 it is evident that the distribution of the urban population by city-size group has altered substantially since 1926. At that time almost half of the Soviet urban population lived in cities of less than 50,000 inhabitants. By the mid-1980s barely 30 per cent did. During this period a substantial number of cities joined the largest city-size category of over 500,000 population. This city-size group more than doubled its share of the total population between 1926 and 1987. Even when the specific cities in this largest city size category at a particular time are taken as the basis of measuring rates of growth, invariably they grew at least as fast as the cities of less than 50,000. In short, policies to check the growth of the largest urban places and to promote the expansion of the smallest have not been terribly effective.

Perhaps the clearest indication of the nature of the urban growth process during the past six decades is given by the number of cities with more than one million inhabitants. In 1959 there were only three: Moscow, Leningrad and Kiev. By 1970 seven more had been added to the roster. In 1987 there were 23 'million' cities and fully one fifth of the urban population lived in them. There is, of course, nothing magic about one million. However, the trends underlying the differential growth rates suggested by the data in Table 9 are significant. Population concentration in large cities was originally perceived to be a negative phenomenon, an inherent feature of capitalist societies where urban growth was both spontaneous and

Table 9: Urban growth by city size group (in millions)

City size group	1926		1939		1959		Population 1970		1977		1987	
	m	%	m	%	m	%	m	%	m	%	m	%
Less than 50,000	12.7	(48.3)	24.9	(41.2)	40.4	(40.4)	47.4	(34.8)	48.7	(30.5)	55.8	(30.0)
50,000–99,000	4.1	(15.6)	7.0	(11.6)	11.0	(11.0)	13.0	(9.6)	15.3	(9.6)	17.7	(9.5)
100,000–500,000	5.4	(20.5)	15.7	(26.0)	24.4	(24.4)	38.3	(28.2)	46.8	(29.3)	51.0	(27.4)
Over 500,000	4.1	(15.6)	12.8	(21.2)	24.2	(24.2)	37.3	(27.4)	48.8	(30.6)	61.5	(33.1)
of which over 1,000,000	N/A		7.7		10.1	(10.1)	19.1	(14.0)	27.4	(17.2)	40.8	(21.9)
TOTAL	26.3	(100.0)	60.4	(100.0)	100	(100.0)	136.0	(100.0)	159.6	(100.0)	186.0	(100.0)

Source: Narodnoye Khozyaystvo SSSR za 60 Let (Moscow: Finansy i Statistika, 1977), 59–68;
Narodnoye Khozyaystvo SSSR za 70 Let (Moscow: Finansy i Statistika, 1987), 395–400.

uncontrolled. It is still the view of many Soviets that 'controlled' urban growth should be one of the distinctive features of a socialist system. Yet as we have seen, despite a flood of decrees establishing limits to city size, the existence of a system of internal passports and *propiski*, and a real need for planners to predict city populations, urban growth, and especially that of the larger centres, has proceeded at largely unplanned rates. One of the principal reasons for this situation is the pattern of investment in industry.

With ministries, and their various departments and enterprises, increasingly preoccupied with efficiency and economy in the allocation of limited financial resources, linked closely to the issue of profitability introduced by the 1965 reform and more recently endorsed by Gorbachev, the financial benefit accruing from the external economies of the large urban centre clearly put a premium on locations there. For the enterprise seeking to expand *in situ* owing to the lower incremental cost than in a new location, a major stumbling block can be the city planning agency which may regard industrial expansion as undesirable. However, as we shall see in the next chapter, the city Soviet and its various regulatory and planning departments are frequently no match for politically and economically important ministries and enterprises. Thus, notwithstanding the numerous regulations restricting the growth of large cities, existing deficiencies in housing, consumer and cultural services, and the negative impact of an unplanned population increase, expansion of the employment base in the large urban centre often goes ahead regardless. At present more than 40 per cent of investment in industrial production is concentrated in the 55 cities with more than 500,000 population. Without more effective intervention this share is likely to continue to increase.

Even when civic authorities are seemingly successful in warding off unwanted increased employment in a particular production facility, there are other means to achieve the same end. If an enterprise is advised it cannot expand its employment, and hence the population of the city concerned, it is not uncommon for production to be increased anyway by simply attracting labour from *outside* the city. Of the 58 million people who commuted to cities in 1980, close to 17 million did so to work. This so-called 'pendulum' migration has grown rapidly, and is having an impact on the city, the rural sector and on the nature of the settlement system itself.

Urban enterprises are easily able to draw upon a labour supply from outside the city because of the substantial improvement to the Soviet ground transportation system which has occurred over the past three decades. Modern commuter trains now disgorge enormous numbers of people compared to the late 1950s. Improvements to the network of bus routes, and the frequency of service on them, have similarly enabled ever larger numbers of rural residents to travel to the city to work, shop or use services not otherwise available to them. Between 1960 and 1980 the total number of commuters increased more than twofold. At the latter date about 7.5 million people travelling each day to work in a city began the trip in a village. Roughly the same number commuted from one city to another. Some workers commuted from village to village or from city to countryside. In general, the zone of influence varies according to the size of the city. In the case of Moscow, for example, it extended some 20 kilometres beyond the city border in 1920. It now encompasses an area at least 50 kilometres beyond city borders, which in turn obviously encompass a vastly larger city than in 1920. Each day some 500,00 people pour into Moscow from surrounding urban and rural settlements, while perhaps as many as 100,000 depart the city to jobs in outlying enterprises. To be sure, a substantial number of people commute long distances, spending as much as two hours each way, because they are unable to obtain a *propiska* for the city in question. But to judge from recent surveys of job satisfaction, many commuters are choosing a 'suburban' lifestyle. The attractions of village life are perhaps greater if one's income and lifestyle are not directly tied to the land. In this regard it is worth remembering that many urbanites have recently relocated from village to city. After all, it was only in 1961 that even half of the Soviet population was urban. Village life therefore remains important. Huge numbers of people regularly visit relatives in the countryside, or travel to the family home in the village, now serving the grander function of weekend *dacha*, or cottage. Whether for recreation, food supply or familial obliga- tion, the connection between town and country remains strong for millions of Soviet urban citizens. The impact of such commutation on countryside customs and values is important, as we will describe later. It clearly influences the nature of the settle- ment system as well.

The planned development of the settlement system has been part of Soviet theoretical formulations almost from the outset. But aside from a few general locational guidelines there has been a notable absence of specific policies and pro- grammes to achieve such an objective. Towns are not to be created in isolation from the settlement system of which they would be part, an objective which found legal expression in a decree of 1933. Since that date more than 1,200 new cities have been added to the Soviet map. Some have acquired urban status through reclassification. But hundreds are literally new towns. By the turn of the century it is planned that there will be several hundred more. Most new town development is not occurring on the frontier of settlement, however. Notwithstanding the many major resource developments and railway construction projects such as the Baykal–Amur line, which are spawning a considerable number of new cities, about three-quarters of new city formation is actually taking place within existing urban agglomerations. Because town planning has traditionally focused on the city, as distinct from the city and its region, and because the authority of the city Soviet and its planning bureaucracy usually only extends as far as the city border, there has been very little done to plan the development of the settlement system as opposed to the individual city within it. It was not until the 1970s that the Central Urban Planning Institute in Moscow formalized a plan for creating an interconnected system of places on a national scale – the so-called General Scheme for the System of Settlement.

As Fig. 16 implies the General Scheme is intended to integrate rural and urban settlements. Comprising a network of hierarchically organized settlement systems, 60 large, 169 medium and 323 small, when complete it was intended to embrace more than 90 per cent of the total Soviet population. Introduced with considerable fanfare, the General Scheme was to provide the spatial frame of reference for the development of the economy between 1976 and 1990. While in practical terms the General Scheme seems not to be of great significance, it does give tangible expression to the growing preoccupation of many Soviet analysts with the long-standing problem of how to eradicate the difference between town and countryside.

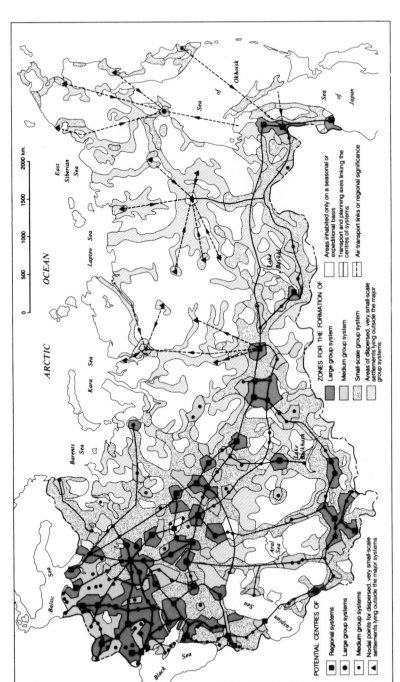

POTENTIAL CENTRES OF

■ Regional systems

● Large group systems

● Medium group systems

▲ Nodal points for dispersed, very small-scale settlements lying outside the major systems

ZONES FOR THE FORMATION OF

Large group system

Medium group system

Small-scale group system

Areas of dispersed, very small-scale settlements lying outside the major group systems

Areas inhabited only on a seasonal or expeditional basis

Transport and planning axes linking the centres of systems

Air-transport links or regional significance

Fig. 16 The General Scheme for a System of Settlement

Source: A. Brown *et al.* (eds.), *The Cambridge Encyclopedia of Russia and the Soviet Union* (Cambridge: Cambridge University Press, 1982), 348–9.

Moreover, it reflects implicitly the growing attention being paid to the role of agglomerations within the Soviet Union.

Since the 1960s there has emerged a concerted effort to turn the attention of all planners away from the individual city to the city region and to the national settlement system. The General Scheme is one manifestation of this tendency, the growing interest in the role of the urban agglomeration is another. As we have noted already, Soviet town planners traditionally have had jurisdiction only within the borders of the city. When their policies have been successfully enforced, outlying settlements have been the recipients of much new, and unplanned, investment. New investment produces jobs, and jobs urban growth. Very frequently the places selected for such investment are part of existing, or nascent, agglomerations. Thus, while controls over population movement limit entry to the major cities, satellite communities are experiencing explosive growth. Even in the case of Moscow where planning authority does extend well beyond the 'official' city border, the growth rate of urban settlements subordinate to the Moscow City Soviet is, for some observers alarmingly high. Between 1959 and 1981 the population of Moscow itself increased from 5.1 to eight million, or by more than 57 per cent. But the population of the subordinate urban settlements increased by more than five times during the same period. As Fig. 17 shows there are many cities in Moscow oblast which have grown at singularly rapid rates. Two cities lying outside the oblast border, but certainly within the Moscow agglomeration in the opinion of most authorities, have also experienced rapid growth between 1959 and 1981 (cf. Aleksandrov and Obninsk, Fig. 17). The same phenomenon is occurring in many other places, but in most cases without the equivalent authority of the Moscow City Soviet.

One of the objectives of urban planning in the Moscow agglomeration has been the containment of sprawl and the protection of the forest park belt as a recreation zone for Muscovites. But it is precisely in this intended green belt where the urban population has increased fastest in both relative and absolute terms between 1959 and 1981 (Fig. 17). The obvious question is, if this can occur in the best planned city-region in the country, what is happening in the majority of cases where planning authority does not extend past city borders?

Two main influences on contemporary Soviet urban development are the so-called scientific-technical revolution and agro-industrial integration. Both demand a perspective on urban development which emphasizes networks or systems of interconnected places. The vast majority of the Soviet urban population now lives within an agglomeration. The definition of the agglomeration varies, but is customarily regarded as a network of urban and rural settlements linked to a city of at least 250,000 inhabitants by a transportation system that permits journeys from dependent settlement to the core-city within a two-hour travel time. While obviously an integral part of the Soviet urban scene, agglomerations are in the main still divorced from the day-to-day jurisdiction of town planners. It is only recently that they have figured prominently in national planning strategies like the General Scheme. The concept of planning for agglomerations has certainly taken root, but it has not yet borne fruit in terms of juridically-based planning regions throughout the country. Meanwhile, the system evolves with a momentum of its own. The costs are considerable.

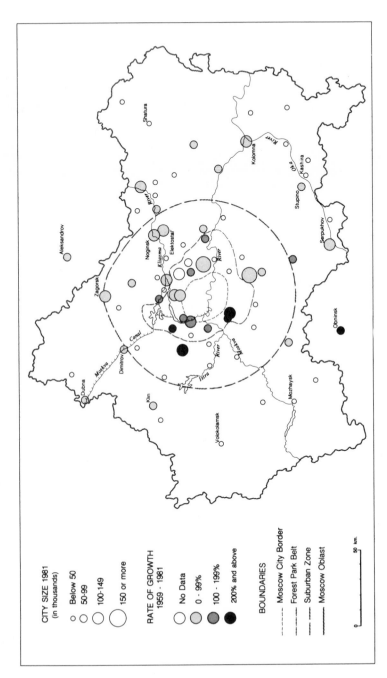

CITY SIZE 1981
(in thousands)

- ○ Below 50
- ○ 50-99
- ○ 100-149
- ○ 150 or more

RATE OF GROWTH
1959 - 1981

- ○ No Data
- ○ 0 - 99%
- ○ 100 - 199%
- ● 200% and above

BOUNDARIES

- ----- Moscow City Border
- ----- Forest Park Belt
- ----- Suburban Zone
- ——— Moscow Oblast

0   50 km.

Fig. 17 Urban Growth in Moscow Oblast

Source: Gary G. Hausladen, 'Containing the Growth of Moscow. Comparisons with London', *Cities*. Vol. 3, February 1985, 65.

The large city and agglomeration continue to gain an ever larger share of the urban population, thus rendering planning more difficult. Indeed, the concentration of population in the central city within agglomerations is notably high in comparison with western countries. This concentration of population in the central city, which rarely is less than one half of the total metropolitan population of the urban agglomeration, is at least partly due to the low level of private automobile ownership and to the preponderance of apartments as opposed to detached, individually owned housing which is typical of North American metropolitan areas for example. Clearly, with such spatial concentration of the metropolitan population the small and remote towns are even further removed from the mainstream of Soviet economic development.

Beyond the two-hour isochrone, that is, the area bounded by two hours travel time from the central city, there are many places which do not enjoy such accessibility to any major urban centre. Such settlements bear witness to lost opportunities. In the current decision-making environment, which tends to emphasize cost efficiency over spatial or regional equity, the small city remotely located often has a sizeable level of under-employment. But the lack of adequate municipal services, the absence of centres of higher and technical education, and a general dearth of consumer and cultural services, which follows from years of limited investment, are more than sufficient to outweigh any possible advantage of manpower availability to ministerial decision-makers. In such communities absolute population decline is not unheard of. Since only a handful of city-regions have been set up as independent planning administrations, since there is as yet no operational plan for managing the development of the settlement system, throughout most of the country the large city grows faster than intended, spawning development in its shadow. The small town outside these burgeoning agglomerations is left to get on as best it can with limited investment and resources since existing legislation directing ministries to locate new facilities in precisely such places is widely ignored.

Consolidation of rural settlements, industrialization of agriculture, stemming the tide of rural depopulation in some regions, while encouraging this same phenomenon in others, also are part of the broader programme of planning the settlement system. Perhaps the major irony is that as the large Soviet city garners an increasing share of the urban population, the small, remote village remains an integral part of the rural landscape. Millions have migrated from village to city during the Soviet era, but many of those who still remain in the countryside live in villages not much different in average size than at the turn of the century. These villages are now part of large, more complex agro-administrative structures to be sure. However, with only 225 inhabitants in the typical village the long-standing objective of making the rural lifestyle more urban-like remains elusive. Many Soviet rural settlements are too small to offer much potential for economic provision of educational, health and other consumer or cultural services, and too distant from a city to permit regular commuting. Such remote small villages are to be abandoned in favour of rural centres of 1,000 or more people. These latter places are each year accounting for a larger share of the rural population. But at present this is barely half of the total.

Clearly, there is much that influences the evolution of the Soviet settlement system aside from official policies and regulatory agencies. At this point we might well ask, what is the nature of the Soviet city itself? Have six decades of Soviet development created a distinctive urban environment and socialist lifestyle?

Recommended reading

Akiner, S., *Islamic Peoples of the Soviet Union* (London: Kegan Paul, 1983), 2nd ed.

Allworth, E. (ed.), *Ethnic Russia in the USSR* (New York: Pergamon, 1980).

Allworth, E. (ed.), *Soviet Nationality Problems* (New York: Columbia University Press, 1971).

Azrael, J.R. (ed.), *Soviet Nationality Policies and Practice* (New York: Praeger, 1978).

Besemeres, J.F., *Socialist Population Policies* (White Plains: M.E. Sharpe, 1980).

Chinn, J., *Manipulating Soviet Population Resources* (London: Macmillan, 1977).

Churchward, L.G., *The Soviet Intelligentsia* (London: Routledge and Kegan Paul, 1973).

Chylinski, E.A. (ed), *Soviet Central Asia: Continuity and Change* (Esbjerg: South Jutland University Press, 1984).

Defosses, H. (ed), *Soviet Population Policy: Conflicts and Constraints* (New York: Pergamon Press, 1981).

Fitzpatrick, S. *Education and Social Mobility in the Soviet Union 1921–1934* (Cambridge: Cambridge University Press, 1979).

Friedberg, M., Isham, H. (eds), *Soviet Society under Gorbachev Current Trends and the Prospects for Reform* (Armonk, New York: M.E. Sharpe, 1987).

Grandstaff, P.J., *Interregional Migration in the USSR: Economic Aspects 1959–1970* (Durham: Duke University Press, 1980).

Jones, E., Grupp, F., *Modernization, Value Changes and Fertility in the Soviet Union* (Cambridge: Cambridge University Press, 1987).

Katz, Z. (ed.), *Handbook of Major Soviet Nationalities* (London: Macmillan, 1975).

Karklins, R., *Ethnic Relations in the USSR: The Perspective from Below* (London: George Allen and Unwin, 1986).

Kerblay, B., *Modern Soviet Society* (New York: Pantheon Books, 1983). Translated by Rupert Sywer.

Kozlov, V., *The Peoples of the Soviet Union* (London: Hutchinson, 1988).

Lane, D., O'Dell, F., *The Soviet Industrial Worker* (Oxford: Martin Robertson, 1975).

Lewis, R.A., Rowland, R.H., *Population Redistribution in the USSR: Its Impact on Society 1897-1977* (New York: Praeger, 1979).

Lorimer, F., *The Population of the Soviet Union* (Geneva: S.D.N., 1946).

Lubin, N., *Labour and Nationality in Soviet Central Asia* (Princeton: Princeton University Press, 1984).

Ryan, M., Prentice, R., *Social Trends in the Soviet Union from 1950* (London: Macmillan, 1987).

Rywkin, M., *Moscow's Muslim Challenge: Soviet Central Asia* (Armonk, New York: M.E. Sharpe, 1982).

Sacks, M.P., Parkhurst, J.G. (ed), *Understanding Soviet Society* (Winchester: Unwin Hyman, 1988).

Tomiak, J.J. (ed), *Western Perspectives on Soviet Education in the 1980s* (New York: St. Martin's Press, 1986).

Wixman, R., *The Peoples of the USSR: An Ethnographic Handbook* (Armonk, New York: M.E. Sharpe, 1984).

Yanowitch, M. (ed), *The Social Structure of the USSR: Recent Soviet Studies* (Armonk, New York: M.E. Sharpe, 1986).

5 The Soviet City

One of the compelling ironies of urban existence is the great gap between the promise of modernity, the vision of abundance and equality, and its fulfilment by the cities which are its agents.

Dyos, 1973.[1]

A half century of rapid urban-industrialization clearly has wrought a massive transformation of the urban scene in the USSR. The dimensions of change are readily apparent from a few statistics. On the eve of World War I no more than one-sixth of the 160 million subjects of the Russian Empire lived in towns, a small share in comparison with the major western European states or the United States. In 1988 two thirds of the USSR's 285 million inhabitants lived in cities and urban type settlements. At present roughly one in ten of the world's urban population lives in a Soviet city. The question immediately arises, what, if anything, is distinctive about the Soviet socialist city?

The Russian revolution of 1917 imposed a new ideological blueprint for a society moulded over the centuries by the values and precepts of an absolute autocracy. Nowhere else was the change to the new social order so palpable as in the city. All resources having been nationalized, land uses were to be planned, not market determined. Most forms of privatism were eventually to be abolished. Meanwhile the ethos of collectivism was actively cultivated. Equality was heralded. Socialism portended new possibilities for charting the course of urbanization, even if the precise direction and tempo of the changes set in motion by the revolution were not always immediately clear. The Soviet city was to become both an agent and an example of directed social and economic change. The extent to which the built environment actually reflects the prevailing ideology is a complex issue to resolve. In this chapter we will attempt to provide some insights by first of all describing the

---

[1] H.J. Dyos, *Urbanity and Suburbanity. An Inaugural Lecture* (Leicester: Leicester University Press. 1973), 5.

ideals which have ostensibly governed the planned development of the Soviet city. Secondly, we will examine the way in which cultural values have shaped the built environment through the residential segregation of specific classes or groups of society, clearly one of the more important ways in which human actions have influenced urban form the world over. Finally, the success of Soviet town planning practice will be assessed.

Soviet town planning – ideals

The transformation of the values of society through the conscious manipulation of the urban-industrialization process is an integral part of Marxist-Leninist doctrine. Thus, the state's relationship to the city was altered from something which had been coloured by deep-rooted distrust in imperial Russia, to positive endorsement. The creation of a new urban form figured prominently in the task of inculcating the values of a proletarian culture. Individualism and privatism in all their manifestations were to be supplanted by the proletarian principle of collectivism. In the first few years of revolutionary fervour this led to much experimentation, especially in art and architectural design. In terms of actual urban development, however, the chaos of Civil War and reconstruction of the national economy meant that little was accomplished outside the municipalization of existing real estate and the reassignment of housing space. Indeed, the massive urban–rural migration, which the chaos of the times occasioned, significantly eased the long-standing housing crisis. The benefits, however, were both relative and temporary.

The fundamental contradiction between city and countryside, which Marxists claimed was produced under capitalism, somehow was to be resolved in a socialist society. Much was said about the role of communal living in the new order, some enthusiasts even arguing that it would eventually replace the nuclear family. These were just two of the many potential social changes introduced by the revolution which had some important implications for urban design. But there were no readily available models to accommodate the profound changes set in motion by the revolution. While not much was actually built during the early 1920s, debate over what form the new Soviet socialist city should take was intense. There emerged two principal and opposing schools of thought, generally labelled the urbanist and de-urbanist schools.

The ideas of the prominent Soviet architect, L. Sabsovich, are typical of the urbanist approach to the socialist city. He proposed a system of essentially self-contained urban centres in which multi-storeyed collective living facilities would de-emphasize distinctions between the various strata of Soviet society. The nuclear family was regarded as a transitional social phenomenon, one which would eventually give way to an entirely communal way of life. Thus, housing would serve essentially a dormitory purpose. Filling the void would be a host of state services such as day-care centres for pre-school children, communal food services and so forth. In order to create a sense of community, if not a communal ethos, it was thought that each city should be of strictly limited population size. A fixed population of about 50,000 was commonly assumed to be the ideal. Within Sabsovich's socialist cities major design considerations included: strict land-use zoning to prevent any form of environmental pollution, proximate development of places of employment and housing so as to minimize the journey to work, a non-commercial city centre, ample green space and recreational facilities, and an emphasis on pedestrian movement within the city.

In the opinion of proponents of the de-urbanist school, schemes like Sabsovich's did not chart a new course for urban development at all, they simply replaced large cities with smaller ones. Despite the emphasis on communal services the urbanists, it was contended, were not proposing a socialist urban environment. The de-urbanists on the other hand wanted an entirely new urban future, one more in keeping with what they regarded as basic Marxist ideology. De-urbanists such as M. Okhitovich and M. Ginsberg, for instance, proposed an essentially townless, socialist society, in which the population would be dispersed over all of the habitable parts of the state. Settlement would occur in ribbon-like developments, individual dwellings being located in natural surroundings, but within easy access to communal centres for dining, recreation and so forth. While some measure of privacy would be provided in terms of living quarters, the lifestyle itself would be communal. All centres of employment and consumer services were to be located in these same ribbon developments, but in such a manner as to minimize travel time to them. Spatial mobility was predicated on universal use of the automobile, a marked contrast to the urbanists' emphasis on pedestrian journeys. Given the radical nature of the town planning proposals put forward by both the de-urbanist and urbanist schools, it is scarcely surprising that few schemes ever got past the drawing board. However, one idea did make the transition from drawing board to bricks and mortar – N. Miliutin's linear city. This scheme merits brief description because it embodied most of the important principles from the leading schools of thought about the future Soviet socialist city.

Miliutin's proposal for a linear city was not original. The concept had been developed by the Spanish architect Soria y Mata and by the late 1920s had a sizeable and international roster of adherents. Miliutin's adaptation of the concept was used in the planning of Stalingrad (now Volgograd) on the Volga river, and in part in the design of the new iron and steel centre in the southern Urals, Magnitogorsk. As Fig. 18 indicates, the linear city incorporated about a half dozen strictly segregated zones. A green buffer served to separate the industrial and transport zones from the residential zone, with due attention in their respective locations to the direction of the prevailing winds. The parallel development of industry and housing was intended to facilitate a short, pedestrian journey to work. The perceived need to create an alternative to the large city and agglomeration, both judged to be inevitable by-products of capitalism, led all planners to try to create urban environments which would generate a sense of community. Miliutin, like so many others, reckoned that the best balance between the economic provision of urban services and the potential for creation of a sense of community was in a town of 50–60,000 inhabitants. Thus, city populations were to be strictly limited. State control over the level and location of consumer and cultural services within the city was intended to ensure spatial equality. Thus, decentralization, not concentration, of items of collective consumption was necessitated.

Whatever the merits of the architectural and town planning schemes produced

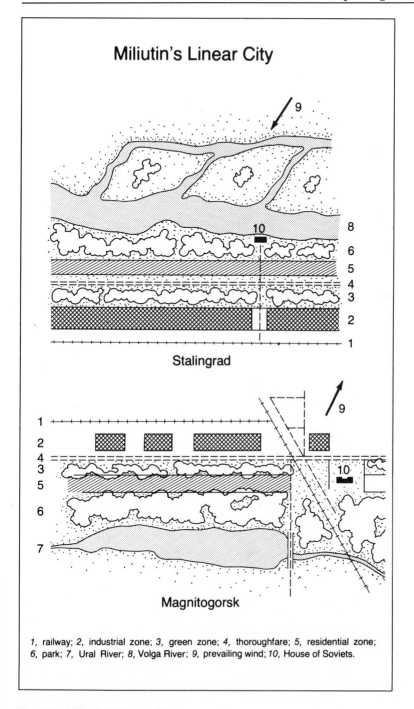

Miliutin's Linear City

Stalingrad

Magnitogorsk

1, railway; *2*, industrial zone; *3*, green zone; *4*, thoroughfare; *5*, residential zone; *6*, park; *7*, Ural River; *8*, Volga River; *9*, prevailing wind; *10*, House of Soviets.

Fig. 18 Miliutin's Linear City

Source: Based on F. Parkins, *City Planning in Soviet Russia* (Chicago: University of Chicago Press, 1953), 22.

during this era of 'cultural revolution', most were denied a place in the real world. As in literature and art, this visionary, utopian and not uncommonly, totally impractical experimentation had little impact on the ordinary Soviet citizen. As was noted in the preceding chapter, only 18 per cent of the population lived in cities at the time of the first Soviet census in 1926. The programme of forced industrialization initiated in the First Five Year Plan of 1928 laid down very clearly the long-term development priorities of the state. A fundamental restructuring of the existing urban system which was common to all the visionary schemes for the built environment of socialist man was simply not included. The debate over the form of the Soviet socialist city ended in 1931 when it was decreed that all Soviet cities must be socialist by virtue of their being part of the Union of Soviet Socialist Republics. While this pragmatic policy statement, coming as it did with the full authority of the Communist Party, served to stifle further public discussion, and especially the oft-cited criticism that the existing urban system being capitalist in origin and in form should be eradicated, it did not mean that the lively debate of the 1920s was without any consequence. In fact many of the basic ideas of the urbanist and de-urbanist schools were incorporated, albeit in suitably modified form, in the Plan for the Reconstruction of Moscow adopted in 1935. The Party limited the terms of reference for the international competition to reconstruct the Soviet capital to a moderate reworking of the existing urban form, and thus ruled out the possibility of a new capital being built from scratch. Still, the principles upon which the plan was based are important because they became the guidelines for town planning throughout the country. Among the more notable were: limited city size; an ideological role for the city centre; state control and allocation of housing; spatial equality in the distribution of consumer and cultural services; and a limited journey to work. Planned urban development and limited city size dictated some mechanism for controlling population movement. The optimal city size was judged to be between 50,000 and 60,000 even though Moscow's already exceeded three million. Public space in general, and central city space in particular, was assigned an ideological, or symbolic, role. The central city had to accommodate massive, orchestrated public ceremony as well as serve everyday needs, a formidable design problem. State control of housing was intended to ensure egalitarian allocation at essentially nominal rents. However, the state evidenced little interest in, and invested little of its scarce financial resources in, housing. By assuming responsibility for provision of a wide range of consumer, cultural and household services, housing per se was envisioned by the state as having a largely dormitory function for future Soviet citizens.

Over the years the general principles for urban development have been translated into myriad norms to guide planners. For example, nine square metres of living space is the sanitary minimum per capita housing allotment established in 1922 for the urban population; the journey to work should not exceed 40 minutes in average size cities; 35 cinema seats should be provided for each 1,000 population and so on. While such a normative approach is intended to ensure an equitable allocation of resources, it does not always meet the needs of a population which is more differentiated ethnically, demographically and geographically than it is homogeneous. In any event, there are numerous problems in fulfilling some of those norms, as we shall describe at a later point.

City and state

Outwardly the relationship between the state and the city was entirely positive. After all, under socialism urban culture was by definition superior to that of the countryside. While the new Soviet city was scarcely the utopia architects and planners of the 1920s envisioned, the planning principles embodied in the Moscow Plan of 1935 nonetheless did constitute a sharp break with the past. The Soviet socialist city was intended to bring into existence a new and higher form of society, one in which collectivism would supplant privatism, one in which the traditional cultural values and religions would be obliterated, one in which the primacy of the family would eventually disappear. While there is no doubt as to the official view of the relationship between the city and the state, what is of interest is the extent to which the official viewpoint is shared by those who live in the city. This line of enquiry, of course, is complicated by a real dearth of information. Still, there is scope for a few observations which will serve as background to the ensuing discussion of the outcome of Soviet town planning endeavours.

For the early Soviet period our perception of what the city was like tends to be clouded by official pronouncements of government and Party spokesmen, and by the voluminous and frequently effusively enthusiastic commentary of contemporary architects and planners. What the average person thought, faced as he or she was with a rapidly deteriorating built environment, and possibly being a part of the sizeable roster of the unemployed, is impossible to ascertain. However, Soviet literature was certainly not always at one with the official view depicting the city as a positive force in society. In L. Leonov's *The Badgers* (1925), for example, the city as a corruptive environment is developed in a Soviet setting. In M. Zoshchenko's *Short Stories* materialism and privatism are the dominant traits of urban dwellers and invariably the acquisitiveness of a would-be bourgeoisie corrupts human relationships. As late as 1930 I.K. Paustovsky's *Moscow Summer* still depicted the city as an essentially negative and oppressive force in society, a stark contrast to the positive spiritual qualities engendered by the countryside. Even in literature with a futurist bent such as V. Mayakovskiy's *The Bedbug* (1928) the portrayal of the city did not echo the official viewpoint. Regimentation and alienation, not selflessness and fellowship, seemingly were the principal feelings of urbanites.

The advent of Socialist Realism and the censor during the Stalin era soon strictly limited the scope of Soviet literary endeavour. The theme of middle class, bourgeois preoccupations was not entirely erased, however. Nor should it have been. Contrary to original principles Stalin began in the early 1930s to entrench a system of privileges, benefits and salary differentials intended to enhance participation in the industrialization drive, and subsequently the war effort and reconstruction. Put simply, in the Stalin era private values were converted into public values. The middle class – the *meshchanstvo* of the imperial era – was legitimized, and hence so was privatism. In censor-approved Socialist Realist literature the hero contributing in his own special way to the development of Soviet socialism could be portrayed as a dedicated, career-minded manager aspiring to own a house, and perhaps a *dacha* (or summer cottage) as well. Not for him the cramped quarters of the average citizen. He could even be depicted as driving his own car! Meanwhile in the real world those who could not, or would not, participate in the now firmly ensconced system of perks and privileges travelled to work six days a week on an overcrowded tram, returning home to scarcely less congested conditions. Indeed, the housing crisis deepened with each passing year. For example, the sanitary minimum allotment of 'living space' of nine square metres was established in 1922 as noted above. At that time the per capita average was about six square metres of living space. By 1940 it was barely four. By 1950 it had dropped below four, in other words, to less than half the national minimum sanitary standard. A family per room was the rule, not the exception, in many Soviet cities in the early 1950s. The portrayal of privilege in literature was not entirely divorced from reality, of course. Positions of perceived importance in Soviet society did bring a variety of special dispensations, including an above-norm allocation of housing. As in the Russian city during the imperial era, however, it seems that privilege and territoriality were not strongly developed. Space, rather than location, was no doubt a more significant consideration given the acute nature of the housing shortage. But there were rituals as well for public behaviour. These helped to distinguish those who had arrived at positions of importance in society from those who were still *en route*, rituals which acknowledged in personal, rather than in geographical ways, one's place in society.

The accommodation, indeed promotion, of a Soviet middle class during the Stalin era spawned *kul'turnost'*. This Vera Dunham has defined as constituting a '. . . program for proper conduct in public', one whose special function was 'to encode the proper relationship between people through their possessions and labels', something which clearly facilitated the declaration of position in society through appearance and behaviour instead of territoriality.[1] The Soviet system sanctioned *kul'turnost'* because it was a means of social control. The growing middle class in Soviet society was thus dependent upon the regime for its perpetuation, and the regime upon the middle class for its support. While egalitarian principles were often cited in official statements concerning the relationship between the city and society, it should not be assumed that ideal and reality in the city were at one during the Stalin era. In a society where scarcity and shortage were the norm, where public space and public values were accorded most attention, privatism not only had a place, it was nurtured.

In Soviet literature since the Stalin era depiction of the reality of Soviet life, the so-called *byt* genre, has emerged as one of the more controversial themes. Important in its own right, it also tends to cast a rather different perspective on the relationship between the city and state than does official ideology. Firstly, there is the village prose tradition in which rural cultural values are frequently juxtaposed with urban values, to the latter's detriment. Fedor Abramov's works, for instance his trilogy *The Priaslins* (1958–1973), figures prominently in this village prose, but many other writers have developed the same theme as well. In it inhabitants of the contemporary Soviet village are portrayed as having retained high moral qualities, as having preserved the essence of important cultural values despite the corruptive impact of widespread urbanization. The apparently wide popular appeal of this literary genre probably has more to do with the fact that a very large proportion of the urban

---

[1] Vera Dunham, *In Stalin's Time. Middle-Class Values in Soviet Fiction* (Cambridge: Cambridge University Press, 1976), 13, 22.

population has itself only recently departed the village than it has to do with it being a realistic portrayal of the countryside. Thus, on the one hand the peasantry is in some Soviet literature, as it is in some late nineteenth century Russian literature, embued with cultural values which the city has corrupted. On the other hand, the literary theme of the reality of urban life which has developed since the 1960s does little if anything to offset the message conveyed.

Yuri Trifonov, perhaps the best known exponent of the city prose tradition, paints a somewhat dismal picture of the reality of contemporary Soviet urban life. The central figures are frequently cast as unethical and acquisitive. Concern with self, with privatism and gaining a larger share of whatever is available, are linked directly to the prevailing values of the urban milieu. Those who get ahead are not the ones who are selfless and sharing, but those who know how to work the system best. There are few instances of story endings in which the spirit of collectivism prevails over privatism. As with the village prose, Soviet literary critics often label such works as unrepresentative, untypical and too much preoccupied with the ordinariness of day-to-day existence. Evidence of cultural advancement, of a communal ethos is overlooked, or down-played, they claim, and perhaps with some truth. But available sociological studies suggest that there is more to Trifonov's interpretation of the relationship between the Soviet city and society than there is substance to the scenario conveyed by official statements and ideology.

Egalitarian principles were to have guided cultural change, were to have shaped the relationship between city and state, but in the process of urban development planners have often been unable to plan. We might usefully explore at this point why this has been so and to note some of the consequences.

Planning the Soviet city

In theory, the city Soviet, or municipal government, and its bureaucracy including an architecture and planning department, is responsible for all that happens within city boundaries. However, in practice the structure of the decision-making system in the Soviet Union is such that municipal government does not figure very prominently in terms of its political influence, in terms of its claim to financial resources, or in terms of its ability to determine the course of actual development. In the Soviet model of centralized sectoral, or ministerial, planning, the theoretical rights of the city Soviet are often subordinated to the interests of particular ministries. Thus, the chief architect, to whom is subordinate the architecture–planning department, and who is responsible for ensuring that physical planning norms are met and that all development conforms to the general plan for the city, is often in an untenable position. Important ministries frequently side-step city planning regulations. As was noted in the preceding chapter, industrial enterprises in most large cities are ostensibly precluded from adding new plant and with it, of course, additional workers. The subterfuges used to get around such restrictions are manifold, but the consequence is that urban growth frequently exceeds what planners anticipate, thereby confounding efforts to satisfy prescribed the norms.

There have been many attempts to strengthen the hand of city Soviets in decision-making. For example, in 1957 legislation was introduced which sought to clarify and strengthen the role of the city in controlling its own affairs. Specifically, the executive of the city Soviet was assigned greater authority. Through a variety of measures, including the affirmation of political power and the recommended transfer of facilities and financial resources to the city, the 1957 reform intended that municipal government in fact be 'master in its own house'. The city was to become the sole agent responsible for contracts for the planning, financing and construction of all housing, consumer and cultural services. While the 1957 reform did produce improvements in the provision of housing, communal and cultural facilities, the continued existence of compartmentalized, centralized and generally tangled lines of decision-making responsibility rendered management of municipal affairs inefficient and irrational. Only in Moscow was there evident success in bringing about what might be described as 'single-developer' status. The lack of action elsewhere eventually prompted another Party and government response. In 1971 a barrage of resolutions and decrees urged city Soviets to exercise more forcefully their legal rights. Emphasized yet again was the need for cities to control the roughly two-thirds of the state-owned urban housing stock which was still owned and managed by ministries and enterprises. Throughout the 1970s resolution after resolution promoted the city Soviet as 'master in its own house'. In 1981 yet another major

Table 10: Urban housing stock by republic, 1987

Republic	Living space* per person (m²)
Slavic	
RSFSR	9.5
Ukraine	10.1
Belorussia	9.2
Baltic	
Lithuania	10.3
Latvia	11.2
Estonia	11.7
Caucasus	
Georgia	10.2
Armenia	8.6
Azerbaydzhan	7.8
Middle Asia	
Kazakh	8.2
Uzbek	7.3
Kirgiz	7.4
Tadzhik	7.3
Turkmen	6.6
Moldavia	8.4
USSR average	9.4

Source: *Narodnoye Khozyaystvo SSSR za 70 Let* (Moscow: Finansy i Statistika, 1987), 374, 518.

Note: living space has been calculated as 67 per cent of useful space.

resolution was issued by the Party and government. The plans of all-union and republic ministries which might impinge on city development were henceforth to be directed to the appropriate city Soviet for examination and approval. There is nothing yet to suggest that this most recent resolution will fundamentally change the nature of the decision-making process, notwithstanding the comparative success of one model experience in the port city of Poti, in Georgia. Here considerable gains were registered in enhancing coordinated planning, but there is little evidence that this particular management model has been widely emulated. We might at this point turn to one of the areas of long standing concern – the provision and maintenance of housing.

The provision of housing across the country has now just satisfied the sanitary minimum of nine square metres of living space for each urban inhabitant, but this is an achievement of the 1980s. Indeed, in 1980 living space per urban inhabitant was still only 8.6 square metres, though by 1987 it had reached 9.4 square metres. In 1987 there was still considerable disparity amongst the various Republics, with the Baltic region being the most liberally endowed, and the Middle Asian region the least (Table 10). The fact that in 1980 a six-decade old sanitary minimum still had not been universally attained is a reflection of the limited investment in housing during the industrialization drive undertaken during the Stalin era. A housing crisis of enormous dimensions was precipitated by this policy, a policy not reversed until after Stalin's death in 1953. Since then enormous progress has been made. Indeed, between 1960 and 1975 fully two-thirds of the population were assigned improved, if not new, housing. But as the figures in Table 11 reveal, as late as 1983 many cities still bore testimony to the years of inadequate, or no, state investment in housing.

The standard approach in the construction of state housing is to use the *mikrorayon* as the organizational concept. Comprising a set of smaller housing units or living complexes (traditionally referred to as super blocks or *kvartali*), the *mikrorayon* usually accommodates somewhere between 8,000 and 12,000 people. Several *mikrorayoni* may then be designated a residential complex. Something of the population and spatial dimensions of this system are indicated by the following figures. Five to eight living complexes, each with a population of 1,000 to 1,500, and a radius of perhaps 50 to 100 metres, comprise a *mikrorayon*. Four to five *mikrorayoni*, each with a population between 8,000 and 12,000 inhabitants, and a radius of between 300 to 400 metres, comprise a residential complex. One variant of this hierarchical system is portrayed in Fig. 19. Standardized apartment blocks occupied by a representative mix of the city's socio-economic and ethnic groups, ample green space, perimeter thoroughfares with public transport facilities, day-care, educational and health services – all are common denominators of long standing in the planning of residential areas. In theory, there is a logic to the spatial allocation of facilities. All day-to-day requirements are to be satisfied by a short pedestrian journey. Higher-order goods and services are to be located strategically within the *mikrorayon* and residential complex. Only infrequent journeys to the central city are anticipated, and then more for the purpose of mass culture than personal consumption.

The *mikrorayon* was intended to provide the physical environment appropriate to the task of engendering a sense of neighbourliness, of collective responsibility; in short, a communal ethos. Sociological evidence suggests that this has not yet occurred

Table 11: Housing stock in selected Soviet cities 1983

City	Population (000)	Living space per person (m^2)
Slavic		
Moscow	8,396	11.2
Leningrad	4,779	10.9
Kiev	2,355	10.1
Kazan	1,031	8.7
Gorkiy	1,382	9.3
Novosibirsk	1,370	8.9
Irkutsk	582	8.9
Baltic		
Tallin	454	11.2
Riga	867	10.6
Vil'nyus	525	9.3
Caucasus		
Tbilisi	1,125	9.2
Yerevan	1,095	7.7
Baku	1,638	7.4
Middle Asian		
Tashkent	1,944	7.1
Frunze	577	7.8
Alma Ata	1,023	8.7
Dushanbe	530	7.2
Ashkhabad	338	7.1

Source: *Narodnoye Khozyaystvo SSSR v 1983g* (Moscow: Finansy i Statistika, 1984), 17–22, 396–97.

Note: Living space has been calculated as 67 per cent of useful space.

on a very large scale. Socializing with neighbours, for example, tends to vary inversely with position in the social hierarchy. The few at the top give little indication of even recognizing their neighbours, let alone socializing with them. Even amongst workers and service personnel who occupy the lower echelons of the hierarchy where socializing with neighbours is most common, more time is still spent with relatives than with neighbours. Alienation rather than a sense of collectivism is a more commonly reported psychological trait of residents of *mikrorayoni*. It is manifested in most of the usual ways – withdrawal from community endeavours, indifference to the maintenance of public space, and of growing concern, vandalism and hooliganism amongst the young in particular. Given the massive scale of rehousing since 1960, it is hardly surprising that the disruption of social networks has generated in some people a feeling of alienation. This is a theme reflected in Soviet literature as well. Indeed, there is a sizeable body of opinion in the Soviet Union that regards the concept of a *mikrorayon* being the focal point of human interaction as a contradiction of the urbanization process which tends to promote greater, not lesser, spatial mobility.

About one-half of the Soviet urban population currently lives in a *mikrorayon*, in housing which seemingly is more standardized than differentiated. However, there

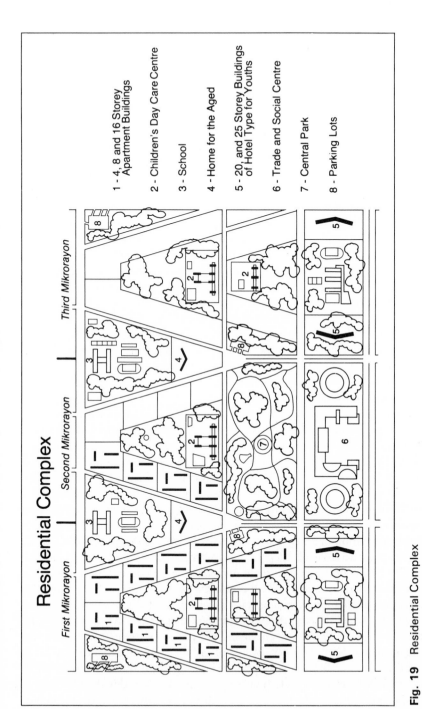

Fig. 19 Residential Complex

Source: Ya. Kravchuk, *Formirovaniye Novykh Gorodov*, (Moscow: Izdatel'stvo Literatury po Stroitel'stvu, 1973), 2.

The following labels accompany the figure:

Residential Complex

First Mikrorayon | Second Mikrorayon | Third Mikrorayon

1 - 4, 8 and 16 Storey Apartment Buildings

2 - Children's Day Care Centre

3 - School

4 - Home for the Aged

5 - 20, and 25 Storey Buildings of Hotel Type for Youths

6 - Trade and Social Centre

7 - Central Park

8 - Parking Lots

has always been variation in apartment design since some groups in society are entitled to above-norm allotments of space. Professionals such as architects, for example, receive an additional allocation, since it is assumed that work space at home is necessary. To be sure, municipal authorities can and do make adjustments in housing allocation purely on the basis of social need as opposed to occupation. But municipalities, in theory the principal arena for decision-making in matters related to housing, in fact control only about one half of the state housing supply. The rest is owned, operated and maintained by ministries, departments and enterprises whose self-interest in attracting labour is often best served by retaining control over housing. Despite years of promoting the concept of municipal jurisdiction in housing matters, central authorities have been unable to persuade ministries, departments and enterprises to turn housing over to city government. But even if this were to happen, the Stalin-era entrenched system of housing perquisites as a reward for career mobility is unlikely to be dismantled. It seems to be too important an element in rewarding incentive, and is now part and parcel of the privatism of Soviet urban culture. Still this has not manifested itself to any great extent in residential segregation within the state housing sector. As we have already suggested, for elites living in state housing, apartment size and furnishings may well matter more than location. And once outside the apartment, a chauffeur waiting with the Volga (or possibly a Zil or Chaika) and the rituals of *kul'turnost'* establish position in society even more demonstratively than territorial exclusivity in housing. In any event, the state however defined controls only 70 per cent of the total urban housing stock. The remainder is made up of cooperatively and privately owned housing. If residential segregation is to be found anywhere in the contemporary Soviet city, it is in these two components of the housing stock.

The construction of cooperative and private housing has had a somewhat chequered history, as might be imagined. In the case of cooperatives, a substantial number were created during the early Soviet period when the state's housing construction efforts were decidedly limited. A need was met, and in an ideologically more acceptable manner than by means of construction of privately owned housing. But official sanction was withdrawn in the late 1930s when all existing cooperatives were taken over by the state. They were, so to speak, nationalized and the former cooperative member became a tenant, albeit one paying the characteristically nominal rent. Given the official recognition of a major housing crisis in the post-Stalin era, the attitude toward the potential role of cooperatives in ameliorating the housing shortage softened. By 1962 cooperative apartment ownership was made legal once more. The state now provides loans to cover 60 per cent of the cost of construction. Information on the location, and intensity, of cooperative housing is extremely sparse. However, it seems that the larger the city, the more common cooperatives are. In Moscow, for instance, 11 per cent of all housing put up in 1973 was cooperative. It is probable that the share at present is even higher. While of growing significance in many major urban centres, the overall share of cooperative housing of the total stock is not likely much above 7 per cent at present. If current trends continue, this share is likely to increase however. In the late 1970s some 25,000 cooperatives housed 2.2 million people. Who they are, how they live, and where, are important issues.

Given the bewildering maze of government regulations, the success of a housing cooperative depends upon the ability to get along with other members in order to get things done. Thus, the membership of cooperatives tends to be drawn from particular socio-economic groups, or strata, in Soviet society rather than from a broad cross-section, official intentions otherwise notwithstanding. The need to have a sizeable down-payment in cash and an income large enough to meet the monthly payments are other requirements for cooperative membership. But these probably are not as significant barriers as the need for organizational expertise amongst the collective and a sense of group identity. Thus, the cooperative apartment block tends to house what might be broadly labelled a segment of the Soviet middle class. Outwardly the state owned and cooperative apartment block may not be easily distinguished. But according to one, no doubt not entirely apocryphal observation, there are some visible signs that the two types of housing accommodate different populations. In the state-owned building, apartment lights go on in the early morning hours as the inhabitants prepare to leave for work. In the cooperative, lights come on later in the morning, a reflection of the different circumstances of their presumably more professional than working social-class composition.

As a rule, cooperative housing while built according to government norms and limitations is nonetheless of higher quality than that available in the state sector. Public space, that is, halls, foyers, courtyards, and so on, tends to be better maintained as well. Since some cooperative members build apartments as large as the regulations permit, they tend to be more generously housed in a qualitatively better environment than would be their lot in the state sector. Where in the Soviet city cooperative housing is built is an intriguing question. If spatially segregated, then in view of its social class composition not reflecting the full spectrum of classes in Soviet society a type of residential segregation may be taking form. Available information on this issue is limited in the extreme, and may not be typical of all Soviet cities. Still it is notable that a study of the social geography of Tallinn revealed a measure of spatial concentration, or segregation of cooperative housing.[1] In 1975, when the study was undertaken, cooperatives comprised 4.3 per cent of the total housing stock. But in areas of recent housing construction, the percentage was rather higher. In two peripheral regions characterized by new housing the share of cooperatives ranged between 15 and 16.3 per cent. Many apartment owners were bureaucrats and professionals. Workers were not necessarily excluded, but they certainly did not dominate the socio-economic composition of cooperative housing membership. Tallinn, with 464,000 inhabitants and capital of the Estonian republic, has a far higher standard of living than is found in most of the rest of the country. Overall, the share of cooperative apartments does not appear to be at all high; thus, the intraurban concentration is particularly noteworthy. Clearly, to the extent that cooperative housing members are separated from society at large, then a form of residential segregation is being created. Yet it would probably be a mistake to regard the cooperative as home to a Soviet elite. Given the nature of the rather generous housing perks for the Soviet government, military, economic and artistic elites, most observers reckon that such groups have every reason not to give up a state apartment

---

[1] V.O. Rukavishnikov, *Naseleniye Goroda* (Moscow: Statistika, 1980), 180.

with its nominal rent for a cooperative costing substantially more.

Privately-owned housing has been permitted throughout the Soviet period, though under various pressures at various times. In the countryside such housing is by far the most common type. In the city its share has been steadily reduced over the years, but with nearly 23 per cent of all urban housing floor space in private hands in 1987 it remains important. Moreover, this share is the national average, and there are substantial deviations from the mean. In Armenia, for example, it accounted for 30 per cent of the urban housing stock. In the Uzbek republic more than two-fifths was privately owned. By contrast only 16 per cent of the urban housing in the RSFSR was in private hands in 1987. As a general rule, the smaller the urban centre and the more remote its location, the higher the proportion of privately owned housing. Since the early 1960s construction of such accommodation has been prohibited in most regional capitals and major cities. In the smaller cities construction continues; indeed, state loans are available to assist with construction. Thus, the supply of such housing increases each year even though its share of the total stock may slip. The privately-owned house is typically a detached, wooden structure, not always in the best maintenance, the overall floor space of which must conform to the prevailing norms. There are examples of well built, well maintained private homes in most Soviet cities, however. The construction of such housing sustains the 'wooden' fabric of so many of the small to medium size cities of European Russia and Siberia. But whether the local building materials are wood, stone, cement or adobe, the land on which such construction occurs remains the property of the state. Private housing to be sure adds much more character to the texture of the urban fabric than either the state or cooperative sectors. By dint of who tends to live in privately owned housing, it perpetuates residential segregation as well. Residential segregation occurs on both ethnic and socio-economic bases.

The legacy of autocracy included territories with distinctly non-Slavic populations, some acquired only late in the imperial era, some in the Middle Ages. The Middle Asian realm is an example of the former. Despite the fact that all major Middle Asian cities are dominantly Slavic, the indigenous population has not been entirely submerged since a sizeable number still choose to live in the traditional quarters. The situation in Samarkand is in many ways typical. The built environment of this city of 388,000 people in Uzbekistan mirrors the cultural values of three epochs (Fig. 20). The traditional quarter is still more or less the exclusive territory of Uzbeks and reflects the centuries-old tradition of social custom and architecture. The colonial outpost of the Russian government now comprises part of the central city. With its broad thoroughfares liberally endowed with shade trees and laid out with some attention to the classical notions of town planning of the eighteenth century, it still stands in stark contrast to the hotch-potch of streets and alleys in the traditional quarter from which it was once separated, much like New Delhi was separated from Delhi. Of course, not all indigenous Middle Asians live in the old quarter. Many have voluntarily taken up residence in the standardized state housing which now surrounds most of the colonial and traditional parts of the city. Still others have had to relocate because of man-made incursions into a housing stock which does not meet contemporary Soviet town planning standards, or because of destruction wrought by the occasional earthquake. But within the remaining traditional quarter the

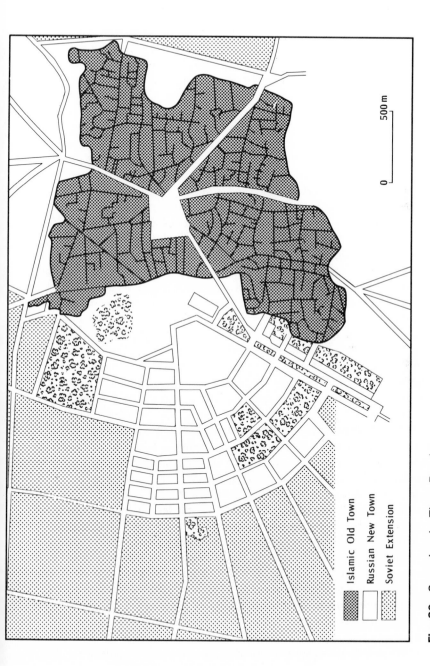

Fig. 20 Samarkand – Three Epochs

Islamic Old Town

Russian New Town

Soviet Extension

0   500 m

Source: Based on E. Giese, 'Transformation of Islamic Cities in Soviet Middle Asia into Socialist Cities', in French, R.A., Hamilton, F.E.I. (eds.), *The Socialist City* (New York: Wiley, 1979), 158.

resistance to change is considerable. Such housing provides the physical basis for the perpetuation of cultural values which are not in any sense mainstream Soviet. Birth rates are high, women have a subordinate role in the family, wives are rarely employed in 'socially productive' labour outside the home and so on. Segregated housing of an ethnic minority provides a cultural staging-post in the transition from village to city. But this phenomenon is not peculiar to Middle Asia.

Kazan', capital of the Tatar Autonomous Soviet Socialist Republic and located at the confluence of the Volga and Kama rivers in European Russia, was brought under Russian hegemony in the sixteenth century. As in Samarkand, the indigenous population presently comprises about one-third of the total population, now just over the one-million mark. While Tatars live throughout the city, a recent study reveals that some areas are still dominantly Tatar in ethnic composition. For the most part the areas of concentration of Tatars depicted in Fig. 21 reflect, in the first place, pre-revolutionary inner-city patterns of residence which have to some extent persisted to present times, and reflect in the second place, former villages which have been engulfed in the process of urban expansion. Thus, while the spatial concentration of Tatars in Kazan' is less than that of indigenous Middle Asians in Samarkand's traditional quarter, such residential segregation as does exist certainly helps to perpetuate the cultural traditions of a minority group. And it is the stock of older, inner city, privately-owned housing and the counterpart on the outskirts of the city which is an important factor in facilitating voluntary segregation.

The private housing which makes up such a large component of the peripheral areas of the Soviet city in general, and its small to medium size version in particular, is, as a rule, the realm of the working class. Many rural migrants apparently find that the privately-owned detached house, with its garden, provides a more agreeable entry to urban life than an apartment or room in the state-owned housing stock. Just how many migrants can afford such accommodation is a moot point, however. Indeed, it often takes several years before the young rural migrant secures a room or apartment for himself and his family. But for those with some capital the possibility to buy or build still exists in many cities, especially the smaller ones. What this leads to, of course, is a kind of socio-economic segregation. The peripheral dominance of workers in Kazan' depicted in Fig. 22 is far from uncommon. Notwithstanding the egalitarian principles endorsed by the state, the reality of Soviet society is that the working class, and most notably the recently arrived peasant and unskilled worker, are more near the bottom than they are near the top of the social hierarchy. A close inspection of Fig. 22 reveals the central city orientation of the professional (*intelligentsia*) group. One reason for this pattern is that the level of amenities provisionment is usually highest in the central city. Indeed, intra-city disparities in consumer and cultural services, public transport servicing, quality of housing, in short, in the quality of life offered by residence in particular neighbourhoods, is reflected in the differential rents charged for state housing. Although the rent is in any event nominal, and the variations to allow for preferred neighbourhood residence small, the fact that such differences exist at all speaks to the reality of the urban environment. Part of this reality is a perpetuation of residential segregation on ethnic and social-strata basis.

It is in the new town rather than in those cities inherited by the Soviet Union

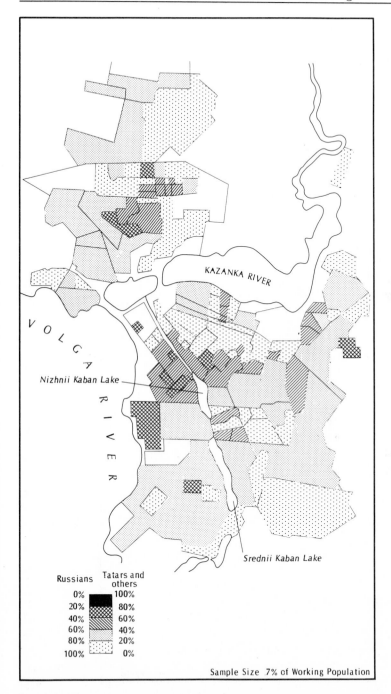

Fig. 21 Kazan' – Residential Segregation of Tatars

Source: After V.O. Rukavishnikov, 'Ethnosocial Aspects of Population Distribution in Cities in Tataria', *Soviet Sociology*, Vol. 8, No 2, 1978, 71.

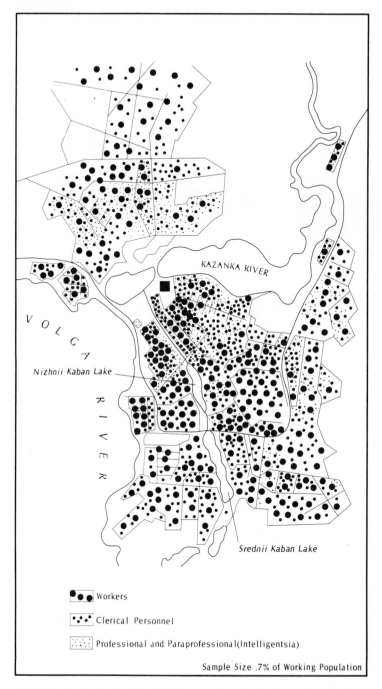

Fig. 22   Kazan' – Residential Segregation by Socioeconomic Group

Source: After V.O. Rukavishnikov, 'Ethnosocial Aspects of Population Distribution in Cities in Tataria', *Soviet Sociology*, Vol. 8, No. 2, 1978, 70.

where reality might be expected to match most closely town planning ideals such as social class heterogeneity and egalitarian allocation of state housing. Akademgorodok, the science town of about 10,000 inhabitants to the south of Novosibirsk, is indeed unique, but so too, in some way or another, are most new towns. But in Akademgorodok there is also residential segregation of the academic elite. Leading academicians occupy semi-detached dwellings of substance in a bucolic suburban environment. Those lower down the academic ladder are usually assigned accommodation in apartment buildings commensurate with their particular status. In Bratsk, a new town of 250,000 inhabitants on the Angara River in Central Siberia, what was to have been a unified settlement has developed into a system of non-contiguous single-industry or company towns built by particular ministries (Fig. 23). A peculiar kind of occupational segregation has ensued. For example, Padun, the original town builders' settlement, lacks a modern industrial base and therefore has a less skilled work force in consequence. The paucity of Padun stores and service facilities reflects this fact. In general, the level of consumer and cultural facilities varies markedly amongst the several settlements which comprise Bratsk. The persistence of a departmentalist approach to new town development elsewhere in Siberia is creating similar built environments and sociological conditions.

The spatial allocation of consumer and cultural services was to be governed by the principle of equal accessibility. The adoption of a normative approach to the overall provision of items of collective consumption was intended to ensure equibility within, and amongst, cities. As noted earlier, for the most part norms pertaining to items of collective consumption are expressed in terms of per capita ratios. But whether the evaluation of norm fulfilment proceeds on a per capita basis for the total urban population, for a specific city, or for a particular *mikrorayon*, it ought to be remembered that the question of accessibility to facilities is as important as the overall level of provision.

In one assessment of the social and economic aspects of town planning it has been noted that in the majority of cities established norms were far from being met. Schools, shopping facilities, restaurants, cultural facilities – all were less than two-thirds, and in some cases less than one-half, the prescribed levels. Over the last decade some progress has been made, but in general the level of provisionment is still a source of frequent complaint. The regional disparity that was shown to exist in terms of housing also exists in the context of collective consumption facilities. It is worth noting, however, that the degree of regional difference in consumer and cultural services between core area and periphery, between large city and small, is rather greater than in the case of housing. The quality of life is affected accordingly, a topic to which we will return in a later chapter.

Differences in the level of provision of items of collective consumption obviously occur within cities as well. A cross-town journey to obtain a particular service may be a major inconvenience, but it is better than no service at all. About half the urban population now lives in *mikrorayoni*, as we noted earlier. While ideally they are planned and built in an integrated fashion, often this is not borne out in reality. Therefore residence in a *mikrorayon*, especially a new one, is no guarantee of access to consumer and cultural services. Indeed, if relocation from a central-city location is involved, there is every chance that access to services will be less. While the central

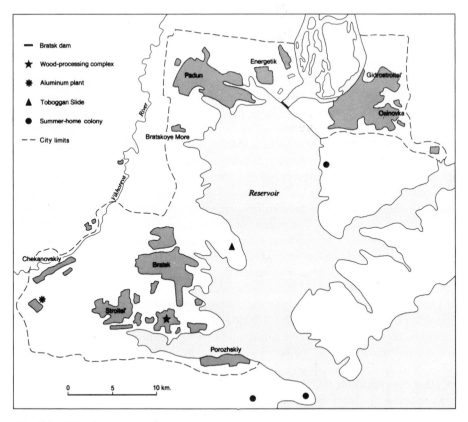

Fig. 23 Bratsk

Source: Norbert Wein, 'Bratsk-Pioneering City in the Taiga', *Soviet Geography*, Vol. 27, No. 3, March 1987, 176.

city was not to be the focus of retailing and services in the early conceptions of the Soviet socialist city, in fact it often affords some comparative advantage in this regard.

During the debate over the future Soviet socialist city in the 1920s the notion that there would be no distinguishable centre was embraced by those proposing a radical departure from past, and indeed contemporary, trends. The 1935 Moscow Plan, however, established the guiding principle which was certainly a pragmatic accommodation with reality. There would be a city centre and it was to become the nucleus of urban social and political life. By means of unified and uniform architectural ensembles, thoroughfares and squares, the city centre was to cater to massive public demonstrations. The design problem was one of striking a reasonable balance between occasional public functions and the day-to-day purposes these same thoroughfares, squares and buildings had to serve. With the emphasis on the cultural and political uses of the central city, the traditional central-city functions were downgraded. While it always needs to be recognized that Moscow is very much a special case, Fig. 24 does convey something of the sense of what was intended. The result was the

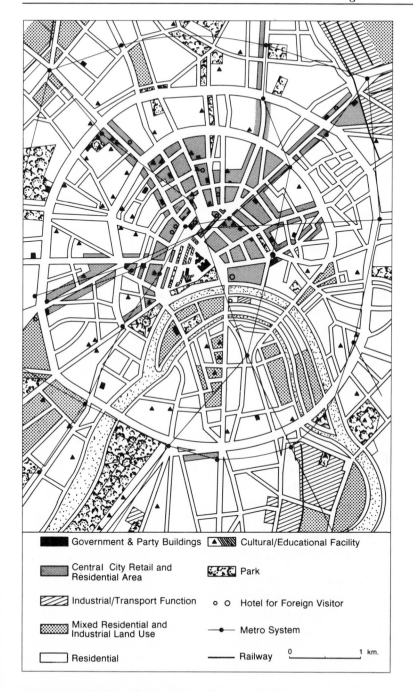

Government & Party Buildings   Cultural/Educational Facility

Central City Retail and
Residential Area   Park

Industrial/Transport Function   o o   Hotel for Foreign Visitor

Mixed Residential and
Industrial Land Use   Metro System

Residential   Railway   0 _____ 1 km.

Fig. 24   Moscow – Central City

Source: Based on *Dierke Weltatlas* (Braunschweig: Georg Westermann Verlag,
1978), 123.

conscious decentralization of administrative and distributive services into fully developed secondary centres. That Soviet central cities do differ in several ways from cities of western Europe or North America is evident upon first setting foot in one.

Unlike western cities, the central core still has a substantial residential, as opposed to day-time, population. While population densities are generally declining, there is no intention of turning the core over to non-residential uses. As in western cities, during the day there is a substantial net inflow of workers, including a good number still employed in industry. The most striking feature of Soviet central-city areas is the comparative paucity of shops. While the Nevskiy Prospect in Leningrad and Gor'kiy Street in Moscow stand out in terms of pedestrian traffic, neither street presently embraces anything like the array of consumer and cultural service enterprises which existed prior to the revolution. Some specialized shops are still located on or near to these historic arteries, but many more have since been located in new *mikrorayoni*. In short, the usual association of central-city location and specialized shopping does not strictly obtain in Soviet cities for reasons already made clear. Those facilities located in the central city, moreover, tend to occupy ground floor and mezzanine only. Multi-storey shopping complexes are anomalies. Indeed, the famous *GUM* in Moscow and the *Gostinny Dvor* in Leningrad are hold-overs from the Tsarist era. Such bazaar-like complexes exist in other cities as well, but rarely in such grand architectural style.

Similarly, dense concentrations of administrative activities are not characteristic features of the core. While Moscow boasts of central government and state planning functions, the various bureaucracies are scattered throughout the core and even beyond (see Fig. 24). This partly results from the swift transfer of government from Petrograd to Moscow in 1918, a time when government agencies were located wherever possible. Since then the policy of decentralization has prevented any significant concentration. Aside from the Kremlin complex, the closest counterpart to concentrated, and literally built-up, offices are those of the state planning agency (Gosplan) which run behind Karl Marx Prospect almost to Gor'kiy Street. Government bureaucracy is pervasive, but its physical manifestations certainly do not overwhelm the senses when in the central city.

While the central city boasts a fair complement of industry, it is more often factory rather than workshop. Indeed, the concentrations of specialized workshops which characterized the central parts of cities like St Petersburg and Moscow at the turn of the century have virtually disappeared. Even the plethora of small printing and publishing enterprises, so much a part still of the central core of western cities, has been greatly diminished as centralization and scale economies have been institutionalized. Traditional handicraft functions still survive in the streets around the central market in the old quarter of Tashkent, for example, but these are rather distinctive anomalies. The workshop/handicraft function very largely has been supplanted by mass production and state-run and state located small-scale repair outlets.

The cultural and symbolic roles assigned the Soviet central city are clearly distinctive. Red Square, the Kremlin and Lenin's Mausoleum in Moscow have a special symbolism, of course, but the function is not unique. The regular use of central squares and thoroughfares for mass demonstrations is an important facet of orchestrated public participation in formal and informal events alike. The evening mass promenade to the central city following the May Day celebration is representative of the latter, while the 7 November mobilization of the masses epitomizes the former. What goes on in Moscow receives most attention, but on a more modest scale the scene is enacted in large and small cities throughout the country. Cultural facilities like theatres, both pre-Soviet and Soviet, are centrally focused, though again the concentration is by no means exclusive as the decentralization of theatres to secondary centres has occurred. Generally speaking, however, for many forms of 'passive' culture for the masses – museums, theatres, parks and gardens – the central core acts as a magnet. In a great many instances what is seen, or sat in, is the legacy of the past, a legacy which reflects a different economic system, one which put a premium on centrality through the market mechanism. What has emerged in the Soviet central city by way of economic, bureaucratic, cultural or consumer activity is there because of a normative planning system in which land 'values' traditionally have played no part. It is precisely the consequences of this system, seen most clearly in the central city, which are now being called into question. Land-use allocation procedures traditionally have given a somewhat patchy quality to the urban landscape. Substantial areas remain underutilized, in some cases unused entirely, after having been allocated to potential users on the basis of some expectation of need and according to prescribed norms. However, once having been allocated land, the user was customarily under no great pressure to develop it. Land, even in the central city, has not always been used intensively. But the situation is fast changing. Why will be explained in the ensuing chapter.

Three broad periods in the evolution of the Soviet socialist city stand out. The first period from the revolution of 1917 through the 1920s was a time of enormous intellectual activity – a time of cultural revolution in the full sense of the word. With only the most general guidelines for the creation of a socialist society, the prospects for the new Soviet socialist city were as exciting as they were uncertain. On the whole, the state tolerated, if it did not endorse, most of the ideas put forward at this time. By definition, urban culture was good. The reality of urban life was quite another matter, however. The massive urban–rural migration which revolution and civil war occasioned was only reversed in the early 1920s. But thereafter unemployment and severe privation was the lot of many who sought a better life in the city. As yet there was little to be shared amongst those who comprised the privileged in the new society. For all the theorizing about the future Soviet socialist city, the unsettled conditions meant that little was actually built. With the onset of the Stalin era, the fluidity of ideas in particular, and personal freedoms in general, were steadily checked.

Under Stalin public proclamation about the leading role of the city and its proletariat in shaping culture went hand in hand with a programme of co-opting privatism in a variety of forms, and legally sanctioning them, on the part of the state. It was in this period of retrenchment that the ground was prepared for the emergence of a middle class, something which had not fully developed during the imperial era. While privilege in the form of housing perks was sanctioned, it is debatable whether it materially altered the form and fabric of the city. Given the continuing acute shortage of housing, it is more likely that, as in the era of autocracy, place in society continued to be proclaimed in personal ways rather than through territorial exclusivity.

The economic reform of 1965 initiated a period in which the material needs of the Soviet population have been accorded unprecedented attention. Notwithstanding the continued shortage of many consumer durables, for those who are consciously successful, or perhaps simply lucky, the opportunities for acquiring the trappings of Soviet middle class materialism have increased enormously. From the ownership of an automobile to a cooperative apartment, the rewards for participation in the system have never before been in such abundant display. Of course, this is a relative change and seemingly not always necessarily a welcome one. Since the 1960s the tensions and anomalies of contemporary Soviet urban life have become almost as evident as the improvements in material well-being. From the pens of sociologists and the literati has issued a stream of statistics and stories suggesting that urban cultural values have not always evolved in the manner intended. But then the Soviet city both as an agent, and as an example, of cultural change has not always evolved according to town planning principle either.

Clearly, the phenomenal urban growth in the Soviet Union since the 1920s testifies to the attraction of city life. In the years since, the urban population has increased from one-sixth to two-thirds of the total population. In the course of a period of extremely rapid urban-industrialization the Soviet city has been transformed. To be sure, much has been accomplished in terms of creating a new socialist urban environment. In general, most people live in broadly similar circumstances, circumstances which have to some extent at least been planned and developed according to egalitarian principles. While change has been part and parcel of the Soviet urban scene, we ought not to lose sight of some important continuities. As we have attempted to show in this chapter, some of the ideas and ideals so clearly set down in the early years have not always been possible to realize. Thus, privatism and privilege have come to shape in subtle and significant ways both the form and fabric of the Soviet city. While privately owned housing has been steadily eroded in terms of its relative share of the total urban housing stock, it is still significant, and in absolute terms grows one year to the next. It is not part of the socialist plan for the city, of course. In light of the long-standing and serious housing shortage it is tolerated. But its continued existence helps to perpetuate more than simply a different physical attribute of the Soviet city, it helps to perpetuate, indeed in some cities to promote, a degree of socio-economic segregation. Residential segregation occurs as well in the cooperative housing stock, but as an obviously unintentional consequence of the decision to legalize their construction in the early 1960s. How much longer such manifestations of personal choice in housing will continue cannot be answered. But it does seem that throughout the Soviet period it has been far harder to change human values and habits than it has been to introduce legislation and establish town planning norms. At the present time incentives of one kind or another are essential to the national well-being, for without incentives it seems that the willingness to work, to participate, to succeed, is blunted. Given the current state of the Soviet economy, it is unlikely that such perks as differential allocations of state housing, of access to cooperative or privately owned housing, could be abolished without negative effects for the national economy. The point is, of course, that as restrictions on individual and collective actions are eased, as economic necessity takes precedence over egalitarian principles, the hard-won individuality of the Soviet city must surely be put at risk.

Recommended reading

Andrusz, G.D., *Housing and Urban Development in the USSR* (London: Macmillan, 1984).

Bater, James H., *The Soviet City: Ideal and Reality* (London: Edward Arnold, 1980).

Chase, W.J., *Workers, Society, and the Soviet State: Labour and Life in Moscow, 1918–1929* (Urbana: University of Illinois Press, 1987).

DiMaio, A.J., *Soviet Urban Housing: Problems and Policies* (New York: Praeger, 1974).

French, R.A., Hamilton, F.E.I., (eds), *The Socialist City* (New York: John Wiley, 1979).

Hamilton, F.E.I., *The Moscow City Region* (London: Oxford University Press, 1976).

Hamm, M.F. (ed), *The City in Russian History* (Lexington: The University Press of Kentucky, 1976).

Harris, C.D., *Cities of the Soviet Union. Studies of their Functions, Size, Density and Growth* (Chicago: Rand McNally, 1970).

Lane, C., *The Rites of Rulers: Ritual in Industrial Society – The Soviet Case* (Cambridge: Cambridge University Press, 1981).

Lewis, C.W., Sternheimer, S., *Soviet Urban Management: With Comparisons to the United States* (New York: Praeger, 1979).

Miliutin, N.A., *Sotsgorod – the Problem of Building Socialist Cities* (Cambridge: Mass: Massachusetts Institute of Technology Press, 1974). Translated by P. Sprague.

Morton, H.W., Stuart, R.C. (eds), *The Contemporary Soviet City* (Armonk, New York: M.E. Sharpe, 1984).

Parkins, F., *City Planning in Soviet Russia* (Chicago: University of Chicago Press, 1953).

Ross, C., *Local Government in the Soviet Union: Problems of Implementation and Control* (London: Croom Helm, 1987).

Savas, E.S., Kaiser, J.A., *Moscow's City Government* (New York: Praeger, 1985).

Taubman, W., *Governing Soviet Cities. Bureaucratic Politics and Urban Development in the USSR* (New York: Praeger, 1973).

Underhill, J.A., *Soviet New Towns: Housing and National Urban Growth Policy* (Washington: U.S. Government Printing Office, 1976).

6 The Management of Natural Resources under Soviet Socialism

Let us not, however, flatter ourselves overmuch on account of our human victories over nature. For each such victory nature takes its revenge on us.

Engels, 1974.[1]

The relationship between man and the environment is clearly influenced by the stage of development attained by a particular society and its fundamental attitudes or values. The revolution of 1917 witnessed the demise of the imperial era with its deeply conservative system of beliefs and the advent of a Bolshevik party ostensibly guided by the principles of Marxism. In the preceding chapters we have described how this political transformation affected the structure of the political-administrative system, the nature of decision-making in managing the economy, and the management of the country's human resource, settlement system and urban environment. Marxist theory also spelled change for the management of natural resources. Once nationalized, natural resources were to be allocated free of charge to designated users who would develop them according to the dictates of the central plan. The need to demonstrate socialist society's ability to conquer, to subjugate, the physical environment was a central theme in the new ideology. Of course, no society remains constant, and the Soviet approach to resources management is no exception since it has changed over the years. In this chapter we will trace the evolution of Soviet ideology and Soviet practice in relation to resources management in general. In ensuing chapters the development of several specific natural resources will be examined in greater detail.

First principles of resources management

According to the Marxist scheme of things, under conditions of scientific socialism the door was open to a future of enhanced material prosperity, if not abundance.

---

[1] F. Engels, *Dialectics of Nature* (Moscow: Progress Publishers, 1974), 180.

Under the new order it was presumed, for example, that the capacity of the soil to feed an ever larger Soviet population was virtually unlimited. Gone was the Malthusian doctrine which envisioned the world's limited agricultural land base incapable of producing enough food to meet the basic needs of an ever growing population. Such pessimistic scenarios were true only if land remained privately owned and therefore exploited by the class of capitalists who controlled its use. Under socialism science and technology would be brought to bear on behalf of society at large, not one privileged part of it. Under socialism there was no teleological order of things in which men and women could be subjugated by the natural environment. Socialist society was not perceived to be in harmony with nature, was not perceived to be in some ordered relationship with nature, rather it was construed as being in conflict with nature. The natural environment was often described by Marxists as being in a state of disorder, or chaos, and it was the task of socialist science and technology to conquer nature, to transform it. For progress to occur, the inherent contradiction between the state of the natural environment as it is, and as it ought to be, must be resolved. Thus, for much of the Soviet period the notion of conquering nature has played a central part in the official ideology. The new Soviet scientist often took literally the clarion call for action espoused by the propagandist.

The private ownership of natural resources was seen by the Marxist as the principal reason for their exploitation and waste. In contrast, nationalization of all resources and their planned development was equated with wise husbandry and conservation. Under socialism resource management conflicts and environmental pollution simply would not exist. Much of the early legislation reflected this somewhat benign attitude. We need only illustrate this point by way of a few examples.

The decree nationalizing land and water resources was issued in January 1918 and followed a decree of November 1917 which transferred the ownership of large agricultural estates from individuals to the state. By June 1918 a decree had been issued which gave to local authorities the responsibility of managing the nation's forest resources. At about the same time the management of wildlife was assumed by the state insofar as the control over hunting and firearms was vested in local authorities. As time passed the scope of state control broadened. Legislation prohibiting the discharge of polluted waters by industrial and commercial enterprises was adopted in 1923. Up until Lenin's death in 1924 at least 15 decrees pertaining to the management and conservation of the state's natural resources were enacted. Many were attributable to the personal interest and initiative of Lenin himself. He was but one of many theorists convinced that state ownership of resources combined with proper and legal allocation of authority for their management was sufficient to remove the possibility of misuse and consequent environmental degradation. The legal apparatus put in place by the state was assisted by educational programmes and voluntary organizations. A central role in this latter regard was assumed by the All-Russian Society for the Protection of Nature founded in 1924. While the concept of conservation or protection of nature was implicit, if not explicit, in much of this early legislation, the purpose of conservation was not simply to set something aside never to be developed by the state. In fact most legislation of a conservationist hue was intended to 'save' resources so they would be available for economic development at a later date. Perhaps the single most important exception was the creation of a system of nature preserves, or *zapovedniki*, which was initiated in 1919.

While environmental degradation was presumed incompatible with socialism, it ought to be remembered that the principal objective of the new state was to develop the domestic economy. With the death of Lenin and the assumption of control by Stalin, industrialization became the single most important goal. The role of science was to facilitate this endeavour and thus the role of technology figured prominently in the planned development of the natural resource base. A more rational management of resources might have been possible had there not been such attachment to the concept of 'conquest of nature'. Similarly, the concept of value in Soviet economic theory also proved to be prejudicial to rational resource management.

In nineteenth century Marxist thought labour was regarded as the basic element in determining the value of commodities. The enhancement of the price of a commodity as it passed from producer to consumer under capitalism did not reflect real value, but simply the manipulation of supply and demand and the exploitation by those who controlled the means of production of those who did not. Put simply, to the Marxist a commodity was without value until labour was applied to it. The value of a manufactured good was therefore equal to the sum of the labour required to make each of its component parts. Natural resources on the other hand were without value until developed by human labour. It followed, therefore, that in the Soviet Union all land, water, forest, mineral and other natural resources were allocated to users free of charge. The consequences of this Soviet interpretation of Marx's labour theory of value were unforeseen. Perhaps not surprisingly the treatment of natural resources as free goods has been inimical to their rational utilization and conservation. Over the years Soviet economic thought regarding value, price and rent has shifted ground rather considerably, as we shall explain shortly. At this point, however, it would be fruitful to examine in greater detail some other aspects of Soviet ideology as they influenced resource management.

Technology and the transformation of nature

The New Economic Policy initiated by Lenin in 1921 lasted until the First Five Year Plan introduced in 1928. This Policy, it will be recalled, was introduced to permit the reconstruction of the national economy. The policy allowed the small-scale entrepreneur and peasant farmer a measure of autonomy, of free enterprise. But the basic components of the national economy, including the natural resource base, remained state-owned and controlled. With the advent of the Five Year Plan and Stalin's industrialization drive the application of socialist science and technology to the resolution of the nation's problems assumed an importance previously unmatched. And so too did the role of ideology.

Typical of the attitude which soon took hold was that pertaining to water resources management. Even during Lenin's time large-scale hydro-engineering projects were promoted enthusiastically. Thus, during the 1920s a number of dams were approved for construction on the rivers of European Russia. These projects were an integral part of the GOELRO Plan, or the State Commission for the Electrification of Russia, one of the earliest of the Soviet regional development schemes. While the Plan included thermal as well as hydroelectric stations, it was the latter that captured the attention of the propagandist. Where else could one find such clear testimony to the ability of socialist man to conquer nature? The first large-scale, for the time, project to be completed was at Volkhov on the Volkhov river in the northwest part of European Russia near Leningrad. It was commissioned in 1926 amidst considerable fanfare. The propagandist was greatly aided by one of Lenin's more famous dictums: 'Communism is Soviet power plus the electrification of the whole country.' Under Stalin such sloganeering was raised to new heights, and so was the assault on nature.

Stalin supported a broad range of initiatives which were customarily publicized in terms of a struggle between socialist science and technology and the vagaries of nature. Large-scale water resource development projects continued to figure prominently in this scenario. Typical of some of the worst features of the Stalin era was the construction of the White Sea–Baltic Canal. For the time it was a huge undertaking, yet it was completed in less than two years thanks to the widespread use of forced labour and little regard for human life. The development of the hydroelectric power potential of the Volga river was accorded high priority and a number of power stations were begun during the 1930s. Conceived as a multi-purpose river basin development scheme it was closely linked to urban-industrialization in the Volga region. As time passed and technology improved the scale of each power station increased accordingly. Even after Stalin's death in 1953 individual power stations were regularly publicized in terms of conquest of nature by Socialist man. While the achievements of technology were customarily lauded by public figures and the media, basic science had an obvious role to play in the creation of socialist society as well. But where basic science became the handmaiden of state ideology there were bound to be problems. Genetic science in particular and biology in general offer a case in point.

The name of T.D. Lysenko is inextricably linked to the early years of experimentation in Soviet agriculture. At a time when the Soviet state had embarked on a vast programme of industrialization there was little money and even less will to invest in agriculture. Thus schemes to improve production which involved limited financial outlay were compelling. If they had overtones of a new science created under the conditions of building socialism they were even more so. Thus, the 'peoples' scientist' Trofim Lysenko was able to gain Stalin's personal support for his projects, most of which were of dubious scientific value. One example was 'yarovization', or the pre-heating of seeds. This sped up the process of germination, thereby permitting crops to be grown in regions not normally suited to them. This is only one of the presumed advantages of this widely applied experiment. Lysenko also contended that by such a process the basic genetic structure of the plants involved would be altered. The seeds of such plants would have 'adapted' to the new, more harsh, natural environment. Lysenko continued to hold an influential position even after Stalin's death. He died in 1976 at a time when a more realistic assessment of his contribution to Soviet science could be made without fear of reprisal. Lysenko is generally credited with blocking real advances in Soviet genetic science for the better part of three decades. Something of Lysenko's scientific opinion is represented in the Stalin Plan for the Transformation of Nature adopted in 1947.

During the 1930s the role of the geographical environment in the development of society was a contentious topic of debate. Stalin eventually dictated the official view of the Party in 1938 by declaring that the economic factor, not the geographic environment, was the dominant influence in the process. He allowed that the geographical environment could accelerate or retard societal development, but that under the conditions of socialism the development of society would 'proceed at an incomparably faster rate than the changes and development of the geographical environment.'[1] What is more, the advancement of science under socialism would permit the acceleration of the process, indeed, would allow the process of change to occur at a fundamentally different level than was possible under capitalism. An example of the thinking of the time was the idea that man could alter the climate over large areas. The notion comprised one element of the Stalin Plan for the Transformation of Nature, namely the creation of a network of shelterbelts. Put simply, science and technology were assumed to be capable not just of bringing order to the environment as in the case of hydraulic engineering, but of actually changing the natural order.

The shelter belt component of the Stalin Plan is outlined in Fig. 25. It, like other ameliorative programmes introduced in 1947, sought to stabilize agricultural production in the critically important south Ukraine and Kuban regions of the North Caucasus. Here the variability of rainfall during the growing season hampered planned levels of output. Part of the problem of unstable yield was related to the prevalence of the *sukhovey*, or very dry air-mass movements from northern Middle Asia during July and August. Originating in the region north of the Aral Sea these air masses tracked west, frequently devastating crops in their path. In the era of Lysenkoism it was thought possible to mitigate the prevailing climatic regime by introducing into a wooded steppe, steppe and semi-desert environment, four huge shelterbelts. The planting of the four major shelterbelts outlined in Fig. 25 was complemented by an equally vast programme of planting windbreaks around individual fields. Such programmes of planting vegetation in agricultural regions had a long history and were employed widely in both the United States and Canada during the 1930s. But in the latter cases, protection of fields at the local level with the expectation that with the moisture thereby provided, yields would be enhanced, was the rationale. In the Soviet Union this reasonable objective was carried a significant step further. Here science and technology in the employ of the state were charged with the task of ameliorating the climate of a vast region of steppe and semi-desert. Clearly, more objective scientific opinion did not support this contention. With the death of Stalin in 1953 the scheme was quietly shelved. The landscape, however, has been changed. A careful perusal of vegetative maps of the region in later decades will reveal relict features of this programme, but only in the zone of the wooded steppe. Whether the existence of these relict features has been of real economic benefit is a moot point. Some studies of the effects of large-scale shelterbelts in other countries suggest that not only do they raise moisture consumption during the summer, they prevent a more widespread distribution of snow cover and hence reduce moisture availability in the regions affected. Since Stalin's time more moderate approaches

---

[1] Joseph Stalin, *Leninism* (London: Lawrence & Wishart, 1944), 604.

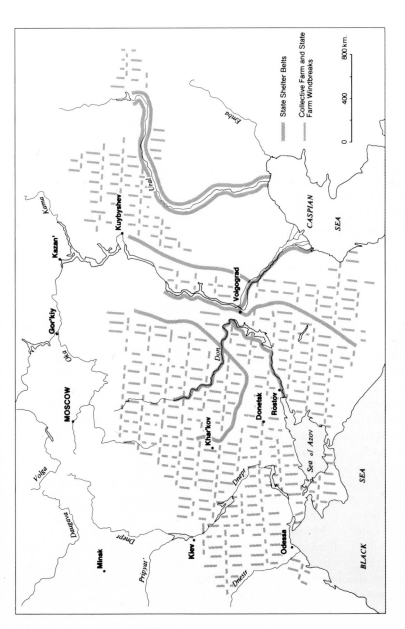

Fig. 25 The Stalin Plan for the Transformation of Nature – Shelterbelt Project.

Source: Albert E. Burke, 'Influence of Man Upon Nature – the Russian View: A Case Study', in Thomas W. L. (ed.) *Man's Role in Changing the Face of the Earth* (Chicago: The University of Chicago Press, 1956), 1043.

have been encouraged. Needless to say the dessicating impact of the *sukhovey* has not been thwarted, and thus the regional climate has not been modified by the Stalin Plan.

During the Stalin period, and for that matter Khrushchev's as well, the attitude toward the environment in official proclamations did not change substantially from the theme of a conquest of nature. If Khrushchev was perhaps more sanguine in his view as to what science and technology could achieve in reworking the natural environment, many of the schemes closely associated with his name were certainly technologically dependent. For example, his promotion of the so-called Virgin Land Schemes entailed the cultivation of a vast area of grassland in Kazakhstan and West Siberia. Huge state farms were established, monoculture of grain introduced and vast amounts of agricultural machinery were dragooned from elsewhere in the country to run the farms. Over 40 million hectares were put under the plough in a few short years. In a region previously the domain of the pastoral nomad, the land was cropped annually. Some of the consequences of this scheme will be examined in the next chapter, but the point to be made here is that the ideology of a technological imperative prevailed. Perhaps in the era of the Sputnik and later the first manned space flight, such a conviction was to be expected. But in the Soviet Union, as elsewhere, there has been a moderation of the view that transformation of the environment can be achieved without cost. Indeed, the reason for the change in attitude, and official policy, had to do with the matter of cost, and how to measure it.

The valuation of resources

Resource allocation procedures became the subject of intensive debate during the 1960s for the same reasons as have prompted similar discussions elsewhere – a growing appreciation of the scarcity of natural resources and the recognition that economy in their extraction and consumption was long overdue. A major stimulus was the 1965 economic reform and the use of profitability as one measure of economic performance, for it was soon recognized that the desired efficiency in resource use would not be encouraged if resources continued to be allocated free of charge. Notwithstanding the legacy of legislation from the early Soviet period, natural resources had not been managed with due regard to their scarcity and value. The all-too-typical pattern was profligate waste and increasingly serious environmental degradation. In virtually every measure of consumption of resources per unit of production, the Soviet Union compared very poorly with western countries. A growing chorus of Soviet voices argued for a reassessment of the ideological obstacles to pricing natural resources. The process began in the 1960s and has continued down to the present day.

As we have noted in an earlier chapter, in the Soviet economic system it is not the market place which influences the price of a good or service, it is instead the State Committee on Prices which determines it. To be sure, in some cases scarcity plays a part in the process but so too does ideology. Thus, the price of bread, for example, has remained essentially unchanged for more than a quarter century. For most of the Soviet period all natural resources were allocated to state enterprises to be developed free of charge based upon some notion of presumed requirements or prescribed norms. There is a growing consensus among Soviet observers that such an approach works against rational resource development practice. The Gorbachev reforms suggest that scarcity, indeed, market pressures, may play a larger role in pricing of all resources in future.

Throughout most of the Soviet period economic growth has been achieved by directing ever increasing amounts of natural resources, financial capital and labour into production. But as we have noted elsewhere, there are now acute labour shortages in some regions and the central task is that of achieving higher rates of labour productivity everywhere. A parallel situation applies in the natural resources sector. Since most resources have been free there has been little incentive for managers to economize in their use. The typical, and entirely rational, behaviour of the extractive industry enterprise manager charged with the task of meeting an ever increasing production quota is by way of illustration, as follows. Having successfully put a mine into operation, the manager is assigned a larger production target each year. Initially these are met, indeed, exceeded, thereby bringing manager and worker alike a bonus payment. The increased production is achieved by hiring more labour and using more capital equipment. At some point, however, it becomes difficult to maintain output let alone increase it, since the mineral deposit begins to be worked out. Cost of production increases. In the post-1965 period, and in the Gorbachev reform era, this means that profitability of the operation declines. So long as the manager is able to successfully argue the need to move the operation to a new site, for which there is no charge and at which the marginal and average costs of production are lower, then there is no incentive to extract from the first deposit the maximum which is both technically and financially possible to achieve. In most mining operations the enterprise would have to pay less than half the geological prospecting costs involved in finding another site. Thus, request to move operations approved, the enterprise relocates. A rational decision for the management and workers, indeed, a rational decision for the ministry concerned since its success is dependent upon the performance of the various enterprises under its jurisdiction. Better to have more enterprises able to meet a demand for increased production imposed by Gosplan, and be profitable, than not. However, from the perspective of the national economy as a whole such decision-making behaviour is sub-optimal because it is obviously wasteful. The absence of a charge for natural resources, it was contended, simply reinforced such manifestly irrational practices. Ideology notwithstanding, since the 1960s Soviet authorities have become much more receptive to the idea that more efficient resource use can be encouraged through the imposition of a charge. While there are still some obvious gaps, there has been real ingenuity in attempting to invoke some semblance of a market situation in price determination. There have also been some small achievements. A few examples will suffice.

In the post-war period the loss of agricultural land to urban development has been considerable. While the legislation which governs land use and conversion includes norms for the amount of land required for particular purposes it does not establish prices. The reason is simple – for ideological reasons land remains a free good. Not only has this situation encouraged rapid conversion of high quality agricultural land to non-agricultural uses, it has biased evaluations of the benefits and costs of large-scale projects such as hydroelectric power stations. More than six million hectares of agricultural land have been lost to reservoirs. In the absence of a price for land, and therefore some ability to determine its discounted value in the future, it is small wonder that the calculation of the cost of a kilowatt-hour of electricity from hydropower stations had been criticized as unrealistically low. Land use within cities, has, according to critics of the present system, been irrationally planned also. In virtually every serious assessment of Soviet town planning in the last two decades the question of how better to allocate urban land uses has arisen. The high proportion of one-storeyed structures is often cited as an example of wasteful use of land. In a number of cities with more than a million inhabitants such buildings still comprise more than half of city land. As the proportion of apartment dwellers increases this share will decrease, but not all such structures are used for housing. Indeed, industrial use of land has come under fire for taking up more land than the norms prescribe. But clearly if land is free an enterprise is encouraged to acquire as much as possible by whatever means simply as hedge against future need. It has been contended that extensive land use has produced abnormally high service costs, thereby adding increasingly to the overall operational and maintenance costs of the urban system. Even in the city centre land use prior to the 1960s was often extensive rather than intensive. The skyline has changed since then in most sizeable cities, but the arrival of the Soviet version of the skyscraper, which rarely exceeds 30 storeys, has not solved what is still regarded by many Soviet observers as an inefficent, irrational utilization of an increasingly valuable resource. The standard argument once again is that in the absence of any charge for urban land there is no incentive to use it economically. A number of possible solutions have been proposed, but one of the most interesting of them entails the use of several surrogate measures to place a value on a number of economic, engineering, social and environmental dimensions of the urban scene. What appears in Fig. 26 is something akin to a land-value surface for the city of Novgorod. Similar maps were prepared to illustrate the spatial variations in the value of land in other cities. The objective of the exercise, which it should be noted entails a considerable amount of subjective evaluation, is to underscore the need to introduce some spatially differential charges for urban land that would reflect the inherently higher value of central city locations. The issue of imposing a differential rent for urban land remains unresolved, but there are moves in this direction in other resource sectors. The prices paid by the state for agricultural commodities such as grain is spatially differentiated. In more marginal regions the price paid is higher than for the same product in more bountiful agricultural areas. While not the equivalent of differential rent, it is nonetheless a vast improvement over the flat rates of payment of an earlier era. The price paid by the state does not necessarily reflect the real value of the commodity, of course, and more significantly it does not reflect prevailing conditions of supply and demand. Revisions of Soviet prices occur very infrequently.

Beginning in the 1960s much of the legislation governing the management of natural resources was revamped. The catalyst in setting this process in motion seems to have been a belated acknowledgement of serious environmental degradation. Air and water pollution had reached crisis proportions in many industrial areas. The former was soon to be linked to respiratory disease and the decline in life expectancy registered during the 1970s. The latter was widespread and had been a serious social

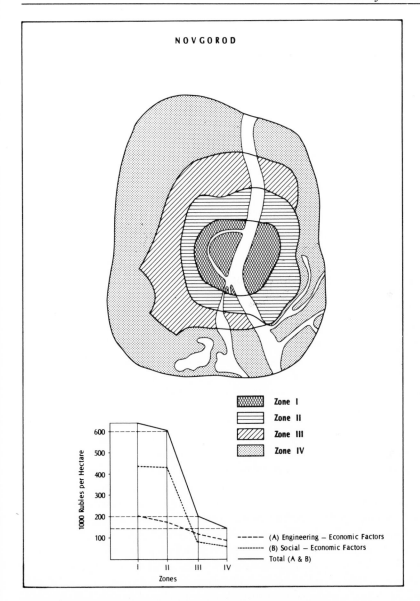

Fig. 26 Urban Land Value – A Non-Market Approach, Novgorod

Source: Based on S.I. Kabakova, *Gradostroitel'naya Otsenka Territory Gorodov* (Moscow: Stroyizdat, 1973), 125.

cost of rapid industrialization almost from the beginning. Environmentalist legislation which on the surface seemed exemplary was not being adequately implemented. The same was true of the myriad legal sanctions intended to ensure an objectively rational and efficient development of natural resources. In a later chapter we will examine the problem of environmental degradation in greater detail. As this point we will focus on those aspects of the recently revised legislation which deal with resource pricing.

Between 1968 and 1980 most of the legislation pertaining to the major natural resources was revised. Included were new Principles for the use of land (1968), water (1970), minerals (1975), forests (1977), air quality (1980) and the animal world (1980). Land remains a free good, as noted. In the case of water it too was to be allocated free of charge to most users. In certain cases token charges could be levied. But in a special joint resolution of the Party and government in 1979 a charge for water used by industry was introduced. This special measure permits a levy of relatively modest proportion to be exacted for consumption up to the maximum stipulated by the norm for the production process involved. Above-norm usage brings a steep surcharge into play. Set at 400 per cent of the within-norm rate, it is intended to force water conservation. Of course, to charge for water requires some mechanism for monitoring actual rates of consumption, something not universally available. For example, domestic consumption is not metered and is paid for through an imputed fixed charge incorporated into rents for state-owned apartments. Perhaps not surprisingly, water in the typical Soviet urban household is not used moderately. Like industry, domestic consumption is greatly in excess of what is registered in western industrial states. While a charge for irrigation waters can be levied, this has rarely been done. Under Gorbachev there is increasing pressure on Middle Asian irrigators to be more efficient, a topic to which we will return in the following chapter. Thus, in general for agriculture, which accounts for about half of the total usage, water remains in practice a free good. In the case of mineral resources there are some measures to encourage full utilization but they are indirect. Aside from a modest levy to cover a proportion of geological exploration costs, the resource 'sites' are still allocated to users free of charge. Clearly some sites are advantageous because of more favourable geological conditions. In such cases higher taxes are imposed by the state on the value of the production obtained each year. But these turnover taxes are in any event not that high. Whether the deliberately lower rates which are imposed on more marginal operations actually encourages enterprises to stay in business longer is a moot point. Certainly the pressure on enterprise decision makers is to gain access to sites more geologically favourable, better located, or ideally both. In the 1977 legislation on the use of forest resources there are direct charges stipulated for the right to harvest a stand of timber. While there is debate as to the extent to which existing prices for natural resources actually reflect their real value, they do represent a gradual shift in policy, and hence ideology, from the position adopted in the early Soviet period. Some long-standing attitudes toward the environment seem to have been modified as well.

From transformation of nature to conservation of nature?

From the middle of the 1960s on there seems to be a much more explicit concern with the environment, at least to judge from some legislative initiatives and recent policy decisions. It would be imprudent to suggest that the traditional belief in the role of science and technology in achieving the state's objectives has diminished. But there is some evidence to suggest that the Stalin-era preoccupation with the conquest of nature, with its purposeful transformation, has been tempered somewhat. In this regard some lessons have been drawn from past experience. We will highlight some recent developments to illustrate this point.

One of the central problems confronting the current Soviet leadership, like those before it, is the state of agricultural production. After decades of undercapitalization a huge investment has been made in this sector since the 1965 economic reform. Agriculture now consumes in excess of one-third of available investment capital annually. Yet production of grain still does not meet planned targets and the Soviet Union has shifted from being a net exporter to a net importer of grain during the past quarter century. The problem is many-sided, as we shall see, but part of it is environmental. Put simply, where there is adequate heat to grow crops there is generally inadequate moisture. This broad relationship is described by Fig. 27. The zone of greatest agricultural potential, that of chernozem soil, is characterized by considerable variability of precipitation during the growing season. Over the years there have been many schemes proposed to fix this vagary of nature. They have ranged from Lysenko-based agronomy, which being essentially unscientific did not work, to vast projects in which the flow of major rivers would be reversed. Such grandiose schemes were obviously perfectly compatible with the Stalin-era preoccupation with transforming nature. As it happened, river diversion projects remained on the drawing board owing to their cost, not for want of enthusiastic support. In the post-Stalin era the basic problems did not disappear, but technological advances made some of the river diversion projects more realistic alternatives and the apparent benefits seemed to outweigh the costs, at least insofar as Soviet economics was concerned. Aside from improving domestic agricultural production, the case for river diversion gained support from some other quarters in the post-Stalin period.

The first was the state of the inland seas. For most of the Soviet period the level of the Caspian Sea had steadily declined. In total it dropped nearly three metres before apparently stabilizing in the late 1970s. The reason for this steady decline appears to have been related principally to climatic change in the Caspian's watershed. But human intervention also played a role. The Volga, which accounts for more than 70 per cent of the inflow, has been extensively developed for water power since the Stalin era. The river is basically a series of huge reservoirs. Urban industrial development at the numerous large-scale hydroelectric power stations has dramatically increased water consumption. In the lower Volga region water has been diverted for large-scale irrigation projects. The same factors have reduced the flow of the Amu and Syr Dar'ya rivers in Middle Asia. As these two streams are the principal sources of water for the Aral Sea, its decline has been even more dramatic. In the last 25 years it has dropped more than 10 metres. Unlike the Caspian it has not stabilized since very little recharge occurs owing to the excessive withdrawal from the Amu and Syr Dar'ya systems. Both the lower Volga region and the areas adjacent to the Amu and Syr Dar'ya offer considerable potential for irrigation. Since 1965 the area under irrigation in the USSR has doubled, but further expansion is constrained by water availability. Thus, the combined pressures to do something about the decline in the level of the country's two principal inland water bodies and to improve agricultural production through expansion of the area under irrigation gave a real fillip to the Stalin-era proposals to divert the waters of several north-flowing river systems. After

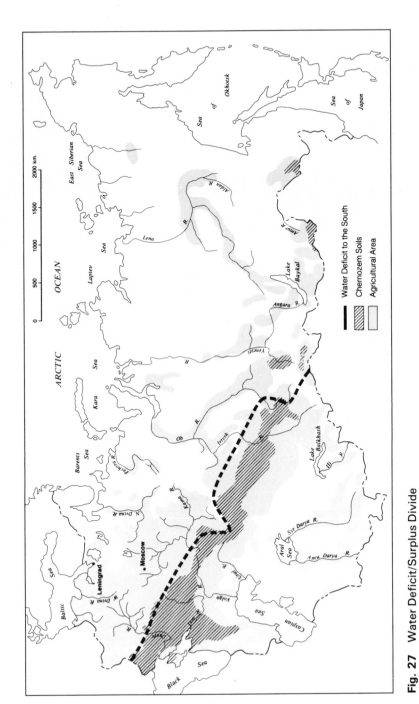

Fig. 27 Water Deficit/Surplus Divide

Source: Adapted from John R. Tarrant, 'The Significance of Variability in Soviet Cereal Production', *Transactions, Institute of British Geographers*, New Series, Vol. 9, No. 4, 1984, 392.

all, was not the northerly flow of such an important resource testimony to the need to rework the natural environment? Preliminary engineering surveys were initiated in the post-Stalin era on the assumption that such massive river reversal was indeed in the national interest.

While in parts of northern European Russia some comparatively minor projects were initiated, they were minor only in the sense that in terms of the volume of water to be diverted and the cost involved they paled in comparison with the proposed diversion of the Ob' and Irtysh systems. As is portrayed in diagramatic fashion in Fig. 28 the so-called SIBARAL scheme entailed taking water from the upper reaches of the Ob' river to the Irtysh and reversing the flow of the Tobol' river at the confluence with the Irtysh. A combination of gravity and pumping stations would see nearly 30 cubic kilometres of water move from the north to the arid south

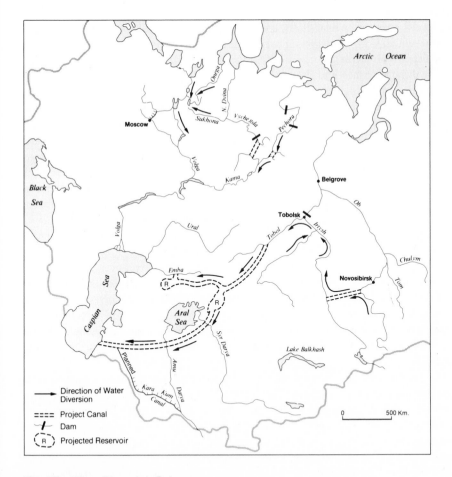

Fig. 28 River Diversion Schemes

Source: L. Symons *et al., The Soviet Union. A Systematic Geography* (Totowa, NJ: Barnes & Noble, 1983), 85.

(see Fig. 27). The cost was estimated to be in the billions of rubles, but the presumed benefits were greater. Not only would the area under irrigation be greatly expanded, bringing with it an increased and predictable level of commodity production, but the problem of the declining levels of the Aral Sea, and possibly the Caspian Sea as well, would be addressed. Up until 1985 the projects seemed to have the full backing of Party and government. It was anticipated that given the advanced stage of engineering design work in the office and in the field, there was every reason to expect to see some of the benefits of the project by the year 2000. Middle Asian political figures and technical personnel alike were enthusiastically in support. Water for irrigation was seen as the key to resolving both the pressure for land and the need to more fully employ the rapidly growing rural labour force. Soviet technologists were keen to see the implementation of the century's most massive example of the transformation of nature. Already a huge amount of time and money had been committed to the scheme. Notwithstanding the environmental benefits to be gained from stabilizing the levels of the major inland seas, and in the process forestalling a change in climatic regime which portended greater aridity, there were costs. And these began to be articulated with increased urgency from the early 1970s on.

The principal concern of those who opposed the project centred on the inadequate attention accorded environmental impact assessment and the apparent absence of a thorough comparative cost evaluation of alternative solutions to the problem. Local concerns were expressed over the loss of significant cultural and archeological artifacts due to flooding. Others were worried about the impact on the tayga, the principal vegetation and the mainstay of numerous local settlements. Climatologists outside the Soviet Union, as well as some inside, expressed grave concern over the potential climatic change for the northern hemisphere. A diversion of fresh water of the scale intended, the argument went, would affect the extent of the ice cap, albedo, and upper air circulation patterns. The fresh water comprises a relatively thin layer above the Arctic Ocean's salt water. As it freezes at a higher temperature than salt water, any substantial reduction in fresh water in the Arctic Ocean would result in a shrinkage of the ice cover. Still others, and probably more persuasively, focused their criticism on the fact that a huge expenditure was required to implement the scheme and that it could be at least two decades before any return on this investment would occur. And all of this expenditure to bring water to a region in which existing irrigation projects were notoriously wasteful of water. A more efficient use of an obviously valuable resource would clearly be of benefit, but the mechanisms to bring this about do not exist at present.

As late as 1984 it appeared that the protagonists had the upper hand in this increasingly contentious debate. The SIBARAL project was included in early discussions of the draft guidelines of the 12th Five Year Plan (1986–1990) which were published in 1984. Throughout 1984 and early 1985 the project appeared to have the full support of the leadership. But the criticism continued and gained momentum with the arrival of Mikhail Gorbachev in March of 1985. By November of that year the 12th Five Year Plan was released for discussion. It was ratified by the Party and government in early 1986. The Plan did not include any reference to the SIBARAL project. In August of 1986 the Central Committee of the Communist Party and the Council of Ministers adopted a resolution to discontinue design and preparatory work not just on the diversion of the Ob' and Irtysh waters (SIBARAL), but on the diversion of part of the flow of northern European Russian rivers into the Volga system as well. Further study of the ecological impacts of such schemes, and of their economics, has been ordered. Meanwhile the various ministries and agencies involved in water management have been instructed to find other means to conserve water and to develop alternative strategies for the intensification of agricultural production. Environmentalists have now turned their attention to the broader issue of large-scale human intervention in natural systems.

There seems to be little doubt that the huge cost of the SIBARAL project was the principal reason for the decision to discontinue work and to drop it and other similar schemes from the 12th Five Year Plan. But there is also a case to be made for the growing importance of an environmental or conservationist perspective. The Gorbachev emphasis on *glasnost'*, or openness, clearly has played a major part in facilitating public discussion of some of these issues. Equally important in legitimizing the environmental perspective is the growing catalogue of examples of mis-management of natural resources attributable to technological intervention. While these are by no means restricted to the management of water resources, certainly some of the more significant examples of resultant environmental degradation are related to water resources and are now widely reported.

In the 1970s it was determined that construction of a huge dike separating the Caspian Sea from its appendage, the Kara-Bogaz-Gol lagoon, would help to stabilize the level of the Sea by preventing an 'excess' of water entering the lagoon and evaporating. However, by the time the dike was completed in 1980 the decline in the level of the Caspian Sea had stabilized, indeed, it had already increased slightly. The dike was also supposed to slowly reduce the area of the Kara-Bogaz-Gol lagoon. This was intended to benefit the chemical industry which had developed on its shore to exploit the vast deposits of salts and other chemicals. These had been created through the evaporation of the salty Caspian waters over the centuries. Most forecasts estimated that the Kara-Bogaz-Gol would continue to exist as a lagoon for a couple of decades. In fact by November of 1983 it had all but dried up, threatening the very future of the chemical industry in the process. Moreover, the creation of a vast salt bed posed a major environmental hazard for the extensive tracts of irrigated land in Middle Asia since wind-blown salts were now a distinct possibility. The solution required construction of a system of aqueducts to once again replenish the Kara-Bogaz-Gol with Caspian waters. Miscalculations have had an equally serious impact on the level of Lake Sevan in Armenia. There water diverted to generate hydroelectricity has resulted in a far greater draw-down than anticipated. Given the historic importance of Lake Sevan in Armenian folk culture this unexpected environmental impact has been widely criticized. Remedial work has been expensive, and not yet entirely successful. The aesthetics of landscape clearly have a value, a value given insufficient weight in the original plans.

The Ministry of Power and Electrification figures rather prominently in many of these controversies. Throughout the country the management of reservoir levels has been severely criticized as having deleterious consequences for other vested interests in river basin management. Economies have often been achieved which are decidedly short-run. For instance, in many of the low-gradient river systems of European

Russia plans to construct dikes or berms around reservoirs to minimize the area affected were shelved in the interest of cost-saving. In consequence losses of agricultural land are in excess of what are necessary. In Siberia 'savings' were achieved by not clear-cutting the forest cover from the intended zone of inundation of the Angara and Yenisey river projects. Not only is the economic loss in terms of unharvested timber significant, but prospects for a reservoir-based fishing industry are compromised. Even the generation of electricity has been affected since the intake pipes to the turbines are frequently clogged with wood, thus reducing the volume of water intended to pass through the plant. Calculations have been wide of the mark in respect of several other operational parameters as well. At the Bukhtarma hydro plant on the upper Irtysh river the reservoir has never accumulated the planned volume of water. The available waters are released during the peak demand for power periods – autumn and winter. In the spring and summer the reservoir is replenished, but downstream there is often a shortage of water for agriculture as a result. This situation has existed for more than two decades. The accumulated loss for agricultural production in the region is in the millions of rubles. Such opportunity costs have not yet been adequately incorporated into the benefit–cost assessments of large-scale projects such as hydroelectric power stations. There are clearly conflicts of interest between the various groups of ministerial decision-makers. It is once again this 'departmentalist' mentality which is currently the target of serious criticism, this time from the environmentalist perspective as well as the Gorbachev-era economic reformers.

The main thrust of so much of the current discussion of resource management projects from the environmental point of view focuses on the absence of a wholistic view of the impacts of technological intervention in natural systems. As in any industrialized state, there are numerous instances of technology developed for its own sake at the expense of other interest groups. There are many contemporary examples. In Leningrad flooding has been a problem since the city was founded in 1703. The reason is related to the fact that the city was built on the delta of the Neva river and is especially vulnerable when heavy autumn rains swell the outflow at the same time that on-shore winds drive water up the Gulf of Finland toward the city. The technological solution was to construct a barrier dike across the Gulf to 'protect' the city. Local scientific opinion that this posed an environmental hazard and not a solution to the problem of flooding was ignored. The dike has been completed (see Fig. 57, page 275). Natural water exchange and currents have been altered. The considerable effluent carried by the Neva is now impounded. The impact in this case is water and air pollution. As a recreation zone the Neva shoreline is very much at risk. Scientific opinion from a different perspective than the protagonists of technology is frequently ignored. There is debate at present as to the need for a Danube–Dnepr Canal. The rationale for its construction is linked to the apparent need to expand irrigated land in the Ukraine. Questions have been raised as to the capacity of the soil in the intended area of irrigation to absorb more moisture when groundwater levels are already rising. Conservation of water figures prominently in the critics' argument. One of the points being made is that 'irrigators' are often remunerated on the basis of the 'volume' of water they process. The more diverted to irrigation the higher their wages. A not dissimilar situation prevailed in the

Khrushchev-initiated Virgin Lands scheme. There the area planted was expanded annually in response to the central plan. The dependence on a high degree of mechanization was related to the huge scale of the individual state farms, frequently in excess of 40,000 hectares of cultivated land. Against the advice of some agronomists the land was cropped annually and not allowed a period of fallow. Both water and wind erosion took hundreds of thousands of hectares of valuable land out of production as a result. In the Khrushchev era public or scientific criticism of high-priority state projects was not common, and thus not especially effective. But since the Stalin era dissenting views have been raised with increasing frequency. *Glasnost'* has certainly opened the door to public scrutiny of all issues, including those concerning negative environmental impact. Yet it would be assuming too much to contend that the Gorbachev-era tolerance of public comment has entirely erased past practices. After all, the environmental disaster by which all others in the Soviet Union that we know about pale in comparison, the nuclear meltdown at Chernobyl', was not reported immediately in the Soviet media. To be sure, it soon had headline attention, but the control over the media by central authorities still remains a fact of Soviet life.

There is much happening in the Soviet Union which suggests that the long-standing preoccupation with transforming nature is undergoing change. Natural resources are recognized as something to be managed wisely. Past reliance on well-intended legislation has been acknowledged to have been misplaced. The record of resource waste and environmental degradation is far from auspicious. As the arguments against the whole concept of science and technology being employed by the state to transform nature gain momentum, there is certainly the possibility of a more explicitly conservationist or environmentalist ethos developing. But there are many obstacles, not least of which are the deeply engrained ideological premises, a deeply entrenched bureaucracy with vested technological interests, and a continuing adherence to the principle of ever increasing industrial production. To facilitate this latter objective the management of the land resource plays a critically important role. To some observers Soviet agriculture is the achilles heel of the system. In the next chapter we will explore the validity of this assumption.

Recommended reading

DeBardeleben, J., *The Environment and Marxism-Leninism: The Soviet and East German Experience* (Boulder: Westview Press, 1985).

Gerasimov, I.P., Armand, D.L., Efron, K.M., *Natural Resources of the Soviet Union: Their Use and Renewal* (San Francisco: W.H. Freeman, 1971).

Goldman, M.I., *The Spoils of Progress* (Cambridge, Mass: Massachusetts Institute of Technology Press, 1972).

Graham, L.R., *Science and Philosophy in the Soviet Union* (New York: Random House, 1972).

Jackson, W.A.D., (ed), *Soviet Resource Management and the Environment* (Columbus: AAASS, 1978).

Jancar, B., *Environmental Management in the Soviet Union and Yugoslavia* (Durham: Duke University Press, 1987).

Jensen, R.G., Shabad, T., Wright, A.W. (eds), *Soviet Natural Resources in the World Economy* (Chicago: University of Chicago Press, 1983).

Joravsky, D., *Soviet Marxism and Natural Science, 1917–1932* (New York: Columbia University Press, 1961).

Pryde, P.R., *Conservation in the Soviet Union* (Cambridge: Cambridge University Press, 1972).

Weiner, D.R., *Models of Nature-Ecology, Conservation, and Cultural Revolution in Soviet Russia* (Bloomington: Indiana University Press, 1988).

Ziegler, C.E., *Environmental Policy in the USSR* (London: Frances Pinter, 1987).

7 Managing the Land: Farming and Village Life

... the commune is the cradle of the social organism.

De Gurowski, 1854.[1]

One of the most striking features of the contemporary agricultural scene is the apparent continuity with the past. Most people still live in villages not much different in average size than at the turn of the century and much of agriculture is run on a collective, if not a communal, basis. At the time of the revolution three-quarters of the population were classified as agriculturalists and most of them conducted their affairs in accordance with the age-old customs of the rural commune, or *mir*. The field work was carried out predominantly by women, as it is now. Seasons and the weather influenced the pace of daily life in obvious ways. While the revolution and eventual socialization of agriculture changed in a fundamental manner the relationship of the peasant to the crops sown and harvested, they did little to alter the tempo of rural life. Much of the Soviet countryside still comes to a standstill during the periods of *bezdorozhnaya*, or roadlessness, associated with the spring and autumn rains. Crops from the land, and the people who harvested them, played a decisive part in the modernization of the Soviet economy. But the simple fact that many tens of thousands of villages are still not accessible by road suggests that the rural sector has not been an equal partner in Soviet economic development. To some people it is no small irony that a country with one-sixth of the world's land area and a huge population still engaged in agriculture has been forced to import substantial amounts of grain and meat during the past quarter century. This development is a key departure from the pattern of the past when Russia, and later the Soviet Union, played an important role as a grain exporter. The reasons for this situation are complex, and have to do with the nature of the agricultural resource base, its management, and the attitudes and aspirations of the more than 96 million people

---

[1] A. De Gurowski, *Russia As It Is* (New York: D. Appleton, 1854), 192.

who still remain in the rural sector. These are some of the topics we will examine in the ensuing discussion of farming and village life.

The physical basis for agriculture

From the standpoint of growing crops there is much that is disadvantageous about the physical geography of the Soviet Union. Despite the huge land mass, an ideal balance between heat, moisture and light is an all too rare occurrence. In Chapter 1 the basic features of the country's physiography, climate and zones of natural vegetation were briefly outlined. The combination of northerliness and continentality mean that permafrost conditions extend over half of the country. Under such harsh conditions agriculture is not ruled out completely, but crop options and types of husbandry are clearly restricted.

The largely latitudinal pattern of the country's vegetative zones is very much a reflection of the impact of climate. The wedge-like strip of productive wooded steppe and steppe which diminishes in north–south extent from the Ukraine and the Kuban through to Eastern Siberia is one example of the influence of climate (see Fig. 3, page 11). The basic pattern of 'accumulated heat', that is, the number of degree-days above the 10 degrees celsius threshold, which tends to be the temperature at which plant growth can be sustained, is perhaps even more striking in this regard (Fig. 29). The desert and semi-desert region of Middle Asia clearly stand out on this map as the principal storehouse of accumulated heat. Tapping this potential climatic resource comprised part of the rationale for the scheme to divert the north flowing Ob' and Irtysh waters to the south, as was noted in the preceding chapter. Unfortunately for Soviet agriculturalists, and their Russian counterparts before them, the distribution of effective moisture (Fig. 30) is roughly the obverse of the distribution of accumulated heat (Fig. 29). Thus, even though the total area which from a climatic point of view could be cultivated is larger than exists in the United States, a much larger proportion of it is decidedly marginal in terms of crop production. Put simply, in the Soviet Union the risk of drought is ever present. Indeed, Fig. 27, page 142, succinctly describes the geographical nature of the dilemma. The area of greatest agricultural potential, namely the belt of rich chernozem soils, also lies within the all-too-extensive zone of potential moisture deficiency.

Having a finally accepted the fact that further expansion of cultivation into marginal areas would not ensure a reliable increase in grain production and that massive transformations of the natural environment are not only extremely costly but also create new environmental problems, greater attention is now being paid to maximizing output from the country's best lands. Since the economic reform of 1965 the byword has been 'intensification' of production. A thorough inventory and classification of soils, something which had not been done previously, was initiated about this time as part of the programme of more rational management. But even with a more scientific scheme for agricultural land management, the harsh physical environment continues to stymie efforts to fulfil planned targets for food production.

Notwithstanding the many environmental problems confronting Soviet agriculturalists, it should be recognized that yields per hectare have been steadily improving in the post-World War II era. According to some authorities the relative increase in

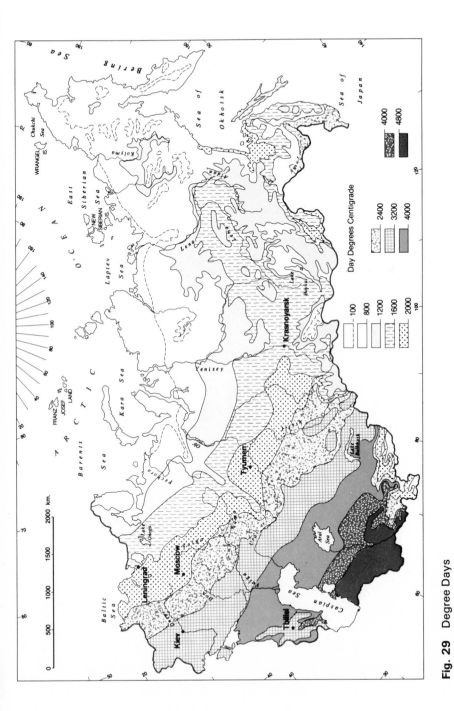

Fig. 29 Degree Days

Source: Leslie Symons et al., *The Soviet Union. A Systematic Geography* (Totowa, NJ: Barnes & Noble, 1983), 40.

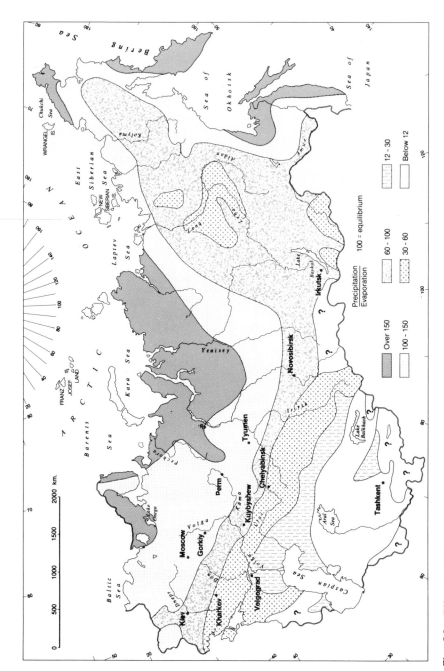

Fig. 30 Effective Moisture

Source: Leslie Symons *et al.*, *The Soviet Union. A Systematic Geography* (Totowa, NJ: Barnes & Noble, 1983), 42.

output in the Soviet Union exceeded that in the United States over the same post-war period. Of course, the base level was much lower to begin with in the Soviet Union. To some extent higher average yields per hectare are the result of taking out of production some of the most marginal land. This was especially evident in the immediate post-Khrushchev years. Khrushchev's enthusiasm for the Virgin Lands Scheme, which saw more than 40 million hectares of former grazing land in West Siberia and northern Kazakhstan put into spring wheat production, was not shared by his successors. Constant cropping of friable chestnut-brown soils in a region with an average of only 30 centimetres of precipitation annually resulted in fairly extensive wind erosion. And when the typical summer thunderstorm did bring rains, the uprooted soil was susceptible to gulleying. Although some of the least productive land was pulled out of production immediately after Khrushchev's ouster, a sizeable area had already been permanently lost to agriculture because of wind and water erosion. Thus, ever since the mid-1960s there has been a consistent effort to increase, and stabilize, agricultural production in the country's most environmentally suitable regions. Part of this initiative involved a vast increase in production of chemical fertilizers. Between 1960 and 1985 there was nearly a tenfold increase in output. Owing to problems in distribution and application not all of this huge increase in output has been of practical benefit. Nonetheless, yields have improved because of fertilization. Another part of the programme of 'intensification' has entailed a substantial expansion of areas of irrigation and drainage. Such ameliorization schemes have not been inexpensive. And while they have also contributed to improved yields they have not solved the basic problem of planning food production from land which, generally speaking, suffers from either too little or too much moisture. The nature of the principal agricultural regions underscores the difficulties which face planners.

As Fig. 31 reveals, the largest agricultural region is roughly coincident with the tundra and northern tayga and is characterized by reindeer husbandry. Where settlement exists, and where local soil conditions allow, some vegetable production occurs. But more often than not, vegetable production is only possible in the artificial environment of the greenhouse. While this is of obvious local importance in terms of both employment and food production, the region as a whole is still a net importer of all food products. To the south is a zone of tayga in which reindeer husbandry is complemented by more extensive pockets of cultivation and livestock rearing. Agriculture here is usually pursued in conjunction with other economic activities and is highly dependent upon inorganic fertilizer supplements to the typically heavily podzolized soils of the forest and marsh. Dairying occurs in the tayga, but mostly in association with major northern settlements such as Murmansk. If these areas are combined with the vast tract of desert and semi-desert pastoralism, it is apparent that for much of the country agriculture is a distinctly extensive as opposed to intensive activity. In order to ensure a balanced diet for the resident population of these huge territories food imports are necessary. Throughout the rest of the country dairying, livestock raising, grain production and market gardening are found in differing combinations as determined by the natural environment, local tradition, and the demands of urban settlement. This 'agricultural wedge', broadly defined by a line joining Leningrad, Odessa and Irkutsk, encompasses the bulk of

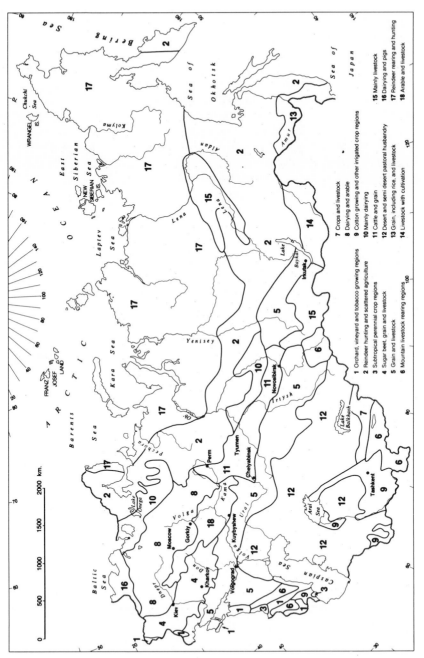

Fig. 31 Agricultural Regions

Source: Leslie Symons et al., *The Soviet Union. A Systematic Geography* (Totowa, NJ: Barnes & Noble, 1983), 120.

1 Orchard, vineyard and tobacco growing regions
2 Reindeer hunting and scattered agriculture
3 Subtropical perennial crop regions
4 Sugar beet, grain and livestock
5 Grain and livestock
6 Mountain livestock rearing regions
7 Crops and livestock
8 Dairying and arable
9 Cotton growing and other irrigated crop regions
10 Mainly dairying
11 Cattle and grain
12 Desert and semi desert pastoral husbandry
13 Grain, including rice, and livestock
14 Livestock with cultivation
15 Mainly livestock
16 Dairying and pigs
17 Reindeer rearing and hunting
18 Arable and livestock

Soviet agricultural production, and not surprisingly most of the population as well. As Fig. 31 indicates, there are relatively few specialized agricultural regions. Most are found in the sub-tropical enclaves of the Caucasus, the more temperate realms near the Black and Caspian Seas, and the oases and irrigated tracts of Middle Asia. A more market-oriented perspective of Soviet agriculture is provided by Fig. 32. The intensity of agricultural activity is obviously influenced by the distribution of the major urban centres. But excluding dairying and market gardening under green-house conditions, the range of agricultural activities is still governed to a large extent by climate and physical geography. To be sure, soil drainage and irrigation, chemical fertilizers, genetic science and mechanization have permitted more efficient use of the existing agricultural land base, but it is still impractical to grow corn in the tayga or cotton in the steppe. Clearly, the nature of the physical environment complicates planning agricultural production. But in some ways so too does the institutional environment which envelopes those whose daily life and labour is tied to the land.

The organization of agricultural production

At present about one-third of the total population is classified as rural. According to Soviet definitional procedures, this is the share of the total population which lives in places *not* qualifying as urban-type settlements or cities. But of the 96 million so defined as making up the rural sector in 1987, about 33 million were workers, and dependents, engaged in non-agricultural pursuits. As we have noted in an earlier chapter, many of these people are part of the urban workforce. They commute from village to town out of necessity, or sometimes choice. The rest comprise workers in branch plant factories located in the countryside and a wide, and growing, range of largely technical personnel (who fall into the *intelligentsia* social class). From school teachers, to scientific personnel, to government bureaucrats, the support structure for the farm population has expanded rapidly in the post-Second World War period. And with the change which this has produced in the official version of the rural social class structure has come a host of other, more subtle, manifestations of social position. For example, those who were amongst the first *kolkhozniki* to hold an internal passport clearly had status. Education and positions in management have brought a wider array of perks and privileges to the countryside as well. And beneath all of this lies the traditional social class structure in which peasant values still count in determining status. Thus, both in the city and the countryside there are many nuances in determining social distance. In the countryside, however, the combination of modernity and traditional folk culture makes for a much more complex social system. The total number of people directly related to agriculture is 63 million, or about 23 per cent of the total population in 1987. By any standard of comparison this is a huge absolute number, and a sizeable share of the total for a modern industrial state. It is worth emphasizing again that until 1961 the rural population exceeded the urban. For a very large number of urban inhabitants then the link with the village is very much a part of their life experience.

Deficient food supply is an inherent and important theme in Russian and Soviet history. Notwithstanding the fact that Russia was the world's largest exporter of grain on the eve of World War I, inadequate internal distribution systems and

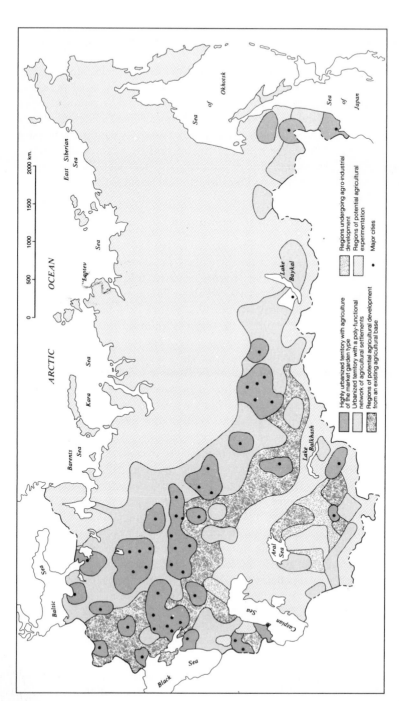

Fig. 32 Agricultural Marketing Zones

Source: Based on V.P. Butuzova, 'Sel'skoye Rasseleniye v Rayonnoy Planirovke' in *Geograficheskiye Nauki i Rayonnaya Planirovka. Voprosy Geografii*, No. 113 (Moscow: Izdatel'stvo Mysl', 1980), 86.

government policy often resulted in both regional food shortage, and occasional famine, at the same time as the export of grain. Thus, to the peasant the Bolshevik call for the dissolution of the large estate and the redistribution of land raised the prospect of a better chance to adequately feed his family. Indeed, during the early Soviet period there was little by way of government policy concerning the country-side that would do other than encourage the peasant to look after his own family first. As we shall see, deficient diet, food shortages and outright famine characterized the Stalin era, along with grain exports. In this regard as least there was a real continuity with the past. It is only since Stalin that the agricultural sector has emerged as a national priority garnering each year a larger share of investment capital and, ironically, in the past quarter century claiming a large share of hard currency expenditure on imports. The relationship of the peasant to the land has played a central role in the chequered history of domestic food production.

To the typical peasant of late imperial Russia legal title to land was often beyond his ken. Functionally illiterate and deeply imbued with the values of the communal lifestyle which the *mir* offered, he went about his tasks with a sense of duty to the community as a whole and secure in the knowledge that what was produced on his various strips of land could be used to feed his family. The Stolypin Agrarian Reforms and estate agriculture, modern and mechanized, were changing the rural scene, but the resurgence of the communal ethos at the time of the revolution and the redistribution of land was a measure of how important centuries-old traditions remained in the countryside. In central European Russia peasants who had opted out of the commune in accordance with the Stolypin Reform often were forcibly returned. For many peasants living in the city an opportunity to return to the land was compelling. No doubt the severe hardships of urban life during the revolution and ensuing years of Civil War were further incentive to leave. Thus, the number of peasant households was larger following the revolution of 1917 than before it (25 million as opposed to 21 million). Many of the western regions traditionally charac-terized by individual farming units were 'lost' to the Soviet Union through indepen-dence movements and border adjustments at the time of the Treaty of Versailles. These included the Baltic States and parts of the west Ukraine and Belorussia. As a result of this process, the role of the commune in agriculture was intensified in the immediate post-revolutionary years. From the European Russian core to the peripheral regions of the new Soviet state the influence of the *mir* declined just as it did prior to the revolution.

While the revolution brought a redistribution of land, the Civil War brought the domestic economy to the brink of ruin and gave rise to forced requisition of foodstuffs from an increasingly beleaguered peasantry. Subsistence agriculture pre-vailed since those who could produce a surplus were disinclined to exchange agricul-tural commodities for currency that was worthless. Lenin took the major step of permitting the peasantry a measure of free enterprise with the introduction of the New Economic Policy in 1921. This had several consequences. It stabilized the domestic economy. Since forced requisition was ended and replaced by taxes in kind or in money, the peasantry was encouraged to produce food for the market. While the government promoted the replacement of the commune by collectives and state farms the lure of profit had an even greater impact on the communal system through the expansion of private farming. The state owned the land, but capitalistic forms of agriculture developed rapidly during the 1920s nonetheless.

The success of the New Economic Policy in restoring agricultural production to pre-World War I levels, thereby ensuring an adequate food supply for the rapidly expanding urban populace, was double-edged. The capitalistic tendencies unleashed by the New Economic Policy were facilitating the rise of a class of wealthy peasant farmers, or *kulaki*, in the countryside, which at the time was home to four-fifths of the total population. The growing commercial significance of the *kulaki* underscored the apprehension of some leaders over the political reliability of the peasant population as a whole. Soviet authorities had formalized the earlier Russian practice of separating the peasantry into three categories, poor peasants (*bednyaki*), middle peasants (*serednyaki*),and rich peasants (*kulaki*). In endeavouring to exercise political control over the massive rural population, the government strategy was based on fostering tensions between the members of the poor and middle peasantry and the *kulaki*. Yet the official position was subject to considerable debate. After Lenin's death in 1924 Bukharin and Stalin represented the two predominant views. Bukharin argued that the nationalization of land, the tax system, and agrarian reform initiated by the revolution, were leading to a genuine convergence of classes in the country-side, and consequent diminution of *kulak* authority. Many took Stalin's analysis as correct, however. He contended that the rural scene was becoming more, not less, stratified as the *kulak* element steadily acquired more rented land and hired labour. The fear that a politically unreliable peasantry might thwart the drive to industrialize the country by withholding food from the cities loomed ever larger. The Stalinist view prevailed. A programme of collectivization was adopted as part of the First Five Year Plan (1928–1932) introduced by Stalin.

In some regions the authority of the commune as a social and economic institution had been challenged by the nascent forms of capitalistic agriculture which flowered under the New Economic Policy. Thus tensions already existed, and were con-sciously exacerbated where possible by Soviet authorities. The initial plan to col-lectivize 20 per cent of the cultivated area made use of the poor peasants (*bednyaki*) in the assault on the *kulaki*. Formation of collective farms entailed the redistribution of wealth and in some villages this objective found popular support. Resistance to collectivization was common, however. Where the art of persuasion failed, armed force eventually brought compliance. In 1930 the tempo of the collectivization drive was escalated, the total elimination of the *kulak* element now being a central goal. By 1935 the programme had transformed the Soviet countryside. The costs were staggering. Population loss cannot be determined with any real precision, but prob-ably amounted to between three and four million. Those people unfortunate enough to be labelled *kulaki*, and often the label had little to do with wealth but rather popularity, were dispossessed, relocated or shot. Famine took hold, notably in the Ukraine, as crop production plummeted in the chaos of the time. Livestock holdings were decimated as peasants slaughtered their animals rather than turn them over to the state. Two-fifths of cattle and horses and two-thirds of sheep, goat and pig holdings were lost. The age-old link with the land was severed. What was ushered in were new institutional arrangements for the management of agriculture – the col-lective farm or *kolkhoz*, the machine and tractor station (MTS), and the state farm or *sovkhoz*.

Superficially the new collective farm may not have appeared different from the commune (*mir*) to the casual observer. Peasants still lived in their own homes in the villages of before, the mix of crops and rotation was determined by higher authority, the collective's well-being was still determined by the weather. The ownership of land in each *kolkhoz* was still held by the state, but it was now formally leased in perpetuity to the *kolkhoz* membership. As before, most peasants worked land they did not legally own. The peasant's movement was now governed by the *kolkhoz* management, whereas in a not-so-distant era the elders of the commune determined who could leave, and for how long. But there were also significant departures from past customs. Peasants were now obliged to work the *kolkhoz* land for a specified, and over time a larger, number of days a year. Each *kolkhoz* had to deliver to the state specific quantities of agricultural product according to the dictates of the plan. Payment for peasant labour rendered was unpredictable since it was based on the assumption that there would be a surplus. Until the mid-1960s the return on peasant labour was based on the concept of the work-day (*trudoden'*). Each task on the *kolkhoz* was measured in work-day equivalents. After the quota required by the state had been met, the remainder of the harvest could be sold to the state at a fixed price or sold at the prevailing market price in the collective farmers markets in the cities, if indeed the surplus commodities were marketable. In any event, either income from the sale of the above quota production or the surplus in kind was shared amongst the *kolkhoz* peasants according to the total individual labour contribution as measured by labour-day equivalents. The steady escalation in the required number of days to be worked for the *kolkhoz* was a reflection of the fact that the payment for labour was completely unpredictable. On the all too frequent occasions when there was no surplus left after the state quota was met, there was simply no return for the time spent labouring in the *kolkhoz* fields. The willingness to work hard on the collective farm land was compromised and yields fell in consequence. As one of the most important institutions in the agricultural sector the *kolkhoz* was clearly deficient. Most peasants toiled instead on their private plots or took care of their privately owned livestock. As we shall describe in detail shortly, it was the personal farming activity legally sanctioned by the Collective Farmers Charter of 1935 which sustained the peasant family for decades. Notwithstanding government restrictions on the personal sector from time to time, and the obligatory tax imposed on presumed income from it, this sector remains critically important in total food production. Thus, the state extracted food and income from the countryside by imposing quotas for each *kolkhoz* to meet, by taxing the personal sector, and until 1958 by extracting payment in kind for the use of machinery provided by the Machine and Tractor Stations (MTS). After that date the MTS was abandoned and the equipment sold to the collective farms whether it was wanted or not.

As time passed the position of the collective farm peasants, or *kolkhozniki*, steadily deteriorated. And in turn so did the diet of the fast growing urban population. As we have seen in the preceding chapter, the prevailing ideology of the conquest of nature resulted in schemes to expand the arable without investing in essential infrastructure, such as an adequate all-weather road system to enable harvested crops to be delivered to the railhead. Given the dismal prospects for the *kolkhoz* operation, especially in the more marginal regions for agriculture, two options were frequently pursued. One was to amalgamate in order to achieve some possible benefit from scale economies.

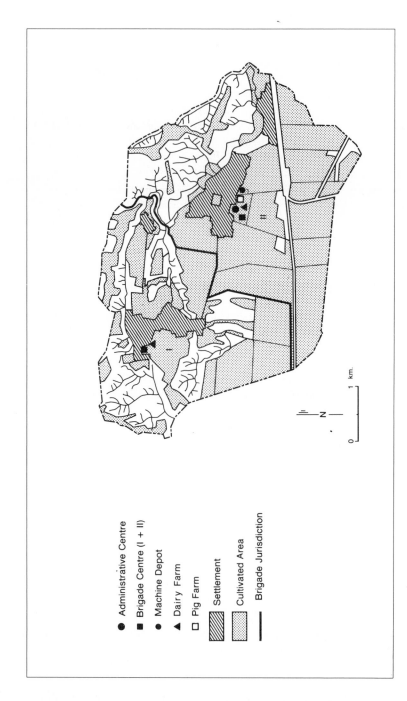

● Administrative Centre

■ Brigade Centre (I + II)

● Machine Depot

▲ Dairy Farm

□ Pig Farm

▨ Settlement

░ Cultivated Area

— Brigade Jurisdiction

N

0   1 km.

Fig. 33   Collective Farm

Source: Based on *Dierke Weltatlas* (Braunschweig: George Westermann Verlag, 1978), 128.

Thus, from 1928 to 1950 the total number of *kolkhozy* was halved; the number of households and arable land in each about doubled. But the larger the operational unit the greater the difficulty to coordinate activities, for as Fig. 33 illustrates, the typical collective farm comprises a number of separate village settlements. The trend has continued, nonetheless. *Kolkhozy* now number about 26,000, down from a maximum of more than 240,000 in the late 1930s. On average each *kolkhoz* has several hundred households under its jurisdiction, and about 6,500 hectares of land to administer, of which 3,600 hectares are under cultivation. Since 1980 the number of *kolkhozy* has remained relatively constant. Members of many collective farms chose a second option to improve their conditions of daily life and labour – changing the institutional organization from *kolkhoz* to *sovkhoz*, or state farm.

The *sovkhoz* offered one distinct advantage to the impoverished *kolkhozniki*. By changing status they became employees of the state. To be sure they were still raising crops, but no longer were they dependent upon the vagaries of nature to produce a surplus over quota in order to obtain payment for their labour. State farm employees are just that – salaried workers who are paid irrespective of the level of production. Some 23,000 collective farms changed status, many of them amalgamating in the process. Prior to the collectivization drive initiated by Stalin there were perhaps 1,000 state farm operations. For the most part they had been set up on former estates and were run as model agricultural enterprises. From the outset they tended to be more specialized, and better equipped than the typical *kolkhoz*. They always owned their own machinery and were therefore not dependent on the MTS during its existence. During the early 1930s some 3,000 *sovkhozy* were created in the open steppe to produce grain. This development was in response to the collapse of grain production from the *kolkhozy* and peasant sector during the chaos and famine of 1931–32. Under Khrushchev the state farm was given another fillip since it was the principal institutional organization associated with the Virgin Lands Scheme. As a result, the cultivated area under *sovkhoz* jurisdiction tripled to more than 22 million hectares between 1953 and 1956. Since that date the total number of *sovkhozy* has increased to nearly 23,000. Inasmuch as the labour force is governed by norms relating workers to arable, or to numbers of livestock, there is not as large a dependent population as on the collective farm. But because of its typically large size the average labour force is substantially greater, and unlike the *kolkhoz* it is predominantly male not female. Each *sovkhoz* administers on average about 16,000 hectares of land, nearly 5,000 of which are under cultivation. Many *sovkhozy* in the steppe region specializing in grain production are huge by any standard of measure. *Sovkhoz Gigant*, portrayed in Fig. 34, is aptly named for it occupies some 48,000 hectares of steppe near Rostovon-Don. It is apparent from Fig. 34 that a decentralized administrative structure exists on this particular *sovkhoz*, a feature in fact common to all the larger *sovkhozy*. By way of comparison, the *kolkhoz* illustrated in Fig. 33 covers barely 2,000 hectares. State farm households are permitted private plots as well. The detailed plan of one *kolkhoz* settlement presented in Fig. 35 is not too dissimilar from a *sovkhoz* in that it has a regularized street plan with a mix of apartment units and individual homes with adjacent private plots. More typical of the *kolkhoz* settlement pattern in fact is the ancient linear village with houses, gable-end to the

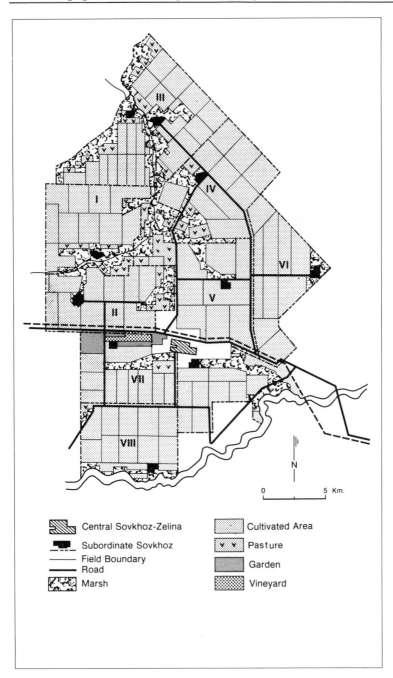

Fig. 34   State Farm

Source: Based on *Dierke Weltatlas* (Braunschweig: Georg Westermann Verlag, 1978), 128.

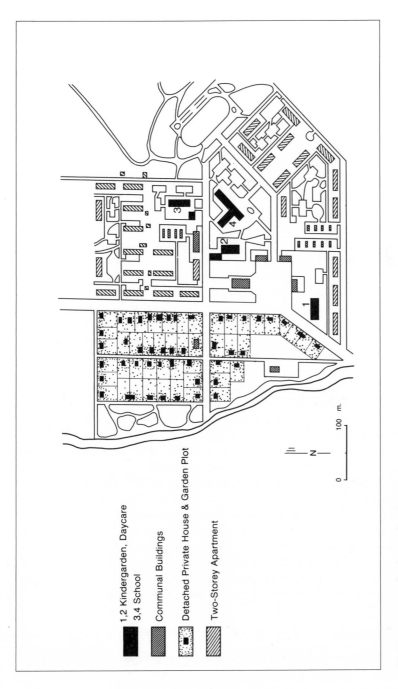

Fig. 35 Collective Farm Settlement

Source: Based on *Dierke Weltatlas* (Braunschweig: Georg Westermann Verlag, 1978), 128.

Table 12: Sown area – 1940–1987 million hectares

	1940	1960	1963	1970	1975	1980	1985	1987
*Sovkhozi**	13.3	73.2	97.8	100.9	112.9	115.2	112.6	112.4
Kolkhozi	117.7	123.0	114.0	99.1	98.2	95.9	92.0	92.2
Personal sector	19.6	6.7	6.7	6.7	6.6	6.2	5.7	5.7
Total	150.6	203.0	218.5	206.7	217.7	217.3	210.3	210.3

Source: *Narodnoye Khozyaystvo SSSR v 1960g (1963g, 1970g, 1975g, 1980g, 1985g)* (Moscow: Finansy i Statistika, 1961, 1964, 1971, 1976, 1981, 1986) *et seq. Narodnoye Khozyaystvo SSSR za 70 Let* (Moscow: Finansy i Statistika, 1987), 225.

*includes other state agricultural enterprises.

road, sometimes stretching for several kilometres. These still number in the many tens of thousands.

Thus, Soviet agricultural production is vested in three types of institutional arrangement, the *kolkhoz*, the *sovkhoz* and the personal sector. The few individual farms missed in the collectivization drive owing to their remote location have now disappeared, but on the eve of the Second World War they still accounted for about one-tenth of the total area under cultivation. The distribution of cultivated land according to institutional type is presented in Table 12. Over the years the principal trends have been a steady reduction in the share of arable under *kolkhoz* jurisdiction owing to conversion to *sovkhoz* status, an increase in the share of *sovkhoz* land owing to conversion, and expansion of the arable in frontier regions, and a steady decline in the importance of the personal sector commensurate with the absolute decline in rural population and number of households. On a more general level the total area under the plow has fluctuated quite substantially. It reached a peak during Khrushchev's last years as leader owing principally to the expansion of the arable under the Virgin Lands Scheme. Marginal land was taken out of production immediately following his demise as leader, as noted above. And some land previously used for grazing but ploughed up during the period of expanding the arable at all costs was returned to pasture. The cultivated area peaked again in the mid-1970s, not quite reaching the apogee of 1963 however. Since then poor harvests, owing mainly to recurrent drought conditions, have resulted in a steady contraction, especially during the early 1980s. The area under the plough clearly has some bearing on the production of agricultural commodities. But yields are obviously the critical factor, and in this respect the attitude of those who till the land is of no small importance. At this point it would be appropriate to look at production trends before examining in more detail the issues of incentive and intensification in Soviet agriculture.

Production trends

As with other sectors of the Soviet economy the basic goals for development are set by the Politburo of the Communist Party and endorsed by the Supreme Soviet. Gosplan establishes the broad range of targets for the plan periods and the Ministry of Agriculture has the responsibility of ensuring that the national targets are met. As we shall see, there have been problems in this latter regard. Centralization of decision-making in the case of agriculture is problematic at best. Historically, the controls from the centre have been excessive. Following the collectivization drive two ministries were responsible for agriculture – the Ministry of Agriculture which was responsible for the *kolkhoz* and MTS operations and the Ministry of State Farms. Up until the mid-1950s detailed planning from Moscow governed the crop mix, and even the time of sowing and harvesting for each agricultural operation. Such detailed control from the centre was finally acknowledged to be pointless. The demise of the MTS along with many other adjustments to the management of agricultural supplies and output signalled the steady shift toward a more rational management system. At present all agricultural operations are under the Ministry of Agriculture. Targets are set nationally for the Five Year Plan by Gosplan, but at the farm level much more discretion is given both *kolkhoz* and *sovkhoz* management teams by the Ministry in determining how their individual operation can best contribute to achieving these targets. In the last decade or so there has emerged a host of other organizations concerned with facilitating agricultural production. Perhaps the most notable of these are the Agro-Industrial Production Associations and Intercollective Farm Cooperatives. The former are associations of farming operations and support services such as factories processing agricultural commodities, distribution and research enterprises. The main purpose of such fundamental groupings is simply to expedite the production and delivery of higher quality agricultural commodities. The Cooperatives tend to concentrate more on improving infrastructure and the management of the land resource itself. At all levels the Party is an integral part of the decision-making process. However, despite decades of exhortation to produce more, the correlation between planned output and delivery of agricultural commodities to the state has never been worse than in this past decade and a half.

As we have seen, Russia, and until quite recently the Soviet Union, were consistently net exporters of grain even if segments of the domestic market had to do without. A more enlightened approach has been followed since the early 1960s, and hence the Soviet Union has emerged as a major market for surplus grain produced in other parts of the world. The shift from net exporter to net importer of grain is in no small way related to the realization that consciously depriving the population during peace time would be politically unacceptable to the masses. It also owes something to the genuine efforts to improve the diet of the average citizen. In the early 1950s the typical Soviet meal was heavy in carbohydrates, light in protein, and generally deficient in both quantity and selection of vegetables and fruit. Since that time there has been a very real improvement in the quantity and quality of the food supply. Basic dietary improvement was closely linked to increasing grain production, especially coarse grain for fodder.

Protein intake in the Soviet Union is inextricably tied up with the size of livestock holdings, and expansion of the latter is dependent upon fodder supply. If fodder supplies are inadequate to sustain animals over the winter, 'distress' slaughtering occurs in late fall or early winter. For years distress slaughtering had frustrated efforts to quickly build up livestock holdings. This situation was exacerbated by the devastation of livestock holdings at the time of collectivization. The impact of the collectivization drive is readily apparent from the general trends portrayed in

Fig. 36. As noted above, for many peasants slaughtering their animals was preferable to turning them over to the state. Even by 1950 the total numbers of cattle and pigs barely equalled the 1929 levels, and the number of sheep remained substantially below. Horses, the principal draught animal during the 1920s, suffered a similar decline, but owing to mechanization of agriculture were destined never to regain their former importance. While there had been a modest recovery by 1950, the population was still worse off than in 1929. Put simply, there were about 50 million more mouths to feed in 1950 than in 1929. Small wonder that recipes of an earlier, more bountiful era, were rendered useless. If in the early 1950s an egg had become a luxury in many urban households, what was a fruit pie with meringue topping? Indeed, the content of Soviet cookbooks eventually began to reflect the new, more austere, reality. In later years when the programmes to improve the diet had begun to have a perceptible impact, cookbooks published in the 1920s and early 1930s became something of a collector's item for in them were recipes no longer easily obtained.

The substantial increase in livestock holdings between the 1950s and 1980s outlined in Fig. 36, was translated into large gains in the production of beef, veal, lamb, and pork. A vast expansion of coarse grain production underlies this change. While silage corn was introduced during the Khrushchev years as a major fodder crop, especially in the south Ukraine and the Kuban region of the north Caucasus, it still does not compete with the traditional Russian and Soviet emphasis on oats and barley. The latter two still represent about three-quarters of coarse grain production, while corn counts for perhaps one-sixth in a good year. This ratio is roughly the opposite of that of the United States. The much more stringent heat and moisture requirements of corn during the growing season underscores the quite different agricultural production potential of the two countries. Given the substantially higher yield per hectare of corn in comparison to oats and barley, it is no suprise that American total coarse grain production remains half again as large as the Soviets', and from a smaller cultivated area. In terms of maintaining, and enhancing, livestock holdings a substantial share of the wheat harvested in the Soviet Union of necessity has to be fed to animals as well.

Clearly the programme to improve the protein intake in the average citizen's diet has not come cheaply. And having once registered substantial improvements, to deprive the population during periods of poor harvests becomes politically intolerable. Food riots have wracked Poland on more than one occasion in the last quarter century. There have been reports of similar, but smaller-scale to be sure, disturbances in Soviet cities over the years. Put simply, tampering with the food supply is especially fraught with risk. Thus, in times of poor harvest the Soviet Union has opted to buy grain in order to sustain livestock holdings and meat production. As well, meat imports have been substantial since the 1960s. During the 1970s they averaged about 300 million tons per year. They have been even larger during the 1980s, a trend which reflects the overall poor performance of Soviet agriculture during most of the decade.

The pattern of Soviet grain production since the early 1960s is presented in Fig. 37. During the 1960s there was a steady, if irregular, increase in production, and save for 1963 and 1965 it was a decade of grain exports. This general trend in

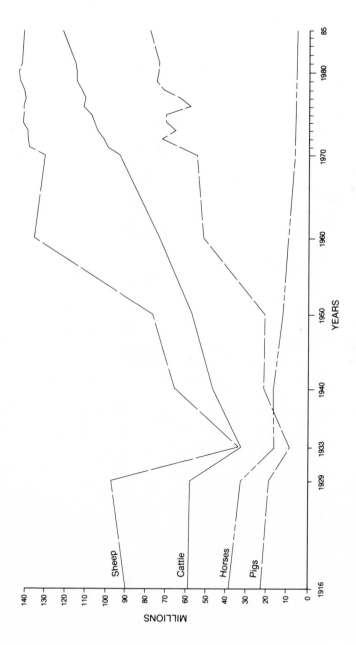

Fig. 36 Livestock Holdings

Source: *Narodnoye Khozyaystvo SSSR v 1965 g (1975g, 1985g)* (Moscow: Finansy i Statistika, 1966, 1976, 1986), *et seq.*

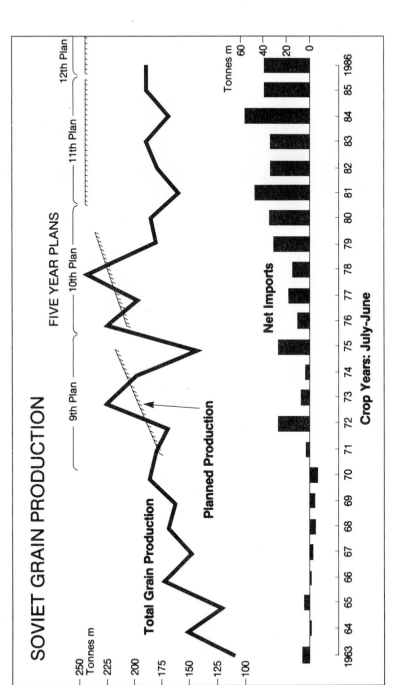

Fig. 37 Grain Production Trends

Source: Based on 'Russian Agriculture', *The Economist*, November 15–21, 1980, 22; *Narodnoye Khozyaystvo SSSR za 70 Let* (Moscow: Finansy i Statistika, 1987), 643.

grain production was a reflection of policies introduced the preceding decade. Over-all, agricultural output was 40 per cent higher in the second half of the 1950s compared to the first half. In bringing about this change the Virgin Lands Scheme figured prominently. But as has been noted earlier, expansion of the cultivated area into marginal lands previously the domain of the pastoralist was a calculated gamble. Constant cropping raised the stakes. The disastrous harvest of 1963 simply con-firmed the informed observer's opinion of the risk involved. Still, recovery was rapid as average or higher amounts of precipitation during subsequent growing seasons produced reasonable yields and the traditional export of grain was resumed, albeit at a relatively small scale. Yields were higher owing to better weather conditions, but they also owed something to a much greater investment in fertilizer, machinery and, as we will discuss shortly, the wages paid to farm workers. What the 1970s and 1980s have brought is quite different. Harsh weather, including too much heat, moisture or cold at critical times, has produced a dependence on world grain markets every year since 1971. What the data presented in Fig. 37 reveal is, first of all, an overall stagnation in agricultural production generally, for poor weather takes a toll of more than just the harvest of grain crops, secondly, by implication a decreasing return on the ever larger investment in agriculture registered in each five year plan from 1965, on, and thirdly, a sizeable outlay of hard currency to pay for grain imports. It is for these reasons that grain production in particular, and agriculture in general, are regarded as the 'achilles heel' of the Soviet economy. At this juncture it would be appropriate to examine briefly some of the economic and social dimensions of the problems confronting Soviet planners.

Investment and incentive

The first steps toward modernizing agriculture taken by Khrushchev were fre-quently at cross-purposes. Massive campaigns to introduce new crops, or new ways to handle old tasks, were introduced only to be changed or reversed a few years later. The scientific and technical personnel in the rural sector were then inadequate in number to educate the *kolkhozniki*, who anyway often knew better what needed to be done than could be dictated by the plan. But Khrushchev's initiation of a price reform for agricultural products was a significant and beneficial step. By the early 1960s the prices paid to collective farms had been substantially increased, the price paid for above-quota production delivered to the state was more attractive still, and of particular importance for collective farms in marginal areas, the first step was taken toward creating a regionally differentiated scale of payments. Thus, collective farms in many areas of inferior quality land were paid higher prices for the same crop produced on a collective farm in a region known for its productive soil. This was a partial recognition of the higher costs of production in the former case. In the years since price regionalization schemes have become more refined, although the zones delimited still reflect to some degree the boundaries of political-administrative units rather than natural geographic regions. Notwithstanding greater procurement price sensitivity to regional variations in soil, climate and agricultural potential, to say nothing of relative location, some collective farms are still hard pressed to turn a profit. The question of accessibility is of no small importance since the prices paid exclude the cost of transportation to the nearest railroad terminal. This must be borne by the collective, or state, farm and for many operations is a major economic burden. The abysmal state of most rural roads simply compounds the problem. Indeed, the ability of producers to deliver agricultural commodities to rail or road terminals prejudices the full recovery of what is actually produced. Even now it is estimated that a fifth or more of the grain, vegetable and fruit crop is lost because of inadequate facilities for transportation, storage and distribution. The massive requisitioning of vehicles from non-agricultural rural as well as urban enterprises which occurs every autumn in an attempt to move commodities from the field to the depot does not solve the problem. Decades of little if any investment in basic infrastructure continues to plague agricultural planners. In the early 1960s perhaps a little more than one-fifth of total investment capital was directed towards agriculture. At present the share is closer to one-third. The absolute number of rubles currently spent on this sector has clearly increased very considerably. That which has gone into the pockets of collective and state farm workers perhaps has been amongst some of the most cost effective.

With the improvement in prices paid for agricultural products has come a commensurate increase in return for the labour expended. On the *kolkhoz* the relationship is quite clear. The more profitable the operation, the larger the payment for the labour invested by the *kolkhozniki*. But until the economic reform initiated by Brezhnev and Kosygin in 1965 there was still a major disincentive for the peasant willing to work on the collective farm instead of on his private plot or with his animals. To reiterate, his annual income was not predictable. Thus, in the late 1960s a programme was introduced in which the *kolkhozniki's* annual income was averaged over a period of several years and a basic monthly wage established. The concept of the labour-day has been dropped. Annual income of collective farmers has drawn closer to that of state farm workers, and the base levels of both have been increased substantially since the late 1960s. Putting state and collective farms on a profit or loss basis as part of the 1965 economic reform was attractive in that it held out the prospect of stimulating higher levels of output. However, it also raised the spectre of farm managers producing only what was most profitable and dropping that which was not. Such local discretion in decision-making was held at bay during the 1970s by the continuing intervention in decision-making by central authorities. With the arrival of Gorbachev, however, ideas regarding decentralization of decision-making responsibility are finding more favourable reception although as yet not much has actually changed. In summary, from the point of view of instilling incentive to work harder for the *kolkhoz* or the *sovkhoz*, the increase in wages and salaries initiated in the 1960s had an impact. Beginning in the late 1960s there was a notable improvement in yields, attributable in part it seems to the attitude of farm workers. Indeed, in some regions the private plot and livestock holdings were let slip. After all, if an adequate income could be had from the *kolkhoz* why put in the additional hours in physically demanding labour on the plot? But overall the role of personal farming still remains an important, and controversial, element on the agricultural scene.

Much of the increased investment in agriculture since 1965 has gone into large-scale 'amelioration' projects, some of which were described in the preceding chapter. In some observers' opinion the proportion of investment directed to rural construction projects of this type is too high. It runs around two-fifths of the total in the Soviet Union compared to about one-quarter in the United States. In the latter, the balance, that is, about three-quarters of the total investment in the agricultural sector, goes into increasing the stock of machinery, a substantially larger share than in the Soviet Union. Thus, despite a cultivated area at least 25 per cent larger than that of the United States there is far less equipment. In 1966 the United States' stock of tractors and combine-harvesters on farms numbered 4.8 and 0.88 million respectively. In 1986 the Soviet tally was 2.8 million tractors and 0.827 million combine-harvesters. Trucks as noted already are in chronic short supply and are requisitioned annually from other sectors. Under-capitalization takes many more forms than just these examples. Given that only 3 per cent of the American labour force is occupied in agriculture, whereas the share is around 20 per cent in the Soviet Union, there are clearly huge differences in the ratio of machine to farm worker. Part of the problem is that improving infrastructure and stocks of equipment necessitates even larger investment. Return on this investment is already unacceptably low. What is not low is the current level of subsidy to agriculture.

In virtually all modern industrial states, and a good many developing ones as well, there exist extensive programmes of agricultural subsidy. But amongst industrialized states few provide as much support for agriculture as the Soviet Union. This was not always the case, of course. During the Stalin years prices paid by the state for agricultural commodities were exceedingly low. For many collective farms, income received did not even cover the cost of seed, let alone provide a source of income for the *kolkhozniki*. Hence, the preoccupation of peasants with the personal sector in agriculture and the drift from *kolkhoz* to *sovkhoz* status were eminently logical. From agriculture, wealth was extracted with short-term gain and little sense of long-term cost. To cheaply purchased agricultural commodities the state applied a turnover tax. Put simply, as the principal intermediary in the process of exchange, the state charged substantially more than it paid for agricultural products. As all prices outside the collective farmers market were determined by the state, supply and demand factors were irrelevant. Income from the turnover tax on agricultural, and other commodities, provided the investment capital to finance the industrialization drive. Eventually, as we have seen, adjustments have had to be made in order to induce greater output from this long-exploited sector of the economy. But this has come to pose a real dilemma. Although the state paid little for such products as wheat, or rye, the final cost to the consumer of bread was low even with the inclusion of turnover taxes. And it mattered little that the price of meat bore no relation to actual cost, if the volume sold by the state was small owing to short supply, if the population inured to such deficiencies was prepared to pay the going price on the collective farmers market when money was in the pocket at the same time that meat was on the counter. Cheap food has long been touted as one of the benefits of socialism, just as low rent for housing and public transportation in cities are taken for granted by the populace. As the wage bill of agricultural workers has risen, as the prices paid for products have been increased, as investment generally in agriculture has jumped ahead since the 1965 reform, the spread between cost of production and revenues received has created a vast chasm into which huge amounts of money are now being poured. Save for the presumed benefits derived from feeding the population better and putting more spending money in the pockets of farm workers the net result is escalating subsidy.

Between 1965 and the mid-1980s state retail price subsidies have increased more than seventeen-fold. The sum involved is fast approaching 50 billion rubles annually. The irony is that while the demand for staples such as bread or potatoes is usually relatively inelastic, that is, only a certain amount will be consumed more or less independent of the price, these products are so cheap that peasants are now able to afford to buy bread and potatoes to feed their livestock. On the other hand, despite the substantial increase in domestic meat production, and imports of meat and meat products, domestic demand is still not satisfied and appears a long way from being so. Increased consumption of meat and dairy products in the last 20 years is a major reason for the jump in the total retail price subsidy. At present it is estimated that prices charged by the state for beef, lamb and butter represent less than half the cost of production. For milk and pork the price covers perhaps as much as 60 per cent of production costs. To substantially increase prices perhaps poses a smaller risk of inciting domestic unrest than artificially creating a shortage of state-subsidized items such as beef and pork in order to lower costs but neither is risk free and thus far the state has simply absorbed the cost. Inadequate supply in the state sector enables peasants to turn a handsome profit on privately produced meat sold at market prices in the collective farmers market. The combination of high prices for commodities sold on the collective farmers market, higher income from the *kolkhoz* owing to price and wage adjustments over the past two decades, and availability of bread and potatoes from the state sector at exceedingly low prices gives rise to the intolerable situation of bread and potatoes destined for humans being converted into meat. For the peasant it is perfectly logical of course to secure feed for livestock this way if the alternatives are to invest a substantial amount of time personally supervising grazing livestock or competing with the collective farm for available fodder. Clearly, those charged with managing the domestic food supply are caught on the horns of a dilemma. While the urban household is the primary beneficiary of cheap food, we might well ask at this point, how has the dramatic increase in expenditure on the agricultural sector affected the conditions of daily life and labour of those who farm land?

Village life and the household economy

In an earlier chapter reference was made to the widespread popular appeal of the village prose tradition in literature. Part of this appeal seems to be related to the juxtaposition of urban and rural lifestyles and values. Fast growing cities are often perceived as producing a sense of anomie, of self-centred behaviour, amongst the citizenry. According to some writers, the village community still retains its original, higher moral values, unless it has somehow been corrupted by the impact of urban-industrialization. Yet if the results of the surveys conducted amongst the rural populations of at least the Slavic and Baltic regions are to be believed, most villagers would change places with urbanites – and with alacrity. Those with skill and more advanced levels of education, and hence with most to contribute to the rural sector, are invariably the ones who express least satisfaction with the quality of life in the countryside, a theme we will return to in a later chapter. Of course, the vast rural–urban migration which has occurred over the past half century simply confirms such survey results. The fact that a very large proportion of the urban population has itself only recently left the village, and no doubt looks back at village life with some nostalgia, may account for part of the popularity of the village prose. But notwithstanding the fact that some people may actually choose to commute from the countryside to the city to work, there is little evidence of movement from city to village to live. The attractions of village life are better savoured through the pages of a book than on a first-hand basis it seems. Thus, in many parts of the Slavic and Baltic countryside there is absolute population loss, growing labour shortage and dim future prospects for those who remain.

In Middle Asia and parts of the Caucasus where rural populations continue to grow rapidly, there is already extensive underemployment and outright unemployment. With both environmental and economic limits on the area which can be irrigated, population pressures will inevitably result in more migration to the city. And as elsewhere, it will be the most energetic and ambitious who leave first. The often stultifying grip of traditional values – subservience, bride prices and the like – on the lives of rural women will eventually loosen, thus further encouraging out-migration. Indeed, for rural women in all regions it is possible that the nostalgic appeal of village prose may be less than for men who were, and are, at the apex of the rural social class hierarchy. In any event, life on the farm is rarely easy anywhere. For most of the Soviet countryside this is certainly the case.

In the Soviet Union the word farmer is hardly ever heard. Farm workers are peasants. Strictly speaking the term peasant is restricted to the *kolkhozniki*, or the more than 33 million members of the country's 26,000 collective farms. But to the urban sophisticate it matters little if the man on the street in front of him sporting knee high, dirty black boots, a tattered, padded jacket and cap and smoking a *papirosa* is a state farm employee, and therefore a member of the country's working class and not strictly speaking part of the peasant class. He is just another in the horde of *kolkhozniki* invading the city to buy goods probably already in short supply or to sell something on the collective farmers market at an inflated price. And indeed he could be right, for each day millions of peasants make the journey to cities for precisely such purposes. To be sure, they are often unsophisticated by contemporary urban standards. But unlike 40, or even 20 years ago, they are no longer as likely to be literally poor country cousins. With the rapid escalation in wages paid farm workers since the late 1960s has come a huge jump in potential purchasing power. The fact that for most of this period there was more money in the average rural savings account than in the urban speaks as much to the dearth of consumer items in rural stores as it does to the propensity to save amongst the rural population.

Rural–urban differences in household incomes have been steadily eroded by the policies introduced since the 1960s. In 1970 urban incomes were on average about one-quarter again as large as those in the countryside. By the mid-1980s, if the earnings from the private plot and animal holdings of *kolkhozniki* are included, the gap is probably less than one-tenth. In peasant households close to major urban centres where agricultural commodities can be easily sold, incomes frequently exceed those of factory workers in the city. But distance is not necessarily a barrier either. For many peasants travelling by airplane to distant, cold climate, urban markets to sell the products of the sunny south is commonplace, and presumably profitable.

Irrespective of locational or climatic situations, much of the activity in the Soviet village is centred on personal auxiliary farming. This incorporates both the cultivation of the individual private plots, which for *kolkhozniki* usually are one-half hectare in size, and tending privately owned livestock. Ostensibly in regions characterized by irrigation the area of the private plot is reduced, but as the membership of the collective farm assembly is charged with monitoring the land so allocated all have an obvious vested interest in pushing the tolerance of regulations to the limit. The typical household plot is adjacent to the home itself. Across much of European Russia and Siberia the household agricultural enterprise comprises a detached wooden house (plastered exterior in much of the Ukraine, sometimes even brick in parts of the Baltic region), with outbuildings, orchard and plot. In the Caucasus and Middle Asia stone and adobe are the more common materials used in private rural house construction. The outbuildings provide both storage facilities and shelter for privately owned livestock. Depending on the region, animal husbandry includes looking after a single cow and calf, sow and piglets and a gaggle of sheep, lambs, ducks, chickens or whatever combination the local culture dictates. Numbers owned are restricted. From time to time the personal auxiliary farming system has come under government pressure or outright constraint. In the late 1950s for example, Khrushchev endorsed policies which severely restricted the personal sector. Peasants could sell produce in the collective farmers markets in the cities, but only at the state regulated price. Roadside stalls and other forms of private initiative in marketing products from the personal sector were prohibited. The result was predictable. The supply of commodities to the urban market dried up and the resultant food shortages produced widespread complaint, and according to some reports riots, in the cities. After Khrushchev's ouster such restrictions were lifted; indeed, in recent years there has been positive encouragement of personal auxiliary farming as part of the campaign to improve the food supply.

At the present time about 3 per cent of the total cultivated area in the Soviet Union is comprised of millions of tiny, private plots. They are not just associated with *kolkhozniki*. The right to grow crops on a private plot extends to all of the rural population. In addition, urban households have the right to apply for a summer garden, a much smaller plot than legally available to the *kolkhozniki*, and one on which no permanent habitable structure is to be constructed. This latter restriction is widely ignored for in the hinterland of many Soviet cities may be found what are rather elaborate tool sheds on such summer garden plots. Not infrequently these so-called sheds serve as a kind of poor man's *dacha*, complete with sleeping facilities and sometimes even a front porch! Produce from these plots, as well as from those tended by rural inhabitants, finds its way into the collective farmers market, and hence onto the kitchen table of the typical Soviet urban household.

While making up only 3 per cent of the cultivated area, the personal sector still generates more than half of the total potato production and around a third of most other vegetables. The personal sector accounts for nearly one-half of the nine million hectares sown to vegetable crops, so its contribution in this regard is not surprising.

Vegetables are of obviously comparatively high value. Not infrequently the production from private plots is compared to that of the *kolkhoz* or *sovkhoz*, to their obvious disadvantage. But it should be borne in mind that the personal sector is not entirely independent of the state sector or the collective farm. On occasion both the *kolkhoz* and *sovkhoz* provide machinery to facilitate plowing and harvesting on the private plot. In recent years such loaning of equipment has been encouraged by the government. A little fodder is grown on private plots, but as indicated, most of the land in this category is used for supplying the rural household with food, the surplus being marketed as opportunity permits.

While private plots comprise 3 per cent of the total arable, or about 6.5 million hectares, there are significant regional differences. In the more bountiful agricultural regions with significant rural populations the share is quite high. In Georgia they represent nearly one fifth of all cultivated land. In the Ukraine the figure is 7 per cent. In the Russian republic the share is below the national average. Over the past quarter century the absolute number of hectares in the personal sector and the share of the total have been steadily eroded. To some degree this reflects a reduced dependence on the household's own labour to supply food and a shift to goods purchased from the state. At present, the personal sector supplies about two-thirds of the rural household's food requirements. Thus personal auxiliary farming continues to account for a substantial share of the rural household's time budget. For women it is a major focus of attention, but even male *kolkhozniki* probably still spend one-quarter of their time in the family farming enterprise. To be sure, even when the rural household is still actively tending a plot and livestock, the women of the household are frequently no longer baking bread or making butter. Indeed, as noted earlier, bread bought cheaply from the state is sometimes used as fodder.

Though the contribution of privately owned animals to the national food supply remains important, it has steadily declined in relative terms. In the space of less than one generation the role of private egg production has dropped from more than two-thirds of the total to barely one-tenth. The development of *sovkhozy* specializing in poultry and egg production between the mid-1950s and early 1970s accounts for the change. The state has increased its share of other traditional markets of the private sector as well. Dairying is a case in point. In 1961 there were approximately 35 million milk cows in the country, of which 47 per cent or about 16 million were privately owned. By 1985 the personal sector still accounted for 13.2 million head, but the total number of cows was 42.9 million, and thus the share of the personal sector had dropped to 31 per cent. Some expansion in holdings had occurred on collective farms, but the most significant growth had taken place on the *sovkhozy* (5.7 to 13.9 million head). As was noted earlier, recent government policy has encouraged production in the personal sector. While the limits on the number of cows, pigs, and so forth have not been increased to any real degree, other ways of tapping the skills of the *kolkhozy* households have been pursued. One successful programme has the collective farm household taking piglets from the collective-farm and fattening them to an agreed-upon weight. Fodder is supplied. The inducement has centred on the household retaining one of the fattened pigs as payment for service rendered or sharing in the profit realized from their sale. By this and similar schemes, including providing peasants with loans to purchase livestock, the state has sought to augment meat production.

In most discussions of personal auxiliary farming much is made of the fact that it still accounts for something in the order of 25 per cent of the value of total agricultural production. But recognition of the state's contribution needs to be taken into account. Privately owned livestock are often supported by fodder from the state sector or collective farm. Indeed, while the monetary payments to *kolkhozniki* have increased substantially in the past quarter century, a not inconsiderable number of peasant households still choose to have part of the payment for their labour in kind. Fodder for their livestock is a frequent choice, if choice exists. Privately owned livestock also graze on state land, whether vested in the collective farm or not. And mention has already been made of the use of equipment to assist with the cultivation of the private plot. In irrigated areas, water is drawn for use on the personal plot free of charge. Notwithstanding such 'assistance', it is apparent that the yield from such a small share of the arable is extremely high. So, too, is the yield from privately owned livestock. It is this feature which supports the argument, increasingly vocal in the Gorbachev era of *glasnost'*, that more family farming needs to be encouraged.

The huge scale of the agricultural enterprise – *kolkhoz* as well as *sovkhoz* – militates against a close link between cultivator and the land. Over the years there have been experiments in which a small area of the *kolkhoz* or *sovkhoz* is turned over to a few men, or contract groups, to cultivate according to their estimation of which crop or crops would do best. Gorbachev sanctioned more of this type of activity in 1983, before taking over as Party Leader. Where such decentralized control has been linked to a share of the harvest, the results have been invariably the same – substantially higher yields than similar areas farmed by salaried *sovkhoz* employees, or regular collective farm labour brigades. In 1987 legislation was introduced which extended the concept of agricultural contracts embedded in the 1983 decree to families. The new legislation permits families to lease land for periods up to 15 years. As yet it is too early to assess the impact of such policies. The incentive of higher personal income combined with autonomy in decision-making is a latent but potentially powerful force in Soviet agriculture.

As the state continues to tinker and experiment with such innovations, daily life for the majority continues in much the same manner as always. The private plot and livestock remain a major focus of activity. However, the income from auxiliary farming has declined as a proportion of total peasant household income. Peasants are now not just paid more, but members of the *kolkhoz* are eligible for benefits such as state pensions. Up until the mid-1960s they had been excluded, the principal reason being that as they were 'owners' of a share of the collective farm's assets, the *kolkhoz* rather than the state should be responsible for their welfare. Thus, the private plot and livestock not only sustained families during the working life of household members, they were assumed by the state to be capable of supporting old-age pensioners as well. In the culture of villages everywhere the aged and infirm were the responsibility of family and neighbours.

With the advent of benefits such as state pensions, as but one instance of the modernization of the rural sector, sociological surveys suggest that something of the old values has been lost. The out-migration, the growing preoccupation with material well-being, the increasing stratification of income and wealth in the rural sector, all have been cited as reasons for the erosion of the solidarity which the harsh years of the past seemed to have forged. Whether such perceptions are correct or not, the reality of village life is in fact a greater reliance on the state. As will be discussed in detail in a later chapter, the fast rising rural household incomes have been spent in part on better equipping the family with consumer durables such as refrigerators, washing machines, television sets, and so on. Indeed, over the past two decades the difference in the ratio of such basic consumer durables per capita between the urban and rural sectors has declined dramatically and is now in some respects insignificant. But available statistics do not allow any analysis of the quality of consumer durables owned by rural households and there is some reason to assume that it is lower than those owned by urbanites. Moreover, service facilities are poorly developed everywhere, but are especially deficient in the countryside. Thus, ownership patterns may be broadly similar, actual usage may not be. There are now more privately owned automobiles, the ultimate consumer durable, in the countryside than in the city. The motorcycle, with or without side-car, is commonplace in all rural areas. Yet for all the signs of marked material progress it would be a mistake to paint too rosy a picture of rural life. In the Slavic realm, that is, the Russian, Ukrainian and Belorussian republics as well as in the Baltic, a vast number of people have been consigned to life in what are officially classified as 'futureless villages'. A growing abundance of consumer durables in the affected households is little compensation for the dearth of state services which accompanies such classification.

Soviet agriculture is managed by fewer than 50,000 collective and state farms, and the related personal auxiliary sector. But in the countryside there are in excess of 400,000 villages. The General Scheme for the System of Settlement described in an earlier chapter affirmed a long-standing policy objective of consolidating the rural population. At present some 350,000 villages have too few people to qualify as a district centre, which brings with it entitlement to state investment in services ranging from day-care facilities to cultural centres. For the 15 million inhabitants of the country's 'futureless villages' isolation, if not deprivation, is exacerbated by the exceedingly slow pace of actual consolidation of settlement. Without adequate state investment in new housing in the centre designated for development, relocation is impeded. Out of sheer frustration with existing conditions in the 'futureless villages', some people have moved of their own volition. Those left behind are further deprived as a result, since they are typically the aged, infirm or the less industrious.

Current problems and policy initiatives

While the agricultural labour force comprises a fifth of the total, its composition and geography pose problems for the future. As the young and ambitious males leave, especially, but by no means exclusively, in the Slavic and Baltic regions, the proportion of women in the rural labour force increases. Characteristically the female rural worker is less skilled than the male, and hence less productive. At present about two-thirds of the agricultural population is female. Given the proportion of the young and the old of the total rural population, those comprising the potential workforce are a smaller proportion than in the urban sector. But even so, it is not everywhere the case that there are too few hands for the work available. In the southern republics underemployment is rife. Indeed, the euphemism for the unemployed, the 'unengaged work-capable' population, has been estimated to be in the order of one-sixth to one-fifth of the potential labour force in the Turkmen and Kirgiz republics. As these are averages for the total republic population, the situation in the countryside where the problem really exists is in relative terms worse still. In the Uzbek republic the number of unemployed is conservatively pegged at one million. This huge surplus labour pool is part of the reason for the continuing intensive use of labour in the fields. For instance, about half of the cotton harvested in the Soviet Union is still picked by hand. It is also the reason for the disproportionate importance of personal auxiliary farming in rural Middle Asia. Even with the inevitable increase in rural–urban migration which the worsening population–land resource ratio will produce, there is a major challenge ahead in terms of making 'socially productive' use of this labour reserve. The diversion of north-flowing Siberian rivers, the SIBARAL project, was very much regarded as a solution to the underemployment, indeed, unemployment, problem of rural Middle Asia. Its cancellation, and hence the demise of any real prospect for substantial expansion of irrigation, will demand other more drastic solutions. One receiving renewed attention is resettlement of rural Middle Asians in labour deficient parts of the Russian republic. To date, however, such resettlement programmes as have been undertaken have had few volunteers. Owing to the growing problems of desertification and secondary salinization in Middle Asia, there has been some resettlement, but typically to other parts of the region. The advantages to the state of resettlement outside Middle Asia are numerous. Not only would the additional labour be welcome, but the process of assimilating mainstream Soviet values would be facilitated. However, there are other ways of approaching the problem, and these are likely to be more favourably received by the indigenous population.

The mis-use of water resources in Middle Asia is widely acknowledged and documented. Immediately following the cancellation of the SIBARAL project charges for irrigation water were introduced on an experimental basis in the Tadzhik and Kirgiz republics. Consumption was halved without adversely affecting production. Indeed, it is entirely possible that greater economy of water in irrigation projects will not only enable the impending acute water deficit to be mitigated, or even postponed, but the annual loss of existing irrigated land to salinization could be reduced as well. Conventional wisdom has it that for every hectare added to the area irrigated one is lost, principally to secondary salinization brought about by overconsumption. If this is anything like representative of the actual situation, the cost of achieving the expansion of irrigated land outlined in Table 13 must have been colossal. The return on the investment may well be considerably less than 2 per cent according to some observers. As the data in the table reveal, the Middle Asian republics still account for the largest proportion of the irrigated land in the country, but since 1965, when the decision to embark on a vast expansion programme was made, the most dramatic change has been in the RSFSR. In the last two decades this republic has almost doubled its share of the irrigated area. The problem of keeping land in production is perhaps highlighted by the situation in Azerbaydzhan. Between 1965 and 1975 more than a tenth of the total area was removed from production. Given the cancellation of

Table 13: Changes in irrigated land, 1965–1985

REGION	1965 000 hectares		per cent	1975 000 hectares		per cent	1985 000 hectares		per cent
MIDDLE ASIA	5,850		59.6	6,950		48.0	8,871		44.5
Uzbek		2,752			3,006			3,930	
Kazakh		1,255			1,648			2,172	
Kirgiz		861			910			1,009	
Tadzhik		468			567			653	
Turkmen		514			819			1,107	
RSFSR	1,510		15.4	3,684		25.4	5,805		29.1
UKRAINE	503		5.1	1,483		10.2	2,456		12.3
AZERBAYDZHAN	1,278		13.1	1,141		7.9	1,318		6.6
OTHERS	671		6.8	1,228		8.5	1,501		7.5
TOTAL SOVIET	9,812		100.0	14,486		100.0	19,951		100.0

Source: *Narodnoye Khozyaystvo SSSR v 1965g* (Moscow: Finansy i Statistika, 1966), 363; *Narodnoye Khozyaystvo SSSR v 1985g* (Moscow: Finansy i Statistika, 1986), 228.

the SIBARAL scheme there will simply have to be more economic, and rational, use of existing water resources. Agriculture is not the only culprit in terms of over-consumption of a scarce resource in Middle Asia, but it is certainly the key one. It is not beyond the realm of possibility that further expansion of the irrigated area could occur in Middle Asia without the SIBARAL project. But it is doubtful that the scale of what it is possible to achieve through better management of existing water resources would materially affect the existing unemployment problem, let alone mitigate what the near future portends. Other strategies will have to be found. Further development of agricultural industries is certainly one of them.

The growth of jobs in factories located in the countryside has been rapid during the past quarter century. On collective farms alone some 17,000 industrial operations occupied nearly three-quarters of a million *kolkhozniki* in 1980. Outside the *kolkhoz* there are obviously other opportunities. To be sure, most of the development of rural industry to date is concentrated in European Russia in the shadow of the major urban industrial agglomerations. But as labour is everywhere in European Russia in short supply, the attraction of rural locations in Middle Asia for certain types of industry is increasingly compelling. Recent developments in agricultural policy may well encourage more by way of rural industrialization in Middle Asia.

In 1982 Brezhnev announced a new Food Programme, a broad policy framework for guiding the development of agriculture until 1990. Interestingly, Mikhail Gorbachev played a major role in its formulation. Gorbachev was the Politburo member responsible for agriculture from 1978 to 1985, scarcely an auspicious period in terms of production. The Food Programme was to a large degree 'old wine in old bottles', that is, there was little fundamentally new that was being called for. The countryside required 'restructuring'. By that was meant the existing level of ser-vices, from roads to cultural facilities, was too low. More investment was needed in order to remove the difference between town and country, the age-old Marxist preoccupation. By so raising the quality of life in the countryside, it is expected that peasants will work harder and produce more. This may well prove to be an illusory response. The Programme fosters more widespread use of various kinds of financial incentive. One of the key elements in this entails putting much more of the rural economy – farming and farm related manufacturing enterprises – on an accounting system that would demand profitable operations. As it is, many *kolkhozy* and *sovkhozy* operate continuously in the red, while still managing to pay the workers and management bonuses. Much effort is spent in devising ways to tap the state's vast array of funding sources, without delivering to the state commodities of equivalent value. Put simply, unprofitable operations are propped up by the state by subsidies of one kind or another, a sizeable cost in addition to the huge retail price subsidy programme discussed earlier. Part of the programme which bears on the pool of reserve labour in rural Middle Asia involves further development of agriculture-related industry in the countryside. Each Middle Asian republic was instructed to expand those branches of industry which process agricultural output. Logically such jobs in processing plants belong in the rural areas where there are both the raw materials and available labour. Taking jobs to the Middle Asian countryside has been a long-standing strategy, one which is likely to receive a fillip now that the planned expansion of irrigated land called for in the Food Programme of 1982 has been effectively scuttled with the SIBARAL cancellation. The problem of surplus labour in rural Middle Asia still awaits some kind of major policy response however.

The dilemma confronting the current Soviet leadership is clearly multi-faceted. There are environmental limits to the area that can be cultivated. Massive programmes to transform the environment in the attempt to remedy this seem once again to be on the back-burner. Aside from calling for more efficient use of existing land, labour and capital, the present policies, including the 1982 Food Programme, do not suggest much improvement beyond what next year's weather might bring. Personal auxiliary and contract farming is being encouraged on the one hand, while on the other hand, the size of income from it has come under closer scrutiny. In some regions bureaucrats have prohibited privately produced agricultural commodities from being transported across district boundaries. Moreover, in the absence of adequate means to transport goods to market, the traditional response of the peasantry has been to bribe underpaid truck drivers to haul sought-after agricultural commodities from countryside to city. Now such illegal movement of goods is being clamped down upon in the campaign to ensure that more people in all occupations take home only legally earned income. The result, as usual, is predictable. Those urbanites who want a better, more balanced, diet and are prepared to pay the going price in the collective farmers market to get the desired foodstuffs are in some cities finding that the flow of commodities has been interrupted. While these are perhaps small matters in light of the size of the agricultural problem as measured by the level of investment, scale of subsidy, or the huge expenditure on imported grain and meat, they nonetheless underscore the fact that very little can be changed without some type of feedback coming into play.

To date the Gorbachev-era initiatives have been far from radical in implementation. Calls for greater incentive in agriculture usually require a greater tolerance of individualism, acceptance of greater disparity in the size of personal income, and acceptance of the possibility of a rural population materially better off than the urban. There is clearly considerable risk in unleashing the entrepreneurial talents which undoubtedly exist in the Soviet countryside. It has often been contended by western observers that a greater reliance on private initiative, rather than state control, in agriculture would largely solve the current problems in food production. But to accommodate that would require change throughout the entire Soviet economic system. As yet the first state to embrace socialist principles has taken only a few short steps in that direction. The final irony is that after decades of the agricultural sector being exploited to support industrialization, the industrial sector is now obliged to pay the bill for the shortfall in agricultural production. There is still some way to go in reforming the management of agriculture and making better use of the agricultural resource base.

Recommended reading

Belov, F., *The History of a Soviet Collective Farm* (New York: Praeger, 1955).
Borders, K., *Village Life Under the Soviets* (Plainview, New York: Books for Libraries, 1976).

Brada, J., Wadekin, K.E., (eds), *Socialist Agriculture in Transition: Organizational Response to Failing Performance* (Boulder: Westview Press, 1987).

Bridger, S., *Women in the Soviet Countryside* (Cambridge: Cambridge University Press, 1987).

Conquest, R., *The Harvest of Sorrow: Soviet Collectivization and the Terror-Famine* (New York: Oxford University Press, 1986).

Danilov, V., *Rural Russia Under the New Regime* (London: Hutchinson, 1988).

Hedlund, S., *The Crisis in Soviet Agriculture* (London: Croom Helm, 1984).

Humphrey, C., *The Karl Marx Collective: Economy, Society and Religion in a Siberian Collective Farm* (Cambridge: Cambridge Univeristy Press, 1983).

Johnson, G., McConnell, K., *Prospects for Soviet Agriculture in the 1980s* (Bloomington: Indiana University Press, 1983).

Joravsky, D., *The Lysenko Affair* (Cambridge, Mass: Harvard University Press, 1970).

Lewin, M., *Russian Peasants and Soviet Power* (London: George Allen and Unwin, 1963).

Litvin, V., *The Soviet Agro-Industrial Complex, Structure and Performance* (Boulder: Westview Press, 1987).

McAuley, M., *Khrushchev and the Development of Soviet Agriculture. The Virgin Land Programme 1953–1964* (London: Macmillan, 1976).

Millar, J. (ed), *The Soviet Rural Community* (Champaign: University of Illinois Press, 1971).

Reston, R., *Aftermath to Revolution: The Soviet Collective Farm* (London: Collier Macmillan, 1975).

Shaffer, H.G. (ed), *Soviet Agriculture: An Assessment of its Contributions to Economic Development* (New York: Praeger, 1971).

Stuart, R.C. (ed), *The Soviet Rural Economy* (Totowa, New Jersey: Rowman and Allanheld, 1984).

Symons, L., *Russian Agriculture: A Geographic Survey* (London: Bell and Sons, 1972).

8 Energy Resources – The Geography of Supply and Demand

Communism is Soviet power plus the electrification of the whole country.

Lenin, 1920.[1]

The importance of energy to the modern industrial economy was apparent to the Soviet leadership from the very beginning. Great emphasis was placed upon expanding production of all forms of energy, renewable and non-renewable. To that end the energy sector commanded a substantial share of the investment capital in each plan period. Such an objective was facilitated by the fact that within the country's borders were to be found the world's greatest fossil fuel and water power resource potentials. By the mid-1980s Soviet production of oil, coal and natural gas ranked first in the world. In terms of both production and consumption of all forms of energy the Soviet Union ranks second to the United States. In recent years energy exports have also grown rapidly, and not just to the traditional East European market. The oil crisis of the early 1970s precipitated by the Organization of Petroleum Exporting Countries (OPEC) resulted in a rapid escalation in the price of oil on the world market. In order to reap some benefit from this situation draconian measures were introduced to expand Soviet oil production to facilitate exports. Proven reserves were run down faster than newly discovered deposits were brought on stream. By the mid-1970s some observers were suggesting that the Soviet Union itself would experience an oil shortage by the mid-1980s. While such pessimistic forecasts have not proven correct, the fact is that production flattened, and indeed dropped slightly in absolute terms in the early 1980s, before increasing again in 1986 and 1987. The Soviet Union remains the third most important oil exporting country. But with the depressed world oil prices which the 1980s ushered in following the collapse of the OPEC cartel it now has to export even more to maintain export

---

[1] V.I. Lenin as quoted in D.G. Zhimerin, *Istoriya Elektrifikatsii SSSR* (Moscow: Izdatel'stvo Sotsial'no–Ekonomicheskoy Literatury, 1962), 3.

earnings. Such external forces have had an impact on energy resource development strategies within the Soviet Union. As in managing the land for agricultural production, greater efficiency in developing energy resources is being demanded by the Party. The problems confronting energy sector planners are complex to be sure, but they are made even more so by the geography of Soviet energy. Put simply, as the more accessible reserves of non-renewable fossil fuels and renewable sources of energy are consumed or developed, the fundamental imbalance between resource location and the market is exaggerated. This basic fact of geography will be a common theme in the ensuing discussion of the various components of the Soviet energy scene.

We will begin our examination of energy resource development and management by briefly describing general production trends in both the renewable and non-renewable sectors. The first topic to be considered is electric power production; the second, the contribution of fossil fuels to the energy balance of the Soviet Union. This will be followed by an assessment of the supply of, and demand for, the key energy resources – coal, oil and natural gas.

Electric power

While electrification is of obvious importance in all industrializing countries, in the Soviet Union the heavy emphasis on it in large measure has been the result of Lenin's integration of the electrification concept with his scientific theory for the formation of a socialist state. The first major regional planning initiative, the State Commission for the Electrification of Russia (GOELRO), was introduced in 1920 in order to facilitate the restoration and reconstruction of the country's industrial infrastructure. Electric power grids served as the planning regions. Within and between each of them increased generation of electric power and the interconnection of the installed generating capacity were seen as essential steps in the industrialization process. As noted in an earlier chapter, hydroelectric power development was accorded considerable publicity since it was often held up an as example of socialist man's ability to transform or conquer nature. Despite the pre-eminent position of the hydraulic engineering project in the public mind during the GOELRO and later the Five Year Plan, era, electricity generated by thermal plants predominated from the outset (Table 14). In fact, the GOELRO scheme fostered the use of any and all local fossil fuel resources within each planning region. Thus, coal, oil, shale, peat and even wood on occasion were consumed in the rapidly expanding network of small thermal power stations. Larger-scale heat and power thermal stations were developed as part of the overall electrification programme after 1931. In these plants the heat produced in the process of generating electricity was converted into steam and fed into extensive urban heating networks. In this manner an otherwise wasted by-product helped to heat factory and new apartment house alike. Heat and power thermal stations now play an important role in the Soviet city, accounting for about half of the total urban heat supply, as well as generating a substantial share of total electricity. The most commonly used fuel in such plants is the comparatively clean-burning natural gas.

As Table 14 indicates hydroelectric power stations presently account for about a fifth of total installed generating capacity, and around 14 per cent of the electricity generated from all sources, a fairly consistent pattern over the past three decades. It is

Table 14: Installed generating capacity and electricity production, 1913–1986

	Total	Hydro	%	Nuclear	%	Total	Hydro	%	Nuclear	%
	Installed capacity (000 mw)*					Electricity generated (billion kwhs)**				
1913	1.1	.02	<1	–	–	2.0	.04	<1	–	–
1928	1.9	.12	6.3	–	–	5.0	.4	8.0	–	–
1940	11.2	1.6	14.3	–	–	48.6	5.2	10.7	–	–
1950	19.6	3.2	16.3	–	–	91.2	12.7	13.9	–	–
1960	66.7	14.8	22.2	N/A	–	292.0	50.9	17.4	N/A	–
1970	166.0	31.4	18.9	.9	.5	741.0	124.0	16.7	3.5	.5
1975	217.0	40.5	18.7	4.7	2.2	1,039.0	126,0	12.1	20.2	1.9
1980	267.0	52.3	19.6	12.5	4.7	1,294.0	184.0	14.2	73.0	5.6
1985	315.0	61.7	19.6	28.1	8.9	1,544.0	215.0	13.9	167.0	10.8
1986	322.0	62.1	19.3	30.1	9.4	1,599.0	216.0	13.5	161.0	10.1

Source: Narodnoye Khozyaystvo SSSR v 1958g (Moscow: Finansy i Statistika, 1959), 215; *Narodnoye Khozyaystvo SSSR v 1985g* (Moscow: Finansy i Statistika, 1986), 155; *Narodnoye Khozyaystvo SSSR za 70 Let* (Moscow: Finansy i Statistika, 1987, 161.

*mw – megawatts
** kwh – kilowatt hours

readily apparent from Fig. 38 that there has been a steady shift toward the eastern regions since the 1930s. Up until the mid-1950s development had been concentrated in European Russia and the Caucasus. The largest projects were on the Volga river and were ostensibly built for more than just the generation of electricity. Improved navigation, flood control, expanded irrigation and fishing were all presumed to be as important as the electricity generated. In practice, however, the management of water levels by hydrostation engineers was often geared to the maximization of electricity produced, to the cost of other users. As was noted in Chapter 6, the influence of the hydroelectric power group was still strong in the 1950s, the counter-vailing environmental lobby having gained momentum and influence only in the late 1960s. The trend toward investment in ever larger-scale hydropower projects was given a fillip with the decision in the 1950s to tap the huge water power potential of the Angara and Yenisey rivers in central Siberia. The lure was the prospect of getting large blocks of hydroelectricity at very low cost per kilowatt-hour. Favourable river regimes, ideal site characteristics for dam construction, and technical innovations in plant design and in the transmission of electric power over long distances have all helped to bring about the changes in distribution depicted in Fig. 38.

The prime function of the large-scale Siberian plants was to provide power to meet the base rather than peak load demand of the regional electric grid system. This was possible because of the unusually regular flow of the Angara and Yenisey rivers. The Angara is especially notable in this regard for there is hardly any seasonable variation in the regime owing to the fact that it is the only outlet for Lake Baykal. While small in surface area, Lake Baykal is very deep: indeed, it contains the largest volume of water of any lake in the world. The combination of a large, regular flow, steep gradient and ideal geological conditions for dam construction permitted the design of hydropower stations which could generate sufficient electricity on a regular basis to

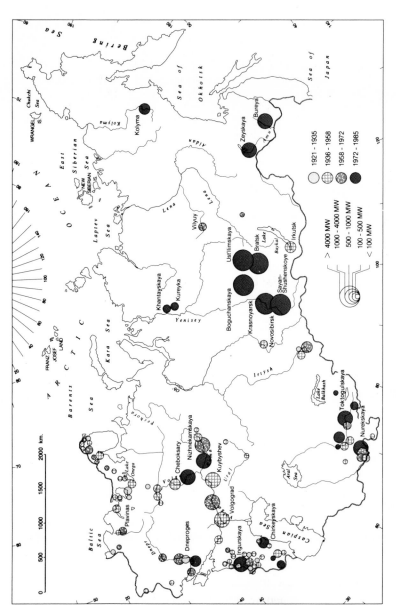

Fig. 38 Hydroelectric Power Development

Source: James H. Bater, 'The Development of Hydropower in the Soviet Union', *Water Power*, June 1974, 216; Leslie Dienes, Theodore Shabad, *The Soviet Energy System: Resource Use and Policies* (New York: John Wiley, 1979). 135.

satisfy the requirements of industry. On most rivers the pronounced seasonal variations in flow make it problematic for hydropower stations to serve the industrial
market, that is, to meet regular, daily base-load demand for electricity. Instead,
hydropower stations are usually designed to meet part of the base load when ample
water is available and to cover the peak load at other times. Because of the storage
capacity of reservoirs and the near instantaneous production of hydroelectricity,
hydropower stations can more easily meet peak daily demand for electricity than
thermal power stations which frequently take a few hours to 'come on stream.'
Thus, around dinner time when urban-industrial electricity requirements commonly
'peak', hydroelectricity is generated to meet the demand. The fact that hydropower
stations stand idle a good part of the time is the reason why they account for about
one-fifth of the total installed generating capacity, but only 14 per cent of total
electricity generated (Table 14).

Because the large-scale Siberian hydropower stations portrayed in Fig. 38 were
built to meet base rather than peak load demand in the regional power system, and
therefore operate on a regular basis throughout the year, substantial economies were
achieved. Proponents of these projects contended that the prime cost of electricity
from them was less than one tenth the average cost of thermally generated electricity.
The peculiarities of Soviet prices, the absence of a proper accounting of costs for
reservoir preparation, infrastructure and so on, ensured that the projects appeared
economically attractive. But the huge blocks of cheap electricity generated required
markets. The water power potential of Siberia would have remained untapped had
there not been a willingness to invest heavily in associated energy-intensive industrial
complexes, new towns and transportation systems. Hydropower developments in
both Siberia, and later in Middle Asia, therefore became the catalysts in major
regional economic development schemes, the nature of which will be explored in the
ensuing chapter. Were it not for the huge hydroelectric power stations in central
Siberia, which together account for about one-third of all hydro generating capacity
in the country, and which because of their base-load function in the regional power
system represent an even larger share of the total hydroelectricity generated, the
role of water power in the electric energy scene as a whole would be decidedly
minor.

The notion of generating electricity from a renewable source of energy as opposed
to those of finite quantity such as fossil fuels is obviously appealing. Over the years
the Soviets have experimented with solar, tidal, geothermal and wind generation of
electricity. As yet they remain of local significance only, but given the very high level
of integration of regional power systems, these less easily manipulated sources of
electricity can contribute quite effectively to overall demand. Because the country
spans eleven time zones, it is technically possible to shunt 'surplus' electricity from
east to west as the peak demand changes geographically. While eminently flexible,
energy in the form of electricity cannot be 'stockpiled' like coal or oil to be used later.
The integration of the European Russian power grid with that of Eastern Europe
and Finland provides even more scope for making most efficient use of electric
power, for it is 'exported' in substantial amount. Given the small potential contribution to total electricity supply from other renewable energy sources, water power
will remain the principal non-thermal source. While conventional fossil fuels like

coal, oil and natural gas predominate in the generation of electricity in thermal power stations, the role of nuclear power stations in electricity production deserves comment at this juncture.

As recently as 1970 the role of nuclear electricity was quite insignificant. It accounted for a mere 0.5 per cent of all electricity generated. But since that date the rate of expansion of nuclear power generating facilities has outstripped that of conventional fossil fuel based thermal stations and hydroelectric plants. By 1986, 10.1 per cent of all electricity generated came from nuclear stations. As Table 14 indicates, total electricity production nearly doubled between 1970 and 1986 and against this background the gain registered by nuclear power is even more impressive. The attractions of nuclear electricity are numerous. Uranium, the basic nuclear fuel, is available in sufficient quantities, it appears, to sustain further large-scale development of nuclear power. Mining of uranium is concentrated in Middle Asia though deposits are found throughout the country. Technology is advanced and involves breeder, fusion, as well as controlled thermonuclear fusion reactors. The breeder reactors afford the possibility of producing more fissionable materials than they consume, thus in terms of conservation of non-renewable energy resources are viewed as a positive technological innovation.

Given the portability of the basic raw materials nuclear plants can be located near the market thereby reducing the loss of electricity inevitably associated with long-distance, high-voltage transmission. Save for the need for an adequate water supply for cooling purposes, there are few locational constraints on where a plant can be constructed. For these reasons as well as the fact that in the pre-Chernobyl' period nuclear power stations were officially proclaimed to be a safe technology, they were most often sited close to the major urban-industrial centres within energy deficient European Russia. The geography of nuclear power stations presented by Fig. 39 obviously stands in stark contrast to that of hydroelectric power development depicted in Fig. 38. Official regulations dictated the specific site requirements such as soil and geologic conditions, prevailing winds, and proximity of suitable land for disposal of radioactive wastes. While most plants are at least 40 kilometres from a major city, housing facilities for power station personnel were customarily within easy reach. On balance, the guidelines controlling location relative to major urban centres were less than precise.

In view of the locational flexibility of nuclear power the high priority attached to its development since 1970 is understandable. The alternative uses of fossil fuels such as oil and natural gas, the high cost of developing ever more remote hydropower sites, all lent credibility to the decision to expand electricity production from nuclear power stations. Notwithstanding the environmental disaster produced by the meltdown at the huge nuclear installation at Chernobyl' north of Kiev in the Ukraine in the spring of 1986 (Fig. 39), the rationale for continued expansion of nuclear electricity production remains as compelling now as before. In Chapter 10 we will examine the environmental and public health consequences of the Chernobyl' disaster, but at this point we need only note that the technology involved has not been officially condemned. Indeed, the disaster has been attributed to errors in management of the facility and those responsible have been dealt with in the courts. Electricity production was quickly resumed at Chernobyl' and a separate

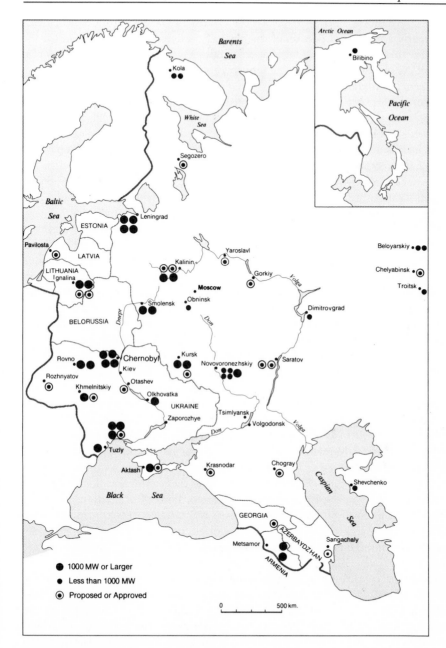

Fig. 39 Nuclear Power Development

Source: Leslie Symons *et al., The Soviet Union: A Systematic Geography* (Totowa, NJ: Barnes & Noble, 1983), 149.

Ministry of Nuclear Energy has now been created to manage future development. Apparently a substantial portion of the power generated at Chernobyl', and at the Ukraine's many other nuclear installations, finds its way into the East European grid system. As most of these countries are energy resource deficient, there were active development programmes under way to expand nuclear power. In the aftermath of Chernobyl' there has been a decided dampening of enthusiasm in Eastern Europe for nuclear energy. The need for electric power, however, has not diminished. It is somewhat ironic that since the Soviet Union intends to continue nuclear development, increasing by five to six times the current level of electricity production by the turn of the century, Eastern Europe probably will be using more rather than less Soviet nuclear electricity. The only difference will be that it will come from Soviet reactors located principally in the Baltic region and the Ukraine – and at a price. The hazard of nuclear fall-out does not stop at the Soviet border, of course.

The combined output from nuclear and hydroelectric power stations comprised about one-quarter of the total Soviet electricity supply in 1986. As the data in Table 14 indicate, fossil fuels have always been the mainstay of electricity production and will continue to be so in the foreseeable future. However, the current mix of fossil fuels consumed in thermal power stations is far from ideal, and is therefore scheduled to change. Unlike the United States where coal has long been, and remains, the dominant fuel for the generation of electricity, the role of coal in the USSR declined sharply between 1960 and 1975. At the former date coal comprised about 70 per cent of the fuel supply for power plants, using standard calorific equivalents as the basis for measurement.[1] By the mid-1980s coal's share was less than one-half. This was an improvement over the situation in 1975, however, when its share was just a shade more than two-fifths. The fuel mix for power stations is considered to be less than ideal because of the sizeable opportunity costs involved when natural gas and oil replace coal. The first two sources of energy can and do command a premium price in the export market. Moreover, as we shall see shortly, the Soviet Union has the world's largest coal reserves. Thus, the current strategy envisions a vast expansion of large-scale, coal-fired thermal generating stations at the resource locations, which are principally in Siberia, the Far East and Kazakhstan. Power from stations fuelled by low-cost, strip-mined coal would be fed into the national electric grid system to supply distant markets. Even with the loss of electricity entailed in long-distance transmission and the risk of acid-rain, the perceived benefits are assumed to exceed the costs.

Across the country there are significant regional variations in the fuel mix of thermal power stations. In European Russia local coal production has long been insufficient to meet the demand for electricity. Hence oil and natural gas are the dominant fuels. While each accounts for a shade more than a quarter of the fuel consumed by all thermal power plants within the Soviet Union, together they meet nearly two-thirds of the fuel demand of European Russia's thermal stations. Increasingly both oil and natural gas must be 'imported' from Siberia because the reserves in European Russia are shrinking.

---

[1] Soviet practice reduces all energy sources to tons of standard fuel equivalent, where one ton of fuel equivalent equals seven million kilocalories or 27.8 million BTUs.

In Siberia coal has been and will remain the principal fuel for thermal electric power stations. Natural gas is used for this purpose in Middle Asia, but there too coal is the pre-eminent fuel. It is likely that natural gas will maintain its relative position as an energy source for thermal power stations in all regions not so much because of a concern for cleaner air, which is one of the side-benefits of its use compared to coal or oil, but rather because of its comparatively abundant reserves relative to petroleum. Together peat and oil shale represent less than 4 per cent of the fuel consumed by all thermal power stations, again using conventional calorific equivalents as a basis for measurement. However, as these fuels are found mostly in the increasingly energy-deficient western part of the European Russian region, their local importance in contributing to electricity production is much greater than their share of the fuel mix might suggest.

Thermal electric power stations are thus a major market for Soviet fossil fuel production. About one-third of all energy consumed by the Soviet economy is converted into electricity at thermal power stations. Obviously, efficiency in using energy for this purpose is a major concern. And as indicated earlier, so too is achieving an optimum mix of fuels. Exporting more petroleum and burning less of it generating electricity is a quite logical strategy for the Soviet Union to pursue. For the time being at least, the low level of private automobile ownership gives the Soviet Union more flexibility in managing domestic petroleum supplies than is the case in the United States for instance. In the mid-1970s about one-fifth of all fuel consumed by US thermal power stations was derived from petroleum, a smaller share than in the Soviet Union, but one which had been similarly steadily edging upward during the post-war period. To be sure, in the United States there is a greater profit to be had selling gasoline at the pump than selling oil to electric power utilities. The continuing emphasis in the United States on coal-fired thermal generation of electricity is thus understandable, if not very sensible given the costs exacted by acid-rain throughout much of the mid-west and north-east regions to say nothing of the trans-boundary effect in Canada.

In summary, electricity has long been the hallmark of a modern industrial economy. In the Soviet Union production has increased at a frenetic rate and is intimately linked to the modernization of the economic system as a whole. At present about three-quarters of electricity production is obtained by burning fossil fuels of one kind or another. The balance of production comes principally from nuclear and hydro-power, with a tiny contribution from other renewable energy sources. But this is only part of the Soviet energy scene. Viewed differently, the electricity generated by hydro and other renewable energy projects, such as solar or tidal power installations, represents barely 3 per cent of the total energy balance, again using the standard calorific equivalents for each energy type as a basis for measurement. At this point we need to examine the most important component of the Soviet energy balance, the production of conventional fossil fuels.

The fuel balance

On the eve of the revolution the fuel balance of the Russian Empire belied its industrial backwardness. Although wood was still an important fuel, it is the role of

Table 15: Fuel balance; million tons of fuel equivalent (MT)*

	Total M.T.	Coal M.T.	%	Oil M.T.	%	Natural gas M.T.	%	Peat M.T.	%	Oil shale M.T.	%	Wood M.T.	%
1913	45.9	23.1	50.3	13.2	28.8	–	–	.7	1.5	–	–	8.9	19.4
1940	237.7	140.5	59.1	44.5	18.7	4.4	1.9	13.6	5.7	.6	.3	34.1	14.3
1950	311.2	205.7	66.1	54.2	17.4	7.3	2.3	14.8	4.8	1.3	.4	27.9	9.0
1953	384.2	252.3	65.7	75.5	19.6	8.7	2.3	15.8	4.1	2.1	.5	29.8	7.8
1965	969.0	451.9	42.9	347.3	35.9	151.3	15.6	17.0	1.7	7.5	.8	30.0	3.1
1970	1,221.8	432.7	35.4	502.5	41.1	233.5	19.1	17.7	1.5	8.8	.7	26.6	2.2
1975	1,571.3	471.8	30.0	701.9	44.7	342.9	21.8	18.5	1.2	10.8	.7	25.4	1.6
1980	1,905.7	484.4	25.4	862.6	45.3	515.7	27.1	7.3	.4	11.9	.6	23.8	1.2
1985	2,137.3	486.9	22.8	851.3	39.8	759.9	35.5	5.5	.3	10.2	.5	23.5	1.1
1986	2,165.7	454.8	21.0	879.1	40.6	792.7	36.6	6.6	.3	9.6	.4	22.9	1.1
1987	2,194.0	450.3	20.5	882.3	40.2	882.7	37.5	8.1	.4	9.5	.4	21.1	1.0

Source: Narodnoye Khozyaystvo SSSR v 1958g (Moscow: Finansy i Statistika, 1959), 200; Narodnoye Khozyaystvo SSSR v 1965g (Moscow: Finansy i Statistika, 1966), 174; Narodnoye Khozyaystvo SSSR v 1980g (Moscow: Finansy i Statistika, 1981), 156; Narodnoye Khozyaystvo SSSR v 1985g (Moscow: Finansy i Statistika, 1986), 157; Narodnoye Khozyaystvo SSSR za 70 Let (Moscow: Finansy i Statistika, 1987), 163.

* A ton of standard fuel is equal to seven million kilocalories or 27.8 million BTUs.

oil which stands out in Table 15. As was noted in Chapter 2, at the turn of the century Russia was one of the world's principal oil producing and exporting countries. Exploitation of the oil deposits around Baku had brought profits to foreign entrepreneurs, taxes to the state treasury and harsh working conditions for those who toiled in the oil fields. The importance of oil in the national fuel balance hinted at modernity, but this was more likely to be found in the industrializing states of Europe which were the principal export markets than in Russia itself. Within the Empire coal and wood held sway as fuels, as they would for decades to come.

During the early Soviet period the industrialization drive was based on the proven, extensive, and accessible reserves of solid fuels such as coal, peat and wood. With the onset of the Stalin-era Five Year Plans and forced industrial growth, coal production in particular was singled out as the critical component in the development process. Each year invariably brought higher output targets, and higher costs of production in the country's predominantly pit-mining operations. The GOELRO plan of the 1920s had fostered the use of all local energy resources, but these were often of low calorific value, difficult to handle and bulky to transport. As the production of lower grades of coal increased in importance, as the extraction of peat expanded, as the use of wood as a fuel continued to be quite important, the burden on the transportation system increased. From the late 1920s to the mid-1950s the fuel balance became even more dependent upon these fuels, as well as oil shale (Table 15). The result of the vast expansion in production of low calorific value coals, peat and shale was scarcely any improvement in the average heat value per ton of fuel produced from 1928 to 1955. In other industrialized states oil and natural gas were of growing importance. With a higher calorific value than those fuels dominating Soviet production, they were providing many economies in extraction and transportation, to say nothing of their diversified range of chemical by-products. Whether because of rigidities in the decision-making environment, a lack of investment capital, or simple inertia, the Stalin-era fixation with solid fuel production was costly. In 1953, the year Stalin died, the fuel balance was dominated by coal. In terms of tons of fuel equivalent it accounted for 65.7 per cent of the total. Compared to 1913 oil had declined in relative importance from 28.8 per cent to 19.6, a slight improvement over 1950 when it dropped to 17.4 per cent. Peat, on the other hand, had tripled its share of the fuel balance by 1950, and still represented over 4 per cent in 1953. Unlike virtually every other industrialized country, wood still figured prominently in the fuel balance at the end of the Stalin era. To be sure, the Soviet Union was industrializing, indeed modernizing, quickly. During the 1950s the economy was expanding at a singularly rapid rate. But it was growth generated by particular sectors, and often at the cost of others, as we have noted in the case of agriculture. It was also a tempo of growth dependent upon a narrowly defined range of inputs. The fuel balance in 1953 is a case in point.

Stalin's death brought a reassessment of many engrained features of the Soviet system. The heavy reliance on solid fuels was one of them. The decision was taken to diversify the fuel balance, to enhance the role of oil and especially natural gas. The outcome of this reassessment is readily apparent from the data presented in Table 15. Between 1953 and 1965 the combined share of oil and natural gas eclipsed coal, although production of the latter had by no means waned. Coal output in actual tons, as distinct from tons of fuel equivalent used in Table 15, rose from 320 million in 1953 to 578 in 1965. But without the contribution of oil and natural gas the sizeable gain registered in the total amount of fuel from all sources, as measured in tons of fuel equivalent (Table 15), would not have been possible. The basis for this expansion was laid in large part during the Second World War when the German invasion threatened the vital and vulnerable oil fields in the Baku region. A crash programme of geological exploration in more secure regions of the country uncovered new reserves of hydrocarbons, and oil and gas in particular. The Volga–Ural oil fields, first discovered in the late 1920s, were to prove of critical importance both during the war and after when production in the Baku fields began to decline. They also comprised a major part of the resource-base inventory for the decision taken after Stalin's death to diversify the fuel balance. As we shall see shortly, production from this region was soon to be eclipsed by that of West Siberia. Natural gas, which often was flared off and thus wasted when found in association with oil deposits, became a significant component of the strategy to modernize the fuel balance. The change in its share between 1953 and 1965 was perhaps the most dramatic consequence of the new Soviet energy policy. As Table 15 indicates, it has continued to grow in importance. Between 1965 and 1985 the full repercussions of the decision to change the structure of the fuel balance become apparent.

The long-standing domination of the fuel balance by coal ended in 1962, and by 1965 it accounted for scarcely two-fifths of total production. Twenty years later its share had been reduced to little more than one-fifth, despite an overall increase in production from 578 to 726 million, 'actual' not fuel equivalent, tons. However, in no sense is coal relegated to a minor position in the overall energy scene. Given the preoccupation with exporting more oil, which followed the OPEC manipulation of world prices after 1973, and more recent concerns expressed by Soviet planners over the volume of domestic oil production, the decision was taken in the 1970s to replace oil with coal wherever possible, but notably in the generation of electricity. Thus, it is to be expected that the share of coal in the fuel balance will at least stabilize, if not increase slightly. After steadily garnering a larger share of the fuel balance until 1978, when it peaked at 45.7 per cent, the relative importance of oil has since waned. Thus far, natural gas production has continued to register substantial increases one year to the next, and will continue to do so in the short term. The remaining solid fuels – peat, shale and wood – while still of some significance in the western flank of the energy-deficient European Russian region are now quite unimportant nationally. Oil shale and wood production levels have been fairly stable since 1970, whereas peat production has declined rather substantially.

At the national level the Soviet fuel balance will be characterized by the following trends for the foreseeable future. Firstly, the reliance on natural gas will increase and at the current rate of expansion could conceivably dominate the fuel balance before the turn of the century. Given the scale of reserves, the decision to place more reliance on coal production is certainly understandable, and this will be reflected in its share of the fuel balance in due course. Clearly, to substitute coal for oil at existing thermal-fired power stations is neither straightforward technically nor logistically. And to bring new coal-fired thermal power stations on stream cannot be accomplished overnight either. Oil production will be expanded if at all possible, but the rate at which net gains can be achieved is likely to be rather lower than that of natural gas or even coal for the simple reason that the proven reserve situation is not nearly as auspicious. As for the other solid fuels listed in Table 15, further erosion of their aggregate position can be expected.

The policies which have been adopted in the post World War II period have had a profound impact on the geography of energy. At this point it would be appropriate to turn to a more detailed assessment of the nature of supply and demand for the three principal components of the fuel balance, coal, oil and natural gas.

Coal

The renewed interest in coal as a source of energy reflects in large measure the opportunity costs associated with the ways in which domestic oil production was being used. But it also reflects changes which have occurred in the mining of coal. Although oil and natural gas are still the preferred fuels from the standpoint of ease of transport, calorific value, and comparative cleanliness when burned, the shift to more strip-mining of coal, the modernization of some pit mines and the closing of other inefficient and expensive pit operations have all combined to make coal a more attractive, if not an altogether economically competitive, alternative. Comparative cost assessments are of course somewhat problematic given the Soviet pricing system for natural resources and final products. But the security of future supplies of coal is not problematic, and it is in this context that the attraction of coal as a fuel is indeed compelling.

Vast areas of the Soviet Union possess the geological features associated with potential coal reserves. Nearly 7,000 billion tons have been estimated to be under Soviet territory, a rather significant share of the world's potential reserves. But much, if not most, of the potential reserve has not been rigorously prospected nor is it likely to be. About half of this huge potential reserve is associated with two enormous basins in Siberia – the Tunguska with about 2,000 billion tons of hard-coal potential and the Lena with about 1,500 billion. Geologically proven reserves exceed 250 billion tons, and are certainly sufficient to sustain planned production in the foreseeable future. Of this total, hard coal comprises nearly 150 billion tons, almost half of which is coking coal quality and therefore of significance to the iron and steel industry amongst others. Just over 100 billion tons of this proven reserve are lignite, a softer, more friable and lower calorific-value coal than anthracite or bituminous, which constitute the hard-coal supply. The difference between hard and soft coal is significant beyond the simple designation these adjectives imply. For instance, while the Soviet Union is the world's largest coal producer in actual tonnage, the smaller output from mines in the United States actually has a higher total calorific value because most of it is hard coal. In 1985 more than one-fifth of the Soviet coal production was lignite, whereas in the United States it represents less than one-twentieth of total output.

The principal hard-coal producing basins in the Soviet Union are outlined in Fig. 40. The largest is the Donets basin in the southeast Ukraine and adjacent part of the Russian republic. This region was the mainstay of the industrialization drive of the late imperial era. By the late 1880s coking coal from the Donets basin supported

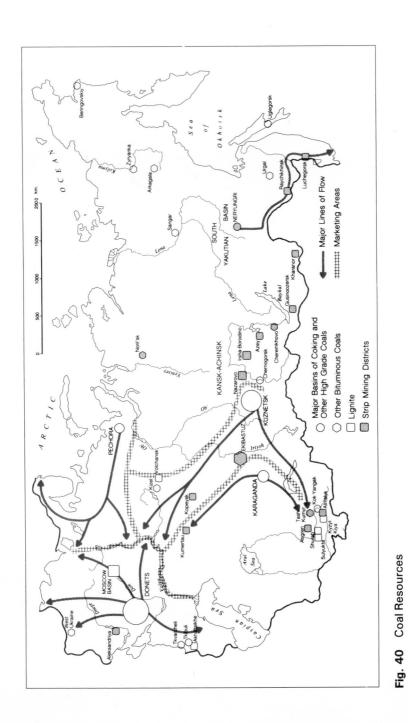

Fig. 40 Coal Resources

Source: Leslie Dienes, Theodore Shabad, *The Soviet Energy System: Resource Use and Policies* (New York: John Wiley, 1979), 109.

most of the iron and steel production in the Russian Empire. A century later it still dominates Soviet hard-coal production, and supports a massive array of local and regional heavy industrial complexes as well as supplying some of the coal requirements of more distant markets. The Donets basin accounts for more than a third of the total Soviet hard-coal output, which was almost 570 million tons in 1985. Still there are problems associated with the basin. Many of the accessible seams have been exhausted, and ever deeper pit mines pursuing the typically thin, discontinuous seams have pushed costs of production higher. Elsewhere there are more economic mining operations, but none possess the locational advantage of the Donets basin with respect to the major, and generally energy deficient, market areas of European Russia (Fig. 40). Thus, the landscape of the Donets coal fields will continue to be modified as new coal tips are added to the hundreds of others which rise up from the steppe. In the west Ukraine the limited production of bituminous coal is of local importance. Most of it feeds thermal power stations, as does the lignite produced in the lower Dnepr river area.

The second most important producer of hard coal is the Kuznetsk basin in Siberia. First developed in the late nineteenth century to supply the coal requirements of the newly developed Trans-Siberian railroad, it was a major component of Stalin's industrialization drive in the First Five Year Plan. Its significance in this context will be described in the next chapter. Unlike the Donets basin, coal seams here are thick, continuous, with a high proportion of that which has to be pit-mined close to the surface. Nearly two-thirds of the reserves are within 400 metres of the surface. In the Donets basin nearly half of the remaining proven reserves lie at depths in excess of 600 metres. Moreover, a significant proportion of the Kuznetsk basin reserves can be strip-mined. The combination of the geological structure of the coal seams and easy accessibility to them results in much lower costs of production. This is reflected in the geographically extensive market area of Kuznetsk coal portrayed in Fig. 40. The long-distance haulage of substantial quantities of coal clearly puts considerable strain on the railroad system, however. Coking and bituminous steam coal from the Kuznetsk basin not only sustain the region's own huge industrial demand, it supplies as well the bulk of the demand of the Urals industrial complex and a portion of the requirements of industry even further west (Fig. 40). Moreover, coal from the Kuznetsk basin accounts for about one-sixth of the country's exports, and thereby could well be transported as far away as North Korea, Japan, Egypt and Western Europe. The bulk of Soviet coal exports, however, are destined for Eastern Europe. As the Kuznetsk basin is expected to both offset reduced output from the Donets basin as its resources dwindle and a substantial portion of the planned increase in output, the burden on the rail system will inevitably increase. Further development of the vast proven reserves north of Novokuznetsk which are easily strip-mined should ensure that the comparative cost advantage of the region's output will be maintained.

Karaganda and Pechora account for the bulk of the remaining hard-coal output in the Soviet Union, but taken together the production from these deposits is not much more than one sixth of the total (Fig. 40). Limited reserves restrict potential future output from Karaganda, while the remote location and harsh environment pose problems for the Pechora mines. The latter were first opened with forced labour during the Second World War when the German invasion over-ran the Donets basin. Coking coal from Pechora played an important role in the war effort by supplying many of the steel mills in the unoccupied regions of European Russia. It still supplies coking coal to mills in the northwest, as Fig. 40 indicates. Development of the Karaganda coal fields began earlier. In order to reduce the huge westward flow of coking coal from the Kuznetsk basin to the steel mills of the Urals, and hence mitigate somewhat the intolerable pressure on the existing rail lines across Siberia, mines were developed in the early 1930s. With limited reserve potential the Karaganda region has not been able to expand production at the high rate of earlier years. Its coking-coal output is increasingly taken up by local steel mills, although several million tons a year still move to the southern Urals, and occasionally beyond. Steam coal supplies local thermal stations and meets a portion of the demand of plants in Middle Asia. Inasmuch as the Karaganda production comes from pit mining operations, as is also the case in the Pechora region, it is more expensive than coal produced in the Kuznetsk basin, where the favourable geology for pit mines and a growing strip mine output keep costs low.

Soft, lower calorific value, coal, principally though not exclusively lignite, is found throughout the Soviet Union. The Ekibastuz deposit in Kazakhstan is the largest in terms of production, and has sufficient proven reserves to sustain a very substantial increase over the present level of production. Its low quality, high ash content sub-bituminous coal feeds thermal power stations in the Urals, Kazakhstan and Siberia. As noted, expansion of coal-fired thermal power stations figures prominently in the current energy policy, but long-distance haulage of Ekibastuz coal on a larger scale than at present poses real problems for the rail transport system. Thus, there are plans for a substantial development of on-site, very large-scale thermal generating capacity for local consumption and export via the European unified grid system to the energy-deficient regions of European Russia. Though located in an arid region, the Irtysh–Karaganda canal is within easy reach and it will provide the cooling water required for the thermal power station complex envisioned. While there is a cost associated with long-distance transmission of electricity, whether by alternating (AC) or direct (DC) current, it is a far more attractive option than hauling even more weight losing, low calorific value coal on an already over-taxed railroad system to feed distant power stations.

The Kansk–Achinsk lignite reserves further to the east are extensive, but at present only produce about half the annual output of the Ekibastuz mines. Coal from the Kansk–Achinsk region is of low calorific value, and therefore it is not economic to transport it any significant distance. Because Kansk-Achinsk comprises the lion's share of lignite reserves, and because the thick seams are readily strip-mined, it has already become the centre of a complex of very large-scale thermal power stations. As in the case of Ekibastuz there are many advantages in supplying energy to other parts of the country in the form of electricity.

The other major soft-coal producing area is the Moscow basin. Production here has been declining in recent years, and while still running about 25 million tons per year it is now less than one quarter the combined output from Ekibastuz and Kansk–Achinsk. Of very low calorific value, the Moscow basin lignite is further disadvantaged since most of it comes from expensive pit-mining operations. But it does sit amidst one of the country's principal industrial regions, and thus in keeping with the long-standing policy of making use of all local energy resources, coal from the Moscow basin mines supplies some of the requirements of not too distant thermal power stations. Increasingly, however, these plants must rely on steam coal from more distant sources, notably those of Siberia.

Elsewhere may be found a number of small-scale coal mining operations whose output accounts for little more than 10 per cent of total production (Fig. 40). Some mines yield coal of coking quality, but most of it ends up feeding thermal power stations. The South Yakutian basin, for example, possesses fairly extensive reserves of both coking and reasonable quality steam coal, which can be strip-mined at low cost. As Fig. 40 implies, output from this region is destined to supply the Far East as well as the export market, especially Japan and North Korea. This basin has become accessible owing to the completion of the Baykal–Amur railroad, the centrepiece of a massive regional development project discussed in Chapter 9. As yet, however, development of the South Yakutian deposits has been limited.

As was noted above, coal is exported to a fairly wide market, extending from the Far to Middle East to Europe, both East and West. In keeping with Soviet policies to export more to earn more, the value of coal exports increased by nearly 50 per cent between 1980 and 1985. The difficulty, of course, is that as the bulk of coal exports are destined for Eastern Europe the opportunities for earning hard currency are accordingly diminished. Still, since 1980 the value of exports to Japan has more than doubled and now accounts for about 10 per cent of the total. While planning higher production for both the domestic and export markets in one sense is straightforward owing to the huge scale of proven reserves of coal, serious problems in achieving these planned increases must still be resolved. In many coal-mining regions it is extremely difficult to retain manpower owing to the outdated technology in the mines themselves and to the dearth of adequate housing, communal and cultural services in the workers' settlements. Coal-mining at the best of times is difficult work, especially in underground pits. Current efforts to boost the production and utilization of automated underground equipment to work the thinner seams are not new but have yet to have much impact. While the technology of Soviet coal mining, whether at ground level in strip mines or underground is not comparable to US technology, for example, it is even a more serious matter in the extraction of the most important component of the fuel balance – petroleum.

Oil

Soviet petroleum production is of particular interest to foreign observers because of the importance of Soviet oil in the international market, the growing dependence of some western countries on it, and the altogether unclear picture of current reserves and future production prospects. Given the dearth of information about energy reserves in general, exacerbated by a late 1970s decision to restrict further the official publication of regional reserves and outputs, it is no small task to accurately assess what the near and mid-term future is for Soviet oil production. What is clear is that at the national level the absolute volume of output has declined in absolute terms in the early 1980s. Before examining some of the Soviet responses to this situation, we need to review briefly the evolving pattern of production and its geographic ramifications.

The early importance of oil in the fuel balance was directly related to the output from the Caucasus, primarily but not exclusively from the fields around Baku. Until the German invasion in 1941 forced rapid exploration and production from other known reserves, the Caucasus accounted for at least four-fifths of the total production. While the Caucasian oil fields were certainly vulnerable to the German advance, in fact they remained in Soviet hands throughout the war. In the post-war period the proven reserves of the Volga–Ural field, roughly the region stretching from Kuybyshev to Perm (Fig. 41), seemed to increase substantially with each exploratory well sunk. By the early 1950s the output from the Volga–Ural fields was already more than three times that from the Caucasus, despite a vigorous programme of off-shore exploration and production around Baku after the war. With the decision to promote oil in the fuel balance, production from the Volga–Ural wells soared. By the end of the Khrushchev period in 1964 nearly three-quarters of a vastly expanded oil output came from the Volga–Ural region. Although the absolute volume of production from the Caucasus increased from 1940 to 1965 owing to the vigorous off-shore programme, and further development of the reserves around Grozny to the north of Baku, its relative role had obviously changed dramatically. In the mid-1960s Caucasian oil represented only about one-fifth of the total. The balance of production was drawn principally from a few small-scale operations in the Ukraine, Belorussia and in Middle Asia.

The locational advantage of the Volga–Ural oil fields in relation to the major market areas in the Soviet Union is readily apparent from Fig. 41. Roughly equidistant from the Moscow region, the industrial belt of the Ukraine and the Ural industrial complex (see Fig. 49, page 233), it satisfied the bulk of the oil needs of each with comparative economy in terms of transport cost. The network of pipelines extended from the Volga–Ural region in all directions, fed as well of course by the output of the Caucasus, and the other smaller fields wherever this was feasible. By the mid-1950s the pipeline system had penetrated Siberia and oil from the Volga–Ural region moved east to the refinery complex established at Omsk. The small-scale production from the Middle Asian fields on the eastern flank of the Caspian Sea helped to satisfy the demands of European Russia and the Urals for the most part. By the mid-1960s oil production from the vast region to the east of the Urals, including that from Middle Asia, accounted for little more than one-twentieth of total Soviet output. The geographical distribution of proven reserves, if not actual production, was already shifting to the east.

The vast west Siberian lowland (see Fig. 2, page 7) had long proffered the lure of oil and natural gas reserves. But geological exploration of this tract of forest and swamp had been slow because it was so difficult to penetrate. It was also some 2,000 or more kilometres further east than the Volga–Ural oil fields. The first really productive wells were developed in the Ob' river valley a few hundred kilometres to the east of the confluence of the Ob' and Irtysh rivers. This complex of oil wells was quickly brought into production with the output first being transported by river tanker to Omsk. A major refinery complex was already in place here to process Volga–Ural oil brought east by pipeline. The river transport of west Siberian oil to

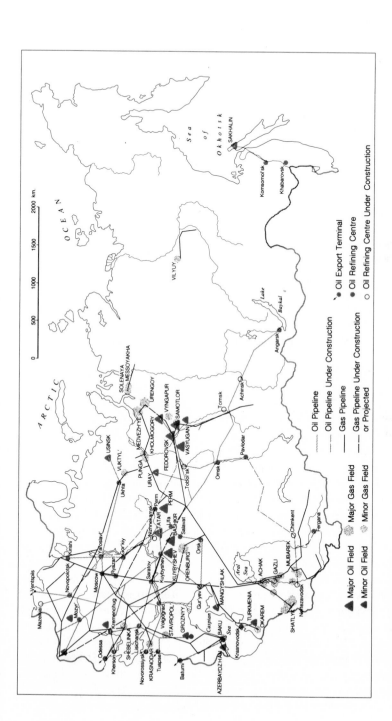

Fig. 41 Oil and Gas Resources

Source: Leslie Dienes, Theodore Shabad, *The Soviet Energy System: Resource Use and Policies* (New York: John Wiley, 1979), 49, 73.

Omsk first occurred in 1964 but was soon replaced by pipeline. This was also the year in which the pipeline carrying Volga–Ural oil finally reached a new refinery in central Siberia at Angarsk, not far from Irtutsk (see Fig. 41). Between the mid-1960s and the present day the development of the west Siberian oil and natural gas fields has transformed the Soviet energy scene. Production of oil from the west Siberian fields, which now extend even further north, accounts for more than three-fifths of total production. About one-third comes from the Volga–Ural wells and the balance primarily from the Caucasus. Oil from west Siberia quickly replaced Volga–Ural oil in the pipeline to Angarsk. Indeed, by the early 1970s the flow from the Volga–Ural fields to Omsk had stopped. The pumping stations on the pipeline were put to work to move oil in the opposite direction. As Fig. 41 clearly indicates, a complex network of increasingly large-diameter pipeline now penetrates much of west Siberia. It takes oil to the markets of European Russia and beyond. It feeds oil to the markets of Siberia and Middle Asia, particularly the Kuznetsk basin and the Pavlodar region of the Kazakh republic. For a long period much of the oil pumped through this rapidly expanding network came from one enormous deposit – the Samotlar field in the Ob' river valley. By the end of the 1970s production from the Samotlar wells began to taper off, prompting even more exploration in the more remote parts of West Siberia and elsewhere. While the offshore oil prospects in the Arctic Sea and along the Pacific coast are promising, as yet no major deposits have been developed. Indeed, given the complex technology involved, extensive development of offshore resources is not likely in the immediate future. Soviet planners are thus confronted with the formidable task of extracting more from west Siberia, a region which in the late-1980s still suffers from a poorly developed land transport system, inadequate infrastructure for permanent settlement, and a climate which by any standard of comparison is severe. Added to the logistic difficulties of getting in and out of the region are those of a technological, incentive, and resource conservation nature. The importance of oil to the Soviet, or any other industrial economy, is self-evident. The drop in annual production which the early 1980s ushered in was thus understandably the cause of great concern.

The dilemma facing Soviet planners responsible for increasing oil production is, as usual, multifaceted. The Party leadership, and specifically Mikhail Gorbachev, has been especially critical of past practices in the petroleum industry. The technology is outmoded, the recovery rates are too low, the labour productivity is both too low and stimulated by the wrong kinds of incentive, the cost of labour is too high, the research and development branches are weakly developed and too little integrated into production both on the field and off, and so the list goes. Meanwhile, throughout the Soviet economy the low level of efficiency in the use of petroleum and derivative products is akin to the profligate attitude to resources management bred during the Stalin-era preoccupation with a technological solution to problems amidst a resource-rich environment, an attitude which persists to the present time. And yet we need only note once again that despite all of the above the country is the world's largest oil producer and the third most important exporter. The question which has fascinated many observers is whether this standing can be maintained. We need only highlight a few details relating to the problems confronting the Soviet oil industry to convey a sense of why Soviet officials themselves are so concerned.

After first suspecting that a site may be oil bearing, exploratory drilling takes place, and if oil is discovered it is eventually pumped out of the ground. However, the basic Soviet technology for drilling is outmoded. In the early 1980s more than two-thirds of all drilling rigs were equipped with turbo-drills, the balance comprising some form of rotary drill. The turbo-drill technology evolved very largely in the pre-World War II era, and has been more or less the same since the early 1950s. Basically the technology involves injecting water and mud under high pressure to weaken and soften the material through which the drill bit then penetrates. As the drill pipe itself does not rotate it is under less pressure and thus can be manufactured with lower quality steel. As a technology it is quite satisfactory to depths of about 3,000 metres. Below that the frequency of breakdown jumps substantially. Rotary drill rigs in contrast must be manufactured from much higher quality steel since the combination of a revolving drill pipe, under pressure, and the bit does the digging. With this technology wells are more easily sunk to much greater depths than by turbo-drilling and equipment failures are less frequent. The problem is that since most exploratory drilling in the Soviet Union is currently below 3,000 metres, the rate of breakdown of the predominant turbo-drill equipment is extremely high. The adoption of the turbo-drill technology, according to some observers, was related to the Soviets' inability to guarantee sufficient amounts of high-quality steel to meet the anticipated large demand for drilling equipment when the decision to rapidly expand the role of oil in the fuel balance was originally taken. The deficiencies of turbo-drill technology are well recognized in the Soviet Union, and since the economic reform of 1965 there have been many decrees to get the industries involved to switch to rotary or other technology. But to do so requires substantial changes in steel production, and to date the turbo-drill remains preeminent.

The Soviet Union's 2,800 or so drilling rigs put down about 9,000 wells a year during the early 1980s. In the United States and Canada 4,500 hundred drilling rigs were able to sink 86,000 wells in 1982. Technology is a major factor in accounting for the difference. Inadequately provisioned drilling rigs and working brigades in the Soviet Union also play a part. Put simply, more workers achieve much lower results. In the critically important west Siberian region the maintenance of existing wells is seriously deficient given the urgency of increasing production. In the case of the Tyumen oil fields, for example, a fifth of the productive wells was not operating for one reason or another in 1985. And throughout west Siberia even where wells are not in need of repair, production is frequently interrupted because the electricity supply is irregular. The irony of an energy rich region unable to meet production targets in part because the pumps and drilling rigs cannot function owing to disruptions in electric power supply in the local grid system is not lost on Soviet authorities. Nor is the fact that there are now more repair brigades in the region than there are production brigades.

As more wells are having to tap ever deeper oil reserves, the technology in drilling becomes more critical. The current level of down-time is not amenable to a superficial solution, hence the emphasis on shifting the drilling technology from turbo to some form of rotary technology. As this occurs, the performance of wells should improve since, as noted, higher quality steel must perforce be used. But whether the recovery rates will improve is still a moot point. All involved in the oil industry have a vested interest in quickly increasing production. For that reason the giant Samotlar field was exploited for short-term results during the 1970s. When one well began to decline in terms of output it was expedient to move to a more productive site. Thus, oil remained in the ground, effectively wasted since to set up operation anew to capture the remaining reserves is prohibitively expensive. On balance, then, recovery rates in the world's largest oil producing country remain well below the prevailing rates in North America or the Middle East under similar geological conditions.

While the downturn in absolute volume of Soviet oil production which occurred in the early 1980s is serious, it is in no sense catastrophic. When major oil producing regions have declined in the past the huge resource potential of the country has yielded up another new source to replace them. Given the favourable geological condition of still vast areas of land and in offshore territory there is the possibility that this could happen again. Moreover, during the push for even greater production which intensified during the 1970s, drilling crews were shifted from exploration to production from known reserves. Thus, the balance between exploited reserves and proven potential shifted ominously. At the same time basic geophysical research to better direct on-the-ground exploration is still quite inadequate. While exploration has been more vigorous during the 1980s than in the preceding decade no finds equivalent to the Samotlar field in west Siberia have been made as yet. Fields discovered tend to be smaller, and almost by definition in more remote and hostile environments, and therefore are more costly to tap. Meanwhile efforts continue to get more from what is known to exist. And in this context improved technology and incentives geared to maximizing recovery certainly can assist. On the broader front of energy conservation generally, the Soviet energy system affords a number of opportunities to make more efficient use of oil. Burning it more effectively in thermal power station boilers is one example. Substituting natural gas for oil is another. For the former at least there is no question that proven reserves can continue to sustain sizeable annual increments in output.

Natural gas

In absolute terms natural gas output has risen from 45.3 billion cubic metres in 1960 to 643 billion in 1985. The proven resource base has more than kept pace with this rather remarkable increase in production. But as in the case of oil, the locus of both reserves and output has shifted to the east, to the west Siberian lowland energy storehouse.

Until the decision was taken during the 1950s to properly exploit the then known reserves of natural gas, much of the production was ancillary to oil production. And even in this case it was frequently just flared off at the well-head since recovery was not part of the plan. Where it was extracted intentionally it was used most often to fuel thermal power stations. Until the mid-1950s production was focused on the Baku region and to a much smaller degree on the Dashava reserves in the extreme western part of the Ukraine. Once part of the new Soviet energy policy, exploration for natural gas proceeded apace and output increased substantially (Table 15). By the mid-1960s a network of large-diameter pipelines had been constructed to transport natural gas from several regions to supply the European Russian market.

From the north Caucasus, especially near Stavropol, natural gas flowed in ever larger volume from the mid-1950s until the mid-1960s when it accounted for just a shade under three-tenths of total production. But the reserve potential was not sufficient to sustain this volume of output and it has since declined in relative and absolute importance. Even better located in terms of accessibility to the major urban-industrial markets of European Russia was the giant Shebelinka reserve in the eastern Ukraine. Combined with the output from Dashava further west, the Ukraine was the country's main source of natural gas for nearly two decades. A pipeline system has emerged which integrates these two main production regions with several others developed since the 1960s. But as in the case of the north Caucasian region, beginning in the late 1970s production waned in relative and absolute terms. The gas produced in the Ukraine not only satisfied a substantial share of the domestic market, but a share of the export market of both Eastern and Western Europe as well. With a pipeline system in place in European Russia, natural gas from points deeper in the Soviet interior could be drawn on to take up the slack as the reserves of the north Caucasus and then the Ukraine were steadily depleted.

Natural gas was a common occurrence at the well-head in the oil fields of the Volga–Ural region, but as elsewhere it too was frequently flared off. By the mid-1960s production was still quite insignificant since few reserves separate from oil deposits had been discovered. This changed with the appearance of data from exploratory drilling near Orenburg. While the gas itself was impure and thus had to be processed before it could be used, the location of this reserve was strategically significant since it was close to the major industrial markets. Natural gas deposits were being discovered and tapped in other locations at this time as well, but invariably the reserves were distant from markets, in a harsh physical environment, or both. Production from the Orenburg gas reserves played a major role in supplying thermal power stations throughout European Russia, and were of sufficient scale that expansion of exports to both Eastern and Western Europe could be entertained. In the former case exports were required as part of the bilateral arrangements which led to the development of the Orenburg gas fields in the first instance. Finances, technical personnel and labour from Eastern Europe were employed in developing the Orenburg deposit and building additional pipeline facilities. At about the same time Soviet authorities were busy linking by pipeline the considerable natural gas reserves of Middle Asia with European Russia (Fig. 41). By the mid-1970s production in Middle Asia accounted for about one-third of the Soviet total. Approximately one-half of production came from the various fields in European Russia and the north Caucasus. The remainder came from the as yet not fully explored west Siberian gas fields. These were known to be substantial already in the late 1960s, but eventually proved to be of colossal magnitude.

The major gas fields in the west Siberian lowland depicted in Fig. 41 account for more than half of the current proven reserves. Most of these fields are in an exceedingly harsh environment and are even more remote than the oil fields. Thus, access to the reserves and transport of natural gas to the major domestic and foreign markets pose major logistical problems. But as Fig. 41 indicates the natural gas pipeline system penetrates this region, and in so doing has helped to make the future Soviet energy scene more secure. But a close inspection of other maps of this region will reveal that there are few settlements and those who inhabit them are frequently there on a 'tour of duty' basis. Tens of thousands of workers in both the oil and gas fields of the west Siberian lowland are transported by special Aeroflot flights to and from the region on a fortnightly schedule. Two weeks on the job and two weeks at home in some more hospitable southern clime is now a standard, if costly, procedure. However, it is contended that while the costs are high, they are still lower than putting in place permanent urban infrastructures near the site of a natural resource of finite quantity. Since the mid-1970s when natural gas from the west Siberian fields made up little more than one-fifth of the total output, development has proceeded apace. While details of specific outputs by field or even region are no longer readily available, there is no doubt that well over one-half of a vastly greater annual production now comes from the west Siberian region.

While the Soviet Union's reserves of natural gas can sustain a steady and significant increase in annual production for the forseeable future, if not always meeting the annual targets set by the plan, the industry is far from immune to the problems confronting the petroleum sector. After all many of these problems are both generic and endemic to the system. Already there is evidence that in the most productive gas fields of the west Siberian lowland recovery rates at some wells exceed the operating norm which will maximize long-term yield. Thus, in the quest to meet the annual output targets, short-term solutions such as exceeding specific rates of extraction are being followed. Clearly this does not augur well for maximizing recovery and thus making most effective use of a non-renewable resource. Once more the really gigantic scale of reserves and the propitious geo-physical conditions which exist in many other regions for expanding the reserve potential cater to a measure of profligacy. But to take geophysical evidence and translate it into proven reserves is to a degree dependent upon drilling technology and we have already noted the problems encountered in drilling below 3,000 metres. In any event once reserves are proven and the necessary facilities for recovering the natural gas are in place, a major task remains – that of moving the natural gas to market.

The fast expanding network of pipeline – both for oil and especially natural gas – has put huge pressure on the Soviet steel industry, amongst others. Oil is moved over long distances in pipelines whose average diameter is less than 30 inches. There are some 48-inch oil pipeline trunk systems, but they do not yet represent a significant share of the total system. More than half of the natural gas pipeline system, however, is in excess of 30 inches, and a sizeable share of the total pipeline length comprises 48 and 56-inch diameter pipe. Clearly there is a vast demand for steel just to meet the requirements of the ever expanding oil and gas pipeline systems. As reserves are discovered in more remote regions (and as Fig. 41 indicates there are production facilities in more easterly locations than the west Siberian lowland), the costs of exploiting them will inevitably increase. Thus far the Soviet Union has shown no reluctance to absorb such costs. Clearly, if oil cannot be depended upon to secure much needed hard currency from exports to foreign markets, the importance of natural gas in this context will grow.

Oil and gas in the world market

Between 1980 and 1985 the total ruble value of oil and gas exports has increased from nearly 22 billion rubles to almost 36 billion. To be sure, part of this increase reflects price adjustments, especially in the case of oil, which are no doubt a reflection of the changing Soviet perception of the balance between domestic supplies and future demand, as well as world market trends. The bulk of the exports of oil and gas are still destined for Eastern Europe, but even these countries can no longer be assured of their supplies. More than once during the 1980s Soviet exports of oil to the Eastern European market have been adjusted to accommodate either domestic demand, hard-currency export markets, or both. The most notable instance is perhaps that which occurred in 1982. At that date it was decreed that exports of Soviet crude oil to Eastern Europe over the next three years would be reduced by 10 per cent from the planned and previously agreed levels. In the case of oil at least this represents a reversal of the trend toward larger exports which began in the 1960s. The attraction of export credits notwithstanding, the days when the Soviet Union could commit as much as 30 per cent of domestic oil output for export, as happened in 1976, are past. If necessary, it seems oil will be directed from the East European market, which customarily generates credits in blocked currencies or goods, to the west for hard currency. In 1985 Italy, West Germany, Finland and France were the principal western markets for Soviet oil.

While the ruble value of natural gas exports was less than one-fourth that of oil in 1985, it had more than doubled since 1980. West Germany has been the principal hard-currency export market in the 1980s, but both Italy and France have entered into long-term contractual arrangements with the Soviet Union to obtain a fixed and sizeable supply of natural gas as well. As the integration and expansion of the natural gas pipeline system binds these markets closer to Soviet supplies there is evidence of growing concern over the vulnerability of the countries involved to Soviet political pressure. But to some this is a calculated risk, and is less than being at the mercy of OPEC and the political instability of the Middle East.

In 1980 the penetration of Soviet oil into the West European oil market was barely one-twentieth of the total consumption. And oil, of course, is but one of several energy sources. Overall the equivalent relative penetration of Soviet natural gas is larger, but this source of energy is much less significant in the total West European energy scene than oil, and thus at this point in time has limited potential as an economic or political lever. Even with their huge reserves of natural gas, Soviet exports were cut back somewhat from contracted levels in the harsh winter of 1980–81, probably to meet an unexpected surge in domestic demand. Whatever the concerns might be over the reliability of Soviet natural gas supplies there is nothing to suggest that present export arrangements have been jeopardized as a result of the 1981 cutback.

There have obviously been some fundamental changes in the Soviet energy scene during the past quarter century. Structural changes in the fuel balance have been pronounced. The geography of energy supply and demand is giving ever more indication of growing tension. Resources and markets have on occasion been proximate, but of late the trend is clearly toward a growing spatial dislocation. The costs of overcoming this imbalance are considerable, though certainly not prohibitive. In most respects, the energy scene is one of the Soviet Union's major strong points. Over the past two decades exports of oil and natural gas in particular, but including other forms of energy as well, have regularly accounted for between one-third and a half of total export earnings. But these are non-renewable natural resources, and are exported in largely 'unprocessed' form at that. If such commodities figure so prominently in terms of exports earnings, what of the output from the manufacturing sector? In the next chapter we will examine the basis for industrialization, and the policies and programmes for ensuring a rational and equitable process of regional industrial development during the Soviet era.

Recommended reading

Campbell, R.W., *Soviet Energy Technologies: Planning Policies and Research*, (Bloomington: Indiana University Press, 1980).

Dienes, L., Shabad, T., *The Soviet Energy System: Resource Use and Policies* (New York: John Wiley, 1979).

Goldman, M.I., *The Enigma of Soviet Petroleum: Half Full or Half-Empty* (London: George Allen and Unwin, 1980).

Hewett, E.A., *Energy, Economics and Foreign Policy in the Soviet Union* (Washington: Brookings Institution, 1984).

Marples, D.R., *Chernobyl and Nuclear Power in the USSR* (New York: St. Martin's Press, 1987).

Raykher, E., *The Economics of the Soviet Gas Industry* (Leesburg: Delphic Associates, 1984).

Sagers, M.J., Green, M.B., *The Transportation of Soviet Energy Resources* (Totowa, New Jersey: Rowman and Littlefield, 1986).

——, *USSR Energy Atlas* (Washington: Central Intelligence Agency, 1985).

Wilson, D., *The Demand for Energy in the Soviet Union* (Totowa, New Jersey: Rowman and Littlefield, 1983).

Young, K.E. (ed), *Decision-Making in the Soviet Energy Industry: Selected Papers with Analysis* (Falls Church: Delphic Associates, 1986).

9 Industrialization and Regional Industrial Development

Now, when the task of evening out the level of economic development of the national republics in our country has been accomplished in the main, it is possible for us to approach economic questions primarily from the standpoint of the interests of the state as a whole. . . .

Brezhnev, 1972.[1]

Within the vast expanse of Soviet territory are to be found virtually all of the energy, mineral and biotic raw materials required by a modern industrial state, and in sufficient quantities to satisfy demand for the foreseeable future. In managing these resources, however, the planner is confronted with what the reader will now recognize as the all-too-typical problem – the location of resources for industry of sufficient scale to sustain long-term development is generally far removed from the main markets of European Russia. The cost of resource development in ever more remote frontier regions simply compounds the cost of overcoming distance. Moreover, for most of the Soviet period there has been a concerted effort to develop the peripheral regions of the country, to spread, geographically, the benefits of socialism. In this endeavour industrial development has been inextricably linked to urban development. Thus, resource-rich regions on the periphery – principally the European Russian north, Siberia and Middle Asia – could not simply be exploited for the benefit of the core region. Spatial inequality in economic development has always been regarded by Marxists as an inherent feature of the capitalist system. The state ownership of natural resources and their planned development in accordance with socialist principles were assumed to break this pattern. And, indeed, over the years considerable progress has been made in reducing regional industrial disparity. In this chapter we will provide a brief overview of the major industrial raw materials, principally mineral and forest. Having acquired some appreciation of the scale and geographical pattern of the industrial resource base, we will turn our attention to the

[1] L.I. Brezhnev, 'On the 50th Anniversary of the Union of Soviet Socialist Republics,' *Pravda* and *Izvestiya*, 22 December, 1972, in *The Current Digest of the Soviet Press*, Vol. 34, No. 51, 1973, 16–17.

main locational guidelines and regional development strategies which have been used during the Soviet era. An overview of the contemporary distribution of the major industries and the transport system will follow. This material will provide the background discussion of the contemporary core–periphery relationship. The changing pattern of regional economic disparity will be assessed in this chapter, while some of the consequences of uneven development in terms of the quality of life will be taken up in the following chapter.

Raw materials for industry

As noted in Chapter 2, a modern iron and steel industry was developed late in the imperial era. The south Ukraine figured prominently since the rich iron ore of Krivoy Rog was located not such a great distance from the enormous coking coal reserves of the Donets basin as to preclude rail shipment. The first major region of iron production during the imperial era, however, was in the Ural mountains. The technology which enabled Russia to emerge as the world's largest producer of iron in the late eighteenth century was based on smelting ore with charcoal, not coking coal. While the Urals provided adequate forest resources for charcoal, they lacked coal. With such technology Russia was not able to maintain its position and was soon eclipsed by production in a number of European states. But the rich magnetite iron ore deposits of the Urals remained. Indeed, it was these enormous, high-quality reserves which provided a major reason for the creation of the Urals–Kuznetsk Combine. The other reason, of course, was the abundant supply of high-quality coking coal in the Kuznetsk basin (Kuzbas). Of this particular regional development project more will be said later. The essential point for our purpose here is that the Soviet Union, and imperial Russia before it, had the necessary resources to develop important iron industries based on prevailing technologies. With more than 100 billion tons of recoverable reserves of iron ore, the future of ferrous metallurgy is secure for several centuries at current rates of extraction. The higher grades of ore, especially in the strategically located and long-exploited Krivoy Rog deposits in the south Ukraine, are nearing exhaustion, however.

Over the last six decades geological exploration has resulted in a number of new iron ore reserves being added to the inventory (Fig. 42). Siberia has figured prominently in these discoveries, but by no means is it the only region. Indeed, from the point of view of strategic location and scale of reserves, the huge magnetite and iron-bearing quartzite deposits associated with the so-called Kursk Magnetic Anomoly (KMA) of central European Russia are of obvious importance (see Fig. 46, page 225). This region has supported a variety of metallurgical industries for centuries, though historically they were primarily handicraft in nature. Ore from the KMA is now shipped to the major iron and steel mill at Lipetsk, to steel mills in the Urals and, because a sizeable proportion of the output is exported, to a number of mills in Eastern and Western Europe. As is the case in the other major iron-mining operations, output from the KMA is of relatively low iron-ore content and thus must be concentrated before shipping. Indeed, the average ore content of Soviet reserves has steadily declined in the post-war period and currently is about 35 per cent. The metal content of ore shipped from mines on the other hand is close to

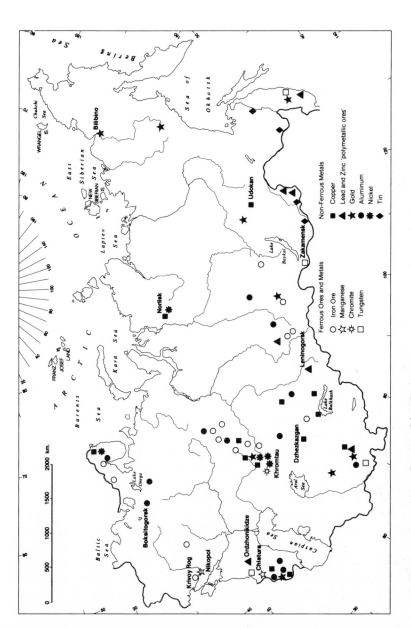

Fig. 42 Ferrous and Non-Ferrous Metals

Source: Leslie Symons *et al.*, *The Soviet Union: A Systematic Geography* (Totowa, NJ: Barnes & Noble, 1983), 155.

60 per cent owing to widespread recourse to various concentration technologies. Together the KMA and Krivoy Rog deposits account for about one-half of total Soviet iron ore reserves.

While Fig. 42 shows the location of the major iron-ore deposits, it does not give any indication of their relative importance in terms of output. The south Ukraine, which has dominated output for a century, is still the largest source of iron ore, accounting for about one-half of the current total annual output of roughly 260 million tons. Production from reserves in the Urals, once second to the Ukraine, declined steadily in the post-war period in relative terms, and in recent years in absolute terms as well. With less than 10 per cent of total production, the Urals now account for a shade less than the output from the Kustanay region in Kazakhstan. KMA production has accelerated at a frenetic rate since 1970 and now represents roughly one-sixth of the total iron ore mined. The Kuznetsk region, and Zheleznogorsk further east near Lake Baykal, are the major Siberian iron-mining regions. Together they represent around 7 per cent of current output. The general pattern of iron-ore flow from mine to mill is portrayed in Fig. 47, page 229. Given that geological exploration of potential iron-ore reserves is still far from complete it is entirely possible that the geography of reserves could change. The most likely consequence of further exploration is that the share of the eastern regions, excluding the Urals, would increase. At present iron-ore reserves are something of a spatial anomaly inasmuch as more than three-quarters are found in European Russia and the Urals. For most industrial raw materials the pattern is reversed.

As Fig. 42 indicates, manganese, chromite and tungsten ores are far flung in distribution. The major reserve of manganese is located in the Ukraine at Nikopol. From mines here more than three-quarters of the total Soviet output is obtained. The other main source is the Chiatura basin in Georgia. Soviet annual production exceeds nine million metric tons, roughly three times greater than South Africa, the next largest producer. Exports to the world market have declined as the highest quality exportable ores from the Chiatura region were depleted. However, Soviet manganese continues to feed the factories of Eastern Europe. Less than one-eighth of current production is now exported, a significantly smaller share of output than two decades ago. The huge chromite deposit at Kromtau in northwestern Kazakhstan accounts for virtually all of the Soviet production of this important metal, which in turn ranks first in the world. Total chromite output was roughly four million metric tons in the mid-1980s. In the 1960s approximately 30 per cent of total production found its way into the export market, principally the hard-currency countries of the west. At present barely one-sixth is exported, and more than half of this amount is destined for Eastern Europe. Technological innovations which now permit lower-grade chromite to be used in the steel industry seem to have benefited most other producers, especially South Africa. Tungsten is mined in several regions, but notably at Zakamensk near Lake Baykal. Less important deposits in the north Caucasus, in central Kazakhstan and in Middle Asia are also worked, but total output from all reserves does not satisfy more than three-quarters of domestic needs. New discoveries have been made in the Zakamensk region which could alter the resource distribution picture.

Amongst the non-ferrous metals, platinum and nickel have been the most important, and consistent, sources of hard-currency income. As data on non-ferrous metallurgy have long been classified it is difficult to be very precise about the level of domestic production. Available information indicates the Soviet Union ranks second after South Africa in platinum output, and second to Canada in nickel production. In both cases the bulk of Soviet output comes from the massive non-ferrous mineral reserves around Norilsk. With more than 180,000 inhabitants the very size of this mining centre located north of the Arctic circle is testimony to both its past and future importance in non-ferrous mineral production. In addition to platinum and nickel, mines here also yield substantial amounts of copper, cobalt, gold and silver. The principal source of copper, however, is the Dzhezkazgan deposit in central Kazakhstan (Fig. 42). Older, but still important copper mines are worked in the Urals. Smaller operations in the Caucasus, Middle Asia and the Kola peninsula also contribute to domestic production. The large reserves near Udokan northeast of Lake Baykal may well shift the centre of gravity of output further to the east once the mines there are in full operation. Current levels of copper production are in the order of 1.5 million metric tons per annum, roughly the same as the United States, the other world leader.

Lead and zinc production is large; indeed, the Soviet Union probably now ranks ahead of the United States, Japan and Canada. Massive reserves have been found in Kazakhstan at Leninogorsk, and the output from mines there now exceeds production at Ordzhonikidze in the northern Caucasus, one of the first deposits to be developed. Fairly significant production also occurs in Middle Asia (Amalyk) and Central Siberia (Salairskoye). Potential lead resources to the east and north of Lake Baykal are apparently very large. If mining is expanded the share of the eastern regions in total production, which in the mid-1980s was close to 600,000 metric tons, could well increase further. Total zinc production was around 850,000 tons. Tin reserves are uncharacteristically meagre. To date tin oxide has been discovered and mined mostly in Eastern Siberia and the Far East regions. Tin production ranks second in the world after Malaysia, but at around 25,000 metric tons annually in the mid-1980s is probably not satisfying much more than five-sixths of domestic demand. Geological conditions in parts of the Soviet Far East are certainly promising however, and as exploration continues self-sufficiency in tin production is not beyond the realm of possibility.

Raw material for aluminium production is found in a number of regions in the Soviet Union (Fig. 42). Bauxite has been the principal source of alumina, but output is inadequate to feed Soviet aluminium factories. Substantial volumes of bauxite ore and alumina, which is the next stage in the production process, have been imported for decades. Probably close to two-fifths of total Soviet aluminium production, which is second in the world after the United States, is based on imported raw materials. Bauxite is mined principally in the European Russian northwest at Boksitogorsk. Import dependence is more a matter of choice than necessity for alumina may be derived from materials other than bauxite. Nephaline, apatite and kaolin for example, can be substituted, and to some degree are. However, the technology involved is more complex. Soviet planners have thus far opted to rely primarily on alumina derived from bauxite, wherever it is sourced, rather than rely on domestically produced alumina from one of the alternatives to bauxite.

Production of aluminium is further complicated since the reduction of alumina requires very substantial amounts of electricity. A number of the country's major hydroelectric power stations have been developed on the premise that alumina reduction plants would comprise a major part of the industrial demand for their output. This is especially so for the Siberian hydroelectric power stations discussed in the preceding chapter. While still dependent upon imported raw materials, the Soviet Union is also a major exporter of aluminium. Perhaps as much as a quarter of annual production, which now probably exceeds 2.5 million metric tons, finds its way into the export market. Eastern Europe is the major destination, but substantial sales are also made to the west. Amongst non-ferrous metals aluminium ranked first in terms of tonnage and accounted for about a third of exports by value in the mid-1970s.

Gold has long been a major source of hard-currency earnings, and annual output is reckoned to be in the order of 325 metric tons. As Fig. 42 indicates, it is found in a number of locations, but the mines in northeast Siberia, of which Bilibino is a major one, account for as much as a quarter of total production. Placer operations on many of the rivers of Eastern Siberia have also yielded substantial amounts of gold over the past century. Indeed, as is the case in parts of Canada and the United States, tailings from earlier worked-out placer operations have been mined again when the price of gold on the world market makes it profitable to do so. While mining of gold underground and extracting it from alluvial gravels is planned just as any other sector of the Soviet economy is, the industry has long been linked to the use of forced labour, especially in the more remote regions of northeast Siberia. Kazakhstan accounts for a sixth or less of total production but ranks as the second most important source on a regional basis. Gold production here is almost entirely related to lead, zinc and copper output from which it is derived as one of several by-products.

Gold reserves are large with best estimates putting the current total near 2,000 metric tons. Sales to the west vary according to the prevailing price and the need for hard currency. In the latter half of the 1970s the volumes sold ranged from an estimated high of more than 400 metric tons per year to a low of 70. Domestic consumption is controlled by high prices at both the wholesale and retail levels. While data are difficult to authenticate the Soviet Union is widely regarded as the world's second largest producer after South Africa.

Non-metallic materials also play an important role in Soviet industrial production and in earning foreign exchange in the export market. Apatite in concentrated form earns almost as much as diamonds in the export market. These two commodities along with asbestos make up just under 2 per cent of all Soviet exports by value. Apatite concentrate comes from reserves in the Kola peninsula in northwestern European Russia. Aside from supplying the export market, it is also an important input for the phosphate fertilizer industry. The Soviet Union is a major diamond producer, second only to Zaire. Mines in Eastern Siberia, for the most part remote and difficult to access, account for much of Soviet diamond production. Prior to the discovery of these deposits following the Second World War diamonds came mostly from placer deposits in the western Urals. Asbestos is the other major non-metallic substance which is exported in substantial quantity. Produced in greatest volume from mines in the central Urals, total production ranks first in the world. Roughly a quarter of domestic production is exported. Substantial deposits of asbestos have been found in Eastern Siberia, and therefore the Soviet Union's premier position in terms of world production is likely to remain unchanged. But given the relatively low value of asbestos, it contributes much less than either diamonds or apatite concentrate to foreign-exchange earnings.

Aside from chemical raw materials derived as by-products, for example from the petro-chemical industry, there are some important elemental chemicals which have been produced in growing quantity since World War II. Prominent amongst the latter is phosphate from Kazakhstan. Plants here account for more than four-fifths of the estimated total annual output of around 600,000 metric tons. Phosphorus is exported, but the principal market is the domestic phosphate fertilizer industry. Given the need to enhance yields in agriculture, it is likely to remain the main market for some time to come. Potash also figures prominently in the fertilizer industry. Production is the largest in the world. Mined primarily in the Urals and Belorussia, about one-quarter of the 20 million metric tons annual output is exported. Along with ammonia and urea, potash ranks among the top three chemical-based exports in terms of value.

The Soviet Union's reliance upon basic industrial raw materials as export commodities is clearly revealed by the wood and wood products group. Traditionally, wood exports have mainly comprised unprocessed roundwood and sawnwood as opposed to higher-value products such as plywood, particle board or paper. Domestic technological innovation could improve this situation, but for some time a more fundamental issue has been the ability of existing forest reserves to supply both the growing domestic demand and export markets. As Fig. 43 indicates, substantial areas already have timber deficits. As a result of decades, if not centuries, of overcutting and inadequate reforestation, the more accessible forest reserves can no longer sustain demand. Logging operations are pushing further north and east into zones of marginal stocks and harsh climate. In the absence of adequate reforestation programmes during most of the Soviet era, environmental degradation in the form of erosion of soil and depletion of natural habitat for fauna is widespread. In recent years, however, there has been a concerted effort to reduce waste in logging operations, and to pursue reforestation programmes more seriously than in the past. At the same time there has been an attempt to shift the emphasis from low-value to higher-value forest products for export. In the mid-1980s at least a quarter of all exports by value was still in the form of roundwood, sawnwood, pitprops and pulpwood. Much of this raw material is destined for hard-currency markets, especially Western Europe and Japan. However, it should be noted that in this group of export commodities the importance of pulpwood has increased over the past few years. Indeed, as several huge mills in Siberia, notably at Bratsk and Ust-Ilimsk, have come on stream, exports of sulphate pulp have surged. This change certainly represents a step towards a higher-value product for export.

Ensuring a sustainable yield from Soviet forests over the coming decades remains a basic problem. Recent efforts to introduce more realistic prices for forest resources represent one attempt to solve it since waste, which has been deplorably high, might be lessened. More scientific management of forests, and continuing improvements in the technology of the forest products industry itself, represent others. Such

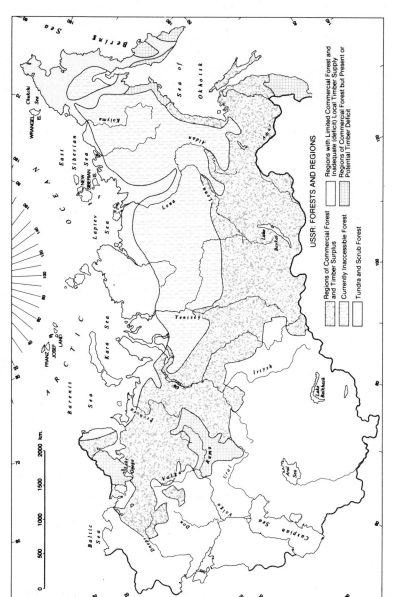

USSR: FORESTS AND REGIONS

Regions of Commercial Forest and Timber Surplus

Currently Inaccessible Forest

Tundra and Scrub Forest

Regions with Limited Commercial Forest and Inadequate (deficit) Local Timber Supply

Regions of Commercial Forest but Present or Potential Timber Deficit

Fig. 43 Soviet Forest Resources

Source: B.M. Barr, 'Regional Dilemmas and International Prospects in the Soviet Timber Industry', in Jensen, R.G., Shabad, T., Wright, A.W. (eds.) *Soviet Natural Resources in the World Economy* (Chicago: The University of Chicago Press, 1983), 428.

developments could reduce imports of paper, and sustain, if not enhance, export earnings by substituting higher-value for lower-value products. As Fig. 43 indicates, the eastern regions of the country will figure prominently as a future source of raw material for the forest products industry.

While reserves of industrial raw materials at any one point in time are fixed in terms of scale and location, the decision to make use of them is obviously contingent upon a number of other factors, including state policy for the development of the national economy. In this context there are some general locational guidelines and control mechanisms which merit brief consideration.

Locational guidelines and controls

To the extent that governments influence the location of economic activity they are all confronted with the dilemma of encouraging either national efficiency and growth or regional equity and growth. In the Soviet Union the general guidelines which have ostensibly conditioned locational decision-making over the years embrace both objectives.

The first group of guidelines deals with technical optimization. The minimization of transport costs by reducing or eliminating long hauls of industrial raw materials or final products is one such guideline. Thus, there has long been advocacy of locating industry near raw materials or near markets, depending on the nature of the production process involved. Hauling long distances weight-losing industrial raw materials such as low metal-content ore makes little economic sense no matter whether the resources are publicly or privately owned. Related to this concern is the promotion of regional industrial specialization. The use of local raw materials, even if the quality is lower, and hence the cost of recovery higher, is viewed positively. Thus, if specialization in industrial output on a regional basis can be combined with some degree of self-sufficiency owing to utilization of local or regional resources, the economy as a whole is presumed to benefit. While the main emphasis in the technical optimization guidelines tends to be on the rational utilization of industrial raw materials, the same general principles apply in terms of making best use of regional labour resources.

The second group of guidelines focuses on spreading the benefits of socialism. A more even distribution of economic activities is sought to ensure that all regions can effectively participate in the development of the national economy. Removing regional inequality involves fostering the urban-industrialization of traditionally backward, largely non-Slavic regions. Eradicating the differences between city and countryside, the ideological significance of which was highlighted in an earlier chapter, is included in this group as well. It is expected that with a higher level of regional economic development there will be a commensurate increase in the political and cultural sophistication of the population. In other words, by ensuring participation in the development of the national economy, socialist, if not communist, values will be more easily inculcated.

A third set of guidelines has to do with strategic factors in industrial location. These guidelines are of obvious importance though precisely what impact they have had over the years is impossible to gauge. Indeed, because of the general nature of all locational guidelines the significance of any single one in locational decision-making clearly cannot. be established with any real certainty. To be sure, there is the possibility that a particular guideline may be used *ex post facto* to rationalize a decision based on trade-offs between various interest groups. Notwithstanding the difficulty of determining how these guidelines have shaped the distribution of industry during the Soviet era, it should be evident that the nature of the Soviet decision-making system permits a potentially close fit between a particular locational guideline and actual development. It would seem that at least some of the industrial development in the eastern regions owes something to the felt need for security from external attack.

Part of the impetus to articulate locational guidelines stems from the perception of early Soviet leaders that the distribution of economic activity inherited from the imperial era was both inefficient and unfair. Differences between the developed core of European Russia and peripheral regions such as Middle Asia were staggering no matter which measures were used. Levels of literacy, life expectancy, infant mortality, income, urban infrastructure, regional transportation systems, industrial production – all these, and many more besides, highlighted the essentially exploitative relationship between core and periphery. The economic and social needs were obvious enough, the regional development strategies to ameliorate them less so. Various programmes of action were considered. Before discussing these, we might usefully review the tools the state had at its disposal to effect the desired fundamental change in the distribution of economic activity.

In a Soviet-type economy investment in industry can be directed to specific regions, or indeed, as noted in an earlier chapter, to specific-size cities. At various times since the 1930s precisely these kinds of decisions have been made. Of course, the corollary of directing investment to new industrial facilities is restricting expansion of existing ones. Along with spatial and city-size priorities for the allocation of industrial development and concomitant social-consumption funds, the state has used a system of wage differentials to encourage migration to regions where economic growth is desired. Regional wage coefficients played an important role in promoting migration to Siberia, particularly the eastern and northern regions, and have been in use since the late 1930s. Fig. 44 depicts the wage coefficient regions during the first half of the 1980s. It is apparent that wage coefficients of one kind or another applied over most of the country. The benefits have always been greatest in the Far North and in those areas accorded the same status as the Far North. It is typically the case that in these zones wage rates are about double those for the same job in areas where coefficients do not apply. Depending on the fortitude of the individual, it is possible to reach retirement age in about half the time required in more southerly and equable climes since every year served counts for two toward a pension. Notwithstanding the attraction of high wages, early retirement, generous holidays, and so on, the fact that there has been a long-standing need for such an incentive system speaks to the problems planners face in attracting, and holding, labour in these climatically harsh frontier regions.

In addition to these positive steps to shape the pattern of economic growth, various forms of coercion have been used from time to time. By the late 1930s labour was often simply assigned to specific locations, there to stay until permission to

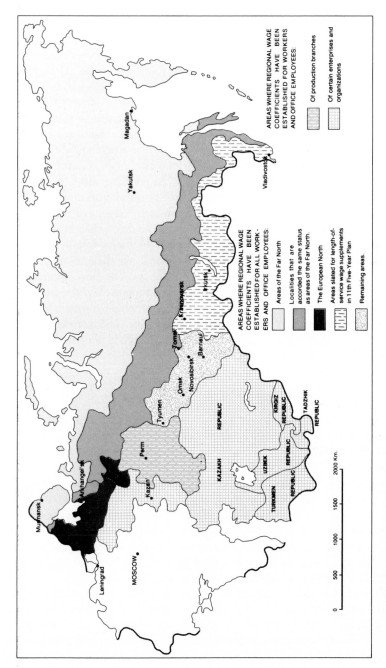

Fig. 44 Regional Wage Coefficients

Source: Adapted from *The Current Digest of the Soviet Press*, Vol. 24, No. 23, 7 July, 1982, 20.

depart was granted, or until sent elsewhere. The substantial number comprising Stalin's peace-time contingent of forced labour was much augmented during the Second World War when some Soviet citizens fell into disfavour because their nationality was suspect. Thus, the Crimean Tatars and the sizeable German population of the Ukraine and Volga region were relocated and assigned to jobs, mostly in the eastern and northern parts of the country where collaborating with the invading German forces was not possible. Prisoners of war were yet another source. Whether or not this pool of forced labour – civilian, prisoner-of-war or simply criminal – ever really contributed to the national economy more than it cost to supervise and support is a moot point. Clearly the diet was bad and general conditions of housing and employment marginal at best. But a vast organization was required to manage the whole enterprise. It was not until the late 1950s after Stalin's death, that this system of forced labour began to be disassembled. As we have noted in an earlier chapter, under Khrushchev the administrative controls over internal migration were eased. Problems of acute labour shortage in the northern and eastern regions were exacerbated in consequence, and hence the perpetuation, indeed enhancement, of the wage-coefficient incentive programme outlined in Fig. 44 was necessary. At present there are still reports of labour camps in remote regions, but these seem to be of a quite different scale than was the case during the Stalin era. Of course, graduates of university or technical-school programmes having been supported by the state while being trained are still liable to be assigned to a period of employment in a remote region. The necessary pieces of bureaucratic machinery for superintending population movements, the internal passport and *propiska*, have been in place since the early 1930s, as was described in Chapter 4.

Regional development concepts

Ideas about regional development have not been lacking during the Soviet period. As has been emphasized on several occasions already, the geography of the national economy under conditions of capitalism in the late imperial era was anathema to the Marxist. The dependence of peripheral, largely non-Russian regions on the core region was regarded as a type of colonialism. Thus, immediately following the revolution a number of proposals intended to foster a more even or balanced pattern of regional development was put forward. The proposals involved both the delineation of regional planning units and ways to stimulate and direct the economic development process. We have provided a broad overview of regional planning in Chapter 3. We will focus the discussion here more on the development strategies which have been followed in attempting to ameliorate regional disparity.

The explicit reliance on electricity as the essential lynch-pin in industrialization in the GOELRO scheme (the State Commission for the Electrification of Russia) not only echoed Lenin's own thinking, but in some ways presaged later concepts in which energy was the integrating element in regional development. While the GOELRO scheme received much publicity immediately following its announcement in 1920, its actual impact on the geography of the country was quite limited. The system of regions which was part of this scheme certainly helped to shape the first attempt by Gosplan to prepare a set of planning regions (1921). The Gosplan regional framework was eventually rejected. In large measure this was because the regions themselves, while reflecting existing, or anticipated, functional linkages, bore little if any relationship to the political-administrative map that was evolving at the same time, but which was based on the fundamental principle of recognizing the distribution of national minorities. By the 1930s the notion that planning regions had to 'fit' the political administrative divisions was well established. However, both the GOELRO scheme and the Gosplan regional system which followed on its heels underscored the need to promote regional specialization and regional integration. With most of the 1920s devoted to rebuilding the national economy according to the economic and political compromise endorsed by Lenin in his New Economic Policy (1921–1928), there were few opportunities to translate regional development strategic thinking into practice. And with the advent of the Stalin-era Five Year Plan and ministerial system of decision-making in 1928, the gulf between principle and practice seemed destined to widen still further. However, the decision to develop the Urals–Kuznetsk Combine did put one type of regional development planning into practice – and on a massive scale.

If the 1920s may be described as a time of intellectual debate over the nature of the regional development process, then the 1930s must be seen as a time of action. What was being acted upon, however, had a long and quite controversial history. The Urals–Kuznetsk Combine was no less than a functional integration of the vast iron-ore reserves of the southern Urals with the substantial, high-quality coking coal reserves of the Kuznetsk basin (Kuzbas). The Urals lacked coking coal; the Kuzbas lacked iron ore. The proposal to integrate the two complementary resources had appeared at least as early as 1916. Envisioned were modern iron and steel complexes at either end. But hauling weight-losing materials more than 1,600 kilometres flew in the face of conventional economic logic and industrial location theory. Some Soviet economists attacked the proposal on the grounds that the resultant transport costs would greatly exceed the presumed benefits. Better to invest, they argued, in the existing iron and steel industry of the south Ukraine. A greater return on investment would ensue, and much sooner. But invoking western industrial location theory to buttress the argument against proceeding with the Urals–Kuznetsk Combine simply invited the obvious criticism that under socialism things could be different and better. The project offered an opportunity to alter quite fundamentally the economic geography of the state, and in a manner which conformed to the notion that under socialism there would be a more equitable distribution of economic opportunity. To invest only in the Ukrainian steel industry would just reinforce the pre-Soviet pattern of development. Besides, with complete nationalization of resources and central planning, rail tariffs and resource prices could be manipulated to suit the proponents. In any event, some observers have suggested that the economics of the project were largely irrelevant because it made good sense from the standpoint of national security. Whatever the real reasons, the Urals–Kuznetsk Combine went ahead notwithstanding a cost which is reputed to be at least equal to one-third of the total investment capital available during the First Five Year Plan alone.

By the mid-1930s large-scale integrated iron and steel complexes had been built in the southern Urals at Magnitogorsk and in the Kuzbas at Novokuznetsk. However, as the opponents of the Combine had predicted, the costs of hauling weight-losing materials over such vast distances soon began to take their toll. Little had been done to bolster the rail system, and thus the operational efficiency of that part of the trans-Siberian railroad linking the two ends of the Combine was greatly reduced. Plans for resource substitution soon emerged. For example, the coking-coal reserves which had been discovered in Kazakhstan near Karaganda were being tapped by the early 1930s in order to supply part of the demand of the southern Urals mills. About half the distance between the Kuzbas and the Urals, the routing of this coal helped to relieve pressure on the trans-Siberian railroad. Eventually iron ore was discovered at Atasu in Kazakhstan, and in combination with Karaganda coking-coal and water brought several hundred kilometres across the steppe by canal from the Irtysh river to the east, the basis for a large-scale integrated iron and steel complex at Karaganda was created. The need to replace at least some of the ore transported to the Kuzbas from the Urals spurred geological exploration in the region. By the end of the 1930s iron ore was being mined in the southern Kuzbas and fed the mills in Novokuznetsk even though it was difficult to use and was of lower iron content. To be sure, the search for local resources helped to foster regional integration, one of the principles of regional development enunciated in the debates of the early 1920s. As well, the Urals–Kuznetsk Combine did foster regional specialization in industrial production. But as a close perusal of Fig. 40 page 196 and Fig. 47 page 229 will indicate, long distance shipments of weight-losing iron ore and coking-coal are still very much part of the Soviet scene.

By the time the third Five Year Plan was introduced in 1938 the Combine had ceased to exist as it was originally conceived, and the underlying precepts which had given rise to its creation were seriously questioned. The cost of overcoming such huge distances was simply too great to be contemplated a second time. In retrospect there is no question that the development of the Urals–Kuznetsk Combine produced a substantial change in the distribution of industry, and economic development more generally. Moreover, some observers reckon that in the absence of the metallurgical complexes in the Urals and the Kuzbas the Soviet Union's ability to mount an effective offensive to counter the German invasion of 1941 would have been seriously hampered. In any event, principles upon which the Combine was based were re-examined and found wanting. While central planning dominated decision-making during the Stalin era, as we have indicated in an earlier chapter, the theory of regional development under conditions of socialism had not been entirely ignored. The work of N.N. Kolosovskiy published during the 1940s carried further some of the ideas which found expression in the more liberal intellectual climate of the 1920s.

Kolosovskiy's scheme envisioned a network of territorial production complexes (TPCs), each TPC having been created on the basis of pre-determined functional linkages. Flows of raw materials for industry and energy were deemed to be the essential unifying ingredients in what he labelled energy-production cycles. While Kolosovskiy identified eight energy-production cycles, later modifications of his conceptual framework have added others to the roster. They range from ferrous-metallurgical, to petro-chemical to agricultural production cycles. In many ways the idea is akin to the notion of growth poles as developed by the French economist F. Perroux in the 1950s. Both ideas focus on the delineation of sets of interrelated, if not directly interdependent, production processes which theoretically could be anti-cipated to generate economic growth. Both, in the first instance, are aspatial. Within the context of a planned economy Kolosovskiy's scheme has some obvious attractions. By concentrating on production cycles, which by their very nature would embrace activities across several sectors of the economy (at the time 'managed' by ministries of one level or another), some obvious efficiencies of integration might occur. The conscious selection of production cycles to suit the resource base of particular regions gives rise to the territorial production complex. Clearly, within a planned economy it is possible to develop interrelated production facilities so as to maximize economies of scale, minimize waste products and ensure some balance between the demands for male and female labour. Perroux's growth-pole concept was similarly extended to regional development planning, though in the absence of direct government inter-vention, the creation of so-called growth centres has been far from successful. Indeed, even where there have been substantial government incentives to encourage firms to locate in designated growth centres there are few examples of permanent spatial change in national economies resulting from adopting a growth centre strategy in regional economic development. Nationalized resources and a planned economy certainly suggest that the Soviet Union provides more fertile ground for such a policy. It is therefore no small irony that during the 1950s and 1960s when Kolosovskiy's ideas about energy production cycles and territorial production complexes were taken up by Soviet academics and planners interested in furthering the role of regional planning, Khrushchev's scheme of 104 *sovnarkhozy* (regional planning councils) was introduced, modified and then abandoned. Part of the official nervousness over the *sovnarkhozy* scheme centred on the fact that it seemed to contribute to national minority group aspirations for greater cultural and political identity and self-determination by facilitating regional economic autarchy. While central planning via the ministerial system was reintroduced by Brezhnev and Kosygin in 1965, the theory behind territorial production complexes has steadily evolved and the TPC is now widely regarded as the principal mechanism for planning regional economic development.

Territorial production complexes are assumed to exist at different scales and to evolve through different stages. Something of the hierarchy of the component parts of a regional production complex is portrayed by Fig. 45. In theory a regional production complex can be conceived as comprising several TPCs, each TPC comprising several functional and spatially integrated industrial nodes. Stages of development run the gamut from regions with latent resource potential for future development, to developing 'pioneer' regions, to regions in which TPCs and indus-trial nodes have been formed, to regions of advanced development, to fully developed regions boasting both specialized and fully integrated economies. That TPCs exist at different geographic scales is apparent from Fig. 46, which depicts those complexes undergoing active development during the early 1980s. What the map also shows is that these TPCs do not conform to the existing boundaries of political-administrative regions (see Fig. 10, page 48). In the absence of an existing regional planning or political-administrative decision-making structure, each TPC has to operate on a more or less *ad hoc* basis in this regard. Since by definition the energy-production cycle upon which it is based spans several different ministerial bodies, and

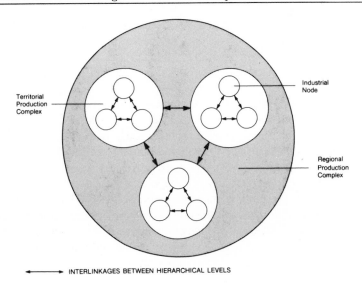

Fig. 45 Territorial Production Complex (TPC) Model

Source: Victor L. Mote, 'The Baikal-Amur Mainline and its Implications for the Pacific Basin', in Jensen, R.G., Shabad, T., Wright, A.W., (eds), *Soviet Natural Resources in the World Economy* (Chicago: The University of Chicago Press, 1983), 171.

sometimes involves ministries at the union, union-republic and republic levels of authority, effective coordination of the functional and spatial development of a TPC has proven to be extremely difficult. As a strategy for regional development there are few in the Soviet Union who would seriously question the relevance of the theory of territorial production complexes. Debate focuses on the exact nature of the energy-production cycles which can give rise to a TPC and whether or not TPCs can be used as the basis for dividing the country up into a single scheme of 'objectively existing' economic regions. At a more practical level there have been numerous suggestions for improving the day-to-day planning of TPC development. To bring functionally related production processes 'on stream' at the right time and at the right place is simple enough in principle. Practice, however, is another matter.

In the absence of a regional decision-making body with sufficient economic and political clout to challenge ministerial authorities ensconced in Moscow or a republic capital city, some rather perverse situations can arise. It is frequently the case that production facilities are created but basic services for the working population are not. Ministerial priorities often take precedence over the proper development of an urban infrastructure, or even a spatially integrated settlement. What happened at Bratsk in the 1960s is all too typical. The TPC approach was used in the Angara river region to plan the development of energy-intensive production processes to utilize the large blocks of seemingly cheap hydroelectric power from the Bratsk and Ust-Ilimsk hydropower plants. At Bratsk, an industrial node within the Angara TPC, aluminium production and wood processing were geared to available regional industrial

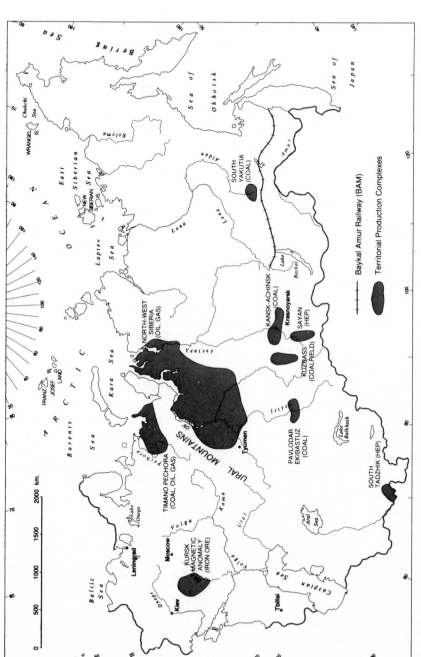

Fig. 46 Territorial Production Complexes in the Early 1980s

Source: Denis J.B. Shaw, 'Spatial Dimensions in Soviet Central Planning', *Transactions, Institute of British Geographers, New Series*, Vol. 10, No. 4, 1985, 407.

resources. A new town was to be created. As was noted in Chapter 5, what is administratively one city of 250,000 people is actually several physically separate settlements, each created by a different ministry (see Fig. 23, page 124). Consumer and cultural services for the population vary considerably from one settlement to another. Given the harsh physical regime all must endure here any unnecessary travel to acquire goods or services is a hardship. More recent TPC projects associated with the construction of the Baykal–Amur Railway (BAM) have not avoided the problems which developed at Bratsk.

Notwithstanding the problems in application, the concept of energy-production cycles and their spatial equivalent, the TPC, remain central to the strategy of Soviet regional industrial development planning. The management innovations described in Chapter 3, such as the *obedineniye*, and the Gorbachev initiatives to enhance productivity and efficiency in resource use are all eminently compatible with this strategy for spatial planning. Having now reviewed the nature of the resource base for industrial development, the locational guidelines and control mechanisms, and the principal regional industrial development concepts it would be appropriate at this point to examine the industrial geography of the country. As noted at the outset, this discussion will provide the principal benchmark for assessing Soviet policies and programmes to ameliorate regional disparities in economic development.

Patterns of industry

The spatial relationship between industrial output and population concentrations in the pre-Soviet era is portrayed in Fig. 6, page 27. During the Soviet period a vast programme of investment in industry has substantially altered the pattern of industry and population distribution. Moreover, this investment has been intentionally skewed away from the consumers goods industries, which in the early 1900s still dominated the industrial structure (see Table 2, page 29), to industries turning out capital goods, industrial raw materials or energy. These latter industries have garnered the lion's share of investment capital from the outset. In the first half of the 1980s for example, about 88 per cent of industrial investment was allocated to the non-consumers goods sector. Investment in both consumer and non-consumer industries accounted for nearly 36 per cent of the 843 billion rubles invested in all sectors of the national economy between 1981 and 1985. The share of investment in industry has not changed much since the mid-1950s, but in earlier years it was even higher. It reached its zenith during World War II (1941–1945) when it commanded over 43 per cent of the total investment funds available. Although the relative share of investment capital allocated to industry has remained fairly constant in recent years, in absolute terms investment has grown dramatically. From 1955 to 1960 about 69 billion rubles were spent on industry of all types. Between 1981 and 1985 more than 300 billion rubles were so allocated. This compares to about 156 billion invested in agriculture and about 128 billion rubles for the housing sector in the same period. An examination of the contemporary distribution of industry may help shed some light on the question as to whether this investment has encouraged national efficiency and growth or regional equity and growth.

While iron-ore reserves are something of a spatial anomaly in that European

Russia and the Urals account for three-quarters of them, the development of the iron and steel industry in peripheral regions of the country suggests that the goal of regional self-sufficiency in key industries has had some practical consequences. As Fig. 47 indicates, ferrous metallurgy is part of the industrial scene from the Caucasus to the Far East. In the Caucasus the mill at Rustavi near Tbilisi began operation in the mid-1950s. Aside from supplying local needs, steel from Rustavi also feeds the rolling mills at Baku. This complements the ouptut from the small steel plant nearby at Sumgait. In Middle Asia steel is produced at Bekobad near Tashkent in Uzbekistan and at the huge mills at Karaganda and Temirtau in Kazakhstan. The Bekobad plant was designed to convert local scrap and imported pig iron into steel. The iron and steel complex in the Kuzbas was a key element in the decentralization drive, as we have already noted. Notwithstanding the dependence on imported ore (Fig. 47), the region possesses some of the country's largest mills. Both the integrated iron and steel plant and the sheet mill in Novokuznetsk rank amongst the world's largest. Smaller iron and steel mills have been in operation for many years at Petrovsk-Zabaykalskiy near Lake Baykal and at Komsomolsk-na-Amure in the Far East. As in the case at Bekobad, they convert local scrap and imported pig iron into steel. With the exception of the iron and steel complexes in the Kuzbas and Kazakhstan, all of these steel works are of comparatively small scale. In total these plants account for less than 20 per cent of Soviet steel production, estimated to be about 160 million metric tons in the mid-1980s.

Plans have been on the drawing board for many years for the creation of a very large-scale iron and steel complex at Tayshet, west of Lake Baykal. Located at the junction of the trans-Siberian and Tayshet–Lena river rail lines it was widely touted during the 1950s as the next major step in the industrialization of Siberia. Indeed, preparatory work was started at the end of that decade, but the project was shelved shortly thereafter. The scheme is certainly feasible for there are huge reserves of iron ore and coking coal of high quality within the region. More recently there has been discussion of a similar size iron and steel complex as part of the BAM project. This would be based on the Neryungi coking coal and iron ore of the Aldan region, resources now more accessible with the completion of the Baykal–Amur railway line. As yet there is no indication that the project will be started. Given the costs of such projects it is more likely that existing plants in the Far East region will be expanded, possibly utilizing local iron ore and coking coal which has not been the case to date. Notwithstanding the real achievements in decentralizing iron and steel production from the European Russian core region, total output from all of the above-mentioned iron and steel mills is comparatively small as we have noted. And perhaps more to the point, the decisions to create these regional centres were taken several decades ago. Changes since have tended to be additions to existing facilities rather than construction of new plants in new locations.

The Industrial South region still accounts for the largest share of Soviet steel production (Fig. 47). In the mid-1980s the steel mills based on Donbas coking-coal and Krivoy Rog iron ore turned out close to two-fifths of total output. Although Fig. 47 suggests a spatially continuous complex of iron and steel plants in the Industrial South, there are concentrations in the eastern extremity centred on Donbas coking-coal and in the west centred on the iron-ore deposits of Krivoy Rog and the KMA. There are some intra-regional specializations in steel fabrication, but perhaps the most significant factor distinguishing the western and eastern flanks is water supply. Fresh water is a vital input in the iron and steel industry and supplies are increasingly problematic in the steppe region of the eastern part of the Industrial South, whereas in the western flank the Dnepr river provides an assured source. The iron and steel plants in the Ural region, which produce about a quarter of total steel production, are now dependent upon both imported coking-coal and iron ore. As was noted earlier, the deficiency in coking-coal was of historical significance. The need to rely on non-local reserves of iron ore is a more recent development. The principal movements of ore are depicted in Fig. 47. Most of the iron and steel mills are located along the highly mineralized eastern flank of the Ural mountains. It is only in the steppe environment of the southern Ural region that adequate fresh water supply has posed a problem. As elsewhere in the country, hydraulic engineers have produced a technological solution to the problem of inadequate or unpredictable water supply. The solution here was to dam the Ural river thereby creating a reservoir of sufficient size to meet the requirements for steel production. This was rather simpler than the solution adopted in Kazakhstan where a several hundred kilometre long canal was created to bring Irtysh river water to the mills located in the arid steppe around Karaganda. The concentration of plants around Moscow in the Central European Russia region is clearly a reflection of market orientation since the bulk of the raw materials is imported from other regions. The main centres of iron and steel production are Tula and Lipetsk, while fabricating plants are found in most major centres in the region. Leningrad boasts a fair complement of steel fabrication plants. Most of the steel comes from the Cherepovets mill which was built in the mid-1950s to supply the Leningrad and Baltic region. Located adjacent to the Rybinsk reservoir, Cherepovets is one of the country's largest plants. It relies on iron ore from deposits in Karelia and the Kola peninsula, and coking-coal from the Pechora region in the European north. There is also a small plant at Liyepaya on the Baltic Sea Coast in Latvia which converts scrap and imported pig iron into steel. In total, these steel plants account for about 15 per cent of total steel output.

For both market and resource location reasons the focus of iron and steel development remains firmly fixed on European Russia. Of the country's ten largest plants, which together account for nearly three-fifths of total Soviet steel production, eight are in European Russia including the Urals. The other two are at Novokuznetsk and Temirtau. The sheer scale of existing investment in the major iron and steel producing regions is alone a powerful reason for adding to existing plants rather than creating new facilities in frontier regions. Indeed, since the Stalin era there have been few major iron and steel developments in the peripheral regions, and with Gorbachev's emphasis on efficiency in resource use the attraction of higher rates of return by adding to existing facilities will certainly be compelling. As the world's largest steel producer, the Soviet Union also exports steel, mostly to the East European bloc. To date exports to the west have not focused to any great degree on the Pacific Rim market, especially Japan. Were such a long-term trade possibility to be developed then the proposed new complex associated with the BAM would take on added importance.

The production of non-ferrous metals differs from ferrous metallurgy in at least

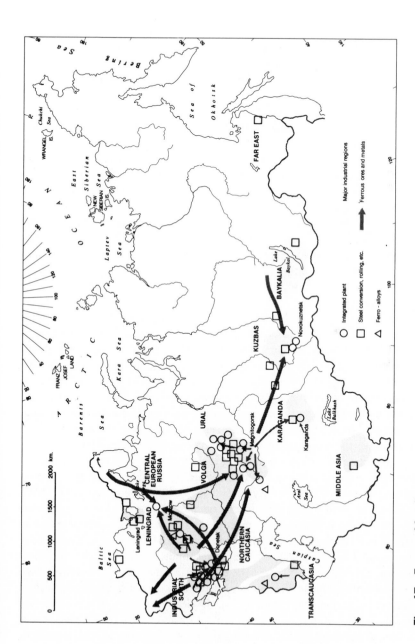

Fig. 47 Ferrous Metallurgy

Source: Based on Leslie Symons et al., *The Soviet Union: A Systematic Geography* (Totowa, NJ: Barnes & Noble, 1983), 166, 180.

two important respects. Firstly, total annual output of all such metals is but a small fraction of the Soviet Union's steel production. At present output is probably no more than 5 per cent that of steel. Secondly, the mining of non-ferrous metals (Fig. 42) is seldom coincident with the production of metals, the latter process being market-oriented, or in the case of aluminium locationally tied to major sources of electricity (Fig. 48). There is a closer spatial link between the location of basic raw materials and the production of steel (see Figs. 42 and 47). While there was some attention given non-ferrous metallurgy in the industrialization drive of the late imperial era, for the most part domestic needs were met by imports from abroad. The Stalin-era industrialization programme gave greater priority to the development of a non-ferrous metallurgical industry, but as we have already indicated some metals are still in short supply and must be imported. Of those that are not, copper is produced in largest quantity. Refining in the pre-Soviet period was localized primarily in the Urals and secondly in the Caucasus. Production in the Urals was given a fillip in the early Five Year Plans, but in the post-war period the locus of production has shifted to Kazakhstan, especially to Dzhezkazgan where a major smelter and refining complex came on stream in the early 1970s (Fig. 48). Copper is also produced in Uzbekistan and Armenia, where there are both mines and smelters. Smaller quantities of copper metal are obtained as by-products from non-ferrous metallurgical complexes at Norilsk, at Ust-Kamenogorsk in Kazakhstan and in the Kola peninsula. Nickel smelters are located in a number of places, but the largest production comes from plants in the Kola peninsula and at Norilsk. Lead and zinc ores are widespread, but smelting has been traditionally associated with the metallurgical complexes in the Ural, Industrial South and Kuzbas industrial regions. Smelting technology has seen coal and coke replaced by natural gas and electricity, and thus the production of lead and zinc metals has shifted to different locations. Refineries at Ust-Kamenogorsk, Leninogorsk and Chimkent in Kazakhstan, at Almalyk in Uzbekistan and at Ordzhonikidze in the north Caucasus complement output from the three main industrial regions. Tin-smelting occurs near Moscow and at Novosibirsk. The very promising reserves in the Far East have resulted in the further development of tin-mining, concentration of ore and construction of a new smelting complex at Solnechniy near Komsomolsk-na-Amure. Aluminium refining, as noted, has been closely associated with major electric power installations, especially hydro, since the reduction of alumina is so heavily electricity-intensive. Production of aluminium occurs in a number of locations, as Fig. 48 indicates. But the bulk of output comes from the Siberian refineries, notably Shelekhov, Bratsk, Krasnoyarsk and more recently the Sayan plant on the upper Yenisey river (Fig. 48). Each is associated with a major hydroelectric power station. To date, Siberian production of alumina is inadequate to meet the aggregate demand of these refineries and therefore long rail haulage from sources in European Russia has been required.

Ferrous and non-ferrous metals are themselves inputs for a vast array of production processes, not least of which are the engineering industries. These have been developed in many regions of the country, as the data on machine tools, transport and agriculture equipment portrayed in Fig. 49 clearly indicates. Some of the key chemical and related synthetic products industries are also shown on this map. Taken together Fig. 47 showing ferrous metallurgy, Fig. 48 depicting non-ferrous metal-

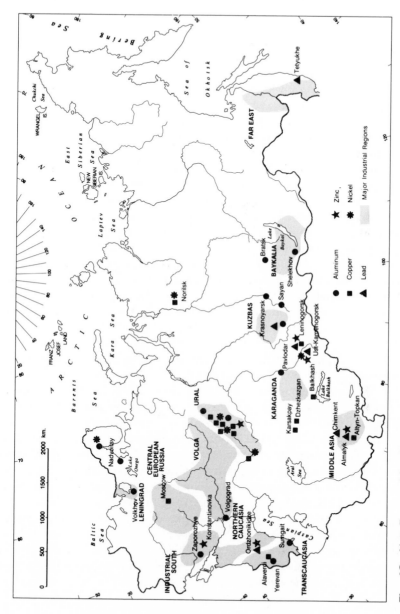

Fig. 48 Non-Ferrous Metallurgy

Source: Based on John C. Dewdney, *The USSR*, (London: Hutchinson, 1978), 93.

lurgy, and Fig. 49 convey a general impression of the major concentrations of heavy industry. What is missing are the many industries which comprise the consumers goods sector, a sector which we noted earlier has consistently received one-eighth or less of the total investment capital allocated to industry. From food products, to textiles, to toys, thousands of goods are produced each year for the Soviet consumer. In terms of location these industries tend to be market-oriented, that is, close to the major centres of population concentration. The distributions portrayed in Figs. 47 to 49 go some way toward providing a general picture of industrial location, however, it is possible to provide a still more schematic regional description of the industrial geography of the Soviet Union.

The most important region in terms of the total value of all industrial production is that roughly delimited by Central European Russia (see Fig. 49). Much of the industry here is market-oriented and labour-intensive. In the early 1970s it accounted for almost one-fifth of the total value of industrial production. In the years since it has not declined in importance. Indeed, if we were to lump in with it the similarly oriented industries of the Baltic zone (primarily the Leningrad region of Fig. 49), then closer to one-third of current Soviet industrial output by value would be represented. As well as having a reasonable complement of those industries turning out capital goods, industrial raw materials and energy, these two regions have a disproportionate share of the country's consumers goods industries. The Industrial South is principally a region of heavy industry and accounts for roughly one-fifth of the total industrial output by value. The Ural region has a similar industrial structure. Although it was eclipsed by the Industrial South in the nineteenth century, industrial development in this region was given a fillip with the emergence of the Urals–Kuznetsk Combine in the First Five Year Plan. Still, the Ural region remains less important than the Industrial South, perhaps accounting for one-tenth of total value of production. The Volga, Kuzbas and Baykalia industrial regions contribute roughly 7, 5 and 3 per cent respectively to total value of industrial output. Industry in the Volga and Baykalia regions is largely the result of post World-War II development programmes and is heavily skewed toward their energy bases, respectively oil and gas and electricity. The Kuzbas, of course, arose as a consequence of the Urals–Kuznetsk Combine and is characterized by heavy industry, as Figs. 47 to 49 indicate. The remaining largely peripheral industrial regions shown in Fig. 49 typically have a reasonable admixture of consumers goods and heavy industries. Transcaucasia and Middle Asia have a higher share of consumers goods manufacturing, but neither of them contributes more than 3 per cent to the total value of industrial output. All of the foregoing industrial regions represent some degree of regional self-sufficiency and specialization. Complementarity of industrial structures requires transportation systems to facilitate inter-regional commodity flows. This topic merits separate, if brief, consideration at this point.

The geography of transport

The integration of the various regions of the Soviet Union demands more than just political power. Power has to be exercised and communication links are the first prerequisite for this to occur. Within the vast expanse of Russia, and now the Soviet

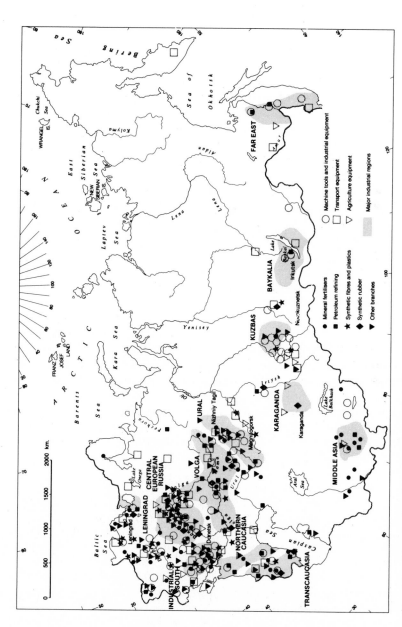

Fig. 49 Chemical and Engineering Industries

Source: Leslie Symons *et al.*, *The Soviet Union: A Systematic Geography* (Totowa, NJ: Barnes & Noble, 1983), 170, 173.

Union, basic transportation systems have evolved to bind the country together. Given the physical geography of the country this has been no easy task. In the nineteenth century it was the coming of the railroad which for the first time permitted comparatively easy internal transport to occur. The imperial system of roads or *trakty*, the rivers, the canals, all were eclipsed when the railroad offered an alternative means of communication. During the Soviet period the railroad has remained the pre-eminent mode within the transport system. While television may inform people even in the most remote corners of the state, the present condition of the Soviet road network is such that the centuries-old phenomenon of *bezdorozhnaya*, or roadlessness, can still bring the movement of goods and people to a standstill for short periods during the spring and autumn. With more than two and one half times the territory of the United States, the Soviet Union still had less than one-sixth of its hard-surface road in the late 1980s. Moreover, there is no comparable system of interstate highways which so greatly facilitate rapid shipment of goods within and between regions in the United States. While road and air transport have become much more important in moving goods and people over the years, they are viewed as complementary rather than competitive modes. In the context of Soviet planning, transport costs are to be minimized wherever possible since transport is regarded as a non-productive activity. What has emerged is often labelled a unified transport system. Interdependence of the different modes is stressed, and to some degree the structure of the Soviet transport system reflects this principle.

As the data in Table 16 indicate, the railroad accounted for the bulk of freight movement from the beginning. Indeed, between 1917 and 1960 its relative importance actually increased slightly, largely at the expense of waterborne freight movement. In view of the limited shipping season on inland waterways and along most of the coastal zone this change is not too surprising. Since 1960 there have been several significant changes in freight movement. The dramatic increase in the role of pipeline movement of oil and natural gas is certainly evident from Table 16. Between 1960 and 1986 this mode increased tenfold in relative importance. At the latter date about one-third of all freight shipment as measured in ton kilometres was accounted for by pipelines. Over the same period there was a fairly substantial increase in the share of

Table 16: Soviet freight movements (billion ton-kilometres)

Mode	1917	1928	1940	1960	1980	1986
Rail	63.0	93.4	420.7	1,504.3	3,439.9	3,834.5
Sea	7.7	9.3	24.9	131.5	848.2	969.7
Inland Waterway	15.0	15.9	36.1	99.6	244.9	255.6
Pipeline – oil	0.01	0.7	3.8	51.2	1,216.0	1,401.3
Pipeline – gas	–	–	–	12.6	596.0	1,240.0
Road	0.1	0.2	8.9	98.5	432.1	488.5
Air	–	–	0.02	0.6	3.1	3.4
Total	85.8	119.5	494.4	1,898.3	6,781.1	8,193.0

Source: *Narodnoye Khozyaystvo SSSR za 70 Let* (Moscow: Finansy i Statistika, 1987), 341; *Narodnoye Khozyaystvo SSSR v 1965g* (Moscow: Finansy i Statistika, 1966), 457.

road freight shipment, but it is still a relatively minor element in the Soviet transport system.

In terms of passenger movement, measured in billion passenger kilometres, railroads traditionally dominated. The pattern began to change in the 1960s when Soviet planners turned their attention to the potential role of cars and especially buses, for short-haul journeys. In 1960 the automobile/bus share of passenger movement was less than 25 per cent; by 1986 it was almost 44 per cent. In the same period the share of rail passenger movement fell from 69 per cent to about 37 per cent. In absolute terms traffic increased from 254.7 billion passenger kilometres to 1057.3 between 1960 and 1986. There was only a marginal change in waterborne passenger traffic. While there is still some enthusiasm, or perhaps nostalgia, for long-distance travel by boat or train, Aeroflot has garnered a large share of the traffic since the 1960s. In 1960 some 12.1 billion passenger kilometres were chalked up by air travellers; in 1986 195.8 billion were recorded. This rate of change exceeded that of any other mode. Given the time required to travel across the Soviet Union by rail it is scarcely surprising that so many choose to fly. If the cost of meals on the rail journey is taken into consideration, then there is probably a saving in rubles as well as in time. On shorter inter-city journeys the fare structure tends to encourage travel by plane. For example, the cost of flying between Moscow and Leningrad is only marginally higher than the price of a soft-class coach seat on the train.

Within the Soviet scheme for transport of goods the road system is viewed as providing a feeder service to rail and water routes. The average distance of goods haulage by road on a per ton basis was barely 18 kilometres in 1986. Rail and waterborne shipments were 940 and 390 kilometres respectively at this date. That the average freight shipment by rail should be so long is partially explained by the fact that coal makes up about one-fifth of the total tonnage. As was noted in an earlier chapter, long-distance shipment of coal is still very much a part of the Soviet scene (see Fig. 40, page 196). The huge demand for construction materials spawned by the frenetic tempo of urban-industrialization ensures that this category of freight dominates amongst all goods moved by rail. While the road network ostensibly dominates in short-haul goods shipment, probably close to one-sixth of all rail shipments are 100 kilometres or less. This is partially explained by the general shortage of goods-hauling vehicles. This shortage is often exacerbated at harvest time when there is a widespread requisition of trucks from rural and urban enterprises as part of the national campaign to move grain from farms to rail terminals. The principal exception to the planned short-haul focus of goods movement by road is in the far north and eastern regions. For example, the Aldan Highway links the trans-Siberian railroad at Never to Yakutsk, a distance of roughly 1,000 kilometres. In terrain such as the Siberian upland the cost of railroad construction is clearly prohibitive. While all-weather roads are complemented by river steamers and barges in the summer, the harsh climate severely limits the shipping season. A costly but necessary alternative is the extensive network of winter roads which ensure a lifeline to the numerous remote northern settlements.

Although the share of goods movement by water has dropped in relative terms, it has continued to increase in absolute volume. The geographic orientation of the major inland water routes also complements the rail system since the former tend to be north–south and the latter east–west. Historically this was an important factor in keeping a sizeable volume of goods shipment on the Volga river system. Indeed, the Volga and related canal/river systems are still the most important routes for waterborne goods movement, accounting for more than three-fifths of the total inland haulage. Coastal goods movement in the Soviet Union is important, but it is the Northern Sea Route which frequently gains most publicity. Despite the short ice-free season there is a sizeable volume of goods moved each season from the west to the Yenisey river. At Igarka transhipment of goods from the ocean going, icebreaker freighter fleet occurs. From here goods can move by river steamer to Dudinka where a short rail line extends to Norilsk, or further upstream. But the main movement of goods, principally forest products, or of late, ore from Norilisk, is outbound. Goods haulage by sea route averaged close to 3,900 kilometres per ton in 1986.

Something of the spatially complementary nature of road, rail and water transport systems is conveyed by Fig. 50. Clearly, much of the country does not have ready access to transport by land or by water. What is missing from this picture is, firstly, the extensive network of air routes. These connect some 3,600 settlements of all sizes in all regions. The growing importance of air passenger traffic has been noted. In the remote far north and east air freight plays an important part in supplying settlements, though to be sure the absolute volume pales in comparison to that moved by land. About three-fifths of all air freight is represented by shipments in the far north and east. Average distance of goods shipment is about 1,000 kilometres. The other component of the transport system which is not represented in Fig. 50 is the oil and gas pipeline network (See Fig. 41, page 201). While there are some possible trade-offs between pipelines and other media, discretion is limited. For example, oil may replace coal shipped by rail or water, but once the technical specifications and route of the pipeline are set there is an upper limit on the quantity that can be delivered. Thus, in creating a unified transport system very careful consideration has to be given the best use for each mode. Unlike Western Europe or North America where duplication of modes, and competition between them, provides a type of safety net in ensuring that products and people do get to their destinations more or less on time, in the Soviet Union there is much less choice as to how shipments might occur. The whole transport system is for example 'inward looking' in that it has been developed with a view to meeting domestic needs. Little attention, or certainly less attention, has been accorded linkages with other countries. Hence, the concept of a land bridge across the Soviet Union which envisioned containerized goods moving between the Atlantic and Pacific realms has been handicapped because there are inadequate facilities to handle containers at the major ports, and more critically perhaps, inadequate rail equipment and trucks to expedite movement of containers across the country. The trans-Siberian railroad has long been one of the most heavily used railroads in the world. Adding an unpredictable trans-national volume of traffic to a system which is barely able to cope with domestic traffic obviously poses problems. The completion of the Baykal–Amur railroad relieves somewhat the pressure on the rail system in the far east, but as it is an essential component of a massive regional development scheme in its own right, there is a real question as to what scope there

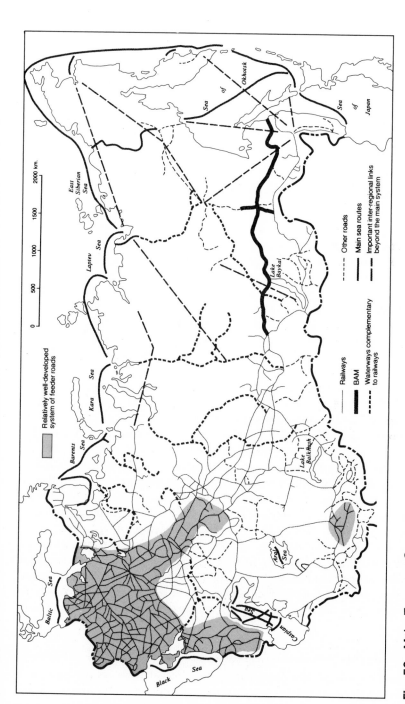

Fig. 50 Major Transport Systems

Source: A Brown et al. (eds.), *The Cambridge Encyclopedia of Russia and the Soviet Union* (Cambridge: Cambridge University Press, 1982), 351.

is for enhancement of trans-national traffic as part of the land-bridge concept.

As Fig. 50 indicates, the European Russian core is especially favoured in terms of the density of transportation systems. Given the distribution of population and economic activities this is scarcely surprising. But the transportation system in the eastern regions should not be underestimated in terms of its impact on the country as a whole simply because it is so sparse in comparison with European Russia. As we have emphasized, it is from these regions that so many of the essential raw materials for industry must now be obtained. The cost of overcoming vast distances has been met. While most regions are now integrated to some degree into the national transport system, the question remains to what extent has the process of regional economic development alleviated regional economic disparity?

Industrialization and regional industrial development

According to the quotation from a speech given by Leonid Brezhnev in 1972 on the occasion of the 50th anniversary of the USSR which introduced this chapter, the long-standing goal of evening out the level of economic development of the fifteen republics had been more or less achieved. This claim was reiterated a decade later in a speech celebrating the 60th anniversary. Of course, in verifying such a statement a great deal depends upon what is being measured, and how. That enormous progress has been made in modernizing the country, in improving the quality of life, is beyond doubt. As Brezhnev himself observed in his 1972 speech, in the 1920s more than 80 per cent of the population of Middle Asia was functionally illiterate; indeed in four of the five Middle Asia republics illiteracy exceeded 90 per cent. Industry and urbanization were at a very low level of development in most regions, but the difference between the most developed region and the least was extreme. In one Soviet study of the level of industrial development in 1926, the range was found to be in the order of 32:1. In the years since 1917 the output from those industries producing capital goods, industrial raw materials or energy has increased more than 700-fold, while consumers goods production is more than a hundred times greater. Concomitantly, the share of the urban population has grown from about one-sixth to two-thirds of the total. Illiteracy has long since been eradicated. In short, there is perhaps something to Brezhnev's claim that 'on the basis of the Leninist nationalities policy and at the price of the intense labour of the entire Soviet people, we have achieved a situation in which the term "backward outlying national area", which was so common in the old Russia, has ceased to exist.'[1] In the remainder of this chapter we will examine this question from the perspective of industrial development.

From what has been said already it is perfectly clear that the distribution of basic resources for industry is far from even. Indeed one of the central themes which has emerged throughout the previous chapters is that of a marked spatial imbalance

---

[1] L.I. Brezhnev, 'On the 50th Anniversary of the Union of Soviet Socialist Republics,' *Pravda* and *Izvestiya*, 22 December, 1972, in *The Current Digest of the Soviet Press*, Vol. 34, No. 51, 1973, 7.

between the distribution of resources of all kinds and the locus of demand. Balancing the need to achieve a measure of regional equality in economic development with the compelling logic of enhancing efficiency in all sectors of the national economy has not been a simple task. In the years preceding Brezhnev's 1972 speech a number of studies attempted to demonstrate which of national efficiency or regional equality was the dominant outcome of Soviet industrial development policies. The critical point is not whether regional differences exist, for clearly they do, but whether over time the differences between regions are diminishing or increasing.

Between 1926 and 1962 there was an appreciable increase in industrial production at the national level, and according to one Soviet source an equally impressive erosion of the gap between the most highly industrialized region and the least. As noted, the difference between the two was 32:1 in 1926. By 1962 it had been reduced to 4:1. By 1968 it was estimated to be only 1:8:1, thus giving some credence to the claim made by Brezhnev in 1972. While western studies are far from being in total agreement concerning the regional dimensions of the standard of living in the Soviet Union, most acknowledge the substantial gains registered in urban-industrial development and concede that the matter of regional equality had been addressed in Soviet policies at least until the 1960s. To be sure, the industrial structure which was put in place was rather narrowly defined and did not embrace overly much in terms of consumers goods production. There is nonetheless general agreement that some amelioration of regional disparity in industrial output took place. Soviet data are illustrative. In the Kazakh republic in 1926 industrial output was barely 7 per cent of the national average. In 1968 it was 79 per cent. Moreover, at this date 14 of the 15 major branches of industry were to be found in the republic. Four other regions had the same proportion of branches represented in their industrial structures. One region, the Baltic republics, had two categories 'unfilled'; the remainder of the economic regions had the full spectrum of industrial operations in 1968.

A more significant measure of regional industrial development, however, is industrial output per capita. Data for two years are presented in Table 17. It is immediately apparent that there are significant regional variations, a scarcely surprising situation given the regional variations in industrial activity and the basic demographic and urban growth trends outlined in Chapter 4. The Baltic, North-west, Centre, Donets–Dnepr and the Urals regions all stand out as having per capita industrial output indices much above the national average. While Middle Asia and the Caucasus are uniformly below average, there are pockets of comparatively under-industrialized territory in the RSFSR (Central-Chernozem) and the South Ukraine as well. These data need to be set against the general performance of the national economy. It will perhaps be recalled that since the 1950s there has been a general downturn in the rate of growth of national income (see Fig. 13, page 63). Part of the reason for this trend was the slowdown in industrial output. As the economy became more technologically complex, indeed more modern, the previous very high rate of growth from the more narrowly defined industrial structure could not be maintained. Of note in this context is the decline in per capita industrial output in traditional industrial regions, the Donets–Dnepr, the Northwest and the Centre between 1960 and 1970. The Volga, Urals and Siberian regions clearly made gains. This was in no small measure related to the decision to exploit the resource

Table 17: Indices of per capita industrial output by economic region, 1960 and 1970 (USSR = 100)

Region	1960	1970
RSFSR		
Northwest	146	131
Centre	162	144
Volga-Vyatka	90	105
Central-Chernozem	68	84
Volga	96	110
North Caucasus	88	85
Urals	135	142
West Siberia	95	104
East Siberia	90	105
Far East	107	108
Ukraine		
Donets–Dnepr	137	132
Southwest	53	65
South	85	89
Belorussia	64	86
Baltic		
Estonia	124	135
Latvia	125	141
Lithuania	79	107
Caucasus		
Georgia	67	65
Armenia	76	78
Azerbaydzhan	76	56
Middle Asia		
Uzbek	61	45
Kirgiz	44	50
Tadzhik	50	41
Turkmen	65	49
Kazakh	66	65
Moldavia	53	64

Source: Leslie Dienes, 'Regional Economic Development', in Bergson, A., Levine, H. (eds), *The Soviet Economy: Toward the Year 2000* (London: George Allen & Unwin, 1983), Table 8–1, 220–1.

base of these regions, perhaps most importantly the oil and natural gas deposits. The data presented in Table 17 reflect some significant regional variations in level of industrialization but to label them regional disparities is to ignore the enormous progress which was registered between the 1920s and the 1960s. As Figs. 47 through 49 revealed, industrial development has occurred in the eastern regions, despite the long-recognized lower rates of return. And not all of this industrial development can be attributed to the exigencies of war-time and locational decisions shaped by strategic considerations. But since Brezhnev's speech of 1972, and especially since the arrival of Mikhail Gorbachev, there appears to be a shift away from regional equity to national efficiency in industrial development decision-making. We might briefly summarize some of the decisions since the early 1970s which tend to support such a view.

The by-words of the Gorbachev era are *glasnost'*, *perestroyka*, and *uskoreniye*, respectively openness, restructuring and acceleration. The latter two have significant implications for decision-making which relate to this question of regional equity or national efficiency. The disproportionate per capita allocation of investment capital in the peripheral regions of the Soviet Union, principally the Caucasus, Middle Asia and the Siberian realm, has long been recognized as generating comparatively lower rates of return than might have been obtained by channelling these monies into the existing industrial regions of the European Russia core region. Industrial investment was regarded as the catalyst for urban development. Thus, in the frontier region resource development went hand in hand with urban development. Communities were to be created where none existed before. Resource exploitation of the periphery to benefit the core region was not then part of the development strategy. In Middle Asia and the Caucasus, industrialization was equally important, but more often as a means of drawing a larger share of the population off the land and into the mainstream of urban-industrialism. To the Soviet planner the transformation of a fast growing, predominantly rural, non-Slavic population into an urban proletariat was compelling on economic grounds given the quest for a larger industrial labour supply. For the Marxist the transformation was equally compelling on ideological grounds. While economic and ideological reasons have lost none of their attraction, the low return on investment in many industrial projects which might have been catalysts in this process seems to have prompted reconsideration.

In retrospect the Tenth Five Year Plan (1976–1980) appears to have been a harbinger of what was to come. Despite massive investment in the development of energy resources in Siberia and Middle Asia and the development of the Baykal–Amur Mainline (BAM) project, a general reorienting of investment between the European Russian core and the peripheral regions was set in motion. The argument for so doing hinged in no small measure on the calculated rate of return on industrial investment in peripheral regions as opposed to the core. But such calculations are based on Soviet prices, which in the main are determined by bureaucrats and not the marketplace. Thus, for example, for Siberia, and especially the oil and natural gas rich west Siberian region, the real worth of the resource base was in effect greatly undervalued in the years following the 1973 world energy crisis. Some Soviet authorities argued at the time that using world energy prices for calculating the contribution to the national economy of industrial, energy related development in Siberia would dramatically increase the rate of return. But as the inputs into the peripheral regions are similarly underpriced, or at least artificially priced in a non-market environment, to attribute world prices to the resource outputs was not deemed to be appropriate. Thus, the rate-of-return argument favouring further investment in the European core region remains intact, even if not everywhere readily accepted. Coupled with the return on investment in industry being comparatively low is the comparatively high cost of creating a suitable urban infrastructure. This is especially significant in the Far North and regions equated to it (see Fig. 44, page 219). Since the early 1970s there has been a dramatic increase in the tour of duty approach to resource development in these zones. In the west Siberian region alone there are now several hundred thousand workers engaged in this type of employment. In an earlier era there was a much stronger commitment to creating a permanent, family-oriented urban settlement in such regions. Both the non-renewable nature of many of the resource development projects in the northern and eastern realms and the huge cost of providing adequately for a permanent population have encouraged this approach.

By the time of the 12th Five Year Plan in 1986 the evidence was much clearer. The massive river-diversion project envisioned for the Ob'–Irtysh river systems was put on hold. As was noted in Chapter 6, up until late 1985 the SIBARAL project had been included in the draft guidelines for the 12th Five Year Plan. The huge outlay, with a long lead time before any return would occur, the need to leverage greater efficiency in water resource management in Middle Asia and perhaps a growing dissaffection with the prospect of yet another massive subsidy to a peripheral and non-Slavic region, all seemed to force reconsideration of the project. Its deletion from the Plan combined with the call for intensification of production in existing industrial complexes in the European Russian core certainly adds weight to the argument that the peripheral regions are garnering less of the investment pot. The BAM project is also less prominently featured in the Plan than might have been expected given the publicity attached to it in the mid-1970s as a regional industrial development catalyst. Many of the ancillary territorial production complexes originally envisioned have not been included in the Plan. Existing urban development remains at a rather low level. For Middle Asia no new projects of any major scale are included. Rather emphasis is on continuing the development of industrial projects from earlier Plan eras. Certainly nothing very substantial has been planned that could be conceived as tackling the growing problem of regional unemployment which, as we have noted already, in the Uzbek republic alone was in excess of one million in the mid-1980s. To be sure, there is a continuing emphasis on enhancing the contribution of the peripheral regions to energy supply. This affects Siberia and Middle Asia most particularly. But even in this instance the investment tends to be rather narrowly focused in that urban infrastructure does not figure as prominently as resource exploitation. Additionally, the role of nuclear energy is scheduled to increase substantially by the end of the century notwithstanding the Chernobyl' disaster. Investment in nuclear energy plants of course will be in the European Russian core region, not the Asian realm.

The call for *perestroyka* and *uskoreniye* adds further spatial emphasis to the long-standing call for intensification of production in all sectors of the economy, but notably the industrial. The benefits of external economies provided by existing urban agglomerations can no longer be ignored. Spatial concentration of industry, especially of a 'high technology' type, is of growing importance in contemporary locational theory and planning. Clearly all of this simply supports the role of the core region within the national space economy. Industrial development will not necessarily be so spatially biased as to entirely deprive the peripheral regions of investment. The raw-material resource base of Siberia and the labour resource of Middle Asia alone will ensure that will not occur. But the conscious effort to expand the industrial base of peripheral regions to achieve a more equitable distribution of industry is certainly going to be muted. More selective industrial investment will have the consequence of welding peripheral regions to the core, but probably at the cost of less well developed urban and social service infrastructure. While this is likely to be most noticeable in the Asian component of the periphery, there are peripheral regions in European Russia and the Caucasus which could similarly be disadvantaged. While it is yet rather too early to speculate as to the probable core–periphery balance in terms of industrial investment in the next Five Year Plan, the trends which have been set in motion over the past decade do not suggest a very auspicious prospect for the quality of life in regions outside the European Russian core.

While there are regional variations in the level of industrial production, the state has at its disposal a host of measures for transferring payments to the populations of peripheral regions which could well result in a rather different picture of regional development. In the next chapter we will examine a number of these with a view to assessing the quality of life in a regional context.

Recommended reading

Ambler, J., Shaw, D.J.B., Symons, L. (eds), *Soviet and East European Transport Problems* (London: Croom Helm, 1985).

Blandon, P., *Soviet Forest Industries* (Boulder: Westview Press, 1983).

Bahry, D., *Outside Moscow. Power Politics and Budgetary Policy in the Soviet Republics* (New York: Columbia University Press, 1987).

Barr, B.M., Braden, K., *The Disappearing Russian Forest. A Dilemma in Soviet Resource Management* (Totowa, New Jersey: Rowman and Littlefield, 1988).

Dienes, L., *Soviet Asia. Economic Development and National Policy Choices* (Boulder: Westview Press, 1987).

Dewdney, J.C., *The USSR. Studies in Industrial Geography* (Boulder: Westview Press, 1978).

Hunter, H., Kaple, D.A., *The Soviet Railroad Situation* (Washington: Wharton Econometrics Inc., 1983).

Koropeckyj, I.S., *Locational Problems in Soviet Industry Before World War II. The Case of the Ukraine* (Chapel Hill: University of North Carolina Press, 1971).

Koropeckyj, I.S., Schroeder, G.E. (eds), *Economics of Soviet Regions* (New York: Praeger, 1981).

Lewis, R., *Science and Industrialization in the USSR* (London: Macmillan, 1979).

North, R., *Transport in Western Siberia: Tsarist and Soviet Development* (Vancouver: University of British Columbia, 1978).

Shabad, T., Mote, V.L., *Gateway to Siberian Resources. The BAM* (Silver Spring: Scripta Publishing, 1977).

Swearingen, R. (ed), *Siberia and the Soviet Far East: Strategic Dimensions in Multinational Perspective* (Stanford: Hoover Institution, 1987).

Symons, L., White, C. (eds), *Russian Transport: An Historical and Geographical Survey* (London: George Bell and Sons, 1975).

Tseplyaev, V.P., *The Forests of the USSR* (New York: Daniel Davies, 1966).

Wood, A. (ed), *Siberia. Problems and Prospects for Regional Development* (Totowa, New Jersey: Rowman and Littlefield, 1987).

ZumBrunnen, C., Osleeb, J.P., *The Soviet Iron and Steel Industry* (Totowa, New Jersey: Rowman and Allanheld, 1986).

10 Social Justice and the Quality of Life

The people's well-being is the central problem in the theory and practice of building socialism and communism.

Sarkisyan, 1983[1]

Enormous progress has been made in improving the material conditions of labour and life for the Soviet population in comparison with the state of affairs which prevailed during the late imperial era. The revolution of 1917 clearly was not a hard and fast watershed separating the imperial era and the societal values which under-pinned it from the new world of socialism. Change came slowly in many instances, and was not universally welcome. Obviously what emerged was a new political, economic and social order. But the new order did not then, and does not now, fully conform to the ideals espoused by those who made the revolution.

Contemporary Soviet society is framed within socialist, not communist, principles. Thus, it is not a classless society in which each member is provided for according to need. This ideal state remains the ultimate goal, but for the time being, formal legal classes and strata define the official social system. All those physically capable are expected to work, and are paid roughly in accordance with the state's perception of the value of their labour to society. Notwithstanding sizeable improvements in wages and the substantial array of free state social services and benefits, a segment of the Soviet population is still poor by any objective standard of measure. With the Gorbachev-era emphasis on *perestroyka* and *uskoreniye*, the existing income differentials by class, occupation and region are likely to be increased rather than narrowed. The effect of *glasnost'* in focusing public attention on such developments remains to be seen, but it seems unlikely that more information about the comparatively large incomes generated by members of the recently sanctioned cooperatives who are capitalizing on a consumers goods and services deficient Soviet economy will promote greater social harmony.

---

[1] G.S. Sarkisyan, *Narodnoye Blagosostoyaniye v SSSR* (Moscow: Ekonomika, 1983), 3.

More information is a key element in Gorbachev's democratization of the Soviet system. But for every bit of good news there has been at least an equal amount of bad. There are clear signs that the quality of life is not what it should be. Perhaps the most notable barometer of something amiss was the absolute decline in life expectancy from the late 1960s until the early 1980s. The trend has been reversed, but as we noted in an earlier chapter this was a unique occurrence amongst modern industrial states. It is our purpose in this chapter to probe some aspects of the quality of life for the average Soviet citizen, and where data permit to do so in a comparative regional context. Our first objective will be to describe briefly the changes in per capita income and social benefits during the Soviet period. In providing a measure of social justice and a reasonable quality of life clearly much more is involved than just rubles to spend and access to state social benefits. Thus, the second objective of this chapter is to examine some other aspects of the quality of life, namely the issues of health care, environmental degradation, recreation and leisure. The chapter will conclude with a brief assessment of some dimensions of social justice in the Soviet context.

Income and expenditure patterns

In Chapter 3 the declining rate of economic growth since the Second World War was highlighted as one of the key problems confronting Soviet economic planners. Official statistics indicate that the growth of national income dropped from a shade less than 8 per cent per year in the latter half of the 1960s to less than 4 per cent in the early 1980s (see Fig. 13, page 63). During the Gorbachev era of *glasnost'* more pessimistic assessments have been rendered by a number of leading Soviet economists. A. Aganbegyan, one of Gorbachev's closest economic advisors during the late 1980s, contended that the decline was from a high of only 5 per cent per annum in the late 1960s to zero in the early 1980s. Whatever the real situation, it is obvious that long-term improvement in the standard of living of the average Soviet citizen can only come from a net addition to the real wealth of the state, a major realignment of existing priorities in the allocation of the state's resources, or a combination of the two. The drive to achieve greater efficiencies in the use of the state's natural, human and financial resources is thus of fundamental importance. And so too – potentially – are the efforts in the international scene to scale down the arms race and to withdraw from costly and intractable military situations such as the Afghanistan intervention. Defence-related expenditures in the Soviet Union are reckoned to consume about 15 per cent of the gross national product, roughly twice the share so allocated in the US economy. This comparison should be qualified by noting that the US economy is probably close to twice as productive as that of the Soviet Union. Nonetheless, the burden of the military still falls more heavily on the shoulders of the average Soviet citizen than on his American counterpart. Four years of the Gorbachev era have not seen a reduction in defence spending, but neither it seems, has there been a significant increase. For the average Soviet citizen the post-World War II period has been one of steady if not spectacular improvements in living standards, notwithstanding the serious problems posed by the decline and possible stagnation in the growth of the domestic economy. Trends in per capita national income are of interest in this regard.

Between 1940 and 1986 per capita national income as measured by wages and social benefits increased by 663 per cent, according to official Soviet statistics. The tempo of change since the late 1960s has been especially notable. It was pointed out in Chapter 3 that the economic reform initiated by Brezhnev and Kosygin in 1965 was premised on enhancing incentives. Enterprises were encouraged to be profitable, and they were permitted to retain a portion of profits for the benefit of workers. More generally, wage rates were improved, particularly in the agricultural sector. Not only was the gap between the average income of collective farm (*kolkhoz*) and state farm (*sovkhoz*) workers significantly narrowed, the gap between the farm worker and the urban industrial employee was also eroded and now stands at less than 10 per cent. While these basic relationships were changing the average monthly wage of all workers and government employees climbed steadily. In 1960 it was 81 rubles; in 1986, 196 rubles per month. Parallelling the increase in wages has been a steady growth in absolute expenditure on social benefits such as education, health, housing, family allowance payments, pensions, and so on. On a per capita basis social benefits amounted to 127 rubles in 1961. By 1986 they totalled 554 rubles. At a rough reckoning wage payments account for about three-quarters of what is described as the 'real income' of the Soviet population. The balance comprises the wide array of state benefits. For the typically two-wage-earner family, this works out to just over 500 rubles income per month from wages and state benefits.

Soviet statistics indicate that per capita national income rose 1.6 times between 1970 and 1985. Expressed in terms of average income per family member, the changes are as follows. In 1970, 18 per cent of the population belonged to families with monthly incomes in excess of 100 rubles per member. By 1985 more than 60 per cent of the population fell into this category. Indeed, by the latter date more than 30 per cent of the Soviet population belonged to families whose monthly income per member exceeded 150 rubles. As already noted, there is stratification in wage levels according to state priorities. Thus, skilled workers in the energy sector, metallurgy or machine construction earn as much as two and one half times more than their counterparts in food processing or textiles. And the system of regional wage coefficients described in the preceding chapter simply serves to compound the potential differences in the monthly wage packet. At the other end of the skill level, in the trade, catering or custodial occupations for example, wages are still quite low. Compared to the highest paid skilled workers they can earn as little as one third, or in extreme cases, one quarter as much.

On a regional basis non-agricultural wage rates vary markedly, as the relative data presented in Fig. 51 indicate. Although these data are only illustrative of republic differences, they nonetheless underscore the importance of disaggregating national-level statistics. In 1986 the average monthly pay for all workers and government employees was 196 rubles, as noted above. But in Estonia the average was 221 rubles; in Azerbaydzhan about 162. In general terms there is a north-west, south-east gradient in average wages. To some degree this reflects differences in the structure of the regional economies. But there is more to the differences portrayed in Fig. 51 than simply a core–periphery relationship. Estonia, for example, has been at the forefront in the economic reform promoted by Gorbachev. It was the first republic to switch from an administrative supply allocation to something akin to a wholesale-

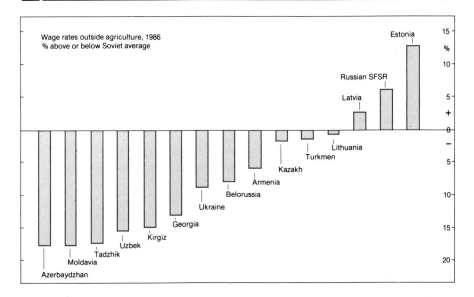

Fig. 51   Non-Agricultural Wage Rates, 1986

Source: 'The Soviet Economy', *The Economist*, 9–15 April, 1988, 6.

trade system. In other words, Estonian enterprises more than anywhere else are market sensitive. In 1988 Estonia moved a step further along the *perestroyka* track by petitioning to have All-Union ministerial control, which emanates from Moscow, turned over to republic-level decision-makers. It seems that cultural factors play a part in the ready adoption of innovations in economic management in Estonia. In other regions cultural values may also play important roles, but sometimes in less desirable ways than the state may wish. The populations of the south, notably the Caucasus and Middle Asia (including the Kazakh region) are comparatively poor in terms of the data on per capita national income presented in Fig. 52. But recent surveys of Soviet emigres suggest that substantial earnings are derived from the second economy in these regions, income which of course does not figure in the official statistics.

The data in Fig. 52 pertain to 1968. In the post-World War II era there was a redistribution of national wealth in one form or another from the more developed to the less developed regions. Since 1968 there have been substantial increases in wage rates and average monthly income, as has been observed already. But in the few studies of regional disparity since the late 1960s there is not much evidence to suggest that the general pattern portrayed in Fig. 52 has altered very much, if at all. Indeed, as was suggested in earlier chapters, there is a real possibility that the Gorbachev-era reforms will exacerbate income stratification by occupation, social group and region. Improvement in the quality of life is implied by larger wage packets and resultant

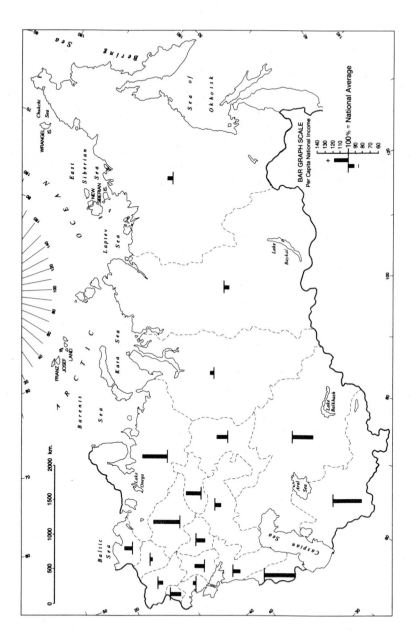

Fig. 52 Per Capita National Income, 1968

Source: L.N. Telepko, *Urovni Ekonomicheskogo Razvitiya Rayonov SSSR* (Moscow: 'Ekonomika,' 1971), 100.

Table 18: Number of consumer durables per 100 households 1970–1986

DURABLE	1970 URBAN	RURAL	1986 URBAN	RURAL
Refrigerators	43	13	101	78
Washing machines	64	26	78	58
Sewing machines	57	54	63	70
Vacuum cleaners	16	3	50	21
Television	61	32	102	94
Private car	–	–	15	17

Source: *Narodnoye Khozyaystvo SSSR za 70 Let* (Moscow: Finansy i Statistika, 1987), 473.

higher per capita income. But this assumes a commensurate increase in goods and services on which consumers can spend money.

While the rubles in circulation increased roughly threefold between 1970 and 1985, production of consumers goods barely doubled. As basic household durables became more commonplace, as opportunities to spend comparatively large sums of money on other consumers goods remained limited, savings, not surprisingly, accumulated. Between the late 1960s and late 1970s registered savings rose fourfold. During the 1980s the pattern has continued. Savings grew by nearly one-third between 1984 and 1988 alone. Too much money chasing too few goods and services clearly produces price inflation. Since the state controls most prices, and can only increase charges for basic items slowly because of long-standing social policy, if not concern over adverse public reaction, inflation has been manifested most in the second economy and in the price of foodstuffs sold in the supply–demand environment of the free collective farmers market and the cooperative. Again not surprisingly, consumer reaction to escalating prices for goods and services not readily available from the state is negative.

There is no question that the average Soviet household is now better off in a material sense that at any earlier time. The data on consumer durables presented in Table 18 certainly make this clear. In 1986 television sets were ubiquitous, though the demand for colour receivers remains strong despite their high cost. Major appliances are commonplace in both the urban and rural households, a rather dramatic change compared to 1970 in the latter instance. Indeed, the growing material prosperity of the rural population is perhaps best reflected by the ratio of private automobiles per 100 households in 1986. But basic statistics such as those presented in Table 18 convey only part of the picture. In many, if not most, rural areas repair services for the growing volume of household appliances are seriously deficient. This facet of the consumer scene is exacerbated by the customarily low quality of such durables. Urban households are similarly disadvantaged in respect of the quality of goods available. However, they have somewhat better prospects of obtaining repairs when necessary, if not from state-run agencies then from the urban *shabashniki* of the second economy, that is, the legion of individuals who provide such repair and other services on the side, often at sizeable personal profit. To put the Soviet consumer-goods supply situation into sharper perspective, comparative data are provided in Fig. 53. Leaving aside the important questions of quality of goods

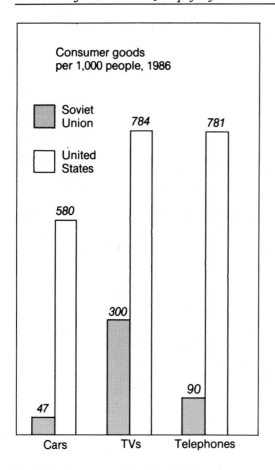

Consumer goods
per 1,000 people, 1986

Soviet Union

United States

784   781

580

300

90

47

Cars   TVs   Telephones

Fig. 53   Consumers Goods, 1986

Source: 'The Soviet Economy', *The Economist*, 9–15 April, 1988, 4.

and availability of servicing, the differences are still striking. For those Soviets who have enough money to buy a car – and there are many in this category – the average waiting time before delivery after payment in full is seven to eight years. Thus, the gains registered in per capita income, in ownership of consumer durables, in general material well-being, while substantial, have not yet satisfied consumer demands. The programme to restrict the production and sale of alcohol has simply left billions more rubles in the pockets and purses of Soviet consumers. In 1984, on the eve of the Gorbachev-era clampdown on alcohol, its sale accounted for nearly one-sixth of all retail turnover. The loss of income to the state because of lower turnover-tax revenue does not make any easier the task of augmenting consumers goods production. An ostensibly more sober workforce has not yet brought about a permanent increase in productivity.

Household expenditure patterns provide some additional insights into the rela-

Table 19: Household budget – worker's family, 1940–1970–1986, per cent

CATEGORY	1940	1970	1986
Food	53.0	34.7	27.9
Alcohol	2.0	3.4	2.4
Fuel	1.2	0.3	0.1
Rent	2.8	2.6	2.6
Clothing	10.9	15.1	14.4
Consumer durables	1.7	5.7	7.8
Social-cultural services*	14.6	20.3	20.6
Savings	4.6	4.0	8.1
Taxes	4.1	7.7	8.6
Other	5.1	6.2	7.5
TOTAL	100.0	100.0	100.0

Source: *Narodnoye Khozyaystvo SSSR za 70 Let* (Moscow: Finansy i Statistika, 1987), 444.

*Includes such state benefits as education.

tionship between the rising per capita national income and general well-being. A basic household budget for an industrial worker's family has long been included in the official Soviet statistical handbook. In Table 19 data for three years are provided for the major components of household expenditure. Again the relative improvement over the years is readily apparent. A larger share of a larger family income goes toward clothing, consumer durables and social-cultural activities than ever before. While expenditures on food apparently have declined in relative terms, there has been a steady improvement in the diet of the population. As noted in Chapter 7, the emphasis since the Second World War has been on improving protein intake by expanding supplies of meat, fish and fowl and reducing dependence on carbohydrates. Thus, per capita consumption of meat has increased from 39.5 kilogrammes in 1960 to 62.4 in 1986. Potato consumption dropped from 143 kilogrammes per person to 107 over the same period. Rent has remained at more or less the same rate over the past half century. Expenditures on alcohol, on the other hand, have fluctuated quite substantially. The data in Table 19 are, of course, national averages and therefore in some categories of expenditure cultural values play an important role. This is certainly true of alcohol. In much of Middle Asia, Azerbaydzhan and parts of Georgia the traditional Muslim interdiction concerning consumption of alcohol is still widely observed. Thus, in the Slavic and Baltic households the level of outlay for alcohol is substantially higher than indicated in Table 19. But everywhere spending on alcohol dropped in the late 1980s as the government programme mentioned earlier took hold. The rise in the share of the household budget directed toward savings, which is especially evident after 1984, is perhaps partly related to the reduction in expenditure on alcohol. However, trends in alcohol consumption are not so simple as to be fully explained by the data in Table 19. Production of *samogon*, or home distilled liquor, has long been part of the Soviet scene, notably, though not exclusively, in the Baltic and Slavic culture realms. As the government programme to cut state production and consumption of alcohol took hold in the mid-to-late

1980s, the sale of sugar suddenly escalated, leaving ordinary Soviet households scrambling to find enough for day-to-day needs. The widespread sugar shortage generated considerable public discussion – and criticism. Conventional wisdom has it that the unpredicted surge in sugar consumption was related to a marked increase in the production of *samogon* and homemade wine.

The data provided in Table 19 are based upon a sample survey of 62,000 household budgets in various regions and include an estimate of state payments and benefits to the average family. There has been considerable discussion in the Soviet Union as to how close these relative allocations by category square with reality. In late 1987 *glasnost'* provided an opportunity for the readers of *Izvestiya*, the main newspaper of central government, to take issue with the official view of the average family budget. The size of the 'average family' budget, estimated to be just over 500 rubles per month when state benefits and payments were included, was felt by many people to be completely unrealistic. It offended the sensibilities of lower-income families to be lumped together with those who have more. Put simply, families with average or higher than average monthly incomes comprise part of the privileged sector of Soviet society. And privilege affords opportunities to purchase goods at state prices in special shops. Thus, the proportion of the family budget needed to purchase food, officially 27.9 per cent in 1986, was widely disputed. Deficient supplies in state shops obliged ordinary households to purchase foodstuffs from the collective farmers markets or cooperatives where prices generally reflect supply and demand. For many families unable to access special shops where foodstuffs are usually available, and at state prices, the additional cost is quite substantial. Official surveys corroborate this state of affairs. It has been estimated that those who earn low or even average wages have to pay almost 50 per cent more for a kilogramme of meat than those with high monthly incomes. In similar fashion that segment of the population with above-average incomes also receives more by way of state benefits simply because they have far greater opportunities to take advantage of them.

The attempt to compile a representative household expenditure budget is problematic in any society. Few people relate well to a statistical average. But there are clearly more difficulties in managing household affairs in a chronically goods and services deficient society than in a more bountiful one, irrespective of how closely one's own circumstances fit the average. Thus, as remarked in earlier chapters, privilege in the Soviet Union is more often expressed in terms of access to goods and services than in terms of money alone. For people born and raised in a society very much conditioned by consumerism, accustomed to accessing virtually any service by no more taxing an exercise than perusing the yellow pages of the local telephone book, the rigours of daily life in the average Soviet household are indeed difficult to comprehend. What compounds the difficulties in household management for many Soviet women is the attitude of Soviet men toward domestic chores.

While in the typical Soviet family both husband and wife have jobs, there has long been an additional burden imposed on working women. Not only do Soviet women living in cities work nearly as many hours as men each week, their contribution to household chores is between two to three times as great. As a rule, the higher the level of education the greater is the male contribution to household duties, but the distinction is relative. The substantial improvement in the ratio of consumer durables per 100 households described in Table 18 certainly has made housework easier, but largely for the wife and mother. Thus, compared to the 1960s when on average 30 hours a week were taken up on household duties – in addition to the 50-odd hours of work and work related activity – the Soviet housewife of the late 1980s is much better off. The work week was reduced in the late 1960s to 41 hours, the six-day work week was reduced to five, thereby providing a free weekend for most workers, and the simple chores of washing clothes, cleaning house and food preparation have been much aided by an improved supply of washing machines, vacuum cleaners and refrigerators. But attitudes obviously change less rapidly than the material circumstances of the household. Married men still spend substantially more time on personal pursuits and asleep each day than women. As perhaps might be expected, the situation for the woman of the rural household is decidedly less favourable than her urban counterpart's. Thus, the Soviet Union shares with many other countries considerable inequality in gender roles in the home and workplace.

While the data on household expenditures go some way toward enhancing our appreciation as to how the average Soviet family lives, it is obvious that a comparative referent would be of value. Even though the statistics are somewhat dated, the message conveyed by Table 20 is clear – the standard of living in the Soviet Union is considerably lower than in other major western industrial states. In the mid-1970s it was roughly one-third that enjoyed by Americans, and not quite three-fifths that of the Japanese. Given the tempo of annual growth in each of the economies for which data are provided in Table 20, it is unlikely that the general relationships would have altered appreciably between then and now. It is notable that only in four instances – all education – were per capita outlays greater in the Soviet Union. Housing and transportation expenditures fare especially poorly in a comparative context. The nature of the housing problem was examined in Chapter 5, and we need only note at this point that it remains a major factor in quality of life

Table 20: Comparative per capita expenditures: The Soviet Union as a percentage of other states 1975–1976

CATEGORY	US	UK	West Germany	France	Japan
Food, beverage, tobacco	58	70	65	54	69
Clothing, footwear	47	76	52	79	68
Rent, fuel	17	30	27	28	43
Household expenditures	19	32	16	17	42
Transportation, communication	12	34	23	24	36
Recreation	30	38	38	46	42
Education	80	144	136	101	121
Health care	33	40	33	34	39
Other	32	42	57	48	53
TOTAL CONSUMPTION	34	54	46	46	59

Source: Data drawn from Gertrude E. Schroeder, 'Soviet Living Standards in Comparative Perspective', in Horst Herlemann (ed.), *The Quality of Life in the Soviet Union* (Boulder and London: Westview Press, 1987), Table 3.1, 15.

surveys at present. Millions of people still await private accommodation while living with relatives, while renting a room or part of one, or while coexisting in communal apartments or dormitories. The data provided earlier on the regional and inter-city variations in per capita allocations of living space demonstrated that there remain significant regional disparities (see Tables 10 and 11, pages 112 and 114). And, of course, the statistics included in Tables 18 and 19 mask sizeable regional variations in quality of life resulting from factors such as climate, cultural values and economic opportunity. At this juncture it would be useful to examine one state service which is ostensibly independent of such factors, but has a direct bearing on the quality of life.

Health care

According to the Soviet Constitution all citizens have the right to free, qualified medical care. The state thus began to assume responsibility for health care from the outset. During the years of Lenin's New Economic Policy (1921–1928) a fair measure of free enterprise was tolerated, as noted in Chapter 3. While the medical profession was not prohibited from providing services for fees, doctors were encouraged to play a role in developing the nascent state socialist medical care system by becoming state employees. In 1922 there were about 5,000 hospitals, 193,000 hospital beds and just over 21,000 medical doctors of all specializations for a population of 136 million. By 1926 the state itself had established polyclinics which charged moderate fees and offered services in competition with doctors in private practice. By the end of the New Economic Policy period some progress in expanding the public health care delivery system had been made. The number of doctors per 10,000 population stood at four, still clearly inadequate but a fourfold improvement over the situation in 1917. The number of beds per 10,000 population increased from ten to sixteen over the same period. In summary, the 1920s witnessed a continuation of the pre-revolutionary era practice of fee for service medical care, the beginnings of a system of special facilities for the privileged, and the attempt to provide free health care for the masses.

The Stalin era produced a vast expansion of the health care system, but one which was more highly differentiated than the relatively simple system which preceded it. Under Stalin privilege was permanently embedded. The delivery of medical care was first of all divided into what are often labelled open and closed systems. The first included all those free facilities and services which are available to the general public according to place of residence. Additionally, since medical doctors were still able to have a limited private practice, those ordinary folk with the necessary wherewithal could avail themselves of private care as they saw fit. The second, closed, system was designed to deliver free medical care to special groups; generally speaking the more important the group the higher the quality of medical attention and facilities provided. So much for the egalitarianism heralded by the 1936 proclamation that the Soviet Union was now officially a socialist state.

By 1940 the number of doctors per 10,000 population stood at nearly eight; the number of hospital beds had increased to 40 per 10,000. A more illuminating statistic in terms of the quality of life is how long the average person could expect to live. At the turn of the century life expectancy was around 32 years. By the late 1920s it was already 44. During the 1930s it improved still more, but there were considerable regional variations, and the difference between men and women was becoming quite pronounced. For millions of people the 1930s were scarcely years of a good, or even adequate, standard of living. Rationing of food was introduced in cities at the beginning of the decade; in the countryside collectivization took a huge toll in human life; and the late-1930s purges put all citizens at potential risk. Nonetheless, officialdom could and did point to the growth in medical care personnel and facilities. For the privileged and the emerging *meshchanstvo*, or middle class, life and, statistically, more of it, had never been better. For the urban masses, and the impoverished peasantry on the collective farms, it was a moot point whether the same could be said.

Over the next 40 years the advances registered in medical care infrastructure and personnel were quantitatively impressive. For instance, the number of medical doctors increased from roughly 155,000 in 1940 to nearly one million in 1980. The number of hospitals nearly doubled, and the number of beds grew from about 790,000 to 3.3 million. Measured in terms of doctors and hospital beds per 10,000 population the changes were 8 to 38 and 40 to 125 respectively between 1940 and 1980. On average the situation in the Soviet Union now compared very favourably with other industrial states. Indeed, on the basis of these two measures alone, no other country was so well off on a per capita basis. However, the health care system in the 1980s was far from homogeneous on a qualitative basis, was far from satisfactory when measured in terms of the health care delivered to the average Soviet citizen, and was far from equally accessible to the inhabitants of all regions.

As Fig. 54 reveals, in the period from 1940 to 1981 there was general improvement in the ratio of doctors per 10,000 population across all regions. Most authorities agree that the relative difference between the best and worst-off regions was ameliorated in the post-war era, as indeed were most other measures of the material conditions of daily labour and life. Still in the early 1980s the Middle Asian realm trailed the other regions. For example, the Tadzhik republic with 24 doctors per 10,000 had less than one half of the number servicing the population of the Centre region. Inasmuch as the Centre embraces the Moscow agglomeration, that there should be a difference is not surprising. However, as Fig. 54 indicates, there were many other regions in which access to medical personnel was substantially better. For the most part these regions comprised the Baltic and Slavic realms. With the notable exception of Georgia, the ratio of doctors per 10,000 people in the Caucasus and Middle Asia was about 20 per cent behind the national average of 38.5 in 1981. Oddly enough, the number of hospital beds per 10,000 Georgians was below the national average (107 as compared to 126), as it was in Armenia and Azerbaydzhan as well. As we will see shortly, the Caucasian peoples are healthier if longevity is the measure to be used. If that is the case, why is there need for so many doctors in the republic of Georgia? In recent years there have been suggestions to the effect that admissions to the republic's medical schools have been less than rigorous. Children of those in positions of authority and privilege seemingly have been amongst the principal beneficiaries. Bribes seem also to have played some part in admissions. The net result is that the number of trained medical personnel exceeds

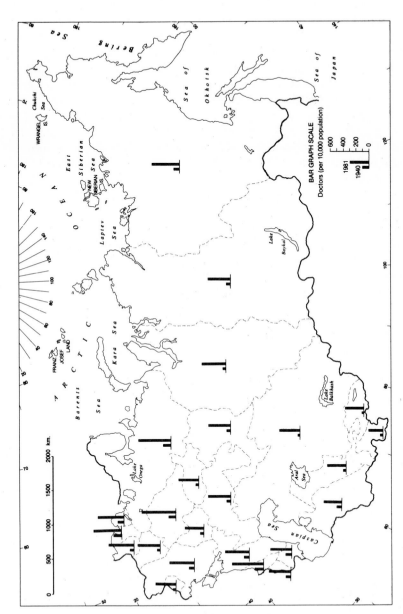

Fig. 54 Medical Doctors per 10,000 Population

Source: T. Buck, J. Cole, *Modern Soviet Economic Performance* (Oxford: Basil Blackwell, 1987), 165.

the number of positions available while in other regions there are critical shortages. In any event numbers of doctors, hospital beds and so forth do not speak to the question of accessibility of the population at large to high-quality health care.

In most western industrial states medical doctors enjoy prestige and incomes commensurate with high status amongst the professions. In the Soviet Union most medical doctors earn less than skilled workers in priority industrial sectors. Indeed, salaries were generally below those for white-collar workers until 1987 when the discrepancy was tackled by a decree which raised salaries of all medical personnel by more than one-third on average. Much is made of the fact that women played an important part in the expansion of medical staff during the Soviet period. However, those sectors of the economy in which a female labour force predominates are usually amongst the lower paid. The medical profession was no exception. Women comprised about 70 per cent of the medical doctor category during the 1980s, a decline from earlier years when their share reached 76 per cent. The relative size of the wage bill for Soviet health care therefore has traditionally been lower than might be expected based on western experience.

More significant than the relative size of the wage bill is the fact that the share of the state budget allocated to health care has been declining for much of the post-Second World War period. About 5.2 per cent of the total budget was devoted to health care in 1950. By the early 1960s it had moved up toward 7 per cent. However, by the end of the decade it had dropped to 6 per cent. A decade later it had fallen a further percentage point. By the late 1980s it had dropped to 4 per cent, and was about half that required. In most western industrial countries it is the growing proportion of the elderly which has been responsible for the steady escalation in the cost of health care. Demographically the Soviet Union is no exception. In 1959, 9.4 per cent of the population was over 60. By 1987 this group represented 13.5 per cent of the total population. By the turn of the century it is anticipated that the over-60 age group will comprise more than 17 per cent. As the population continues to age the demands on the Soviet health care system will increase, and so will the cost. Therefore, the contraction in the share of total state expenditures on health care since the 1950s raises serious questions as to what sort of care is currently provided.

The increase in the number of fee-charging health care institutions which occurred in the late 1980s is symptomatic of the dilemma facing the state. From fee-charging hospitals and polyclinics, to doctors more vigorously pursuing private practice, there has been a liberalization of health care delivery from the bureaucracy of state planning. In many ways this development simply expands on the existing system of differentiated health care. Money, rather than privileged position or the nature of the organization where one works, is increasingly acknowledged as sufficient condition for access to better care. In 1987, for example, visits to fee-paying hospitals and polyclinics represented less than 3 per cent of the 123 million visits paid to state-supported institutions. The expansion of fee-for-service medical care has not been introduced without controversy, however. There is a growing chorus of criticism directed at all forms of privileged access to something which many people firmly believe is a right – as indeed the Soviet constitution so stipulates. Why should one have to endure a second-rate system simply because power in one form or another is absent? From both Soviet and western reports there is little doubt that the open system for the public at large is severely underfunded.

To the degree that *perestroyka* results is some changes in the management of the health care system it will likely be changed at the margin rather than through a major reorganization. And yet some reorganization of the management system would be in order. Most medical care is allocated according to specific norms. Certain types of operation, for example an appendectomy, require a specific period of time in the .hospital. Early departures are usually prohibited. Lengthier stays are discouraged. Medical personnel are expected to perform their tasks in terms of number of patients attended to per shift or even per hour. Death rates for hospitals are prescribed. Stories abound, no doubt not all of them apocryphal, about hospitals not admitting patients with terminal illnesses if the established quotas might be exceeded in consequence. The nature of the facilities available to the average person would seem likely to assure any new fee-paying enterprise a steady clientele.

Notwithstanding the traditionally comparatively low salaries, surveys reveal that medical doctors are nonetheless perceived as having prestige amongst all occupations. But clearly the territorial, public system of health care is a much different environment than that established to cater to one or another of the myriad special groups. Salaries, equipment, facilities and ultimately the quality of health care are better in the latter than the former. And special payments to doctors 'with reputations' are extremely common as well. Thus official salaries are somewhat misleading. And so possibly is the male–female ratio for the medical profession as a whole. Although there are no data, it is certainly not beyond the realm of possibility that the proportion of male doctors is higher in the closed health care delivery system than in the open public one.

Whether public or special-group oriented, medical attention will be conditioned to some degree by the quality of instruction which all doctors are provided. And in this context there is growing concern. Soviet medical schools have been separate from the universities since the late 1920s. Standards for admission have been altered over the years in accordance with the state's social development priorities. Applicants to medical schools who have work experience in production are likely to be more readily admitted than students just graduating from the Soviet equivalent of high school. In terms of life experience and potential commitment to medicine this policy is not entirely misplaced. However, it seems that academic standards have been compromised in the process of encouraging applicants from the real world. Not only are entrance standards lower now than in the past, but the number of exams taken while in medical school have been steadily reduced in number and comprehension. Regulations regarding the number of times candidates may sit the few exams now remaining are often ignored. The net result is that many medical doctors are not well trained. Of some 350,000 doctors assessed for medical competence in the mid-1980s, nearly a tenth were deficient in one way or another. It is argued by some Soviets that returning medical training to the universities would ensure higher standards and a better knowledge of recent research developments and medical techniques.

Once graduated, medical doctors are subject to state regulations regarding deployment of all trained professionals. But as we have already noted, there is far from a uniform per capita distribution of doctors across the country. Many enter the public health care system only to stay until a position in one of the myriad special clinics or hospitals becomes available. Those who remain earn less, have higher patient workloads as a rule and endure poor facilities. For example, of the nearly 23,500 hospitals in the country in 1986 about 3,900 were district-level institutions. Of the latter 65 per cent lacked a hot-water supply. Perhaps more serious, in excess of a quarter of them were dependent upon septic tank systems of one type or another. Nearly a fifth (17 per cent) did not even have running water! The condition of the 18,000-odd rural polyclinics may be imagined. Recent criticism of medical facilities being the source of infectious disease is less surprising in light of such statistics. Thus, for the ambitious doctor the less time served in the 'public' health care system the better. The combination of questionable training of doctors in medical schools and the poor facilities available to the average person requiring medical treatment obviously impinges on the quality of life.

Preventative health care is confronted with major challenges, just as it is in all industrialized societies. About two-thirds of the population does not regularly exercise, about one quarter of the population smokes, and worryingly, two-fifths of the 15–16 age group. As yet the Soviet national anti-smoking campaign started in 1988, the equivalent of which is having a major impact in reducing secondary smoke inhalation in the public places of North America, has not made significant progress. Health warnings on packages of cigarettes have been around since the late 1970s and in common with practice elsewhere, Soviet fire regulations prohibit smoking in auditoriums and arenas. Hockey fans, for instance, must leave the building itself and stand outside in the depths of a winter freeze for between-period puffs. The abrupt and sizeable jump in the price of alcohol over the past few years, however, has not been matched in pricing tobacco. Indeed, production and sale of tobacco products has steadily increased, while that of most alcoholic beverages has declined since 1980. Despite the steady reduction of carbohydrates in the diet of the average Soviet, about half the population is described as overweight. And as suggested earlier, the reduction in official output of alcohol may well have been offset by production of illegal homebrew. Put simply, alcoholism remains a serious social, and economic, problem. It also has obvious health-care consequences.

Soviet studies indicate that average life expectancy of alcoholics is 15 to 20 years less than the norm. Of the adult population, a total of 15 per cent are classified as alcoholics (3–4 per cent) or heavy drinkers (9–11 per cent). For some medical authorities there is a clear link between alcohol abuse, resultant deterioration of health and the recent, unwelcome drop in life expectancy. However, since the population may well be consuming as much alcohol now as before the 1984 anti-alcohol campaign brought a significant reduction in official production, the relationship between consumption and longevity is far from clear. By 1986 Soviet women were once again living as long as they did in the late 1960s, while men were surviving to 65 on average, a year less than the earlier high. The pattern across the republics varies quite considerably, as Table 21 indicates. As Slav and Baltic males are reckoned to consume more alcohol than the people of the Caucasus their lower life expectancy is not surprising. The Muslim traditions of Middle Asia militate against consumption of alcohol, yet the life expectancy of males in those republics was one year less than Slavs in 1985–86. Indeed, the situation in Middle Asia remains distinctly worse

Table 21: Life expectancy by republic

REPUBLIC	1969–1970 All	Male	Female	1979–1980 All	Male	Female	1985–1986 All	Male	Female
Slavic									
RSFSR	68.8	63.1	73.3	67.5	61.5	73.0	69.3	63.8	74.0
Ukraine	70.9	66.5	74.4	69.7	64.6	74.0	70.5	65.9	74.5
Belorussia	72.4	68.1	75.8	71.1	65.9	75.6	71.4	66.7	75.5
Baltic									
Estonia	70.4	65.5	74.5	69.4	64.2	74.2	70.4	65.5	74.9
Latvia	70.2	65.5	74.4	68.9	63.6	73.9	70.2	65.5	74.5
Lithuania	71.1	67.0	74.9	70.5	65.5	75.4	71.5	66.8	75.9
Caucasus									
Armenia	72.9	70.1	75.4	72.8	69.5	75.7	73.3	70.5	75.7
Azerbaydzhan	69.2	65.3	72.6	68.1	64.2	71.8	69.9	65.7	73.4
Georgia	71.9	68.1	75.2	71.2	67.1	74.8	71.6	67.4	75.1
Middle Asia									
Kirgiz	67.9	63.6	71.8	66.0	61.1	70.1	67.9	64.1	71.1
Tadzhik	69.9	67.8	71.6	66.3	63.7	68.6	69.7	67.2	71.8
Uzbek	71.8	68.5	74.6	67.6	64.0	70.7	68.2	65.1	71.0
Turkmen	68.4	65.2	71.3	64.6	61.1	67.8	64.8	61.4	67.8
Kazakh	70.1	64.1	74.9	67.0	61.6	71.9	68.9	64.0	73.3
Moldavia	69.1	66.0	71.8	65.6	62.4	68.8	66.4	63.1	69.5
USSR	69.3	64.4	73.4	67.7	62.2	72.5	69.0	64.2	73.3

Source: Narodnoye Khozyaystvo SSSR za 70 Let (Moscow: Finansy i Statistika, 1987), 409.

in the mid-1980s than in the late 1960s (Table 21). The Uzbek and Turkmen republics stand out rather conspicuously in this regard, for both men and women. The abysmal state of medical care facilities in these republics combined with environmentally-related illness may well play a part in these statistics. We will return to both issues shortly. While the quality of life as measured by life expectancy seems now to have turned a corner, serious problems obviously still remain. Citizens of the Soviet Union do not live as long as their counterparts in many other western industrial states. A disproportionate share of those just born do not survive at all.

With the emphasis accorded free medical care after the revolution, infant mortality rates dramatically improved compared to the levels which obtained in late imperial Russia. In 1913 it is reckoned that 273 out of every 1,000 infants did not survive the first year, but this is likely a conservative figure given contemporary methods of reporting such deaths. By 1940 the ratio stood at 184 per 1,000. During the 1950s it was more than halved, and by 1960 was just 35 per 1,000. By 1971 health care improvements had reduced infant mortality to 22.9 per 1,000. During the 1970s the situation deteriorated, however. In 1980 the ratio had risen to 27.3. By this date official statistics on infant mortality had been classified information for a half dozen years. It was not until improvements were registered in the mid-1980s that such statistics were again included in official Soviet publications. But even in 1986 when infant mortality was 25.4 per 1,000 the state of affairs was still far from satisfactory

Table 22: Infant mortality by republic: Number of deaths before one year of age per 1,000 births

REPUBLIC	1970	1980	1985	1986
Slavic				
RSFSR	23.0	22.1	20.7	19.3
Ukraine	17.2	16.6	15.7	14.8
Belorussia	18.8	16.3	14.5	13.4
Baltic				
Estonia	17.8	17.1	14.0	16.0
Latvia	17.9	15.4	13.0	13.0
Lithuania	19.4	14.5	14.2	11.6
Caucasus				
Armenia	25.3	26.2	24.8	23.6
Azerbaydzhan	34.8	30.4	29.4	30.5
Georgia	25.3	25.4	24.0	25.5
Middle Asia				
Kirgiz	45.4	43.3	41.9	38.2
Tadzhik	45.9	58.1	46.8	46.7
Uzbek	31.0	47.0	45.3	46.2
Turkmen	46.1	53.6	52.4	58.2
Kazakh	25.9	32.7	30.1	29.0
Moldavia	23.3	35.0	30.9	26.4
USSR	24.7	27.3	26.0	25.4

Source: *Narodnoye Khozyaystvo SSSR za 70 Let* (Moscow: Finansy i Statistika, 1987), 408.

and was cause for widespread concern. Indeed, the actual figure might have been higher than 25.4; for example, 30 per 1,000 has been mentioned in some official statements. The latter figure put the Soviet Union at around fiftieth in the world in terms of combatting infant mortality.

As the data in Table 22 indicate, the pattern of infant mortality also varies markedly from one republic to another. Moreover, the general improvement noted above has not been consistent year on year in all republics. For example, in the Estonian, Azerbaydzhan, Georgian, Uzbek and Turkmen republics infant mortality was higher in 1986 than in 1985. Although the ratio improved between 1970 and 1986, for the Soviet Union as a whole infant mortality was still higher in 1986 than in 1970. In the Uzbek and Turkmen republics infant mortality rose dramatically during this period. The Turkmen figure was about the same as the World Health Organization records for Guatamala and Madagascar and was higher than Mexico or the Philippines. While faring poorly in such international comparisons, the actual situation may be worse still. Soviet statistical procedures only count infants weighing more than 1,000 grams or 35 centimetres in body length as live births. Smaller babies are deemed miscarriages and do not enter the statistics on infant deaths. The World Health Organization criterion is 500 grams. The range between the best and worst ratios by republic was fivefold in 1986. The ratios in Middle Asia are especially poor, but there are many other areas where there is also good reason for concern (Table 22).

Amongst the reasons for the abysmal statistics for Middle Asian republics, the poor, indeed, insanitary state of local hospitals and clinics figures prominently. Overcrowding of facilities simply compounds problems raised by unhygenic conditions. The Uzbek republic, for example, requires an additional 29,000 pediatric beds to fulfil existing norms. In the Turkmen republic three-fifths of the maternity clinics, maternity wards and pediatric hospitals cannot provide hot water. Septic tanks service about two-thirds of the republic's hospitals. Inadequacies in these systems for handling waste are thought to be a major reason for pollution of the water supply for a substantial number of the 127 hospitals in the Turkmen republic which make do without piped water. Intestinal infections, viral hepatitis, toxaemia and septicaemia all take an inordinate number of the new born in Middle Asia. Deficiencies in training medical personnel are also acknowledged to figure in the exceptionally high levels of infant mortality. A crash programme in the summer of 1987 brought 1,400 doctors and nurses to Middle Asia to train local medical personnel and to provide care for infants. Whether or not the trends evident in the data presented in Table 22 simply reflect a more accurate reporting of deaths of infants in Middle Asia since 1970, as some authorities suggest, rather than an increase in actual deaths, the fact is that this and other Soviet regions compare miserably with most western industrial states.

The current state of Soviet public health and its obvious relationship to the quality of life has received widespread critical assessment in the past few years. In a number of sociological surveys of public opinion regarding quality-of-life issues, the need to improve medical and dental health care delivery is noted by a substantial share of respondents in cities large and small. In the countryside deficiencies are obviously more acute still. To be sure, rising expectations play a part in expressions of dissatisfaction with the status quo. But data on life expectancy and infant mortality make plain that there are real problems. Inasmuch as these data are averages across a differentiated health care system – poor facilities for the masses, better facilities for special groups – there is much scope for bitterness on the part of the disenfranchised segment of society. The sanctioning of more fee-paying clinics and hospitals for the public at large willing to use them would at first glance seem unlikely to lessen discontent. If recent reports are accurate, however, three-quarters of the population already make 'payments' to medical personnel in the open system with the expectation of better treatment in return. Thus, the publicly accessible system has long sustained an unofficial fee for better service practice. The so-called closed system of medical care clearly provides a more sanitary environment and, one presumes, less busy if not more proficient medical personnel. Highly differentiated itself in accordance with the importance of ministry, enterprise, or special interest group represented, it is not insignificant in terms of its contribution to health care of the Soviet population. A recent report indicated that such closed facilities employed about 40 per cent of Moscow's physicians. The situation in the capital is atypical, but by the same token Soviet society comprises a substantial number of special interest groups. Under Gorbachev's policy of *glasnost'* such facilities have come under close scrutiny and public discussion. Comparisons are frequently made with publicly accessible facilities, which are not always physically separate, but which are invariably poorer.

The nature of the Soviet health care system has a direct bearing on the quality of life. In at least two important and interrelated ways, life expectancy and infant mortality, the system does not seem to measure up to those in other industrial states. These are not the only measures of quality of life. Environmental factors also play a role, both positive and negative.

Environmental degradation

Since one of the traditional advantages claimed for the Soviet socialist system of priorities and decision-making was that the common good takes precedence, an obvious question is why should environmental degradation occur at all? Indeed, as was remarked in Chapter 6, for a long time the problem of environmental degradation was assumed to be the inevitable by-product of the quest for profit under conditions of capitalism, and that such a problem almost by definition could not exist under socialism. While this premise may have some merit in theory, given what has been said already reality is rather different. From the perspective of the quality of life of the average citizen there is good reason for the growing concern regarding the relationship between health and environmentally related disease. A few examples will suffice in illustrating some of the dimensions of the current concerns.

There are major deficiencies in the water and sewage treatment facilities upon which many polyclinics and hospitals in Middle Asia are dependent. However, these alone do not account for the disproportionate number of infants who do not survive the first year or for the nature of the health problems which afflict the population at large. Environmental hazards, in the opinion of some people, have been contributing factors. Widespread use of toxic chemical pesticides in labour-intensive agricultural systems doubtless has taken a toll. For example, much of the cotton crop in Middle Asia is harvested by hand, perhaps not an entirely unreasonable use of labour in a region distinguished by a surplus of labour in the countryside. Indeed, as was noted in an earlier chapter, sizeable unemployment is now acknowledged to exist. At any rate, the combination of intensive use of female field labourers and regular application of such toxic defoliants as Butifos, an agent-orange like chemical, is presumed to have some relationship to the high level of infant mortality in the region.

On a more general level, questions arise as to both the appropriateness of standards to be followed in the application of chemical substances in agricultural production and to the efficacy of their enforcement. Given the penchant for over-consumption of water in the irrigated areas of Middle Asia, excessive application of chemical substances in the quest for higher levels of output is not beyond the realm of possibility. Testing of food products in Middle Asia, as elsewhere, is neither widespread nor a regular occurrence. There are reports that some knowledgeable medical personnel in the Turkmen republic choose not to eat local melons precisely because of a perceived abuse of chemical fertilizers and the lack of testing. Such problems are not unique to the Soviet Union, of course. In Western Europe and North America the popularity of foodstuffs produced without chemical additives is related at least in part to the concern over the relationship between chemicals and personal health. The difference seems to be that in the Soviet Union the level of public awareness and concern over such issues was until recently comparatively low. Chernobyl' and its aftermath have certainly helped to focus public attention on this facet of man and his environment.

The nuclear meltdown at Chernobyl' in late April 1986 had international as well as domestic consequences. In Lapland reindeer herders are still unable to market animals fed on lichens and moss which contain unacceptably high levels of radioactive contamination. The same problem exists in some upland English sheep farming areas. The short-term costs within the Soviet Union are considerable. It is estimated that clean-up costs in the more than 1,000 square kilometres around the nuclear power station, the loss of production from affected farms, factories and Chernobyl' itself, exceed two billion rubles in total. More than 30 deaths have been attributed to the accident, and several hundred other people are suffering from various radiation-related illnesses. At least 100,000 people will be permanently resettled since a substantial zone immediately surrounding the Chernobyl' plant has been removed permanently from agricultural production. Notwithstanding the spirit of *glasnost'*, the Chernobyl' disaster was not immediately reported to the Soviet public. Attributed to human error, the State Prosecutor's Office has since secured convictions for a number of the key personnel in the plant as well as other responsible officials in the nuclear power industry. The creation of a new ministry to manage the industry, the resumption of operations in the remaining reactors at Chernobyl', the continuing official proclamation that it is a safe industry, have done little to allay growing public concern and criticism of the role of nuclear energy in the Soviet Union.

Under the auspices of *glasnost'* various groups in several Soviet regions have questioned the operation of existing facilities and the planned construction of new nuclear power stations. From Armenia to the Baltic republics nuclear power stations have been the focus of public attention since Chernobyl'. By early 1988 public protests were reputedly successful in halting construction of a major installation near Krasnodar in the Kuban region of the north Caucasus (see Fig. 39, page 189). Since a sizeable investment had already been made this was regarded as a rather significant concession on the part of the officials concerned. While it may be business as usual for the remaining Chernobyl' reactors, there are clear signs that Soviet public opinion regarding environmental degradation is figuring much more prominently in management decisions previously influenced more by basic economic than environmental considerations. The issue of air pollution is a case in point.

There have long been legal prohibitions against air pollution by industry. Indeed, attempts to limit industrial growth in the major cities which date from the early 1930s were related in part to the felt need to improve the quality of the urban environment through reduction of both air and water pollution. Laws to protect the environment were enacted even earlier. Yet over the years air pollution has continued to affect all major urban-industrial centres. As the data in Table 23 indicate, there are significant regional variations in air pollution. A cursory review of the distribution of some of the major industries (Figs. 47 to 49) will provide some clues as to the geography of air pollution. Industrial emissions are frequently singled out as the main source of air pollution, although by no means is industry the sole cause. While there is a rough correlation between expenditure on pollution control facilities and volume of pollutants, measured in terms of per capita or area, what the data in Table 23 do not indicate is whether these levels represent a hazard to public health, and if so in what way. From press and other scientific and technical reports there is an emerging consensus that air pollution in many industrial regions is linked to such

Table 23: Air pollution indices, 1984

REPUBLIC	Installation of pollution control facilities rubles per capita	Pollution tons per capita per year	Pollution tons per km² per year
Slavic			
RSFSR	90.0	.410	6.00*
Ukraine	66.0	.360	31.10
Belorussia	48.0	.213	10.65
Baltic			
Latvia	33.0	.115	4.73
Estonia	98.0	.666	41.00
Lithuania	35.0	.191	10.60
Caucasus			
Armenia	3.6	.100	23.85
Azerbaydzhan	26.0	.169	12.60
Georgia	15.0	.142	14.20*
Middle Asia			
Uzbek	19.0	.117	4.84
Kirgiz	10.4	.078	1.80
Tadzhik	9.5	.046	2.97*
Turkmen	8.2	.305	4.78*
Kazakh	64.0	.592	4.70*
Moldavia	24.0	.199	24.00
USSR	70.0	.360	6.87*

Source: 'Local Problems', *Environmental Policy Review. The Soviet Union and Eastern Europe*, Vol. 1, No. 1, June 1987, 25.

*estimate for an area 'economically developed' in respective republics.

conditions as a higher than average incidence of respiratory ailment of one kind or another. Concern over public health, doubtless more acute since Chernobyl' than before, has served to bring about change. And the more publicity each such challenge to established procedures is accorded, the greater the demonstration effect. There have been enough instances of direct links between air pollution and public health problems to legitimate public concern.

At the centre of many debates over air and other forms of pollution is the time lost to production when pollution abatement facilities are put in place. While finances are everywhere a problem, it is a rare year when the total allocation by the state for pollution control is used entirely. With the system of economic accountability which has guided enterprise operations since the mid-1960s, there has been little if any incentive to reduce annual output in order to install new or improved equipment to mitigate the environmental impact of the operation. Dulling incentive further is the scientific methodology for measuring pollutants. There have been major problems in addressing the potentially harmful consequences of the mixture of chemical pollu-tants. The Law on the Protection of Atmospheric Air introduced in 1980 is a case in point. This law established maximum permissible discharges for some 400-odd chemical substances. Standards are geared to individual chemical substances which might be emitted safely, but do not address the more toxic chemical interactions which might occur. Monitoring is undertaken in about 500 cities and the major industrial areas. Monitoring, however, is one matter, implementation of legislation is sometimes another.

Even where evidence of a direct negative impact on public health seems irrefutable, industry response is customarily slow. For example, a pharmaceutical plant in Kirishi, a small town of about 60,000 near Leningrad, was recognized as a major polluter since it began operation in 1974. Not only was the plume of smoke issuing from the factory chimney a visible eyesore, the allergens being pumped out in hazardous quantity were eventually acknowledged as a major contributing factor to the abnormally high levels of disabling respiratory ailments. Bronchial asthma, for example, increased 35-fold over levels evidenced by the inhabitants of Kirishi before the plant began operation. The rate remains some five to ten times greater than in other cities in the region. Lung and skin diseases were one thing, an unusual spate of infant deaths was another. The latter, taken in conjunction with years of curiously high levels of respiratory disease of one kind or another, led to local demonstrations and public complaint in 1987. Ministry of Public Health officials eventually corroborated local claims regarding the health hazard of emissions from the plant, and ministry pressure has helped to force further modifications to the pollution-abatement equipment at the plant. The problem in Kirishi is unique only in its local circumstances.

Across the Soviet Union the working environment in the plant, and the quality of the environment in the community at large, are coming under closer, critical public scrutiny as a result of *glasnost'*. Women have been prohibited from working in a number of jobs owing to potential health risks. For example, in the early 1980s certain jobs in mining were decreed male only. There is still need for close monitoring and further restrictions. Premature births amongst employees of the rubber, paint, plastic and artificial fibres industries are nearly twice the national average, and this raises questions as to the nature of the work environment. Public health hazards are obviously not limited to the work environment within the factory. As noted earlier, agricultural field workers are also in a potentially hazardous situation. The questionable use of Butifos as a cotton defoliant eventually produced sufficient public and 'expert' complaint that the Ministry of Public Health reassessed it. Aside from the noxious odour, Butifos was proven to be linked to a deterioration in measurable standards of public health amongst all those directly exposed to it. This group included farm workers, those involved in one stage or another of its aerial application, and those living in the areas in which it was regularly used. For the latter, impairment of water-supply sources was a major concern. It was formally banned as a cotton defoliant in early 1987. What the long-term effects of its widespread use in rural Middle Asia are remain to be seen.

External diseconomies of industrial development are not specific to any one political-economic system. The fact that land and water are at best only nominally accounted for in the Soviet price system and accounting practices perhaps makes accurate determination of the benefits and costs of a particular development more difficult, but the mere existence of a set of market-determined prices for such resources is certainly no assurance of easy and accurate benefit-cost calculations. There is still the fundamental question, from whose perspective should benefits and costs be calculated? Simply contending that the best choice is that of the common good does not resolve the problem of determining whether cleaner air is preferable to a higher standard of living. The systemic weakness of the Soviet approach to environmental management and protection has traditionally been the absence of an environmental interest group within the upper echelons of the Party apparatus where fundamental policy decisions are taken, and the absence of a single authority at the level of an All-Union Ministry which could serve as a countervailing influence to the economically and politically important industrial ministry. But there are signs that environmental issues are being given greater attention, as the discussion in Chapter 6 suggested. The potential global consequences of some Soviet resource development projects certainly served to heighten awareness. So too has the threat to specific ecological environments popularly perceived to be part of the state's unique resource heritage. Of the many in this latter category, Lake Baykal ranks amongst the best known and publicized.

The Lake Baykal controversy emerged in the late 1960s. For the time it represented an issue of public debate, though the public was largely restricted to the scientific community, ministry officials, the Writers' Union and a handful of other official environmental bodies. The latter were clearly of little potential clout, though the various official organs of the cultural establishment, such as the Writers' Union, were important. Put simply, the controversy arose over the decision to locate two huge pulp and paper mills on the southern shore of the lake. Because of its particular geological history, Lake Baykal supported a vast array of unique flora and fauna. It represents the largest single volume of fresh water in the world. The purity of Baykal's water, plus the local and regional forest resource wealth, were the principal locational advantages for the proposed pulp mills. The threat to the purity of the lake was recognized immediately, if for no other reason than across the lake from the proposed plants was a major institute of linnological research. Ministry officials at first rejected the scientific community's contention that effluent from the plants would threaten the existence of many unique species of life associated with, and dependent upon, the pristine quality of Baykal water. Eventually the debate became a national issue, indeed, it attracted international attention. The plants went ahead, modifications were made to the effluent treatment system, the government responded by legislating a zone around the lake to be immune to the forester's axe and by banning the movement of logs on the lake itself. The latter were a particular hazard since Siberian larch, the predominent specie, is heavy per unit of volume. Estimates of potential losses during rafting of logs to the mills were high. Limnologists argued that the amount of oxygen required to decompose the anticipated volume of wood and bark added to the lake through rafting would seriously alter the chemical composition of the water and thereby put at risk much of the unique vegetative and aquatic life. Since the legislation was introduced in 1966 the worst environmental impacts of the pulp mills have been avoided, but effluent from them has polluted the lake nonetheless. The problem, in the opinion of some Soviet observers, is the traditional case of production taking priority over preservation and conservation. The

Baykal experience has served to inform other more vocal, environmental interest groups in recent years.

In many ways one of the key obstacles in implementation of environmental protection legislation is that for a long time responsibility for environmental management was turned over to the ministries themselves. Internal, subordinate administrative units were assigned the task of implementing and monitoring environmental protection legislation. Fragmentation of authority often results in vital standards being ignored if they impinge on the overriding ministerial goal of meeting production quotas. Thus, antediluvian factories continue to produce and pollute, non-conforming locations of factories in cities are overlooked when closing or relocating them could jeopardize production goals. From the standpoint of industrial managers, the choice is perfectly rational *within* the context of their priorities. Additionally, the proliferation of environmental monitoring agencies within different ministries, and on an *ad hoc* basis amongst various public interest groups, led to a fragmentation of effort at best and outright conflict of interest amongst groups with ostensibly identical objectives at worst.

These systemic problems did not pass unnoticed, but it was some years after the Baykal *cause célèbre* before an institutional arrangement was introduced to ameliorate the problem. The creation of the USSR State Committee on Hydrometeorology and the Environment was really too little, too late. Lacking the status of an All-Union Ministry, it did not have the necessary clout to radically change practice simply by enforcing existing regulations. Its specialist staff worked with other agencies in an effort to ensure compliance with legislation. From the Ministry of Public Health, Ministry of Land Reclamation and Water Conservancy, amongst others, evidence of violation of state laws was procured. While it was not without some success as an institutional arrangement, it was overtaken by events. The 1980s have witnessed a growing preoccupation on the part of the public at large with quality of environment issues. As we have already remarked, large-scale social surveys, and more recently public opinion polls, have all supported the quest for more stringent controls. Lake Baykal caught the imagination and evoked widespread public concern as an environmental problem in the 1960s. Since then the diversion of north-flowing rivers, the pollution of Lake Ladoga, Lake Sevan and a host of smaller water bodies, desertification of Middle Asia, to name only a few, have been added to the list of problems of concern to the public, if not the authorities. Fragmentation of responsibility in monitoring and regulating continued to be regarded as one of the reasons for environmental degradation. In 1988 another administration arrangement was introduced as a solution.

The formation of a USSR State Committee for Environmental Protection, along with Union-Republic equivalents, is aimed at ensuring more rational use of natural resources and better environmental protection than has thus far been achieved. Separating environment from the State Committee on Hydrometeorology is no doubt a step in the right direction, but as before it begs the question of ministerial status and authority. Mandated to improve both the monitoring and protection of the environment, it has a huge task. Environmental concerns are to be fully integrated into future economic and social development plans for the country as a whole. From gathering data, setting new standards, revising existing standards, goal setting, establishing education programmes, supervising existing nature preserves – the list of responsibilities rolls on. Ostensibly its decisions are binding irrespective of ministry, department, enterprise or geographic location. It is to have the right to levy charges in order to build up the financial resources to expand its operation as need arises. Research departments are to be transferred to it from other agencies, ministries and enterprises in order to facilitate its scientific work. In conjunction with the USSR Ministry of State Law, the new state committee was to prepare a draft law on environmental protection for consideration by the Council of Ministers within one year. From the work environment to the global scene there is much that needs to be done. One or two specific examples of the nature of existing problems will suffice.

In the republic of Georgia the areal impact of air pollution is quite severe, as Table 23 indicates. Water pollution is also serious. Most of the republic's water bodies are heavily polluted by industry, urban settlements and agriculture. The Kura river, which winds its way through the capital Tbilisi, receives waste daily from some 200 industrial enterprises. Most of it, apparently, is dumped untreated. Owing to extremely high coliform counts a local lake has been closed for recreational use since 1983. This is not a problem unique to Tbilisi. Untreated domestic sewage continues to find its way into many of the country's water bodies. Indeed, close to 40 per cent of all urban settlements do not yet have adequate sewage treatment facilities, and therefore closure of recreational water bodies is not exceptional. In the city of Kazan' near the confluence of the Volga and Kama rivers, a decision to locate a biochemical plant in the city's protected green belt has produced a substantial public outcry. The ministry's assurance that this plant would be equipped with the latest pollution-abatement equipment has not been well received. Local environmental protection agencies, as well as city planning authorities, were by-passed – an all too common occurrence over the past decades notwithstanding the legal authority of the city Soviet over all local development decisions. In short, from one end of the country to another may be found examples of serious pollution of air and water, in violation of existing legislation. To date, the primacy of production over environmental protection has not been thwarted. Whether the quest for an enhanced quality of life under Gorbachev's *troyka* of *perestroyka, uskoreniye* and *glasnost'* will be realized is certainly the object of considerable speculation. For the average Soviet citizen the quality of the environment clearly influences the conditions of daily life and labour. As leisure time has increased, environmental matters have come to play a more important role in patterns of recreation.

Recreation and leisure

During the Soviet era considerable progress has been made in providing the population with an extensive infrastructure for organized forms of recreational activity. As leisure time has grown in consequence of shortening the work week from six to five days in the late 1960s, and as disposable income has increased, as indicated earlier in this chapter, the potential demand for recreation facilities has similarly increased. In fact, tourism has emerged as an economic activity of some importance in a number of regional economies.

Prior to the revolution recreation was a pursuit of the leisured classes, those with the time and money to repair to the summer *dacha*, estate or spas in one of the more agreeable climatic realms of the Empire. Thus, along the shores of the Baltic Sea, the Black Sea, especially those of the Crimean peninsula, resort-type facilities arose to meet the needs of the affluent. For those inclined to combine rest with the pursuit of improved health, taking the waters at one of several popular locations in the Caucasus was another option. Notwithstanding the widely acclaimed medicinal value of Caucasian mineral hot springs, many members of the elite preferred to journey to the spas of Europe. The masses, of course, simply endured circumstances as they found them.

For the new Soviet government recreation was no longer to be the perogative of the rich. While the average worker would not experience much leisure time for years to come, organized forms of socially acceptable recreation soon came to play an unprecedented role in life. One of the first steps taken to create the necessary infrastructure involved the confiscation of all resorts, spas and private homes in zones of potential recreation. The facilities along the Baltic and Black Seas, and in the mountains of the Caucasus, soon catered to a new clientele. By the mid-1920s the need to provide sanatoria facilities for workers was well recognized. Summer camps for children also received considerable attention. Thus, by the late 1920s the notion of an annual holiday was no longer entirely foreign to the working family. It had been adopted by the rapidly escalating members of the new bureaucracy with little difficulty. Since the 1920s the physical infrastructure for rest and recreation has progressed steadily. General sanatoria for adults and children numbered only a few score in 1917. By 1939 there were nearly 3,000 with accommodation for almost 340,000. As of 1986 the country could boast of nearly 16,000 sanatoria and rest homes with beds for about 2.5 million people, a ratio of roughly nine per 1,000 population.

As outdoor activities have come to figure more prominently in the recreational pursuits of the average Soviet family, an extensive network of camping grounds has developed across the country. And, as a result of the growing use of cars, motels have been added to the Soviet hotel scene since the 1960s. But there are still too few of all types of holiday facilities to satisfy current demands. It was estimated in the late 1970s that the appropriate norm for 1990 would be seven recreational 'places' per 1,000 population. In 1971 the actual figure was 0.58 per 1,000.

With the growing importance of the role of recreation and leisure in Soviet society, steps have been taken to develop planning strategies and development tools. The concept of a territorial recreation complex (TRC) has taken root. It has a clear relationship to the idea of a territorial production complex as outlined in the preceding chapter. The example of the Apsheron-Kobystanskiy TRC in Azerbaydzhan is presented in Fig. 55. While the climate in this region is certainly favourable, the area does suffer from periods of strong wind and dust storms. As well, parts of this region still wear the visible scars of a turn-of-the-century oil industry. Nonetheless, what is planned will be an important complement to the existing facilities in Azerbaydzhan. In the late 1970s only two 'places' per 1,000 population were available in tourist, sanatoria and rest home facilities, excluding those dedicated to the use of children. The aforementioned norm of seven places per 1,000 is for the country as a whole. For

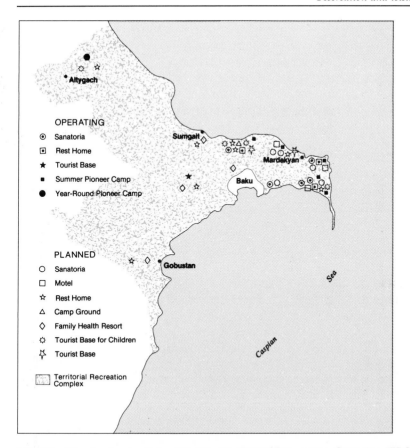

Fig. 55 The Apsheron-Kobystanskiy Territorial Recreation Complex (TRC)

Source: E.A. Kotlyarov, *Geografiya Otdykha i Turizma* (Moscow: Mysl', 1978), 117.

areas such as the TRC depicted in Fig. 55, which boasts a comparatively equable climate and seashore attractions, the norm should be higher. For Azerbaydzhan as a whole the recommended norm is 37 places per 1,000. Each year the state invests more in such facilities, but there is still some way to go.

As Table 24 indicates, some republics are better provided with recreation and tourist facilities than are others, a not surprising situation given the regionally distinctive climatic regions and scenic potentials. While there is a variety of accommodation types, not all facilities are open to the public at large. Many sanatoria, for example, are owned and operated by particular ministries, departments or even enterprises, and are for the exclusive use of their own employees. For members of one of the many special groups – writers, artists, sports figures, military officers, and so forth – there are equivalent special recreational opportunities as well. Thus, as is the case with health care, the infrastructure for rest and recreation is similarly structured to cater to the needs of one or another privileged group. Still, in

Table 24: Selected recreational facilities: sanatoria, rest homes, hotels, 1986

| REPUBLIC | SANATORIA AND REST HOMES | | | HOTELS | | |
	NUMBER OF ESTABLISHMENTS	NUMBER OF BEDS (000)	BEDS PER 10000 POPULATION	NUMBER OF TOURIST BASES	NUMBER OF PLACES (000)	PLACES PER 1000 POPULATION
Slavic						
RSFSR	7,355	1,263.7	87	487	228.5	16
Ukraine	3,537	666.6	130	196	81.7	16
Belorussia	383	49.3	49	25	10.2	10
Baltic						
Latvia	1,125	60.4	228	21	4.2	16
Estonia	392	18.6	119	19	3.6	23
Lithuania	1,333	65.4	180	21	6.6	18
Caucasus						
Armenia	103	22.5	66	23	5.8	17
Azerbaydzhan	134	29.0	43	12	5.0	7
Georgia	394	100.0	190	77	38.5	73
Middle Asia						
Uzbek	319	51.1	27	28	8.0	4
Kirgiz	136	33.1	80	8	3.2	8
Tadzhik	77	13.4	28	4	2.3	5
Turkmen	34	6.6	20	3	0.9	3
Kazakh	422	64.6	40	30	9.8	6
Moldavia	112	21.5	51	17	8.0	19
USSR	15,856	2,465.8	88	971	416.3	15

Source: Narodnoye Khozyaystvo SSSR za 70 Let (Moscow: Finansy i Statistika, 1987), 374, 600.

1986 some 50 million people were accommodated in sanatoria and rest home facilities. Not all were members of the privileged groups in Soviet society. From the small beginnings in the 1920s the state system of pioneer and school summer camps has evolved into a huge operation. In 1986 about 30 million children and teenagers were involved in some form of organized summer camping activity. For the urban child especially this experience is an important adjunct to whatever family holiday might be arranged. For the children of many families this summer sojourn constitutes the only holiday since both parents customarily work full-time and therefore holiday schedules are not always easily arranged. Given the dearth of 'open' hotel accommodation and the restricted access to many of the country's sanatoria and rest facilities, the difficulties may be easily imagined (Table 24).

With about 22 working days annual holiday, retirement age at 55 for women and 60 for men, and a near universal five-day work week, there are considerable opportunities for recreation of one type or another for all age groups. Within cities the planned development of parks, gardens, sports and recreational facilities for mass consumption has long been a high priority. And there has been considerable success in this regard. Most Soviet cities provide a reasonable area of parks and gardens for passive recreation. The norm has long been 25 square metres of greenery per person. Virtually all cities have sports facilities for the various levels of league activity. Soccer, hockey, horse racing, all the activities represented by the Olympic games, and many more besides, are available to participants in huge number, and even larger numbers of armchair enthusiasts. On a daily basis some 30 million people are involved in one form of sports activity or another. However, the huge investment of the state in these facilities has not yet adequately met demand, just as it has not satisfied the demand for the holiday plans of millions of Soviet citizens. In the case of sports, however, demand is dampened somewhat owing to the fact that about two-thirds of the adult population does not exercise on a regular basis.

For many people access to a *dacha* is an important adjunct to the state system of sanatoria, rest homes, camps, hotels and so forth. The *dacha*, or second home, is scarcely a new phenomenon. In the late imperial era suburban trains provided access to thousands of *dachi* in the outskirts of St Petersburg and Moscow. Today Leningraders and Muscovites carry on the tradition, renting a room in a *dacha* for part of the summer when, as is most often the case, they do not own such a luxury themselves. Despite administrative controls on their further development, the *dacha* has left its impress on the countryside around most Soviet cities. Private car ownership has made weekend travel to a *dacha* easier for thousands of the better-off Soviet citizenry.

Although customs vary from one region to another, most urban Soviets enjoy being able to get out into the countryside. In the major cities sizeable tracts have been set aside for this purpose. The concept of a green belt with fingers of open space penetrating the built up area has been widely employed as one means of ensuring ready access to the 'outdoors' for urban inhabitants. But the pace of urban development, the traditional departmentalist approach to development which customarily overrides town planning principles and environmental considerations, and the sheer weight of humanity now contained in the country's major cities, is having a negative impact on such zones of recreation.

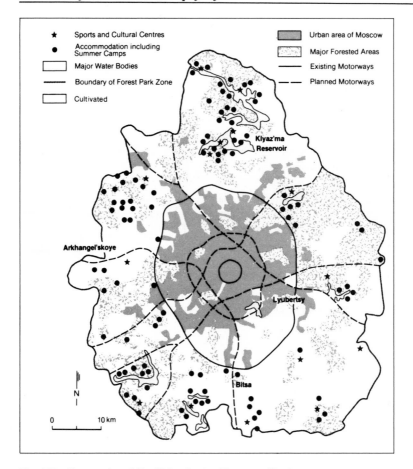

Fig. 56   Recreational Facilities in the Moscow Region

Source: Denis J.B. Shaw, 'Recreation and the Soviet City', in French, R.A., Hamilton, F.E.I. (eds.), *The Socialist City* (New York: John Wiley, 1979), 134.

Fig. 56 depicts the recreational facilities and general land use in the Moscow Forest Park Zone in the mid-1970s. It is apparent that a sizeable area is still under park or wood, as well as cultivation. Recreational facilities are also well developed. But the pace of urban development in the Moscow green belt beyond the ring road depicted in Fig. 56 has taken its toll of such green or open space, as was noted in Chapter 5 (for example, see Fig. 17, page 100). Satellite data provide an opportunity to assess the land conversion process, and in Fig. 57 the changes in general land use in the greater Leningrad area between 1975 and 1987 are presented. As in the case of all major Soviet cities where planners have been able to stem the expansion of existing plants, and prevent the location there of new ones, the customary reaction has been to locate enterprises in the immediate urban hinterland. And this process feeds urban expansion. Leningrad, like Moscow, was to have limited population growth within

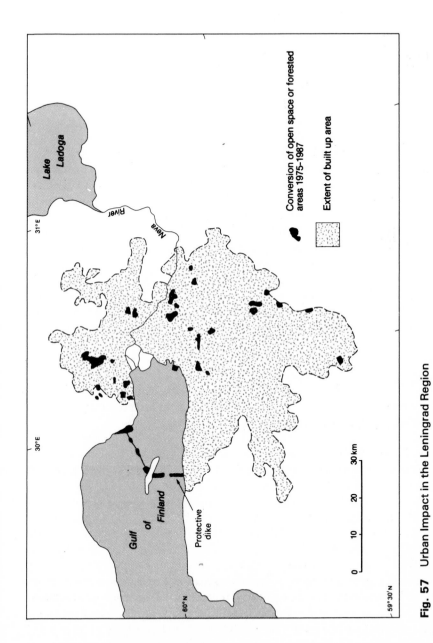

Fig. 57 Urban Impact in the Leningrad Region

Source: Compiled from Landsat Images 1975, 1987.

the urban region. Ample green space for recreation was to be permanently set aside. Because of inadequate planning control what has emerged around Leningrad is a vast urban agglomeration covering several hundred square kilometres. Aside from huge problems in commuting from home to workplace, to highlight only one, the quality of the regional environment has deteriorated as a result of the urban growth process. *Dacha* communities have come under increasing pressure as the number of people wishing to rent a room, or indeed perhaps just a bed, has grown tremendously. Some have been converted to permanent use. As a private form of recreation and leisure, the *dacha* does not enjoy official endorsement, but it is certainly tolerated since most members of the Soviet elite also aspire to own one. Moreover, in the absence of an adequate supply of such alternatives as hotels, or indeed motels, the *dacha* fulfils an important need for many Soviet urbanites. In any event, for passive recreation activity the loss of green space and agricultural land depicted in Fig. 57 is clearly a disbenefit of urban growth for all Leningraders. Leningrad, of course, is not unique in terms of the huge exodus of weekend day-trippers to local woods for such benign pursuits as berry and mushroom picking or a simple picnic.

On a different but not unrelated front Soviet authorities have had rather more success in protecting the natural environment. Shortly after the revolution they took steps to secure parcels of the natural environment as protected areas. *Zapovedniki*, or nature preserves, pre-dated the revolution, but were created in many parts of the country during the early years of Soviet rule to facilitate research in the natural sciences. The Soviet government inherited a handful of *zapovedniki*, but added another 20 or so in the 1920s alone. By the 1960s the number had increased to nearly 70. While still serving as scientific research areas, tourism in and around *zapovedniki* increased steadily. Notwithstanding the attraction of *zapovedniki* to tourists, these natural areas are not the same as North American or European national parks. The demands of tourism eventually resulted in a Soviet version of the national park. They were first created in the 1960s. By 1985, 14 national parks had been added to the list of *zapovedniki*, which then totalled 144 across the country.

While the differentiated systems of health care and recreation afford opportunities for those in positions of privilege to access something other than the ordinary, environmental degradation obviously affects all citizens irrespective of their position in society. As in all industrial societies, a reasonable balance between development and environment is elusive. In somewhat similar fashion the pursuit of social justice in the Soviet Union continues.

Social justice

The notion of social justice inspired those who made the revolution of 1917. It has since found expression in the constitutional framework of the world's first socialist state, in the policies which were formulated for the development of the state, and in countless programmes of action. The principle 'from each according to his abilities, to each according to his work' was viewed as an interim arrangement preparatory to the advent of communism when each would be rewarded not in accordance with his work but in recognition of his need. Much has been accomplished since the early days of Soviet socialism. But as we have noted in this chapter, and in earlier ones as well, there is sometimes a gap between ideal and reality. Within contemporary Soviet society the principle of social justice has emerged as a central issue in critical assessments of the conditions of daily labour and life. At this juncture we will briefly review three key dimensions of what is an exceedingly complex topic. These are the systemic, spatial and nationality dimensions of the task of realizing social justice in the contemporary Soviet state.

The systemic facets of the quest for social justice pertain to the nature of government policies and practices. From the beginning, but especially during the Stalin era, the state put in place the legal foundations for a privileged group within society. In an earlier chapter we noted how the accumulation of wealth was facilitated during the 1930s when the laws regarding inheritance were changed. The intent, it seems, was to co-opt the critically important managerial elements in society. Without their effective participation in the spheres of production and the Party, the realization of national objectives could well have been compromised. Thus, Soviet society is much more than the simple array of classes and strata recognized by officialdom. Privilege in one form or another finds expression in a host of ways, but by definition not all members of society are participants. During the Gorbachev era of *glasnost'* the sundry perks granted the members of the various privileged groups in Soviet society have come under unprecedented public scrutiny and complaint. Having once acquired a privileged status, the natural tendency of course is to attempt to ensure its perpetuation through one's children. Thus, it should come as no surprise that there are instances of parents using whatever influence they have to ensure that educational and occupational advantage is provided sons and daughters or members of the larger family network.

Salaries and wages also differentiate the members of Soviet society. Given the necessary steps before communism is realized, this is entirely consistent with the theory of socialism. Further differentiated by wage coefficients, the monthly discretionary income can vary very considerably from one region to another for the same job. From the standpoint of social justice such differences are not of great concern provided there is a socially acceptable guaranteed minimum income and standard of living. The various social benefits thus play a potentially important role in ensuring social justice. However, the current practice of deriving a good many of these social benefits through one's place of employment leads to inequities. For example, the quality of housing, health care, access to sanatoria and rest homes, even foodstuffs, are often dependent on the nature of the enterprise for which one works. Certain sectors of the Soviet economy are advantaged by prevailing methods of accounting and their place in the list of national priorities. Almost by definition those who work for enterprises, departments and ministries dealing with extractive and heavy industries, defence or energy, are better off than those who do the same type of job in the consumers goods or food-processing sectors. The profits generated by different sectors of the economy often play a critically important part in the social benefits bestowed upon the workforce. Thus, built into the system of economic management are factors which militate against the concept of social justice.

Perestroyka has also unleashed a number of initiatives which challenge the status quo and no doubt will exacerbate efforts to promote greater social justice. One of the basic tenets of the Soviet version of socialism has been the abolition of unemployment. Now enterprises, departments, ministries and even the Party itself are being encouraged to shed labour reserves. To enhance labour productivity is an essential step in the drive to resuscitate the national economy. For those people whose lives thus far have been based on the right to draw a wage more or less independent of the work done, the prospect of becoming redundant is a major change. Already several million people have been deemed redundant. By the turn of the century some authorities are predicting that as many as 16 million people will have been retrained or dispatched to a new enterprise to do the same job as before. In the major cities, and certainly in Moscow, many people face the prospect of being directed to a position in another, and one presumes, less desirable location. Temporary, or even long-term, unemployment is now no longer beyond the realm of possibility. How this aspect of *perestroyka* will affect people's lives has yet to be determined.

At the same time *perestroyka* has legitimated a wide array of activities for individuals or small cooperatives. Having provided an outlet for entrepreneurial talent unequalled since the New Economic Policy of the 1920s, the government soon found itself having to deal with a new group of privileged people, only on this occasion privileged because the rewards for their labour were often vastly in excess of what could be earned in the employ of the state. As noted in Chapter 3, the response was to propose a maximum tax bracket of 90 per cent on incomes exceeding 1,500 rubles per month, sufficient it was argued to keep free enterprise on a fairly tight rein. But having once legitimated private taxi service, small restaurants, the manufacture of consumers goods of various kinds, and so on, the opportunities to avoid such taxes have multiplied correspondingly. The proposal to significantly increase the maximum tax on personal income was partly in response to public complaints about these new entrepreneurs taking advantage of the consumers goods and services deficiencies, the very deficiencies of course that they were encouraged to offset through their own initiatives. At any rate the potential for vastly greater incomes than possible from the state will do little to ameliorate existing inequities in the system.

Many of the foregoing features of the Soviet system itself which contribute to inequity are further exacerbated by the very real spatial dimensions of the social justice issue. Opportunity is not only conditioned by position in society and type of employment, it is influenced by location. Within the urban system there are clear differences in the quality of life, as discussion in earlier chapters has indicated. Invariably the fulfilling of the various norms for the provisioning of the population with goods and services improves from small place to large. The compelling attraction of life in the major cities, and especially Moscow, Leningrad, and the republic capitals is easy to comprehend. Having gained access to a major city, one is recipient of a wide variety of benefits. Not only are cultural activities and consumers goods more abundant, housing, transportation and the myriad facets of the urban infrastructure are much better. Once legally resident in a major city the advantages are perpetuated inter-generationally. For example, education is the key to social mobility in the Soviet Union as elsewhere. However, the educational system, like health care, has been allocated a declining share of national investment funds in recent years. From 11 per cent in 1970 the share of government income directed toward all levels of education dropped to 8 per cent by the late 1980s. The system sorely needs improvement of various kinds, not least of which being the refurbishing of physical facilities. In the late 1980s about one-fifth of all schools lacked central heating. About two-fifths are not integrated into a proper sewage-treatment system. About the same percentage do not have any physical education facilities, save for out door playing fields. A vast number of children cannot be accommodated in existing pre-school facilities, and once in the system in many regions two, and occasionally even three, shifts of young children are necessary. Not surprisingly, the smaller, the more remote the urban centre, the more likely it is that some of the problems confronting the national educational system will be found. And it is not always possible to enrol children in the better schools of larger cities even if private accommodation can be arranged. In many of the large urban centres the number of out-of-city students permitted is limited to available dormitory space. The latter is not sufficient to meet even a small share of the potential demand, thus bright children from smaller, less well endowed cities cannot access better schools. Those that are admitted often have far higher academic qualifications than the local counterparts. Thus, the city in which one is born can figure very prominently in determining one's future. Such a situation is in many people's view a far cry from social justice.

The situation of all residents of the large city is far from equal inasmuch as a sizeable number are ostensibly there on a limited-term basis. These so-called *limitchiki*, however, are often long-term residents, but have no real rights. Without permanent residence status they exist mostly in dormitory accommodation, sometimes in rented accommodation, since access to an apartment is precluded. Prospects for marriage amongst the mostly young *limitchiki* population are dim given their status and their customarily low or unskilled occupations. While filling a real employment need they are in every sense a marginalized group within Soviet urban society. The numbers again tend to vary directly according to city size.

On a more general level the quality of life measures we have used in this chapter also vary according to rural or urban scene. While in a material sense the rural family has made considerable progress over the past quarter century, there is still a vast gulf between the marginal agricultural region and the major urban centre. The scale of the rural–urban migration since the Second World War certainly speaks to the attraction of the city and the disbenefits of the countryside. Where access to the larger centres has not been possible, migrants frequently gain a legal foothold in a smaller settlement within relatively easy commuting distance. While contributing to urban production of one kind or another, the growing commuting population is at best tolerated by urban officials bent upon ensuring that the basic needs of their constituents are met. Hordes of workers taking food and clothing to the smaller, less well provided, centres simply complicates their task. But more fundamentally, what this process reflects is the comparatively impoverished state provisionment of the rural population *vis-à-vis* the urban.

During the Soviet period much has been achieved in reducing regional disparities, but from the data presented it is apparent that the task has not been completed. In broad terms there is a core–periphery relationship in the standard of living as reflected in most of the usual measures. From per capita income, to level of health care, to the material circumstances of daily life, there is still a gradation from the Baltic and

European Russian Slavic realm to the south and east. The Caucasus and Middle Asia offer a style of life moderated by climate which is no doubt the envy of many who live in Siberia or the Far East regions. However, seven decades of Soviet socialism have not homogenized all regions and all peoples, thus life for the migrant Slav or Balt is not always easy in these regions. But it is most certainly more amenable in the city than in the countryside where age-old traditions still shape many facets of daily life. Thus, to be born in the south, for example, confers certain climatic amenities, but by the same token the new-born member of urban society in Tallinn, Riga, Moscow, or Leningrad has the prospect of a higher standard of living simply by virtue of where his or her parents reside. Under *perestroyka* (and indeed as under all of the economic reforms which have been introduced since the Second World War), there is every chance that this basic core–periphery pattern of economic and social development will be strengthened. Thus, the urban hierarchy, and rural–urban dimensions of the quest for social justice are further exacerbated by the long-standing differences between core region and periphery.

The Soviet Constitution acknowledges in a variety of ways the rights and poten-tial aspirations of the country's many distinct nationalities. It also guarantees equality of opportunity and treatment to all irrespective of national background. For many national minorities the legacy of the Great Russian chauvinism of the late imperial era is still a factor in inter-nationality relationships. The riots in Alma-Ata in the Kazakh republic highlighted the sensitivities felt by many national minorities to the dominant positions occupied by immigrant Russians. Indeed, where national minorities have gained access to positions of power they have used them to advantage their own nationality at the expense, seemingly, of the migrant population. At any rate, the net out-migration from Middle Asia in the early 1980s suggests that for some Slavs, and perhaps other non-indigenous nationals, life in Middle Asia is less than enticing. There have long been suggestions that treatment of Middle Asian and Caucasian republics reflects Russian attitudes and aspirations. Certainly the differ-ences in standard of living across the republics would tend to reinforce such a view, whether or not it is correct. Relations between nationalities should not be couched simply in terms of Russians, or perhaps Slavs in general, *vis-à-vis* the others. There are certainly cases of tension between Ukrainians and Russians and Belorussians and Russians. While not usually manifested in an inter-personal manner, they often centre on the question of cultural imperialism. The use of Russian in place of Ukrainian or Belorussian in education in general and literature in particular has been a long-standing bone of contention. The same general accusation of Russification of culture is frequently levied by representatives of the Baltic culture realms of Latvia, Lithuania and Estonia. But nationality issues are much more complex, as the riots in Azerbaydzhan in 1988 indicate. Here Armenians *en masse* demonstrated in support of the return to the fold of the Nagorno-Karabakh Autonomous Oblast which has been part of Azerbaydzhan since the 1920s (see Fig. 10, page 48). Nationality differences which are grounded in religion as well as language resulted in a related modern-day pogrom in the city of Sumgait near Baku. While some people have been brought to trial on charges of murder, the nationality issue throughout Armenia and Azerbaydzhan is far from resolved. From the standpoint of social justice such outbreaks of violence, while isolated in Soviet history to be sure, nonetheless raise serious questions as to the cohesiveness of society at large. The quest for social justice and a socialist solution to the problems of contemporary life continues.

Recommended reading

Atkinson, D., Dallin, A., Lapidus, G.W. (eds), *Women in Russia* (Hassocks: Harvester, 1978).

Dellenbrant, J.A., *Soviet Regional Policy: A Quantitative Inquiry into the Social and Political Development of Soviet Republics* (Stockholm: Almqvist and Wiksell, 1980).

Friedberg, M., Isham, H. (eds), *Soviet Society Under Gorbachev: Current Trends and the Prospects for Reform* (London: M.E. Sharpe, 1987).

Herlemann, H.G. (ed), *The Quality of Life in the Soviet Union* (Boulder and London: Westview Press, 1987).

Komarov, B., *The Destruction of Nature in the Soviet Union* (White Plains, New York: M.E. Sharpe, 1980).

Lapidus, G.W., *Women in Soviet Society* (Berkeley: University of California Press, 1978).

Matthews, M., *Privilege in the Soviet Union: A Study of Elite Lifestyles Under Communism* (London: George Allen and Unwin, 1978).

Matthews, M., *Poverty in the Soviet Union: The Life-Styles of the Underprivileged in Recent Years* (Cambridge: Cambridge University Press, 1986).

McAuley, A., *Economic Welfare in the Soviet Union. Poverty, Living Standards and Inequality* (Madison: University of Wisconsin Press, 1979).

McAuley, A., *Women's Work and Wages in the Soviet Union* (London: George Allen and Unwin, 1981).

Millar, J.R., *Politics, Work and Daily Life in the USSR. A Survey of Former Soviet Citizens* (Cambridge: Cambridge University Press, 1987).

Nelson, D.N. (ed), *Communism and the Politics of Inequalities* (Lexington: Lexington Books, 1982).

Sacks, M., *Women's Work in Soviet Russia* (New York: Praeger, 1976).

Singleton, F. (ed), *Environmental Misuse in the Soviet Union* (New York: Praeger, 1976).

Volgyes, I. (ed), *Environmental Deterioration in the Soviet Union and Eastern Europe* (New York: Praeger, 1974).

Yanowitch, M., *Social and Economic Inequality in the Soviet Union* (London: Martin Robertson, 1977).

Zaslavsky, V., *The Neo-Stalinist State. Class, Ethnicity and Consensus in Soviet Society* (Armonk, New York: M.E. Sharpe, 1982).

Zemtsov, I., *The Private Life of the Soviet Elite* (New York: Crane Russak, 1985).

Zuzanek, J., *Work and Leisure in the Soviet Union. A Time Budget Analysis* (New York: Praeger, 1980).

11 A 'fin de siècle' Agenda

Like the history of the past, that of tomorrow depends upon the choices people make....

Kerblay, 1983.[1]

Throughout the preceding chapters we have stressed the importance of an appreciation of history in attempting to understand something of the present. As well, emphasis has been placed upon the relationship between principles or ideals, policy implementation and the nature of the decision-making process in shaping the geography of the Soviet Union, in determining the material conditions of daily life and labour. Our approach has been necessarily rather selective. In attempting to sum up some of the more pressing problems, and likely prospects, to the turn of the century, we can do no more than touch upon a few issues.

In the absence of any prior experience, or model, for translating socialist ideals into reality, it comes as no surprise that the Soviet Union often manifests a sizeable gap between what in principle was to be and what in practice was actually done. Throughout the Soviet era, pragmatic accommodation with the particular circumstances of time and place has often taken precedence over principles and public proclamations. We need only mention the New Economic Policy (1921–1928) introduced by Lenin in order to forestall the collapse of the domestic economy and the legislation introduced during the 1930s with Stalin's approval which enabled the emerging managerial *cum* middle class, upon which the technical success of the industrialization drive was dependent, to accumulate wealth and leave it intact to heirs. These are perhaps minor aberrations in the course of Soviet history, but along with other developments of a similar kind, many of which have been noted in the preceding pages, they have helped to give a particular texture to the fabric both of Soviet society and Soviet geography. In all likelihood the Gorbachev-era initiatives will leave an indelible impress on both. From an economic perspective much depends

---

[1] B. Kerlay, *Modern Soviet Society* (New York: Pantheon, 1983), 305.

upon the success of the current reforms. And in this context the ability of the Soviet economy to compete more effectively on the world scene is undeniably important.

Gorbachev's attempts to disturb the somnolent status quo has been justified by the promise of a higher standard of living. By working harder and more efficiently, Soviet society will inevitably be better off in a material sense. And, indeed, there is a great deal that could be accomplished through a more efficient management of the domestic economy. Much has been made of the numerous problems confronting Soviet agriculture. Waste alone is an enormous burden on society at large. Simply getting a higher proportion of what is grown to the table of the ordinary family would have a significant impact, as noted in Chapter 7. Were the Soviet agricultural labour force able to produce at the rate of its major international competitors there would be sizeable savings in hard currency since imports of basic foodstuffs would

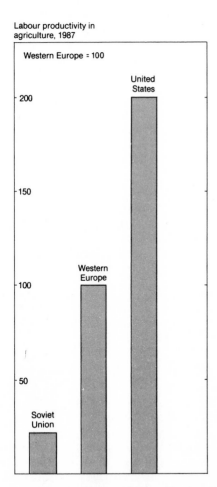

Fig. 58   Agricultural Labour Productivity

Source: 'The Soviet Economy', *The Economist*, 9–15 April, 1988, 9.

diminish. As Fig. 58 indicates, there is much room for improvement. While Soviet industry does not fare quite so dismally in international comparisons of productivity as Soviet agriculture, there is also considerable scope for improvement. Put simply, waste takes many other forms than just vegetables rotting in the field or at the rail depot for want of adequate processing and transport facilities. For Gorbachev, and his supporters, *perestroyka* and *uskoreniye* proffer a solution to a host of domestic economic and social problems. But as we have emphasized throughout, for untold numbers of others, putting what is in hand at risk for future, uncertain benefits, is not something to be embraced with enthusiasm. Revolution and socialism notwithstanding, Soviet society and Russian before it, has a distinctly conservative hue.

Being more efficient would set the stage for fuller participation in international trade, surely the litmus test of modernity in contemporary industrial, or post-industrial, society. Since 1950 Soviet foreign trade has increased more than 40-fold in value. But in 1986 two-thirds of Soviet trade was still with other socialist countries, primarily, but not exclusively with the East European Bloc or Comecon. Barely a

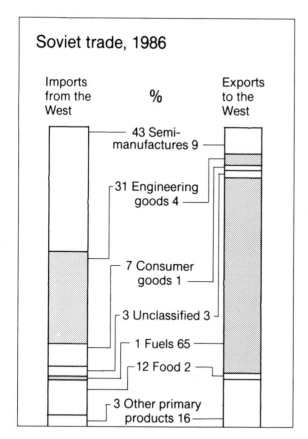

Fig. 59   Soviet Trade

Source: 'The Soviet Economy', *The Economist*, 9–15 April, 1988, 13.

fifth was conducted with what are described in official Soviet statistics as capitalist countries, the remainder being with the developing states. While foreign trade accounts have customarily been in surplus, what the Soviet Union actually exports is important. Raw materials, energy and semi-processed goods dominated the ledger in 1986. At the turn of the nineteenth century, the export list did not look so radically different, save of course for grain, which is now a major import rather than export item. Soviet manufactured goods find their way principally to the other socialist countries, and to a lesser extent to the developing regions of the globe. Despite its economic, political and military significance, Soviet trade with western industrial states reflects a fundamental structural imbalance (Fig. 59). Less than one-twentieth of Soviet exports comprise what are described as engineering goods. By contrast 31 per cent of imports are so classified. And some of the engineering goods exported are part of bilateral trade agreements which reflect less the competitive worth of the product and more the nature of selling to the Soviet Union. The export–import mix depicted in Fig. 59 has often been described as more representative of a developing country than a world super-power. *Perestroyka* is certainly aimed at changing the structural mix of exports and imports. But for the time being, dependence upon foreign technology to re-equip industry, and foreign consumers goods and services to sustain public support for the disruption and uncertainties caused by the Gorbachev reform initiative, is necessary. Thus, the Soviet Union is likely to become more rather than less integrated into the world economy. And therein lies a dilemma we have noted on a number of occasions in preceding chapters.

In the late 1980s the ability of the Soviet Union to generate foreign-exchange earnings to purchase goods and services is compromised by the very nature of the export mix. Energy in one form or another figures prominently in the export column in terms of value. Save for electricity, it is a raw material rather than a 'manufactured' good. Yet as Fig. 60 graphically indicates for crude oil, the slide in the value of the American dollar during the 1980s in relation to European currencies has compounded the problems caused by the slide in the dollar value of a barrel of oil since the 1970s. Trade in oil is customarily pegged to the American dollar, payments are made accordingly, but to purchase goods from Western Europe in particular is increasingly expensive. In 1988 three times as much oil had to be sold as in 1985 in order to purchase the same value of goods from West Germany. Soviet dependence upon foreign goods and services to realize the goals of *perestroyka* brings with it the harsh realities of the world economy from which for decades it had been consciously shielded. Yet too much should not be made of the cost of doing business with the western industrial world. By any standard Soviet net external debt is comparatively small. The resource wealth of the country is huge, if difficult to develop at times. And there are real economies to be realized through greater efficiencies in managing domestic affairs. For the Gorbachev-era reformers the difficulties are not so much finding ways to resuscitate the domestic economy as they are in sustaining broad support throughout all sectors of society – from Party to peasantry – during a period of potentially turbulent change.

That innovation has not been readily embraced by the Soviet system that has evolved over the years is perhaps most directly revealed by the structure of employment. In 1985 more than a third of all industrial workers were classified as unskilled.

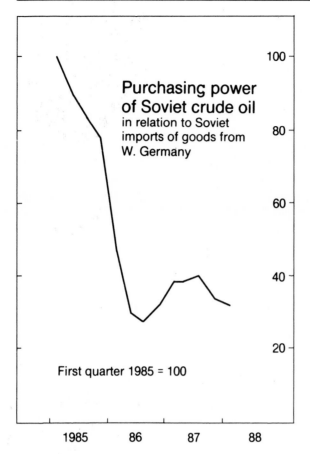

Fig. 60   Purchasing Power of Soviet Oil

Source: 'The Soviet Economy', *The Economist* 9–15 April, 1988, 13.

Less significantly, more than half of all construction workers were similarly classi-fied. But in agriculture, which typically employs less than a twentieth of the labour force in Western Europe and North America, more than two-thirds of the Soviet Union's much larger workforce were unskilled. A direct comparison between the USSR and the United States highlights the point (Fig. 61). Innovation will find more fertile ground when there is less reliance on muscle and more on strategic planning. The latter requires widely disseminated information systems and ready access to data. In a state where telephone books are at a premium, where city maps are intentionally inaccurate or bereft of information, where copying machines are not publicly accessible, where both information technology and information itself are primitive by contemporary western standards, there is an enormous gap to over-come. Despite military technology and space research of the highest possible quality on an international level, those involved in the more mundane sectors of the economy have great difficulty at times just placing an inter-city telephone call or using a com-

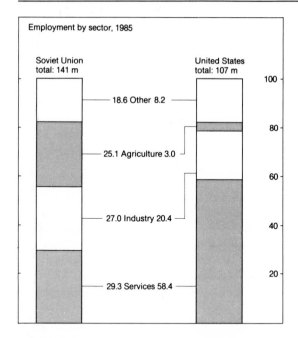

Employment by sector, 1985

Soviet Union
total: 141 m

United States
total: 107 m

18.6 Other 8.2

25.1 Agriculture 3.0

27.0 Industry 20.4

29.3 Services 58.4

Fig. 61   Employment by Sector, USA and USSR

Source: 'The Soviet Economy', *The Economist*, 9–15 April, 1988, 11.

puter. Control over information and its manipulation or transmittal was one means of ensuring control over the potentially contentious elements in society. In restructuring the domestic economy rather more is required than simply providing the appropriate technology. Fundamental attitudes and values have similarly to be changed, and this doubtless poses the greatest challenge during the last years of the twentieth century.

The years between the revolution and the dead hand of the Stalin era are sometimes aptly described as a period of cultural revolution. There was still scope for serious debate on all topics. Experimentation was tolerated if not endorsed by the state. The Gorbachev era hints at the same possibilities – and more besides. It is no accident that in common with earlier reform efforts the lack of initiative or misguided efforts of past leaders are now publicly attacked and criticized. Khrushchev denounced some of the Stalin-era excesses. As a result the place-name geography was reworked as one superficial example of a fundamental process of change which was set in motion. Brezhnev and Kosygin were quick to discredit some of the legacy of the Khrushchev era as hare-brained at worst, ill-informed at best. Gorbachev now has likened the Brezhnev era to a twentieth-century equivalent of an Oblomov state of mind, that is, a period of indolence and lack of initiative which the nineteenth-century writer I. Goncharov so vividly characterized as being quintessentially part of the Russian character. While Brezhnev, like Stalin, found satisfaction in seeing his name appear on signs and cities across the country, this has been an equally ephemeral legacy since under Gorbachev name changes have also occurred. But unlike earlier reform movements, under Gorbachev there seems to be a much more explicit connection with Lenin, and his ideals. Indeed, there are many commonalities between the New Economic Policy of Lenin and the Gorbachev-era reforms. Whether these conscious links with the past are merely attempts to legitimize current reform initiatives by tying them to Lenin, or are of fundamentally the same nature and therefore legitimate historical analogies, remains to be seen. But once again the themes of historical continuity and change stand out as having relevance to the contemporary Soviet scene.

Implicit in much of the discussion in earlier chapters, and indeed explicit in segments of it, is the concept of internal differentiation, both spatial and non-spatial. An example of the latter is the class system and its current embellishment as opportunities to earn larger incomes than can be obtained from employment in the service of the state are taken up by individuals and collectives alike. This simply adds a further layer to a class system that is already complex by virtue of privileges which are bestowed upon certain segments of society. Inevitably, such differentiation will produce further grounds for dissension during a time of change. The Gorbachev-era reforms are intended to reinforce the merits of the socialist system not change the system itself. But in realizing the goal of greater economic efficiency there are associated costs. Ensconced privilege will not easily be removed, for few people are inclined to be altruistic when the material conditions of their own circumstances deteriorate, while those of others improve. *Glasnost'* has made public what was already common knowledge – that the status quo benefits some much more than others, and often for no particularly sound reason. In managing change over the next decade, the economic factors will be decidedly less problematic than the human. The nationality issue is surely evidence of the veracity of this statement.

Tensions within Soviet society have been exacerbated because of the growing sense that public demonstration and personal criticism of the affairs of state are less likely now to precipitate a punitive response on the part of officialdom than before. The nationality issue in the Soviet Union will certainly not just go away. The 1980s have witnessed increasingly serious outbreaks of inter-ethnic conflict, and not always involving Russians as recent events in the Caucasus indicate. As more by way of public demonstration occurs without draconian reaction by the state, the more are other nationality issues likely to bubble over. The next decade will certainly test the current bounds of tolerance by the state. But nationality issues are rarely simple, and the further polarization of the spatial economy could well be an additional point of dispute.

As we have argued in earlier chapters, the current attempt to reform the national economy, to make it more efficient as a system, will likely result in enhancing the economic power of the core region of European Russia at the expense of the peripheral regions of the country. The latter are the national territory of the non-Slavic elements of the Soviet Union. If economic power is polarized to the degree that national minorities perceive that their own situation is not improving as quickly, let alone stagnating, then an economic dimension could well be added to the already highly charged nationality problems in many parts of the country. And yet in many ways the very success of *perestroyka* in the short run is dependent upon garnering greater returns from increasing investment, where resource availability permits, in the core as opposed to the higher-cost periphery. And, of course the European Russian core is far from providing all of its inhabitants with enhanced opportunities for there are many rural areas and many small towns as disadvantaged as parts of the periphery. In the development process attitudes and values are exceedingly important and the current reform initiatives presuppose a gathering of all peoples in the resolution of common problems.

As the first experiment in the planned development of socialist society, there is ample opportunity to point to the divergence of ideal and reality. A legitimate exercise in its own right, it is nonetheless necessary to keep in mind the nature of the society inherited by those who made the revolution. Autocracy and grinding poverty went hand in hand in imperial Russia. The material circumstances of daily life and labour amongst the masses were such that for many the revolution portended real opportunity to improve one's lot in life. Some seized the opportunity to bring about change. Others had change imposed. This was a society whose values were deeply conservative in the main, a society shaped more by the beliefs and habits of the countryside than by the city. It was after all a dominantly rural society, one that required more than four decades of planned socialist development, which ideologically is urban-industrial in complexion, before the majority of its citizenry was classified as urban. Notwithstanding the sizeable environmental costs of Soviet development practices, in terms of quality of life in a material sense there can be no question that the Soviet era has witnessed enormous progress. Traditions, however, still run deep. The celebration of the millenium of Christianity in 1988 is but one example. The residual elements of the Muslim religion amongst large numbers of Soviet citizens is another. Put simply, there are many examples of both continuity and change.

In raising a few issues which are likely to influence the direction and possibly the tempo of change in the Soviet Union to the end of the century, we have sketched a rough scenario with a broad brush and few strokes. There is much yet to be filled in. If what has been presented in this book serves to stimulate more interest, and more enquiry, its purpose will have been served.

Recommended reading

Beissenger, M., Hajda, L. (eds), *The Nationalities Factor in Soviet Society and Politics: Current Trends and Future Prospects* (Boulder: Westview Press, 1987).

Brown, A., Kaser, M. (eds), *Soviet Policy for the 1980s* (London: Macmillan, 1982).

Colton, T.S., *The Dilemma of Reform in the Soviet Union* (New York: Council on Foreign Relations, 1986) revised ed.

Conquest, R. (ed), *The Last Empire: Nationality and the Soviet Future* (Stanford: Hoover Institution Press, 1987).

McCauley, M. (ed), *The Soviet Union Under Gorbachev* (New York: St. Martin's Press, 1987).

Medvedev, Z.A., *Gorbachev* (Cambridge: Cambridge University Press, 1986).

Motyl, A.J., *Will the Non-Russians Rebel? State, Ethnicity and Stability in the USSR* (Ithaca: Cornell University Press, 1987).

Yanov, A., *The Russian Challenge. The USSR and the Year 2000.* (Cambridge: Cambridge University Press, 1988).

Index